The Ideological Origins
of Nazi Imperialism

The Ideological Origins of Nazi Imperialism

WOODRUFF D. SMITH

OXFORD UNIVERSITY PRESS
New York   Oxford

Oxford University Press
Oxford   New York   Toronto
Delhi   Bombay   Calcutta   Madras   Karachi
Petaling Jaya   Singapore   Hong Kong   Tokyo
Nairobi   Dar es Salaam   Cape Town
Melbourne   Auckland

and associated companies in
Berlin   Ibadan

First published in 1986 by Oxford University Press, Inc.,
200 Madison Avenue, New York, New York 10016

First issued as an Oxford University Press paperback, 1989

Oxford is a registered trademark of Oxford University Press

Library of Congress Cataloging in Publication Data

Smith, Woodruff D.
The ideological origins of Nazi imperialism.

Bibliography: p.
Includes index.
1. Germany—Foreign relations—1971–1918.
2. Imperialism.   3. National socialism.   4. Germany—
Foreign relations—20th century. I. Title.
DD221.5.S758   1986   943.08   85-10555
ISBN 0-19-503690-5
ISBN 0-19-504741-9 (PBK)

2 4 6 8 10 9 7 5 3

Printed in the United States of America

Acknowledgments

This book is the result of a convergence of several different directions in research that I have taken during the past fifteen years—research into German colonial history, Wilhelmian politics, the nature of ideology, and the history of social science. My obligations are therefore broadly distributed.

I should particularly like to thank the following individuals for their advice and assistance: Ralph A. Austen, John Booth, William Cohen, Lewis H. Gann, Robert Hess, Sharon King, Wm. Roger Louis, Rodler F. Morris, David J. Schneider, Claudio Segré, and my wife, Jane H. Smith.

I should also like to thank Dr. Hartmut Pogge von Strandmann for his helpful comments in a review of my earlier book, *The German Colonial Empire,* and for permission to use his microfilms of German Colonial Office documents maintained at the Hoover Institution; Dr. Gerald Kleinfeld, editor of the *German Studies Review,* for permission to include portions of two articles originally published in that journal; the National Endowment for the Humanities, which supported part of the research for this book (especially Chapter Seven) with a fellowship and a summer stipend; the German Academic Exchange Service (DAAD), for further support (again for Chapter Seven); the Shelby Cullom Davis Center for Historical Studies at Princeton and its director, Professor Lawrence Stone, for a fruitful semester during the writing of part of this book; the College of Social and Behavioral Sciences, University of Texas at San Antonio, and its dean, Dr. Dwight F. Henderson, for assistance with the cost of preparing the manuscript; the staffs of the *Bundesarchiv* in Koblenz, the National Archives and the Library of Congress in Washington, D.C., the Hoover Institution, and the Frobenius Institute of Frankfurt University; and the staffs of the libraries of the University of Texas at San Antonio, the University of Texas at Austin, Frankfurt University, Princeton University, Harvard University, and the College of William and Mary. I should also like to thank Mr. Andrew Yockers, who edited the manuscript.

Typing the various manuscript versions of the book was the work of many different people, to all of whom I am grateful.

San Antonio   W.D.S.
March 1985

Contents

The Ideological Origins
of Nazi Imperialism

CHAPTER ONE

Introduction

Among the most popular subjects of modern historiography are Hitler's attempt to expand Nazi Germany and the consequences of that attempt in World War II. This book, however, is not primarily about the Nazis or the Second World War. Hitler and his expansionary policies enter the discussion only in the concluding chapter and then rather briefly because of the extensive historical work that has already been done on the details of Nazi war aims.

Most of the book is devoted instead to the argument that Nazi imperialism was in many important respects the culmination of a complex process of ideological development extending back to the first half of the nineteenth century, a process that went through its most important phases well before the Nazis established their program in the 1920s. The main focus is on the Wilhelmian era, the period of greatest innovation in German imperialist ideology.

Continuity and Ideology in the Historiography of German Imperialism

Although the prehistories of most of the other components of Nazi ideology—racism, *völkisch* thought, anticommunism, and so on—have been studied in great detail, this is not true of the imperialist aspects of Naziism. With a few important exceptions, historians of Naziism have tended to see Hitler's expansionary aims as products of thoroughgoing opportunism, as consequences of his other ideological predilections, or as manifestations of underlying continuities in German foreign policy. The pure-opportunism hypothesis has largely been discarded as an explanatory device because it begs the question of Hitler's intentions.[1] There was an important element of opportunism in practically everything Hitler did, but it was circumscribed and directed by strongly held convictions about the ultimate goals of policy. The other two approaches to Nazi policy cannot be so readily discounted.

There is ample evidence that Hitler and other leading Nazis, indeed, expected the acts of aggression that made up much of their foreign policy to serve multiple ends conceived in terms of different parts of their ideological program. Thus an attack on the "Jewish-Bolshevik" Soviet Union was, in part, a consequence of the anti-semitic, anti-communist, and anti-Slavic aims of Naziism.[2] These aims alone, however, did not define for Hitler the total significance of invading Russia. His announcement that Germany sought "living space" in Russia indicates the presence in his program of a distinctly imperialist element. The *Lebensraum* element was a product of an extensive tradition in German imperialist ideology—a tradition related to other constituents of the Nazis' radical-conservative worldview but not defined by them. The Nazi program also contained expansionary goals derived from quite different traditions of German imperialist ideology.

The question of whether or not there were continuities between the expansionary aims of the Third Reich and the foreign policies of previous German regimes has attracted the attention of numerous historians. The question has arisen directly in studies of Nazi policymaking and implicitly in many analyses of politics and imperialism in the *Kaiserreich*. Several East German and Soviet scholars have attempted to demonstrate such continuities, representing them, indeed, as extending into what they call the neoimperialism of the present German Federal Republic.[3] These attempts have been on the whole unsatisfactory, mainly because of the deficiencies of the Marxist-Leninist framework of analysis on which they have perforce been based. The "orthodox" Marxist-Leninist view is simultaneously too broad and too narrow: too broad because imperialism is defined as the entire political, social, and economic order of late capitalism, which means that any continuity at all in modern German history (outside the German Democratic Republic) is automatically a continuity of imperialism; too narrow because of its dogmatic and often distortive concentration on the organized structures of finance and industry as the prime motivators of policy. It is probably not, however, an accident that Marxist-Leninist historians have often led the way in suggesting connections between Naziism and earlier German imperialism. Their framework of analysis, whatever its deficiencies, has the virtue of providing a ready-made concept of underlying historical continuity that can be used to relate developments in imperialist policy to sequential steps in the evolution of German and international capitalism. Successive German governments from Bismarck to Hitler are held to have followed expansionary policies in response to the demands of organized big business for assistance in solving the crises and contradictions that arose within industrial capitalism. Imperialist policies changed to some extent over time because the nature of those crises and contradictions changed, becoming generally worse. Inconsistencies between imperialist programs were the results of fissures within the industrial and financial bourgeoisie, fissures that were themselves products in the last analysis of the inherent contradictions in capitalism.

Most Western historians, including Marxist ones, have rejected the Marxist-Leninist approach because of its limitations. Nevertheless, a great many of them, especially those who emphasize domestic policies as the main determinant of foreign policy, have focused on similar types of social phenomena and similar power relationships. Some have constructed explicitly neo-Marxist analyses on broader and more flexible foundations than Marxism-Lenininsm.[4] The best-known of these approaches, however, have concentrated instead on the concept of socioeconomic *modernization*. The modernization approach has proven to be particularly fruitful in the study of imperialism in the *Kaiserreich* and its relationship to the coming of the First World War. It has not, however, been used effectively as yet to link Nazi imperialism to its Bismarckian and Wilhelmian predecessors, except by suggestion.

The modernization concept became a prominent feature of the postwar study of German imperialism with the attempts of Fritz Fischer and his students to demonstrate continuities between expansionary ideas current in government, political, and business circles in the decade or so before 1914 and the aims of the German government during the First World War itself.[5] In depicting such continuities, Fischer attracted widespread attention by arguing that Germany had, in fact, started the war to achieve the goals developed by its elite before 1914. He implied also that the expansionary aims of the Nazis were to some extent continuations of these goals.

Although Fischer did not extensively use the term *modernization* and concentrated on a rather limited range of economic changes as the underlying forces behind Wilhelmian imperialism, the essence of the modernization approach was present in his analysis. According to Fischer, the course of Germany's rapid industrialization in the late nineteenth century created severe problems for the various German elite classes. For the leaders of finance and industry, modernization led to a need to invest outside the boundaries of the Reich in competition with foreign (especially British and French) business. Germany was, however, perpetually short of capital because of previous heavy demands of rapid industrialization. In the years before the First World War, German financial institutions found that they could not protect their enterprises abroad when they were threatened with foreign takeover. German business therefore turned to the government, formulating different versions of a program of external expansion to secure and enhance investment. This program was transmitted to Bethmann Hollweg's government and to other sectors of the elite through a network of personal and institutional connections. During the war, the same network functioned to create a series of discrete war aims that became, in essence, the policy of the Reich government.

Fischer's students and the large number of historians influenced by his work have extended the approach that he pioneered, noting, for example, the importance of a growing community of interest between segments of the industrial and the Junker agrarian elites in the face of the perceived threat from socialism in the years just before World War I. This community of interest served to enhance the ability of the business elite to affect policy, but it also meant that the interests of the Junkers had to be incorporated into war-aims discussions. Historians of the Fischer school have also taken into account an increasingly wide range of political factors that influenced Wilhelmian imperialist policy.[6] Whatever the specific interests at work, however, the conscious motives leading to imperialism are represented as stemming directly from the process of economic modernization. The resulting expansionary program is regarded as essentially uniform—a product of elite consensus in which disagreements appeared only on matters of detail. Germany was to create an organized system through which her economic domination of central Europe would be assured. She was to annex European territories with industrial and mining capacities or lands that were needed for strategic reasons. Germany was also to expand her overseas empire, especially through the establishment of a single German colony that included most of central Africa. These aims, frustrated by the result of the First World War, were, so it is argued, essentially those of the Hitler regime as well.

Critics of Fischer have found a great many problems with his analysis, especially with his extremely narrow conception of the policymaking process and of the reasons that elite interest groups turned to imperialism.[7] His students, by extending the scope of the analysis, have avoided some of this criticism. But the assumption of the entire Fischer school that German expansionary aims, and thus German imperialism, were basically uniform is not borne out by a close examination of the very statements of those aims that they cite. We shall see presently that before and during the First World War there were at least two different aggregations of imperialist ideas current in German politics. These aggregations overlapped to a considerable extent but were contradictory in many fundamental ways—and they were perceived at the time as contradictory. We shall see further that German imperialism in the Wilhelmian era, far from being the product of elite consensus, was rather the result of attempts to *create* consensus—attempts that failed, at least up to the time of the Nazis.

The Fischer school shares with most other historians of the subject not only the assumption of the fundamental uniformity of German imperialism, but also a particular notion of the nature of the evidence for the continuity of imperialism: the recurring use of a certain vocabulary to denote expansionary ideas. For example, most segments of German imperialist opinion during World War I advocated the establishment of a German-dominated economic union in central Europe. All used Friedrich Naumann's catchword for the idea: *Mitteleuropa*. The Nazis also included *Mitteleuropa* in their catalog of national policy aims as early as the mid 1920s, and Hitler sought central European integration (together with a great many other things) during World War II. Is this continuity? In a sense, yes (as we shall see), but not as the concept of continuity is used in most of the literature on German imperialism, including that of Fischer and his followers. On closer examination, it becomes clear that more than one version of the *Mitteleuropa* idea existed and that the imperialists using the term during the First World War meant quite different things by it. The Nazis, in fact, attempted in their version of *Mitteleuropa* to tie together the earlier highly contradictory views of economic integration. This is a complex concept of continuity that involves consideration of the interaction between political ideology and the structure of politics over time, which the Fischer style of analysis does not permit.

The idea that modernization was the ultimate source of continuity in the history of German imperialism has been employed most explicitly by historians who focus on the phenomenon of "social imperialism," especially Hans-Ulrich Wehler. Wehler and the rest of the social imperialist school argue that Bismarckian and Wilhelmian imperialism were primarily political responses by threatened elites to the domestic class conflict generated by German industrialization. According to Wehler, Bismarck briefly adopted colonialism in the 1880s because he believed that it would permit him to consolidate bourgeois and worker support behind his regime, which Wehler interprets as standing ultimately for continued autocracy and semifeudal Junker rule.[8] The reason that such an instrument of cooptation was available was that colonialism had previously emerged among certain segments of the upper bourgeoisie. German business leaders faced with the post-1873 depression used the demand for colonial expansion as the opening wedge of a campaign to acquire government support for market expansion abroad. Also, the concepts of colonialism and aggressive market expansion provided the business elite with a potential weapon against social democracy: such policies could secure German industry against downturns in the business cycle and thus protect workers' jobs and incomes. Revolutionary socialism, even trade unionism, could not promise the workers so much. According to Wehler, Bismarck turned to colonialism not because of his belief in its inherent validity but because of his desire to use it in the politics of class conflict. The proponents of the social imperialist explanation argue that much the same thing was true of the later history of German imperialism, from the era of *Weltpolitik* to that of Hitler. According to some interpretations along these lines, Germany was led into the First World War by elite groups that sought to use wartime conditions to maintain the loyalty of subordinate social classes.[9]

The social imperialist approach has also been heavily criticized on a number of grounds, most notably because evidence to support it, although available, tends to be somewhat scarce. In Germany as elsewhere, people who advocated imperial expansion pointed to the potential utility of imperialism in deflecting class antagonisms. Nevertheless, it is quite difficult to demonstrate that such considerations weighed more heavily in the minds of imperialists than did many other factors. Wehler and his followers have also been accused of not taking into account other sources of imperialist motivation, especially those arising from the operation of the system of international relations, in order to exaggerate the importance of social imperialist motives.[10] These are not fatal flaws in the social imperialist approach, however. They merely show that the phenomenon in question—imperialism in the industrial age—contained more complexities than the rather broadly defined categories of Wehler's model can accommodate. A great deal of the social imperialist analysis can be readily employed in explanatory frameworks that take other factors into account.

From the standpoint of the present study, the deficiencies of the social imperialist approach lie in rather different directions. Indeed, most of the attempts to explain imperialism as a direct consequence of modernization suffer from the same difficulties. In the first place, there is a strong presumption that imperialism as a set of ideas and distinctive political actions was a result of the aims of a small number of segments of the social elite. These groups wished to achieve relatively clear and straightforward economic ends; at the same time, they wanted to maintain their elite status against potential rivals and against the industrial proletariat. Although much of the politics and ideology of any country revolve around such aims, elite classes are not, in fact, the only participants in the political process, nor is it at all clear that broad social-class categories are the most meaningful ones for defining political action. Geoff Eley's analysis of the politics of the German Navy League, one of the most important imperialist pressure groups in Wilhelmian Germany, has demonstrated the complexities of imperialist politics and the variety of the groups involved.[11] Eley has also shown that the creation and use of ideologies in imperialist politics were not the exclusive prerogative of clearly identified elite classes; important elements of navalist politics reflected the resentment of various middle-class groups against the very elites that were supposed, in many of the social imperialist analyses of Wilhelmian imperialism, to have invented navalism as a means of rallying the support of the bourgeoisie.

Connected to this problem with social imperialism is the one that has already been noted in the discussion of Fischer's modernization argument: the Wehlerians, like Fischer, take an essentially unitary view of German imperialim. This has caused Wehler and some of his followers, for example, to downplay the importance in the German colonial movement of the argument that Germany needed settlement colonies to solve the problem of emigration. In fact, the settlement idea played an extremely important role in German imperialism, a role that is not easily explained by the Wehlerian model.[12] The multiplicity of those who used the idea of imperialism in German politics is matched by the multiplicity of German imperialist ideologies. The social imperialist framework of analysis does not readily explain this phenomenon. We shall argue that social imperialism as Wehler describes it, rather than being the dominant form of imperialist ideology in Germany or even a particular imperialist ideology in itself, was actually a component of practically all varieties of imperialism in the nineteenth and twentieth centuries, including ones that were overtly opposed to each other. Social imperialism was, in other words, one of a number of idea-sets that could be tied together in various ways to make up a composite imperialist ideology—a process about which we shall have more to say shortly.

As with most of the approaches to the history of German imperialism that concentrate on the immediate social effects of modernization, it has proven difficult to apply the Wehlerian analysis of social imperialism to Nazi expansion. The evidence of apparent similarities in expansionary vocabulary and ideas is there, but the logic of the social imperialist argument requires that these continuities be matched with some form of continuity in the response of threatened elite groups to modernization. This, in turn, requires that the Nazis be accorded essentially the same status as Bismarck and the other defenders of the nineteenth-century social order or, at least, that they be portrayed as the willing instruments of capitalism. Although some have ascribed Hitler's acceptance of colonialism to pressure placed on him by the capitalist interests that supposedly stood behind the German colonial movement, the whole idea of the Nazis as the front men for a threatened capitalism is difficult to maintain in the face of the considerable evidence that exists about the revolutionary character of Nazi aims. Unless one can postulate a strong, uniform Nazi connection to elite social interests, it is extremely hard to demonstrate a continuity between the different eras of German imperialism on the basis of the standard social imperialist argument.[13]

These difficulties illustrate what is probably, from the standpoint of the subject of this study, the greatest weakness of most of the explanations of German imperialism that portray it as a series of immediate responses to modernization. By assuming the primacy of *direct* connections between the socioeconomic processes of modernization on the one hand and political action on the other, such explanations oversimplify the workings of politics and the effects of the politics of one period on its successors. There are, indeed, ways of showing the kinds of continuity that the Wehlerians assume, but it requires a substantial broadening of their approach to politics to do so. It requires, in fact, the explicit recognition of a political sphere of human social existence that acts as, among other things, an intermediary between direct perceptions of socioeconomic change and specific instances of political action and that links those perceptions to one another. Moreover, an appropriate structure of explanation that connects modernization to political phenomena such as imperialism must also account for the fact that things other than responses to modernization also influence politics.

Before we turn to the problem of creating such a structure of explanation, we must also note that not all attempts to link Nazi expansionary and foreign policies to those of preceding governments have focused on modernization. Much of the discussion has taken place in the context of more-or-less traditional political and intellectual history. Historians of Nazi foreign policy such as Hildebrand, Weinberg, and Rich have concentrated on the evolution of Nazi policy ideas from the 1920s onward through the interaction of the Nazis' thinking and the pressures of external political reality.[14] We shall consider these approaches in the final chapter. For the most part, however, they postulate a relationship with previous German imperialism based on an apparent continuity in stated expansionary aims or, in the case of Hildebrand's analysis, a continuity founded on the existence of a limited set of policy alternatives available to German governments from Bismarck's time onward. According to the latter view, Hitler, like his predecessors in World War I, chose an extravagant imperialist alternative as opposed to the more pacific (and effective) one chosen by Stresemann. In none of these approaches, however, is the nature of pre-Nazi imperialism closely examined nor is a comprehensive explanation of continuity or discontinuity given in terms of the structures of German politics and society.

Only a few historical works have focused on ideological aspects of imperialism in Germany. This is unfortunate because ideology is crucial to an understanding of the relationship between imperialism and the social and political systems, the motives of imperialists, and, especially, the question of continuity. If continuities exist between the politics of one era and those of the next, they must necessarily involve the adoption of similar patterns of thinking about politics. Obviously, each generation is to some degree socialized with the political attitudes and values of its forebears. People, whether policymakers or more casual political participants, cannot help but work within the intellectual frameworks they inherit, even though they may substantially modify those frameworks to suit their peculiar circumstances. At a certain basic level, any examination of continuities in German imperialism must involve a consideration of political ideas organized into apparently coherent structures, or ideologies. The evidence for continuity that is most often cited—the repetition in one period of imperialist formulas from a previous one—is essentially ideological evidence.

Neither the Marxists nor the Wehler and Fischer schools ignore ideology, but they take a rather limited view of it: ideology is one of the means by which a group of political participants, usually a social class or organized interest group, represents its own interests in politics both to itself and to other people. On the whole, ideology is held to derive from the particular socioeconomic and political environment in which the group finds itself at any time. This brings one back to the problem of explaining the intellectual aspect of continuity between periods in cases in which the environment of politics has changed.

Historians such as Heinz Gollwitzer and Wolfgang Mommsen take a different approach, one in which some of the standard assumptions of intellectual history are directed toward politics and ideology. Ideas are considered to be the products of an intellectualizing sphere of human activity in which intellectuals, formalizing their own attitudes in systematic statements, develop social concepts that are then adopted by political actors to define the objects that the latter seek.[15] This approach, however, does not give an entirely satisfactory account of the relationship between politics and ideology, especially over time. Standard intellectual history, with its relatively narrow conception of the causal link between ideas and action, finds it difficult to deal with the complex interplay among formal ideas, individuals' perceptions of social reality, and the immediate problems faced by political practitioners. Thus, for example, Gollwitzer discusses "social Darwinism" and the concepts of "world-political thinking" as real intellectual phenomena that affect the behavior of policymakers without sufficiently considering the specific circumstances that led politicians to adopt or (more importantly) to modify these phenomena over time to correspond to perceived political needs. Some sort of framework of explanation is required to relate the imperialist ideas Gollwitzer has described to the factors of politics and socioeconomic change that are the prime concerns of most historians of imperialism.

In reaction to the explanatory limitations of much of the contemporary historical literature on German imperialism, there have been a number of recent attempts to take a comprehensive view of the phenomenon without adhering to any particular theoretical line. The most impressive of these is Paul M. Kennedy's study of the development of the antagonism between Britain and Germany that existed before 1914.[16] Kennedy attempts to examine all aspects of the Anglo-German relationship before 1914, weighing the claims of domestic politics, social change, economic rivalry, and diplomacy to being the prime sources of the impending conflict. In the course of his study, Kennedy says much of importance about the relationship between German imperialism and politics. His work helps to break down the artificial (and by now largely deleterious) distinction made in German historiography between analyses of policy based on domestic politics and analyses that emphasize diplomacy. He demonstrates convincingly that, although a great many complex domestic political forces affected the actions of German (and British) policymakers, most policymakers also genuinely responded to their perceptions of the imperatives of foreign politics as significant considerations in themselves. Kennedy does not, however, tell us much about some of the major concerns of the present study—especially the relationship between the politics of the Wilhelmian period and those of the Nazi era.

Imperialism and the Autonomy of Politics

One main deficiency most historical analyses of modern German imperialism share is the failure to recognize in a systematic fashion the existence of an autonomous *political sphere* of social activity: the area of human interaction that comprises political systems and the patterns of thought and action that are characteristically associated with them. The political sphere is no more clearly defined than such other sectors of society as the economy or class structure (the fundamental concepts of most of the analytical approaches previously described) but it is no less clearly defined either. The recent appearance of the new "political economy" has made it respectable again in historical circles to talk about the independent impact of politics on social change. For present purposes, it is not necessary to claim for politics the preeminent place in the determination of change. We need only to recognize the relative autonomy of the political sphere, as we do that of any of the other major elements of perceptible social reality, and to recognize also some of its characteristic roles. It is primarily in the political sphere that individual interests and motives are stated and assembled and where groups compete, compromise, and sometimes integrate with one another. It is in the political sphere that desirable community actions are identified and consensus for their undertaking is created. Contrary to the assumptions implicit in many of the analyses of German imperialism reviewed here, politics is not just a conduit through which the broad underlying forces of socioeconomic change or the demands of elite-interest groups pass as they transform themselves into specific actions. Politics, or the political sphere, is a highly complex social entity in itself, which, although it responds to such influences, also generates motives and a logic of action on its own. It is essential to the argument that follows that we recognize late nineteenth- and early twentieth-century German imperialism, or at least imperialist ideology, primarily as a phenomenon of the political sphere.

A substantial part of German imperialism consisted of ideologies developed and employed by various groups attempting to function under the unprecedentedly complex political circumstances of the late nineteenth and early twentieth centuries. The circumstances that made politics difficult, especially the high degree of fragmentation in the political system (a factor that will be heavily emphasized in our study), were in many cases ultimately the products of the rapid process of modernization that Germany had undergone since the 1850s—but this connection was far from being a simple or exclusive one. A great many other factors also influenced the political context, not least of which was the set of ideologies and formalized social attributes that remained in the public consciousness from the earlier preindustrial periods. Ideologies used for building consensus, formulating policy, or simply attempting to understand the nature of current social conditions had, if they were to be successful, to encompass links to many of these other factors. This is the general vantage point from which the following examination of the origins of Nazi imperialism will proceed. It will concentrate on domestic roots and will in many respects parallel the social imperialist approach. But it will be distinct from the latter, among other ways, in that it will take as its focus the world of politics, both as an intermediary between social change and social action and as a relatively autonomous sphere of social existence in its own right.

One of the keys to the operation of any modern political system is the function of the ideologies within it. Not only do ideologies play a vital role in the conduct of most political processes—from framing the aims and methods of political action to creating consensus and establishing the legitimacy of institutions—but they also act as bearers of political ideas and patterns of behavior from one period to the next. The whole question of continuity in German imperialism (as with any other form of historical continuity within the political sphere) must in some way revolve around the ideologies that are the instruments of continuity. The emphasis in our discussion will be on the evolution of ideologies of imperialism in Germany that culminated in Nazi expansionism. It is necessary that we employ a concept of ideology as an element of a political system that avoids the problems inherent in the other studies we have reviewed. The concept need not claim universal applicability; it must, however, provide a framework within which we can account for most of the functions that an ideological aggregation like imperialism performs in modern politics.

Ideology in Modern Political Systems

There exists no consensus among social scientists and historians about the meaning and societal role of ideology. One school of thought regards ideologies as analogs of philosophical systems, as formal structures of social understanding directed toward policymaking and political action. This approach concentrates primarily on relatively clearly stated and easily recognized ideologies such as Marxism and nineteenth-century liberalism; it tends to have difficulty in explaining more loosely organized sets of political ideas such as Naziism.[17] Another approach sees ideology mainly as a disguise for the particular interests of social classes and groups of political participants or as a means of transforming narrow interest into a general, objective-seeming worldview. This is the approach of the classic sociology of knowledge associated with Karl Mannheim, which is applied implicitly to German imperialism by Fischer, Wehler, and most Marxists.[18] Yet another approach regards ideology in a broad sense, as what Clifford Geertz calls a "cultural system": a cognitive framework—universal in its general type but taking various specific forms in different cultures—through which people structure their knowledge of social reality.[19] These categories are immensely varied within themselves; they are neither mutually exclusive nor exhaustive of the ways in which the concept of ideology has been examined and used.

The lack of consensus about the meaning of ideology entails at least one advantage: one can, to some extent, select the view of ideology that best suits the kind of analysis that one is undertaking. For the purposes of this study, the definition that is used must focus particularly on major functions of ideology within political systems, especially in the context of a rapidly modernizing and highly fragmented society such as that of Germany at the turn of the century. In the following pages, ideology will be treated as a set of ideas employed to facilitate the accomplishment of political action and to justify particular social orders—past, present, or future—by associating such actions and orders with a notion of the general good. This is, of course, only the starting point of a functional definition; it is by no means either original or comprehensive of all possible societal functions of ideology. The definition tends toward a purposive, manipulative conception of ideology. There is no necessary contradiction between this approach and those that see ideologies as widely shared structures of social cognition. Purposive, deliberately constructed political ideologies may be considered in some senses to be subsets of broader ideologies or myths accepted by the community as a whole. But the kinds of political and intellectual phenomena with which we shall deal are primarily ideologies defined in the narrower political sense.[20]

However, it does not make sense from a political standpoint to restrict the concept of ideology to the few relatively clear and, up to a point, logically consistent ideologies such as Marxism and classical liberalism or to force the analysis of other ideological phenomena into a pattern appropriate to these ideologies only. Among the sets of ideas that could qualify as ideologies under the general definition that we are using, Marxism and classical liberalism represent quite a rare type: ideologies with structures similar to formal philosophical systems that have, nevertheless, managed to survive exposures of contradictions in their central tenets, exposures that the very clarity of those tenets encourages. It is not primarily the logical consistency and coherence of a set of political ideas that identify them as an ideology; it is rather their functions in a political system and the relationship of their collective structure to the performance of those functions. Most ideologies, including Naziism and the ideologies of imperialism in Wilhelmian Germany, are not logically consistent, and it may well be that one of the functions of many ideologies is to disguise the inconsistencies among a set of ideas to promote political consensus.[21]

Structure

This is not the place for a detailed analysis of the many forms of ideology, but we can at least identify the structural and functional characteristics of the most important ideological type in modern political systems: the *aggregate* (or *composite*) ideology, of which most forms of nationalism, imperialism, fascism, and, indeed, modern socialism and liberalism are examples. Aggregate ideologies tend to be *congeries* of ideas connected to each other to form what are purported (usually wrongly) to be logically coherent intellectual wholes. Most ideologies offer an analysis of past and current social conditions, a prediction of future social change based on this analysis, and a statement of what should be done either to encourage the predicted change or to prevent it from happening, depending on the judgment of the relative values of the past, present, and future that the ideologies contain. Most modern ideologies are made up of sets of concepts that were originally independent of each other.

The logical structures of such ideologies are consequences of their aggregate natures and their political functions. The logical connections between the constituent elements of aggregate ideologies are often quite loose, depending typically on similarities in image and impression, nonrigorous analogies, the employment of symbols, and similarities in descriptive language. Occasionally, these connections depend on the constant sequential repetition of two unrelated or inconsistent statements so that it comes to be assumed over time that the two statements "belong" together. One of the keys to the political success of particular ideologies is their capacity to incorporate weak logical elements with stronger ones in a single package. The same thing holds for statements that might, in their separate formulations, be regarded by the public at large as narrowly selfish, wrong, or illegitimate. If these can be presented, with or without logically valid connections, in the same set with statements that are widely believed to be true, legitimate, and conducive to the general good of the community, they will have a good chance of finding broad acceptance.

Another characteristic of many political ideologies, one closely related to their composite structures, is a strongly pronounced circular pattern of reasoning and justification. The individual elements of an ideology, as they are fitted over time into the structure of the whole, are usually represented as being supported by the conclusions or assumptions of some of the other elements. In turn, the new elements are used as supports, not only for still other new elements, but also for the original ones. Ideally, an ideology aims at becoming a complex tautology in which the component elements are apparently justified by other elements and no external support (especially empirical verification) is necessary. Although few ideologies succeed in insulating themselves completely from external logic and external tests, the tendency of ideology to remove itself from the sphere of the real and the falsifiable is important to its functioning in the political system.

It is a commonplace that ideologies are oriented toward action. Certain actions proposed by an ideology may sincerely be desired by the advocates of the ideology; others may be included because of the political effect that *proposing* them—not performing them—is supposed to have. The idea of action itself can produce strong images with great affective appeal. The constituent ideas of a composite political ideology legitimate actions, but some proposed actions in themselves also help to create consensus among different groups and individuals. To an extent, such proposed actions legitimate the ideas that lead to them.[22] Action, therefore, plays a complex role in many ideologies, both as an object that ideologies seek to attain and as a means of achieving various political results.

Another commonplace is that ideologies tend toward simplistic ideas. This may be partly because ideologies, having to appeal to a wide variety of people, must aim at a fairly low common denominator of understanding. Probably more important, however, is the fact that to produce the mental images that elicit desired social behavior, ideologies must produce clear-cut, simple diagnoses of what is wrong with society and how, in straightforward, programmatic terms, things can be changed. Simplicity may partly be the result of a need for clear public images that can be shared.

The images advanced by an ideology are typically "displaced" in some way from the society in which they are employed. Mannheim's differentiation between "ideologies" (which employ images of the past) and "utopias" (which employ images of the future) refers to this common ideological characteristic—but *temporal* displacement is not the only form that ideological displacement can take.[23] If one wishes to mobilize people for political action through appeals to dissatisfaction with conditions presently experienced, one way to do so is to present images of different conditions, whether in the past or the future or in some other physical location. Ideologies containing imperialist elements, for example, tended in the nineteenth century to employ a kind of *geographic* displacement, usually in connection with a temporal one. Thus one important form of German imperialist ideology sought to establish in overseas colonies an idealized and re-created peasant agricultural community of a sort that was practically dead in Germany by 1900. Many Europeans have seen colonies as places where needed government reforms (in other words, the political future) could be first introduced.[24] Among other things, displacement allows the employers of an ideology to make statements in terms of a social reality that, because not directly experienced by an ideology's "audience," can be readily manipulated with words.

Functions

The structures of modern composite ideologies are, of course, closely related to their uses in politics, both intentional and unintentional. Within the scope of the definition of ideology used here, one particular ideological function stands out: that of creating *consensus,* either within particular social groups, among different self-conscious social groups, or throughout a society as a whole. Broadly ranging composite ideologies are the intellectual common grounds in modern societies that allow different groups and individuals to undertake joint political action on a regular basis. They are the means by which political parties define the aims, and thus the actions, of their members and by which they seek the support of different segments of society with potentially differing interests. They are also one of the means by which national governments and political elites attempt to create the basis of consent for national political action.

The eclectic and aggregative nature of modern ideologies, their lack of logical rigor, their tendencies toward logical circularity, and their heavy emphasis on emotional and affective appeals are all largely due to their consensus-building function. Such ideologies are usually created from elements that were previously the more limited ideologies of smaller groups that the instigators of action seek to mobilize. These ideological elements are linked in order to bring the smaller groups together for political purposes. At any particular time, political organizations with similar, but not identical, aims may attempt similar forms of ideological amalgamation, thus creating together the impression of a general ideological tendency or, alternatively, of a single highly diffuse ideology. Complete amalgamation into a uniform ideology may or may not eventually occur. For example, before 1914, German radical conservatism was not one ideology but several, with differences more or less corresponding to the differences between the organizations that formed and employed them. By the 1930s, it could be argued that radical conservatism had essentially amalgamated into a single composite ideology to which the National Socialists were the heirs. This is not to say that the process of amalgamation eliminated contradictions from radical conservative thought. German radical conservatism, especially under the Nazis, was shot through with contradictions of all sorts, partly because its proponents originally drew their program together from different, sometimes highly antithetical, earlier ideologies. They did so, of course, to acquire the support of the different groups to whom the earlier ideologies were supposed to appeal.[25]

The lack of logical rigor characteristic of composite ideologies is particularly apparent in the linkages between constituent elements that were originally separate ideological entities. These linkages and their logical weaknesses are frequently glossed over with emotional images and ill-defined vocabulary. Because the motive for ideological aggregation is not primarily the desire to create an accurate model of the social world but rather to establish consensus, an ideology can develop and function quite successfully, up to a point, despite the fact that it may really be a collection of contradictions, non sequiturs, and vivid but empirically ungrounded symbols and analogies. What the employers of an ideology must avoid is the *appearance* of illogicality, contradiction, or inaccuracy. They must attempt to avoid occasions on which the structure of the ideology as a whole can be tested by events—hence the characteristically circular pattern of reasoning and justification in ideologies and hence, also, the need for an ideology to identify scapegoats to be blamed if something goes wrong (as it usually does) when the ideology is turned into policy.

If an ideology turns out to be successful in creating consensus and achieving some of the immediate aims of its users, it can take on a life of its own over time. That is, the ideology may become a continuous element of the political system as a whole, constantly influencing political attitudes at all levels of society. Successful ideologies can find their ways into the process of socialization and education in a society, at which point they can come to be believed more and more uncritically. They may also bear with them—from the periods of their origins on into a changed social world—a considerable burden of unreality and illogicality.

This is crucially important because ideologies play other roles in a political system besides aggregating support and creating consensus. They are also used (consciously or unconsciously) by policymakers in setting the goals of government action, in defining the range of policy options available to achieve these goals, and in evaluating the effectiveness of policies. Whole composite ideologies are not the only conceptual frameworks that are, or can be, employed in this way. As we shall see, policymakers often refer to them merely as justifications for policies that actually represent belief only in some of an ideology's elements. (Indeed, politicians who use large-scale composite ideologies in the creation of public consensus often believe only in a part of what they say or else implicitly prioritize the elements of the ideologies to which they subscribe according to criteria of relative validity.) An ideology deliberately adopted to create consensus may, in the first instances of its use by a group in authority, influence policy because the group believes in the importance of part of the ideology or because it is forced to deliver to the public some of the results that the ideology promises, not because the whole of the ideology is held to be correct. But over time, as composite or aggregate ideologies that have been shaped in part by the needs of consensus creation come to be embedded in the socialization processes of institutions or of society as a whole, newer generations of policymakers may come to believe in them in toto.[26] In such cases, the logical and factual contradictions lurking within an accepted ideology, which are almost inevitably there because of the structures of aggregate ideologies and the processes by which they were created, can cause parties, governments, and peoples to pursue ends that are pointless by means that are self-defeating. We shall observe numerous instances of this, culminating in the disaster of Naziism.

The use of this general view of ideology in the present study can be summarized briefly. In Chapter Two, it is argued that two lines of early German imperialist ideology developed from the responses of different groups of midnineteenth-century liberals to changes in the circumstances of German politics at the onset of rapid industrialization. One of these, migrationist colonialism, emphasized Germany's need for overseas settlement colonies as solutions to the problem of emigration. The other, economic imperialism, called for formal and informal imperial expansion in support of Germany's growing industrial sector. These two rather limited imperialist ideologies were adopted—sometimes individually, sometimes together—by various political organizations in the 1880s that sought ways of building support in what appeared to be an increasingly (and dangerously) fragmented political system. One result of this was Bismarck's sudden foray into colonialism in 1884–85. Another was that imperialism attracted widespread public attention, both as a desirable set of policy aims and as a domestic political tool.

In Chapter Three, the relationship between rapid modernization and the fragmentation of politics in the Wilhelmian era is briefly explored together with the implications for Germany of some of the characteristics of aggregate ideologies. Chapters Four and Five describe the two main Wilhelmian ideologies of imperialism, here called *Weltpolitik* and *Lebensraum,* in structural terms. *Weltpolitik* was essentially an extension of economic imperialism to which other ideological elements were added in the 1890s. As an aggregate ideology, it was shaped, developed, and employed by groups (especially in government and business) attempting to create consensus among segments of society that consciously favored modernity and change but opposed political revolution. *Lebensraum,* an outgrowth of migrationist colonialism to which many elements of nascent radical conservatism were attached in the 1890s, was fundamentally a means of appealing simultaneously to a great many otherwise divergent political groups and social strata that perceived themselves to be victims of modernization. Unlike more extreme conservative ideologies, *Lebensraum* did not completely reject modernity and industrialism; instead, it offered the prospect of retaining much of what was reputed to be valuable in preindustrial German culture through a policy of external settlement, both overseas and in Europe, that would create colonial societies to counteract the effects of inevitable industrialization at home.

Chapter Six describes, through examples, the ways in which the two imperialist ideological aggregations were employed by competing political groups before 1914, how this usage prevented the effective integration of the ideologies, and how the dichotomous nature of German imperialist ideology made it difficult for imperialism to be used as an instrument of nationwide consensus building. Chapter Six also analyzes the process by which the two imperialist ideologies came over time to be accepted by ever-wider arrays of elite and nonelite social groups as accurate guides to policy, quite apart from illusory notions of their political effectiveness in assembling political support for their employers. Chapter Seven discusses the propagation of imperialist ideas in Wilhelmian Germany and various attempts to legitimate and integrate the imperialist ideologies. These attempts, although politically fruitless before 1914, showed the direction that the ideologies of German imperialism would follow in the future.

The careers of the imperialist ideologies in World War I are considered in Chapter Eight. *Weltpolitik,* already ensconced in the official government structure and a major influence on policy before the First World War, strongly informed the aims and assumptions of Bethmann Hollweg's wartime administration. Conservative groups such as the Pan-German League pushed a *Lebensraum*-oriented war-aims policy that featured immense territorial annexations in Europe as part of their campaign to generate conservative opposition to the Bethmann government, which was moving dangerously close to the idea of democratic reform as the price of working-class cooperation in the war effort. In turn, many liberals who favored a degree of democratic reform rallied around an economic imperialist policy based on *Weltpolitik* as their consensus-building weapon. After the overthrow of Bethmann in 1917 and the inauguration of a hidden army rule, the *Lebensraum* connection gained the upper hand. Thereafter, national policy, as manifested in the Treaty of Brest-Litovsk, tended strongly toward *Lebensraum.*

The reign of *Lebensraum* imperialism was cut short by Germany's loss of World War I. Chapter Nine discusses the ways in which both *Weltpolitik* and *Lebensraum* maintained themselves as elements of German politics in the 1920s, *Weltpolitik* as a highly attenuated and modified influence on Weimar governments, *Lebensraum* as a significant integrative ideology on the political right. Also, during the 1920s, a variety of conservative writers and politicians worked with increasing success to integrate many of the concerns of *Weltpolitik* into an overall ideological framework defined by *Lebensraum*. Chapter Ten brings us at last to the Nazis. Hitler is portrayed as a politician attempting to assemble widely dispersed, fundamentally inconsistent ideological entities into a structure that could elicit consensus among the many different segments of society to which the Nazis wanted to appeal and that could at the same time provide a coherent guide for Nazi policy. The latter function included the resolution of the contradictions present in Hitler's own worldview. From the mid-1920s, Hitler's imperialist ideology, which was largely an amalgam of elements from the *Lebensraum* and *Weltpolitik* traditions, played an increasingly important role as an instrument of political integration. Hitler tended to assign temporal priorities to the various prescriptions of the two ideologies—indeed, this was his prime means of combining them. It is clear, however, that he and at least some other leading Nazis genuinely believed in the validity of practically all elements of their version of imperialism. When in power, they moved as systematically as they were able to put the imperialist part of their program into effect. Imperial expansion was in some ways the linchpin of their whole ideological universe, an action that appeared to reconcile the numerous contradictions in the program they put before the public and in which they themselves believed. Thus the Nazi period saw the culmination of the development of German imperialism in a grand scheme of aggression that encompassed no less than the intended subjugation of the entire world. Because Nazi imperialism contained, as a legacy of its history, a multitude of logical and empirical weaknesses, it could not help but be a formula for disaster.

This study is organized as an extended essay rather than a detailed examination of the varieties of German imperialism. It concentrates on the continuities in imperialism afforded by the development of imperialist ideologies as functions of politics. For that reason, much of the discussion concerns the general characteristics of the aggregate imperialist ideologies rather than particular variations or the full range of their political uses. The need for detailed substantiation is met by the inclusion of extended examples to illustrate the major points of the argument. Thus, in Chapter Six, the interaction between Wilhelmian politics and imperialist ideology is displayed in two cases (the emergence of colonial-development policies and the genesis of the Moroccan crisis of 1911) rather than in a treatment of all the major issues that concerned imperialism in the *Kaiserreich*. It is hoped that this approach together with the references to both primary and secondary materials in the notes has made it possible to maintain the coherence of the basic argument without avoiding the requirements of responsible scholarship.

CHAPTER TWO

The Origins of the German Imperialist Ideologies

By the mid-1870s, two distinct varieties of thought about Germany's possible relationship with future dependencies beyond her borders had gained common currency in popular political literature. Both could be traced back to earlier decades in the nineteenth century. Although they had not always been completely separate from each other, their processes of development, their internal logic, and the social outlooks they represented were sufficiently distinct so that they can be considered as at least the nuclei of two different ideologies in the sense discussed in Chapter One.

These two ideological tendencies had no particular names in the general usage of the time. To employ such terms as *Weltpolitik* for one or both of them before 1890 would be rather anachronistic and misleading. I have therefore named them myself on the basis of some of their central ideas, calling one migrationist colonialism and the other economic imperialism. Both had foreign cognates, although migrationist colonialism was the more distinctly German. Neither was a really major political force in the mid-1870s, although migrationist colonialism had come close to being one in 1848 and both would greatly affect politics in the 1880s. To a considerable extent, migrationist colonialism and economic imperialism constituted the central elements of the ideological aggregations that emerged at the end of the nineteenth century which will later in this study be designated, respectively, as *Lebensraum* and *Weltpolitik*.

Migrationist Colonialism

Migrationist colonialism originated as one of a number of ideological responses to the *Auswanderung,* the massive emigration from Germany that continued in cycles throughout the nineteenth century.[1] The early forms that migrationist colonialism took were largely determined by the ways in which its creators perceived the *Auswanderung;* its later development depended on its coincidence with the social perceptions of much broader segments of German society and on the ways in which writers and political organizations were able to link it to other similar ideological formulations.

The most important early body of theories about the *Auswanderung* and of recommendations for what to do about it arose from moderate pre-1848 liberalism, particularly in the western German states that experienced the first waves of emigration directly. To liberals of the 1830s and 1840s such as Hans von Gagern and Robert Mohl, emigration was fundamentally a police problem—in the widest nineteenth-century sense of the term.[2] This probably reflects the much-remarked connection between early German liberalism and occupational groups closely attached to the state administrations.[3] The cycles of emigration that had commenced with the end of the Napoleonic wars seemed to threaten depopulation for large areas of Baden, Württemberg, and Westphalia and raised the possibility of social disorder. Because many emigrants were young men of military age, emigration might weaken the state's defenses. The money that emigrants took with them reduced the availability of capital. Mohl worried particularly about this last point and wanted to forbid the emigration of the well-to-do. Moreover, it gradually became clear in the 1840s that the *Auswanderung* was in some way connected to yet another disturbing social phenomenon: urbanization. At first, some observers thought that the rapid spread of slums in Hamburg and Bremen was due mainly to the influx of immigrants seeking passage to America; but, by the time of the 1848 revolution, most had come to realize that emigration and permanent urban settlement were parallel, not sequential, phenomena—both impelled by the forces that were driving people from the western German countryside. All of the police problems associated with early industrial urbanization were thus somewhat unclearly attached in the minds of liberal politicians and theorists to the problems already spawned by overseas emigration.[4]

It had, moreover, become widely known that conditions of emigrant travel at sea were often terrible, that *Auswanderer* were often cheated by emigration agents, and that conditions in the Americas were not as they had been represented in Germany. In the 1840s, liberal commentators began to complain that *Auswanderer* in the United States rapidly lost the traits of their German culture—their language, their characteristic behavior patterns, their literature—and became, in fact, cultural Anglo-Americans.[5]

The *Auswanderung* presented liberals not only with problems to decry, but also with political opportunities to realize. In the 1840s, liberals could claim that emigration was a social phenomenon with which existing political regimes had failed to deal satisfactorily and that liberal administrations could handle better. Also, if the liberals could offer reasonable programs for improving the conditions of emigration, they could make a substantial claim to the support of the lower and middle social levels of the rural population, the groups from which most emigrants came and the ones whose willingness to accept liberalism was, in the 1840s, questionable.[6]

Moderate liberals concerned with the *Auswanderung* took several directions in their thinking about the problem, but most of them shared certain general ideas. Unlike many conservative government officials who wanted to limit or ban emigration as a whole, most liberals believed that the *Auswanderung* neither should, nor could, be stopped. Emigration reflected a real condition of the rural economy, and trying to prohibit it altogether would have the same deleterious and ultimately futile effects as other forms of fundamental economic interference by the state.

Originally, most liberal commentators conceived of the cause of emigration in rather crude Malthusian terms: the inevitable tendency of rural society toward overpopulation. The result of attempting to constrict the outlet provided by emigration would be economic disintegration in the countryside, misallocation of resources, starvation, and possibly widespread rural violence.[7] More sophisticated analysts related overpopulation to the changing structure of the rural economy. The influential economist Friedrich List, for example, argued that migration both to the cities and to America was due to the appearance of "dwarf economies" in southwestern Germany; these were created by the subdivision of peasant farms through inheritance into smaller and increasingly inefficient units.[8] As the phenomenon of emigration spread to other areas of Germany, however, List's explanation became inadequate, as did most of the simpler overpopulation arguments. In East Elbian Prussia, for instance, the motivation for rural migration was connected to the modernization of agriculture on the larger *Junker* grain estates and the inability of the smaller peasant farmers to compete with them. By the 1850s, liberal commentators increasingly portrayed the *Auswanderung* as a phenomenon connected to complex long-term economic changes.[9]

The importance of emigration as a *symbolic* consequence of modernization helps to explain the nature and political significance of migrationist colonialism as an ideology. From the time that the connection between emigration and ongoing structural economic change was made, proposals to deal with the problems raised by emigration were often, by implication at least, regarded as the proper political responses to change itself. This was, in part, a consequence of the liberal framework within which migration was discussed, but the implicit assumption that action to deal with emigration also addressed the underlying problems of socioeconomic change remained part of migrationist colonialism even after it lost its connection to the liberal framework that gave the assumption its logical coherence.

Most liberals at midcentury regarded major economic trends as essentially unalterable or at least unalterable without severe damage to the social system as a whole. Whatever people like Mohl and List thought of economic modernization (and the example of English modernization made them ambivalent about it), they did not believe that it could ultimately be prevented or that it would be a good idea to try to do so. It was necessary, therefore, to attempt to direct the process by which the *consequences* of economic change worked themselves out along lines designed to maximize the benefits of change and to minimize social and cultural damage. Despite the possibility of contradiction—between laissez-faire liberalism and the idea of government regulation—that manipulating the consequences of change implied, this sort of view became highly characteristic of a great deal of liberal social thought around the middle of the nineteenth century and thereafter.[10] Migrationist colonialism was thus but one part of a larger trend.

Migrationist colonialism is, in its origins, probably best regarded as a specific offshoot of the general moderate liberal approach to the *Auswanderung* that developed in the first half of the nineteenth century, an offshoot that focused on settlement colonies as solutions to the problems of emigration. From the time of the extensive debates about emigration and colonialism at Frankfurt in 1848, the relationship between the main trend and its subset became increasingly strained, until they came to be seen as competing approaches to the *Auswanderung* by the late 1850s.

The essence of the proposals of those who did not go all the way to colonialism was that German states and private organizations should undertake a comprehensive program of improving the conditions of emigration through projects to educate potential *Auswanderer* about the outside world, through the close regulation of emigration agents and emigrant shipping, and through diplomatic pressure on countries such as the United States and Brazil to protect German settlers. Organizations were to be established in Germany to endow German schools abroad to prevent the de-Germanization of the emigrants' children.[11] Those most oriented toward state action also wanted the states to encourage emigration selectively, concentrating on the classes that most needed the outlet (the rural peasantry and the village artisan class).[12] During the 1848 revolution, the projected role of a united German state in accomplishing these goals caused modifications in some aspects of "standard" migrationism, but not fundamental ones. The basic idea remained the same down to the 1880s: emigration should be encouraged and facilitated as a response to socioeconomic change in Germany and regulated only to protect the states, German culture as a whole, and the *Auswanderer* themselves.

The colonialist variant of migrationism grew out of the belief of a number of moderate liberals that the problems caused by emigration and even some of the problems that caused emigration itself could be dealt with more effectively by means other than regulation alone. Colonialists such as Mohl and Friedrich Hundeshagen were concerned, for example, that the standard regulatory proposals would not prevent the draining away of capital needed for economic prosperity and of men needed for labor and military defense. If German colonies could be set up in the kinds of places to which *Auswanderer* went—temperate areas suitable for European-style farming—and could remain economically and culturally attached to the mother country, they could not only protect the emigrants better, but also become permanent partners for German trade and continuous positive influences on German society.[13]

This was, however, not all there was to the idea. At a deeper and more significant level, migrationist colonialism must be viewed as a conscious response to social and cultural change. It was this aspect that eventually developed into the key element of the ideology and its prime link to conservative ideologies in the last third of the nineteenth century, thereby detaching migrationist colonialism from its original liberal context. The ideal migrationist colonies were to be settlement areas in which traditional small-unit agriculture could be established together with the kind of society that such agriculture supported. The emphasis that many migrationists placed on the maintenance of German culture referred not only to the national and intellectual aspects of culture, but also specifically to the cultural patterns characteristic of peasant societies—patterns threatened in Germany by socioeconomic change.[14]

The reasoning behind this aspect of migrationism was thus ultimately conservative. Modernization was inevitable in Germany, but as much of the old social system as was worth saving had to be preserved. If this could not be done within the German states themselves, then it must be done in other parts of the world where conditions were more favorable. The benefits of having a peasant agricultural sector could be guaranteed to Germany through a colonial attachment. Because they would draw on the same sources of population pressure that filled the newly expanding cities, the overseas settlement colonies would, in essence, reduce the ill effects of urbanization and direct potential slumdwellers to areas in which they could practice their traditional rural vocations in ways that benefitted both themselves and their country. Friedrich List, extending this kind of reasoning beyond colonialism, argued in the 1840s that overseas colonization was such a problematic affair that it would be better to direct migrants to "unused" land in eastern Germany, where the same results would be obtained closer to home.[15] This was the germ of the inner colonialization idea that gained great currency in the 1890s.

Migrationist colonialism, although clearly an outgrowth of pre-1848 German liberalism, was on the whole a product of liberalism's most moderate side and incorporated within itself a quite conservative, but not reactionary, view of social change. It should be noted that little in the many formulations of migrationist colonialism around 1848 or in the period up to the 1870s was overtly anticommercial. The colonies were to be agricultural settlement areas but they were supposed to trade with Germany and to augment the incomes of her states. Emigration to colonies was supposed to preserve social order in Germany and the culture of the people displaced by economic change, but it was not fundamentally intended to prevent economic and social modernization.

Migrationist colonialism, like the general migrationist idea-set of which it was originally an offshoot, became momentarily a matter of intense public discussion during the 1848 revolution. The apparent imminence of a united Germany made the possibility of effective emigration regulation and colonial acquisition seem more likely than before. Although most of the colonial proposals before and immediately after 1848–49 were for "colonies" without clear political attachments to Germany or to individual German states, colonial expansion became in 1848 part of a rather violent and multifaceted formal imperialism that caught hold of the imaginations of nationalist liberals.[16] All of this imperialism, of course, went for nought when the revolution failed in 1849.

Migrationism did not entirely die out after 1849. The migrationist colonial idea was further refined and "standard" migrationism and migrationist colonialism developed into separate and increasingly antagonistic ideasets. "Standard" migrationism—the idea that migration should be open but regulated—came to be one of the main foundations for liberal *anti*colonialism during the 1880s.[17]

There were probably a great many reasons that both the colonial and the noncolonial forms of migrationism maintained their positions in German public consciousness after 1848. One was, of course, that the phenomenon with which they dealt—the *Auswanderung*—continued to exist, greatly expanding in volume and geographic incidence in the 1850s. At the same time, schemes for the establishment of more-or-less private colonies in America continued to be put forward. Some of them were actually carried out.[18] But the most important factor preserving migrationist colonialism and encouraging its development toward the status of a fullfledged ideology appears to have been the rapidity of economic change in Germany in the 1850s and 1860s—the period of Germany's real industrial revolution. Rapid change produced a potential mass audience for migrationist colonialism by increasing the kinds of socioeconomic pressure to which migration, by the midnineteenth century, was conventionally supposed to be a response.

Several different segments of German society were affected by this process, but the most important, at least in the minds of politicians and writers who employed migrationist ideas, were the peasants and rural artisans who traditionally supplied the majority of emigrants. Rapid economic modernization in ever-widening areas had substantial, and often quite complex, effects on people in these categories—mostly by intensifying the factors that had been dissolving the peasant sector of the rural economy since early in the nineteenth century. In East Elbian Prussia, accelerating demand for agricultural products from expanding urban areas throughout western Europe increased the disproportion of economic power between the owners of extensive tracts and the peasant farmers. Many of the latter, unable because of lack of sufficient capital and land to compete for widening markets, found themselves driven into debt, into seeking employment on larger estates, and into migrating to urban areas or America. In other regions, the backwardness of the peasant economy and the availability of urban jobs accentuated the flight from the land that had earlier spawned migrationist thinking. There is evidence that the idea of migration as a response to personal or general economic misfortune was widely discussed in rural communities at midcentury.[19] Journalists and politicians who recognized this could try, by using the migrationist ideologies, to organize peasant attitudes toward emigration and direct them to the support of particular political movements.

After 1848, it became clear to politicians of all political persuasions that rural artisans and small property holders were an important key to political success, especially in Prussia.[20] Rural violence had strongly affected the course of the 1848 revolution, and the loss of rural revolutionary fervor had helped lead to the conservative revival in Prussia late in 1848. Conservative expectations of retaining power and preventing further liberal reform, like liberal hopes of gaining the political initiative in the 1850s, depended, in part, on building bridges to the peasantry. The Prussian government and the leaders of Junkerdom adopted a much-publicized program of legal protection of the peasantry against the ravages of capitalism and used the educational system to instill loyalty to a paternalistic, social-conservative state among the peasants. Conservative publicists such as Wilhelm Riehl put together the first elements of a romantic agrarian ideology with the peasant as hero-figure. To advance their cause, liberals of various stripes made their own pitches to the peasantry. Those on the liberal left pushed democracy and antagonism toward hereditary aristocracies. Others made use of migrationism, arguing as they had in the past that liberal governments, committed to freedom of movement, could better facilitate successful emigration than could conservative ones.

We have no way of telling the extent to which migrationist arguments really succeeded in attracting rural support. There is evidence, however, that the politicians who used them believed well into the 1880s that they had broad appeal.[21] The version of migrationism most in evidence in the political literature of the 1850s and 1860s, and thus perhaps the version best known to the public at large, was the "standard" or noncolonial one. Migrationist colonialism also had its adherents, however—people such as the economist Wilhelm Roscher and the publicist Julius Fröbel.[22] At least in theory, their position had a great deal to recommend it as a means of assembling rural support under the political circumstances of the period. It connected the notion of emigration as a response to economic hardship and social dissolution with the ideas of nationalism and patriotism (Prussian and otherwise) that were becoming increasingly important in the struggle for political consensus.

Migrationist colonialists of the 1850s and 1860s did not simply argue that migration was good for Germany in the negative sense of ridding the country of unwanted people. They also claimed that migration to *colonies* was positively patriotic because it augmented the strength and wealth of the home country.[23] Emigration by itself presented an image that was difficult to square with patriotism; it smacked of desertion. But emigration to a German colony (however defined) put the emigrant into the vanguard of Germany's attempt to take its place among the leading European nations. The appeal of this kind of argument could potentially be very strong, despite the fact that there were few real colonies to which emigrants could move—just the scattered settlements of private colonial organizations in North and South America, which had no official political affiliation to the German states. Active subscription to an ideology that accepted the need of many people to emigrate now and connected that need to a political process that would eventually produce real German colonies had the effect of justifying emigration in terms of nationalist assumptions.

Probably even more important in establishing the appeal of migrationist colonialism—not only to the peasantry, but also to substantial numbers of middle-class and lower middle-class town dwellers—was its implicit criticism of modernity and the fact that colonialism provided an apparently *active* response to change. As we have seen, at the heart of migrationist colonialism was an image of a society in a colonial setting overseas in which the small German farmer could pursue his traditional occupation profitably in connection with a commercial economy in which he was an independent participant, not a victim. It was an image of a peasant society shorn of all the things that were making such a society seem doomed in Germany: encroaching Junker estates, competition from producers within and outside the country, the spectre of indebtedness if capital improvements in agriculture were implemented and of unprofitability if they were not. Colonies would be situated on good, scientifically selected farming land, unencumbered by rents, dues, and excessive mortgages, where labor and careful planning would yield sufficient profit to permit capital improvement. The availability of nearby virgin land would create opportunites for the sons of farmers, thus reducing tendencies toward List's "dwarf economies."

The publicists of migrationist colonialism, like an increasing number of other German intellectuals after midcentury, tended to idealize the peasants and their culture as the solid foundations for virtue and stability in German society. Such an image was of course flattering to small farmers. It was formulated in terms of an overt comparison with the urban industrial proletariat, who were represented as something less than human because of their environment.[24] The set of images incorporated into migrationist colonialism did not, of course, closely reflect an existent social reality. If the society of independent, virtuous small farmers that the romantic agrarian imagery of midcentury presented ever existed, it certainly had ceased to do so by then—so the supposed benefits of settlement colonization were largely illusory. But from a political standpoint, this hardly mattered. Migrationist colonialism survived and flourished because its component ideas and images caught the attention of several different kinds of people, not just the peasantry—although small farmers were the central figures in the imagery. It focused fears and resentments of economic change and connected them to a program of political action, which politicians could employ to attract attention to larger ideological programs to which colonialism could be attached.

The criticism of modernity and industrialization implied by early migrationist colonialism was indirect and conditional; it was in no sense tied to a reactionary social view or before the 1870s to conservative politics. The ideology focused on economic change in general, not on industrialization per se. The implied villains were the bankers, the lawyers, and in eastern Prussia, the expansionary Junkers, not necessarily the industrialists. The urban industrial image was usually presented as a horrible alternative to migration and colonialization, not as yet as the force that was destroying rural society. Migrationist colonialism did not, as we have seen, reject all elements of industry and commerce. In other words, although migrationist colonialism was not likely to appeal to industrialists or entrepreneurs on the basis of its specific content, it *could* be used as part of an ideological construct that claimed to offer grounds for reconciliation between an industrial Germany and a certain range of traditional social and cultural images with great political appeal.

From the 1850s at the latest, writers and politicians who employed migrationist arguments were conscious of speaking to an audience of *Kleinbürger* (urban lower middle-class people) as well as peasants.[25] *Kleinbürger* also emigrated, but not as readily as peasants. A large part of the appeal of migrationist colonialism to them probably resulted not so much from the fact of emigration as from the nature of the images that migrationist colonialism conveyed, even though most of these were agrarian, not urban, images.

This phenomenon was clearly connected to a larger development that has been much remarked by historians: the growth of antimodern, antiindustrial sentiment among the German lower middle classes as they confronted the problems of socioeconomic modernization in the second half of the nineteenth century. Hans Rosenberg has discussed some of the factors of cyclical economic change in the 1870s that may have given this sentiment a particular ideological form. But even before that time, romantic literature idealizing the peasantry had become popular among urban lower middle-class readers.[26] This popular agrarianism became an important root of radical conservative ideologies at the end of the nineteenth century. The images associated with migrationist colonialism appear to have focused the same sort of unease with industrialization, occupational obsolescence, and economic concentration that encouraged middle-class romantic agrarianism. Migrationist colonialism had, however, a definite advantage over romantic agrarianism as a potential means of creating political consensus: it contained a seemingly practical plan of action (colonial acquisition and development) that did not entirely exclude commercial interests.

Migrationist colonialism found a place in the spectrum of German political ideology in the 1860s and 1870s as one of the ideological tendencies that grew out of *Vormärz* liberalism but developed political directions of its own. It was by far the best known variety of colonialism in Germany in the 1870s. Most Germans discussing colonial expansion before 1880—either pro or con—normally assumed that they were talking about agricultural settlement colonies.[27] Migrationist colonialism was not, however, the *only* form that imperialist ideology took in Germany in the 1870s.

Economic Imperialism

The main ideological alternative to migrationist colonialism that accepted the basic idea of overseas imperial expansion was the idea-set I have labelled economic imperialism, the specifically colonial component of which is probably best referred to as economic colonialism. Economic imperialism became the central element of the broader imperialist ideology of *Weltpolitik* after 1890.

Economic imperialism was much less uniquely German than was migrationist colonialism. It borrowed most of its constituent concepts from common European imperialist traditions, especially those of Britain.[28] Its main underlying assumption was that overseas policy for a united Germany should be oriented primarily toward improving the prospects of German trade. Increased trade would lead to increased domestic prosperity, to higher industrial and commercial profits, and to higher real earnings for the working and commercial middle classes.

This basic focus was capable of being turned in various directions, encompassing, in fact, economic positions as different as free trade and protectionism. But economic imperialists all generally agreed that, on the whole, the process of economic modernization in Germany was a good thing that ought to be fostered actively. Germany was fated to become an industrial country and therefore what was good for industry was good for Germany, up to a point. A government campaign, for example, to encourage exports by subsidies, by placing political pressure on other countries and influencing their tariff policies, and by setting up a system of consulates abroad would benefit all of German society. So would trading colonies.[29]

Many of the major elements of economic imperialism were enunciated in the 1840s by the ubiquitous Friedrich List. List argued that overseas colonies were needed to supplement his favorite scheme for economic development: a central European economic union.[30] He foresaw an economic organization with an industrialized Germany as its center and a periphery of other central and eastern European states that would supply food and raw materials for German industry and would purchase German industrial products. A semiautarkic structure would thus be created; it would have the advantage of permitting control, or even exclusion, of British competition, thus allowing central Europe to industrialize successfully in an orderly, planned manner. List was not always enthusiastic about industrialization, but he thought it inevitable and, on the whole, desirable as long as government supervision and the economic union could constrain the excesses of free enterprise and prevent severe damage to society in the process of modernization. List did not therefore stand greatly apart in terms of basic attitudes from the liberal migrationists.

Only after his death in 1847 and the development of new attitudes and ideologies in the wake of full-scale German industrialization did the implications of the kind of view expressed by List come to be seen as very different from the implications of migrationist colonialism.

As to colonies, List presented the classic view of overseas dependencies as adjuncts to the home economy. Actually, they played a relatively small role in List's overall thinking. Colonies were supposed to be conveniences for trade, established only where necessary for specific limited commercial reasons. Colonies might stake the claim of Germany (or the central European union) to a share of trade with a particular area and they might provide the facilities for the importation of commodities not available in Europe, but List did not see them either as a means of solving Germany's social problems or as symbols of Germany's prestige. List's solution to the *Auswanderung* was not to create overseas colonies but to direct emigration eastward—to establish strong farming communities in the eastern portions of Prussia and the Austrian empire in order to build an agricultural periphery of the economic union.

List was not the only proponent of economic imperialism in Germany, nor did all of his ideas eventually find their way into *Weltpolitik*. List did, however, express forcefully many of the most important ideas advanced by later economic imperialists: the necessary centrality of industrialization in all economic planning, the belief that stimulating industrial production by expanding and integrating industrial markets would increase overall German prosperity, the related belief that maintaining prosperity depended on an uninterrupted flow of goods between an industrial center and a dependent periphery, and the designation of overseas colonies as elements of that periphery. Like most later economic imperialists, List heavily emphasized the active role of government in economic modernization. Governments were supposed to intervene to prevent social and cultural damage from economic change, and they were supposed, if necessary, to use military power to create the central European union and acquire colonies. Many later economic imperialists reversed some of List's priorities, emphasizing, for example, overseas trade and colonies and downplaying continental economic expansion, but both elements were always present to some degree. For example, although few economic imperialists actively pushed for a *formal* continental economic union in the 1890s, they did generally advocate *informal* German dominance over a large area of central and eastern Europe. The most controversial part of List's proposals—the adoption of high tariffs on manufactured goods—was the aspect least characteristic of later economic imperialism. Later economic imperialists were, for the most part, neither doctrinaire free traders nor protectionists. Whichever side they took on later tariff disputes, they tended to regard tariffs only as a certain type of instrument (and a rather crude one) available for use in support of a broader economic and imperial policy.

List's version of imperialism had few immediate practical effects, although his ideas were widely discussed during the 1848 revolution and influenced Austrian economic policy during the 1850s and 1860s. They did, however, make up an important part of the body of economic literature that supplied ammunition to the various sides in the disputes over German industrialization and unification before 1871. Borrowing from List and from non-German writers, several publicists and politicians in the 1860s took up the notion of colonies as adjuncts to a unified German industrial economy. Lothar Bucher, for example, an 1848 liberal who became one of Bismarck's most prominent spokesmen in the 1860s, publicly advocated economic imperialism and trading colonies. In 1867, Bucher talked Bismarck into allowing him to put a series of articles into the semiofficial *Norddeutsche Allgemeine Zeitung* that favored colonial acquisition as a means of enhancing German trade. The placement of the articles probably meant nothing more on Bismarck's part than another tentative feeler in the direction of the liberals and commercial interests during the politicking over the formation of the North German Confederation, but it does indicate Bucher's economic colonialist leanings and his belief that such ideas appealed to at least a part of public opinion. During the late 1860s and in the wake of Germany's defeat of France in 1870–71, the idea of setting up a colonial empire for commercial purposes was fairly widely discussed, but Bismarck decisively rejected all such proposals.[31]

By the 1870s, economic imperialism with a colonial dimension had emerged—again, largely out of moderate liberal social and economic thought—as a rather minor element of German politics. When the press considered the possibility of building a colonial empire, it was usually the migrationist, not the economic imperialist, version that was emphasized. The later part of the decade, however, brought with it circumstances that pushed economic imperialism to the forefront of public consciousness.

The Colonial Movement of the 1870s and 1880s

The process by which Germany became a colonial power is a familiar subject to students of German history, as is the controversy over Bismarck's "conversion" to colonialism. For this reason, it is only necessary to outline briefly the events leading to Bismarck's colonial initiatives in 1883–85 and to discuss their significance for the later development of the imperialist ideologies.[32]

In the late 1870s and the early 1880s, there appeared in Germany a political movement that called on the government to seize colonies abroad. The movement achieved substantial support among business interests and among the leaders of several political parties, especially the National Liberals and the Free Conservatives. At some point, perhaps in 1880, Bismarck was persuaded that it would be advantageous for himself and for the government to be aligned with the colonialist movement. Treading softly at first because of the opposition of the Reichstag majority to colonial adventure, Bismarck laid the groundwork for German colonization in Africa and the South Seas during 1883 and early 1884 through covert arrangements with entrepreneurs interested in colonies. In 1884 he abandoned secrecy. He dispatched a warship to declare protectorates over the coastal regions of Togo and Cameroon in West Africa; he declared, after diplomatic controversy with the British, a protectorate over Southwest Africa; and he also claimed territory in northeastern New Guinea and adjacent islands. In addition, he reluctantly gave official sanction to the treaties of "protection" signed by Carl Peters with local chiefs in present-day Tanzania. Taking advantage of widespread, if temporary, enthusiasm for colonies, Bismarck also convinced the Reichstag to accept the new state of affairs. For better or worse, Germany had entered the ranks of the imperial powers.

For present purposes, it is probably best to regard the appearance of the colonial movement and the political process leading to the seizure of the colonies as separate phenomena. There were, of course, vital connections between them: Bismarck's decision to create a colonial empire is inconceivable without the prior appearance of the colonial movement; the colonial movement, on the other hand, was never sufficiently strong to force Bismarck's unwilling hand. In essence, what happened was that the formation of the colonial movement in the late 1870s and early 1880s presented Bismarck with a problem (how to deal with a new political force, however temporary it might be) and a set of political opportunities that he seized, but did not have to seize. The prior existence of the imperialist ideologies and their potential for affecting politics help to explain what those opportunities were.

The German colonial movement was one of the first attempts in Germany's postunification history to create a political movement centering around ideologies that appeared to lie outside the traditional dichotomies of German politics. Unlike the *Kulturkampf,* which had pitted doctrinaire liberals against the Roman Catholic Church, and unlike the issue of protection versus free trade that raged around the 1879 tariff, the question of colonialism seemed to cut across ideological and social boundaries. Although both major colonialist ideologies in Germany were originally products of liberalism, neither was exclusively bound to liberalism by the late 1870s; indeed, the major ideological opposition to colonialism in the 1880s came from the ranks of the orthodox free-trade liberals and from the liberal proponents of free emigration. The fact that colonialism appeared to transect liberalism was one of the things that attracted Bismarck to it. It appeared to politicians and political commentators of all sorts that, because of the contents of the existing imperialist ideologies, colonialism could be used to appeal to many different classes and social groups simultaneously in a way that no other readily available ideological set could do.[33] An interest group or party or even Bismarck's government itself, whether or not it had any real concern for actual colonial acquisition, could still anticipate that, by identifying itself publicly with a movement toward imperial expansion and colonization, it could build public support for other objectives that it sought. Colonialism was thus, first and foremost, a tool to counter the political fragmentation that was beginning to appear as the main problem of German national politics. Its utility in this respect depended, of course, on the capacities of the imperialist ideologies for attachment to many different sets of political goals and aims as well as on the credibility with which a movement to acquire overseas colonies could claim to be a major political force.

The actual formation of a colonial movement began in the late 1870s with a series of actions taken by particular business-interest groups to obtain government support in the face of the post-1873 depression and cutthroat competition in international markets. After the Reichstag passed a tariff schedule in 1879 that mainly benefitted the domestically oriented metals and coal industry and big Junker agriculture, economic interests such as the overseas shipping industry and import/export-dependent manufacturing enterprises perceived themselves to be in need of immediate assistance.[34] Adolf Woermann, for example, the head of a Hamburg shipping firm specializing in West African coastal trade, wanted government protection against a possible exclusion of Germans from British-dominated areas of the African coasts, which might be Britain's form of retaliation for the tariff. Woermann also envisioned benefits such as government mail contracts that would accompany the establishment of direct German rule over some parts of his marketing area.[35] The backers of the nearly bankrupt Godeffroy shipping firm, the major investor in plantation agriculture in Samoa, wanted similar kinds of help.[36] The only way that such interests could see of achieving their aims was to get the German government to involve itself directly in the expansion of overseas trade, especially through subsidies and through official intervention in places such as Samoa and West Africa. But the shipping industry was not strong enough politically to turn the trick by itself, especially as Bismarck had up to 1880 resolutely refused to allow Germany to engage in active overseas imperialism. The shippers needed allies, and they found them first among the leaders of export/import-dependent industries such as cotton. Light industries in Saxony and the Rhineland had already begun to organize associations devoted ostensibly to promoting exploration, the spread of geographic knowledge, and the investigation of new overseas marketing opportunities; in addition, they formally pressured the government into undertaking what Hans-Ulrich Wehler has called an "export offensive" throughout the world.[37] The attachment of shipping interests to this movement gave it added strength and depth; moreover, it helped to turn the movement fairly decisively in the direction of formal imperialism and colonialism.

Why colonialism? In part, because the interests of the shipping companies could best be served in their limited trading areas by the establishment of an official German presence. To some extent, this was the price of the accommodation between the light-industrial export groups and shippers like Woermann. But there was a great deal more to it than that.

The formation of an interest in favor of export expansion under government sponsorship required that some connecting set of ideas be recognized as the ideological basis of the interest, as the source of the policies the interest sought. Because the shipping and light-industrial interest did not have great political power at the national level, it was also imperative that ideological means be found of attaching what the shippers and exporters wanted to some broader structure of interests to elicit wider support. It was, furthermore, necessary to provide the political parties and the government with an argument that would allow them, if they chose to respond favorably to the export-expansion pressure, to justify such a policy in terms of the general good. Bismarck, party leaders, even directly concerned parties such as Woermann might or might not believe in the objective validity of the broader ideological justification, but it was absolutely vital that the justification be available. The only existing ideological framework within which the export-expansion interest could operate was economic imperialism; only the colonialist element of economic imperialism could promote the aims of shippers such as Woermann. Hence, as the organizations pushing for export expansion grew in size and in the scope of their activities in the early 1880s, they increasingly formulated their arguments around the tenets of economic imperialism, with a heavy emphasis on colonialism.[38]

A crucial role in giving the movement to expand exports and protect markets an ideological grounding—indeed, the crucial role in actually organizing the movement—was played by a small group of publicists with personal connections to most of the interests involved. Most prominent among these were the Protestant mission director Friedrich Fabri and the Hamburg lawyer Wilhelm Hübbe-Schleiden. Fabri, in particular, was one of the first to note the political utility of certain implications contained in economic imperialism: the elements that Wehler calls "social imperialism" and emphasizes heavily in his explanation of the success of the German colonial movement.[39] A wide variety of propertied and elite groups in German society could be attracted to an imperialist movement by the argument that active overseas expansion, by creating new markets, would increase prosperity and employment at home, and thus cut the ground from under the feet of the Socialists and other radicals seeking more extraordinary responses to the economic problems facing the working class. In a general sense, so Fabri and others argued, active imperialism could serve as a unifying force within a badly fragmented nation—a force rallying the nation behind the "responsible" classes. If workers could be shown the direct benefits to themselves of overseas expansion under the leadership of the established elite, the threat of revolution (and perhaps trade unionism) could be avoided.[40]

Although Fabri clearly believed all this (and a good deal else, as we shall see), the main function of his and other publicists' use of social imperialism was in the conduct of short-term politics. It gave the export-expansion movement, as it was evolving into a colonial movement, the means of making a generalized appeal to people who, regardless of their specific economic interests, identified with employers and property owners on social questions and who shared these groups' fixation on the threat of revolution. Most particularly, it connected the movement to the ideological position taken by the powerful lobbying organizations of heavy industry—especially the *Centralverband Deutscher Industrieller* (CDI), which had been the most important force behind the 1879 tariff. The CDI's general secretary, Henry Axel Bueck, was attracted to the colonial movement by the social imperialist argument and also by the possibility that imperialism might prove to be broadly popular, which would give the CDI a handle on public opinion if the organization could be identified with colonialism. In no real sense, however, was heavy industry an initiating force in the colonial movement. The CDI and other heavy industrial lobbies, in essence, saw political opportunities in the colonial movement in the early 1880s and jumped aboard.[41]

The publicists of the colonial movement used other aspects of economic imperialism as means of cementing the tie to heavy industry—means that had little to do with the idea of acquiring trading colonies for present commercial purposes. Small colonies on the coasts of Africa and in the Pacific were represented as guarantees of access to developing markets in the future when the export interests of the metals and engineering industries extended beyond Europe.[42] More immediately, the concept of economic expansion in eastern Europe through a German-centered customs organization—List's old idea—was beginning to have appeal for heavy industry.[43] The CDI and its heavy-industrial backers had pushed for the tariff of 1879 to protect their domestic German market against British competition. But to get the industrial tariff, they had been forced to agree to substantial tariffs on the import of grain as a protection for Junker agriculture. Partly in response to the grain tariff, the Russian and Austro-Hungarian governments had slapped prohibitive tariffs on German industrial imports, which effectively cut much of German heavy industry off from its most obvious area of market expansion in the immediate future. The economic imperialist idea-set offered the possibility that if Russia and Austria-Hungary could be enticed into an economic union, the union could be used as a vehicle for giving heavy industry what it wanted: maintaining effective protection of the German market while gaining access to eastern European markets. At the same time, the idea of an economic union was sufficiently vague that advocating it did not necessarily constitute an attack on Junker agriculture, which would have upset the uneasy alliance between "rye and iron." Because the concept of regional economic integration had for some time been associated with economic imperialism, it was not difficult to include references to it in the literature of the colonial movement and thus to build a further potential ideological bridge to big business.[44]

Even as the elements of the existing economic imperialist ideology were being mustered to the fullest extent possible in the early 1880s, it was clear to most of the publicists and organizers involved with the colonial question that economic imperialism and colonialism were not sufficient by themselves to create a popular political movement. A truly popular movement was necessary to acquire Bismarck's complete backing and to secure the support of a majority of the Reichstag, which had to approve any new expenditures for a market-expansion policy—with or without colonies. In 1880, the Reichstag rejected a proposal sponsored by Bismarck to subsidize a private consortium to take over Godeffroy interests in Samoa—a test case for the economic imperialists' view of overseas policy.[45] Something else was needed, and it was obvious to Fabri, Hübbe-Schleiden, and many others what it was: migrationist colonialism.

Some of the people who had been attracted to the imperialist market-expansion organizations of the late 1870s, including Fabri and Hübbe-Schleiden themselves, actually tended to conceive of overseas expansion much more along the traditional lines of migrationist colonialism than economic imperialism. In Fabri's case, at least, the tension between the economic imperialism of the main backers of the early expansion movement and Fabri's own migrationism is fairly evident.[46] As the need for popular support became clear, Fabri and Hübbe-Schleiden separately attempted to create a broad popular colonialist appeal. They applied arguments from both the economic imperialist and the migrationist tendencies but heavily emphasized the migrationist elements with which they clearly felt most comfortable. The organizations to which they belonged quickly followed suit, increasingly trumpeting the need to acquire overseas colonies to settle Germany's population overflow and to protect valuable social classes against economic change.[47]

The rapid movement toward a migrationist mode of argument in colonial propaganda in 1881 and 1882 appears to have been one of the causes of the sudden spurt in the popularity of colonialism among diverse, mostly middle-class groups during those years.[48] Success in finding audiences and members encouraged the colonialists to employ migrationism to a greater extent. It gave additional strength within the movement to people like Fabri who actually believed in migrationist colonialism and identified themselves with it. The export-expansion and colonial movement had finally, through migrationist colonialism, made contact with the framework of thought within which most Germans conceived of colonies and also with a set of attitudes that could be used to influence broad public opinion.

The migrationist element of 1880s colonialism has not been given the attention by recent historians that it deserves.[49] It was not until the colonial movement turned decisively in its public propaganda toward migrationism that colonialism became a popular political force. If the colonial movement had not demonstrated that it could affect public opinion—and do so in a way that other ideologies could not—it is difficult to see why Bismarck would have paid particular attention to it. As it was, in the mid-1880s, the acquisition, either immediately or eventually, of settlement colonies in temperate climates became the central conscious focus of the German colonial movement. In some cases, such as those of Woermann and the rising star of German imperialist propaganda, Carl Peters, acceptance of migrationism was cynical and halfhearted. In others, pre-eminently Fabri, it was entirely sincere. In any event, when the colonialist organizations combined into a single umbrella organization—the *Koloni-alverein*—at the end of 1882, both economic imperialism and migrationist colonialism were encompassed within the *Verein* but with the propaganda emphasis strongly on the latter.[50]

This co-location of the two thrusts of the pre-1890 imperialist ideology within the same movement and organizational framework was free neither of tensions nor of costs. Migrationist colonialism and economic imperialism were not actually integrated into a single coherent (or even apparently coherent) framework in the 1880s. The elements of each were simply propounded together. Over time, of course, had no splits occurred in the colonialist movement, integration would probably have occurred gradually. But, in fact, most of the leading proponents of colonialism and imperialism in the 1880s realized that they were talking about different things; this realization caused frequent disputes within the movement. There were bitter arguments between the proponents of trading colonies and the advocates of migrationist colonialism at the founding meeting of the *Kolonialverein,* arguments that were repeated throughout the organization's existence.[51] In 1884, capitalizing on this tension, Carl Peters formed a rival colonial society, the *Gesellschaft für deutsche Kolonisation* (GfdK), which openly advertised itself as the vanguard of migrationism and attacked the *Kolonialverein* for pandering excessively to special interests (i.e., economic imperialism).[52] Peters intended his organization to be a vehicle for his own political advancement. He used it to back the expedition to East Africa in which he more or less forced Bismarck to add an East African protectorate to the ones Germany had declared elsewhere. The latter had been chosen because they fitted into a very limited model of economic imperialism. When the euphoria of apparent success wore off after 1885, the imperialists committed to migrationism felt particularly cheated and antagonistic toward the advocates of trading colonies. With the rather unpromising exceptions of Southwest Africa and parts of German East Africa, Germany had no colonies that could be regarded as potential settlement areas in the near future, and Bismarck had made it clear that he contemplated no further expansion. A tension between the two ideologies was perpetuated in the Colonial Society—the successor to both the *Kolonialverein* and the GfdK—after 1887.[53]

The colonial movement did not, however, accomplish the actual seizure of an overseas empire (except to some extent for East Africa). It merely made it expedient, although by no means politically necessary, for Bismarck to do so. The much-debated question of what Bismarck hoped to accomplish through colonial expansion goes beyond the scope of this study, but there are some aspects of it that must be considered.[54]

Before the early 1880s, Bismarck had taken a dim view of colonies as wastes of a country's resources. His turn to active colonialism was hedged about with his desire to make sure that the colonies Germany took did not become financial burdens. He insisted that no area be acquired that could not be governed by (and at the expense of) the German merchants already trading there or else by chartered concession companies. He adhered, even at the height of his very brief "enthusiasm" for colonies, to the most narrow possible economic imperialist conception of colonies as adjuncts to overseas trade. He was far more willing to countenance the informal aspects of an "export offensive" such as steamship subsidies, the establishment of export banks, the expansion of the consular service, the active pursuit of trade agreements, and so on, than he was to see the colonies that he had claimed in 1884–85 expanded.

Why then did Bismarck turn to colonialism at all? Probably for a variety of reasons: his desire to start a scramble for colonies that would maintain tensions (but not excessive ones) between Britain and France; his apparently genuine concern for the German trading interest in West Africa should the British and French decide to turn the area into protectorates; and his desire to do favors for political and financial supporters such as Woermann and Adolf von Hansemann. But Bismarck was also clearly responding to domestic political opportunities created by the emergence of a popular colonial movement. By publicly accepting colonialism and performing the minimal amount of action necessary to prove the sincerity of his acceptance, Bismarck could appear to be associating himself with all of the other concepts, images, and ideas that had become attached to the colonialist ideologies. He could thereby appeal for the general support of the diverse interest and social groups that responded favorably to some aspect or other of imperialism. We cannot really tell whether he was primarily interested in using imperialist ideology to goad the left liberals into coming out strongly against migrationist colonialism and thus forfeiting some of their peasant and *Kleinbürger* support or whether he thought, as Wehler suggests, in socially more cosmic terms: that a social imperialist colonial policy would reconcile workers and bourgeoisie to an autocratic regime.[55] Probably Bismarck hoped for these results and more. Certainly, he was attracted by the notion that the question of colonies cut directly across German liberalism in a peculiarly debilitating way. Regardless of what his primary intentions were, Bismarck used colonialism as a means of embarrassing the anticolonial left liberals. But the important point is that Bismarck briefly perceived colonialism and its attendant ideologies as potentially integrative forces in politics, as a partial solution to the problem that lay at the root of his own political difficulties: the acute fragmentation of German politics. The ultimate purpose of using imperialism to draw workers away from the Social Democrats and to divert support from the left liberals was not to win short-term gains in the Reichstag but rather to create a broad consensus behind Bismarck's regime. In 1884 and 1885, Bismarck believed that imperialism could do the trick.

He was, of course, wrong, and, well before his fall from power in 1890, he realized that he was. The bloc of Reichstag parties that had supported colonial expansion and other Bismarckian legislation in the mid-1880s and that organized itself into a political cartel in 1887 proved to be impermanent and unmanageable, and public interest in colonial affairs waned considerably after 1885. Bismarck's colonial gambit had little effect on working-class voters; although the left liberals suffered a substantial loss of electoral strength in the 1880s, there is little evidence that their embarrassment over colonial expansion had much to do with it.[56] Even worse, Bismarck found himself in political difficulties that were due, at least in part, to the ideological structure of German colonialism. He had accepted a minimal economic imperialist notion of colonialism and had agreed only to territorial acquisitions that could be justified as immediate adjuncts to German trade and that would be, so he was led to believe, financially self-supporting. In fact, Bismarck discovered that he had been misled. Not only would the government for some time to come have to pay for colonial administrationn, but it was also required to bear the costs of exploring and securing the hinterlands of the African colonies to prevent competing powers from isolating and economically destroying them. Because colonialism had not produced the political benefits Bismarck had hoped for and because he could not abandon the colonies without paying an excessive political price, his only recourse was to try to keep colonial expenses to a minimum, to limit colonial competition with Britain and France, and to set his face against any further colonial expansion.

Bismarck's colonial policies in the late 1880s naturally brought him into conflict with migrationist colonialists such as Fabri. These colonialists had supported Bismarck's seizure of colonies as a first step in the right direction, but they now insisted that Germany take the next step by making massive land acquisitions in temperate regions suitable for large-scale European settlement.[57] This Bismarck adamantly refused to do, just as he refused to establish a separate Reich colonial administration and to support Carl Peters's post-1885 efforts to expand German holdings in East Africa. A large part of the colonial movement therefore turned on Bismarck in the late 1880s, attacking him for weakness in asserting Germany's imperial presence. Bismarck discovered to his cost that imperialism was not really an adequate integrative force in domestic policies, in part because of the inherently dichotomous nature of German imperialist ideology and the fact that competing social groups and interests assembled around one or the other of the main thrusts of imperialism. Bismarck learned this lesson quickly. His successors after 1890 did not.

CHAPTER THREE

Wilhelmian Politics: The Role of Ideology in a Fragmented Society

Before we can pass on to the careers of the imperialist ideologies in the period 1890–1914, we must first discuss some of the characteristics of the Wilhelmian social and political order that help to explain why those careers took the turns that they did. Because the relationship between the socioeconomic structure and the political system of imperial Germany has been studied in some detail in recent years and the historical work on the subject is both copious and well known, the present discussion will be limited to observations of particular relevance to the central concerns of the rest of the book. I shall make no attempt to present even a summary of the literature on Wilhelmian society and politics in general.[1]

Perceptions of Change

In the late nineteenth and early twentieth centuries, Germany experienced rapid socioeconomic change—change so complex that modern historians (like their Wilhelmian predecessors) profoundly disagree about its dimensions. In discussing Wilhelmian politics, it is important to distinguish between the *actual* long-term changes that were occurring in Germany's economic and social structure and the *perceptions* of these changes registered in the minds of Germans. Although these aspects of change were obviously related, their correspondence was far from exact. It was in some of the discontinuities between social perceptions and the remainder of social reality that political ideologies, including imperialist ones, played their most important roles.

One of the most important sources of this discontinuity was ideology itself. Much of the framework of thought with which groups of Germans attempted to understand their society was constructed from ideologies to which they subscribed. Thus, for example, small shopkeepers and master artisans, confronted with problems created by economic modernization, tended collectively to try to comprehend their problems through ideologies that gave legitimacy to their occupations and social roles and assigned the blame for their difficulties to particular culprits—especially industrialists and financiers.[2] These ideologies were put together from various preexisting elements between the 1870s and the 1890s and came to compose one segment of the general ideological set that will be called radical conservatism here. Such ideologies were as much reorganizations of old ideas as they were statements of new ones. They were to be found, by the 1890s, in practically every part of the social structure that had had a clear place in the preindustrial social order and was now confronted with new social and economic conditions. The real structural connection of these groups with an older social order was one of the reasons that ideologies that appealed to them tended to represent society as it had been in the past rather than as it was at the moment.[3]

But the "pastness" of ideological frameworks was a more general phenomenon, applying in some degree to practically all Wilhelmian ideologies—including economic imperialism, which was not notably oriented toward segments of society out of tune with the present. Instead, almost all ideologies tended to represent social processes that had already largely been completed as though they were still going on, as though their outcomes were still in doubt, and as though problems that had arisen with them still required fundamental settlement. On the whole, ideologies tended to ignore very new social problems, and when ideologues did have their attention drawn to them, they tried at first to integrate the problems into existing intellectual structures.[4]

In Chapter One, we saw why this should have been so. Ideologies are not, on the whole, accurate reflections of a social reality external to themselves. They are in themselves discrete elements of social reality, alongside many others, that contain selected and often distorted representations of other parts of the social environment. To the extent that they are conscious creations, they are primarily intended to elicit action rather than produce accurate social understanding. They owe their contents to processes of idea and image aggregation over time; thus they incorporate mainly perceptions of *past* social problems and conditions. Aspects of contemporary reality will, of course, break through this pattern in the cases of ideologies that maintain their political utility as aggregators of support and their popularity as means of framing social perceptions. But, on the whole, contemporary realities are fitted into preexisting patterns; the impingement of external reality usually works to bring the patterns up to date only very slowly and only partially—and, by the time that it does, the overall configuration of social reality is likely to have changed again. In the Wilhelmian era, which followed a period of very rapid and general socioeconomic change and in which modernization was still occurring comparatively quickly, this characteristic of ideology is particularly noticeable. It appears to have been a major cause of the gap that existed between Wilhelmian society as contemporaries perceived it and Wilhelmian society as it can now be understood.

Did this discontinuity between perceived and existent reality mean that all action based on common social perceptions was fruitless, a meaningless manipulation of outdated symbols and images? By no means. Often political actions based on ideologies had very real, although sometimes unintended, social and political effects. But, whether they realized it or not, the actual segment of social reality to which most Wilhelmian Germans responded when they moved mentally from social perception into the realm of structured action was more than anything else a *political* reality. It was not solely that the social factors that people perceived were to a large extent those presented to them through the medium of political ideologies, which thereby invested the facts with both an overt and an implicit political character. More importantly, although the content of ideologies tended to be made up of outdated social perceptions, the motives largely determining the specific form and the selection of elements of the ideologies that would be featured in popular discourse resulted from the more-or-less immediate operation of the political system. Therefore the specifically *political* features of the current social environment were much more likely to be reflected accurately in an ideology than were other, perhaps broader, social factors, and they were likely to be given a more immediate priority by the employers of the ideology.

It was, for example, perfectly possible in the 1890s for a politician to believe sincerely that the fate of the East Elbian peasantry was still an open question (in fact, it probably no longer was) and that government action could bolster eastern peasant society, yet, at the same time to remain fully conscious of the short-term political opportunities for himself and his party in pressing such views. Supporting peasant settlement in the east connected the politician to an ideological set of very real usefulness for assembling support from a wide variety of social groups. The same politician, in analyzing the practical political problems he faced every day, could then integrate these problems into his overall ideological posture by presenting the immediate political problems as obstacles to be overcome before the general social goals identified by the ideology could be attained. Thus the prerequisite to "saving" the East Elbian peasantry was the creation of a consensus within Germany as a whole in favor of the conservative parties that advocated peasant support, a consensus that could coincidentally be used for a great many other political purposes (e.g., raising tariffs).[5] Sometimes, of course, this was conscious flummery, but not always. In the long run, it probably made little difference whether the politicians involved were hypocrites or not. The effect was still that the *political* concerns encompassed by their ideologies tended to be more accurate and real than the broader social or historical ones and to take temporal precedence. From another standpont, one could say that the major ideologies of the Wilhelmian era tended to be employed not so much in response to socioeconomic modernization itself as in response to major political problems, especially that of political fragmentation (discussed later in this chapter). In turn, these problems were largely, although not exclusively, the result of general modernization. But the historical role of the ideologies has to be explained mainly in terms of the structure of politics—however contingent on broader social factors that structure might be—rather than the gross effects of social change. This is a necessity largely missed by many analysts of social imperialism in Germany. They tend to consider imperialist ideology to be a fairly immediate manifestation of direct, accurate perceptions of "real" social change rather than the product of a complex process of interaction among individual and group perceptions, preexisting ideologies and frameworks of social thought, and the circumstances of practical politics.[6]

For these reasons, we must focus now on the Wilhelmian political system and trace some of its connections to general social change and to ideology.

Wilhelmian Politics and Political Fragmentation

We can begin with the perception, common both to Wilhelmian commentators and to modern historians, that the practice of politics had become immensely difficult in late nineteenth-century Germany because the political system was so fragmented and that this fragmentation was the result of an insufficiently integrated society.[7] Although the meaning of political fragmentation is, in general, rather vague, its sense in the case of the *Kaiserreich* can be readily comprehended. Within the German political system, power was shared by a wide variety of institutions and groups. Some of these were legally constituted governmental authorities such as the monarchies, civil services, and executive institutions of the German states, the Reich government structure, and the Reichstag. Others were more informal institutions such as the political parties and the plethora of interest organizations. No single assembly of interests, no single coalition of organizations was regularly able to dominate German politics, and therefore the making of consistent policy and the forwarding of the interests of any particular group were difficult and complex processes. They characterize all modern pluralistic political systems and are, in some degree, simply manifestations of the complexity of modern society. There are, however, some vital differences between the present and the turn of the century that must be kept in mind, particularly in the case of Germany.

In the first place, modern Western political systems function despite a high degree of political and social fragmentation because they possess institutions and ideologies that act to integrate the interests and points of view of substantial numbers of the groups into which society is conventionally divided.[8] These institutions and ideologies did not appear overnight. In the case of practically every modernizing country in the advanced industrial world, there has been a considerable period of experimentation before a political system has been constructed, usually around a framework of representative parliamentary democracy, that provides a means of aggregating organized interests and creating the popular acquiescence needed for politics to function despite the complexities of modern society. The consciousness of how such a system should work also took time to develop, in a climate, usually, of social tension, political conflict, and confusion. In no case has the end result been without obvious flaws.

The historical route toward functioning pluralism is strewn with the wreckage of ideologies and institutions that were tried and discarded—or partly discarded. The Caesarist monarchies of Napoleon III and William II lie along the way together with their more radical descendant, the Fascist leadership state. Alongside them are many of the classic late nineteenth-century composite ideologies: political racism, radical nationalism, imperialism. All of these ideologies were adopted by major political groups—and often by governments—in most modernizing countries in the late nineteenth century. Their most important intended function was, in one way or another, to create sufficient consensus for successful national political action in systems featuring wider political participation than ever before, systems in which the increasing multiplicity of organizations, interests, and political ideas made collective action difficult.[9] Most of these ideological approaches to integration failed, often because they harmed society more than they facilitated integration. This was the ultimate fate of German imperialist ideology in 1945. But realization that imperialism as a guide for policy undid whatever advantages it might seem to display in consensus building took a long time to emerge; as is the case with most other composite ideologies, the realization has never been complete.

If Germany was in any sense unique among the modernizing countries of the nineteenth and twentieth centuries in its ideological response to fragmentation, it was in the unusually wide variety of ideological forms that gained currency there. This was, in part, the result of a second circumstance that separates the world of the turn of the century from modern Germany: the fact that Germany in the course of modernization up to the First World War had preserved practically every important premodern social group at the same time that new groups, largely products of industrialization, had appeared.

This observation is, of course, one of the commonplaces of the modern historiography of the *Kaiserreich*.[10] It is argued that from the top to the bottom of German society, modernization and industrialization created new social classes with new interests. These classes organized (especially at the upper- and working-class levels) to advance their interests against the classes associated with the older, more traditional aspects of economic life; they also organized against each other. Thus the growth of liberal political organizations in the third quarter of the nineteenth century can, in part, be explained as a form of mobilization for new mercantile and industrial elite groups in their competition for power with the landed aristocracy. The emergence of social democracy and the labor movement was clearly the result of a need for a defense of its interests on the part of the new industrial working class. But the old order in Germany had a great many weapons at its disposal as well, some of them of quite recent provenance. Its topmost elite, the landed Junker nobility of Prussia, possessed in its inordinate share of power in Prussia and in its close relationship to the highy efficient Prussian bureaucracy strong capabilities of defending itself. Until the 1870s, the Junkers had responded to the economic pressures of modernization most efficiently, increasing the productivity of their grain estates to supply the growing industrial cities. They permitted the bureaucratic Prussian state to become a major force in encouraging, and simultaneously regulating, the economic modernization of the country. Only with the appearance of American grain on the European market in the 1870s did the economic viability of Junker agriculture, and therefore of the Junkers as a class, begin to diminish rapidly. Their political power, however, remained very great, and they learned a variety of new tricks in order to maintain it.[11]

Other preindustrial social groups also felt the onslaught of modernity and eventually organized around it. The ideological response, for example, of master artisans and small shopkeepers to economic modernization was paralleled by the formation of interest organizations to express their viewpoint and by the attempts of political parties to appear, at least, to be defending them.[12] Here, also, political weapons were available, the most important of which were the extended franchise of the German federal states and the system of universal manhood suffrage established for Reichstag elections at the formation of the North German Confederation (1867) and the German Empire (1871). The same broadened franchise, however, also gave the vote to the "new" middle classes—those with a perceived stake in modernization—and to the mass of the industrial working class, whose voting reflected resentments against both the older and the newer social orders.

In other words, in the late nineteenth century, German society became highly fragmented as a result of rapid economic modernization. In part because of the political resiliency of the older elites, social fragmentation turned into unusually extensive political fragmentation. The political institutions of Bismarck's Reich initially did little to alleviate political fragmentation. In the first place, they had been established to a large extent to defend the power of the old elites. The federal structure of the Reich was supposed to give traditional elites—especially the Junkers in Prussia—the means of protecting their privileged political and economic positions within a united Germany by allowing them to dominate politics at the local level. The Reichstag, which was the most obvious candidate to become a locus for interest aggregation and consensus building, was hamstrung because of the limited power and responsibility it was given under the imperial constitution. Similiar circumstances prevailed throughout the political structure of the Reich as it had been established under Bismarck. Moreover, the very rapidity of German economic modernization had not allowed the social structure of Germany to catch up with the economy, as it were. Both class relationships and perceptions of class relationships tended to be framed in terms of the preindustrial order for some time after the beginnings of Germany's full-scale industrialization process.

The preceding analysis is currently the orthodox explanation of the social basis for politics in the *Kaiserreich*. It needs, however, to be supplemented by some further considerations. One of the most notable characteristics of political and social fragmentation in Wilhelmian Germany was the high level of consciousness that Germans (or at least the Germans who commented in print on political issues) displayed of the apparent fact that Germans were increasingly separated into many social groups with few interests in common. Social factors making for separation between groups tended to be far more widely recognized than the many forces for integration that existed in German society even at the period of most rapid socioeconomic change. This concentration of attention on the existence of fragmentation probably explains why Wilhelmian social observers continually harped on the need for massive efforts to elicit feelings of national unity from the population.[13]

On what was a group's consciousness of its separation from the rest of society based? Germany, like all European countries in the nineteenth century, still possessed, of course, the heritage of a hierarchical, class-conscious social order, an order the general format of which had proved to be highly adaptable to the first stages of socioeconomic modernization.[14] It also goes without saying that regional identities were very strong in Germany, so recently and so violently unified. Most important were the varieties of group consciousness that revolved around the shared perception that one's own group was being particularly disadvantaged by the course of economic change or else the perception (in the case of "new" classes) that one's group was being unfairly prevented from assuming the social role to which its economic function entitled it by the unwarranted power of the older social elites. Groups such as the Junkers, master artisans, small shopkeepers, peasants, and academics in liberal disciplines all expressed the former sense, in their own ways. At various times industrialists, business managers, journalists, and engineers displayed the latter attitude. The particular form of expression that a group adopted depended not only on the actual measurable impact of change on the majority of the group's members, but also on the configuration of politics and the ideological structures available to facilitate perception and expression.

The impingement of economic change on preindustrial classes and groups was certainly real enough by any measure. The Junkers saw their relative share of national wealth and, after the 1870s, their real income diminish markedly, presaging the dissolution of the social order that gave them status and prestige. The independent peasant had been declining in income and status in many parts of Germany long before the last quarter of the nineteenth century. The master artisan and the small shopkeeper both had obvious difficulties with economic change and apparently limited prospects in an industrial society.[15]

As many studies have pointed out, these groups were clearly not threatened in the same way by economic change nor, indeed, even by the same kinds of change. The Junkers were hurt by foreign competition in grain production in very different ways from smaller farmers; the latter, at least those east of Elbe, were historically threatened more by the Junkers than by anyone else. Master artisans simultaneously feared large industrial enterprises and the labor movement; small shopkeepers were threatened by monopolistic suppliers and retail chains. All were disadvantaged by the recurring depressions of the late nineteenth century, but the causes of these depressions were many and complex. The tendency to blame an abstract entity such as capitalism for all of their problems was not so much a result of immediate social perception as it was a product of attempts in the late nineteenth century to tie the various sources of social disaffection together by advancing ideologies that presented capitalism as the villain of economic modernization.[16]

Thus, even when one considers the social and economic foundations of political fragmentation, one cannot avoid the effects of ideology on the operation of the political system: first in creating differences in the perceptions and behavior of individual groups and then in providing images that could be used to reconcile those perceptions and behaviors. Ideological factors strongly influenced conscious definitions of the memberships, social boundaries, and problems of groups affected by economic change. Thus, for example, on grounds of actual economic circumstances and social functions, the group to which we customarily refer as Junkers or the Prussian landowning nobility would better be described as several groups or strata rather than as one, ranging from titled owners of large grain-growing *latifundia* to nonnoble gentlemen farmers with small holdings. The different strata experienced quite different economic circumstances in the late nineteenth century.[17] Master artisans were also an extremely heterogeneous group in terms of actual occupations and standards of living; changes in their income levels in the course of industrialization, although seldom wholly favorable, were far from uniform.[18] Therefore, even for the conventionally recognized "traditional" groupings in German society, the interests and identities of the groups were to a considerable extent the results of accepting ideologies that defined them and not solely of uniform impingement of economic reality on particular classes of people.

Many of these same considerations apply to the "modern" side of German society and the German economy as well. Clearly, the most fundamental example of fragmentation—the antipathetic differentiation between employers and industrial workers—was based ultimately on a very real difference in economic circumstances and in the differing impingements of economic change on the two groups. On the other hand, the attitudes of group identity on each side of the fundamental social divide, what Marx calls "class consciousness," were clearly products of ideology as well as immediate perception because the actual experiences of individuals and subgroups varied considerably. It could be argued, in fact, that one of the reasons that the "social question" (the employer-worker class conflict) loomed so large in the politics of Wilhelmian Germany was that the images and ideologies claiming to reconcile the two sides were not as effective as the integrative ideologies that operated in the "traditional" social sector. Midnineteenth-century liberalism had claimed to be able to reconcile the interests of all elements of the modern social order, but liberalism had lost its ability in practice to do this at least by the late 1870s.[19] Many of the newer ideological approaches of the latter part of the century—Marxian socialism and some versions of Social Darwinism—represented the modern bourgeoisie and the modern proletariat as inevitable enemies. One reason such figures as Max Weber and Friedrich Naumann experimented with imperialism was a desire to find an integrative ideology for the modern sectors of society that could realize the unfulfilled promise of German liberalism.

Consciousness of fundamental social fragmentation in Wilhelmian Germany was therefore not simply an external social fact that affected the realm of politics and ideology: it was partly, but not wholly, influenced by politics and ideology themselves. Ideological factors helped to shape and accentuate the consciousness of separateness on the parts of social elements. On the other hand, these factors also helped to build consciousness of common identity within and among some social groups. Thus one cannot argue that the fragmentation and complexity of German politics at the turn of the century were simply manifestations of a society increasingly fragmented in "objective" economic and class terms. They also resulted from the inability of the ideological, structural, and technical mechanisms available to German politics in the era of William II to meet the requirements placed on them by circumstances of increasing social complexity and rapid economic change.

The Search for a New Politics

The period 1890 to 1914 was characterized by a widespread recognition among German politicians that the tools of their trade were inadequate to their purposes. None of the older ideologies of national integration—liberalism, monarchism, nationalism—had showed itself capable by the 1890s of creating images that could take precedence in people's minds over the narrow concerns of individual group membership. A plethora of attitude-sets characteristic of particular groups had begun to attain the status of limited ideologies, defining the constituencies and aims of the groups and thus accentuating the problem of fragmentation. From the standpoint of ideological development, the Wilhelmian period saw a hectic scramble both by established political organizations and by new ones to construct composite, aggregative ideologies that would, under such circumstances, allow them to build consensus. A sense of bewilderment about how to operate in a pluralistic political system pervaded the political literature of the era—in all areas of the ideological spectrum.[20] At the same time, the Wilhelmian era was one of massive political experimentation, which is one of the reasons that so much of twentieth-century political discourse and ideology can be traced back to the 1890s. Politicians and political organizations cast desperately about for integrative ideologies. Some candidates were found among protoideological attitudes of lower middle-class groups that seemed to appeal to a variety of *Mittelstand* organizations. The widespread adoption of anti-semitism by conservative parties and political organizations in the 1890s represents this kind of development.[21] Others sought to update liberalism, socialism, monarchism, and so on, combining as many as possible.

In this context, the apparent success of the colonial movement of the 1880s attracted the attention of politicians and publicists throughout the German political system. For longer or shorter periods of times, many of them perceived in imperialism at least part of the answer to the problem of ideological integration and consensus building.[22] At the very least, it was thought, imperialism might provide a structure of ideas that could maintain its appeal across the boundaries of the subelements of German society and to which other political programs could be added or adapted. This was approximately what had happened on a limited scale with the colonial movement of the 1880s. Why should it not happen at the level of the political system as a whole?

Politicians and others, of course, turned first to ideological solutions to their perceived problems—as politicians will if they can. Most political problems are conceived in ideological terms to begin with, so that it is conceptually easier to visualize a new ideology as a means of political integration than it is to imagine changes in the structures and techniques of politics. Ideological changes also give the impression (often quite false) of being less costly to implement than others. It should be kept in mind, however, that both in terms of contemporary political perceptions and in terms of retrospective political analysis, the inadequacies of the German political system were general ones. Not only were current ideologies incapable of creating sufficient political consensus, but the structures and techniques of politics were equally deficient. The political parties in Germany had an extremely difficult time learning the procedures and techniques of modern mass politics. The first really effective "modern" party in a technical sense in Germany—that is, the first party organized to employ modern means of mass communications to the fullest extent possible—was the Nazi party. Nevertheless, the 1890s saw attempts in practically all political organizations to improve their effectiveness in public relations.[23]

The same difficulties confronted the official institutions of government as well. In the Wilhelmian era, the personnel of government departments became aware, slowly but inevitably, of the importance of public relations in modern government and of their own deficiencies in that area. Adjustment took a long time—at least through the First World War—but the lead was taken as early as the 1890s by Admiral Alfred von Tirpitz and the navy.[24]

Other institutions, especially the Reichstag, began slowly to respond to an awareness of their own ineffectiveness. The standard view of the Reichstag holds that, because the Reichstag was not responsible for the government and had only limited powers of legislative initiative, it could not easily play the central role that parliaments performed in several other western European political systems: that of acting simultaneously as the arena and the catalyst of developments in the direction of political integration.[25] It is also held that the parties that composed the Reichstag had little motivation to broaden their voting bases or to ally permanently with other parties to form coalitions to dominate an assembly that was relatively powerless. This view, however, is contradicted by the facts that party politics in the Reichstag were quite active, that all parties demonstrated strong desires to widen their bases of support, and that coalitions, although admittedly unstable ones, were in fact formed. Evidence from quantitative analysis of Reichstag roll calls at the turn of the century seems to indicate that, although the Reichstag was not rapidly turning into a true parliament on the British or French model, it *was* beginning to perform some of the functions of interest aggregation and compromise that are associated with legislative bodies in parliamentary systems.[26] Thus even in the case of the Reichstag, Wilhelmian politics displays not only confusion and impotence in the face of complexity and fragmentation, but also experimentation, adjustment, and a certain amount of innovation. Despite some appearances, it was by no means a static political system. The German imperialist ideologies came into their own in the 1890s in a dynamic, highly complicated political environment in which many political participants believed that imperialism could play a vitally important role.

In the next chapter, we shall examine the two most important of the composite imperialist ideologies that emerged in the 1890s in Germany, each of them put together by a particular set of political groups and interests and each an extension of one of the contrasting imperialist idea-sets that were involved in the colonial movement. We shall begin with the better known of the two: the ideology that is denoted here as *Weltpolitik*.

CHAPTER FOUR

Weltpolitik

Weltpolitik is one of those well-known but ill-defined catchwords with which the vocabulary of politics abounds. It is not clear who first coined the word, but the responsibility for its widespread use and popularity in the late 1890s is most often assigned to Bernhard von Bülow (foreign secretary, 1897–1900; chancellor, 1900–1909). The term was (and is) often used to mean nothing more than Germany's assertion of its role as a world power. This usage is not unimportant, both because it denotes a significant and highly destabilizing force in international politics and because the image of aggressive national self-assertion that it encompasses was a common element of political appeals in Germany.[1]

A large proportion, however, of the writers, politicians, and officials who used the term *Weltpolitik* had a conception of German imperial policy in mind that, despite variations, conveyed something much more specific than just aggressive images. They understood the term to refer collectively to the elements of a relatively clearly defined imperialist ideology that took shape toward the beginning of the Wilhelmian era, an ideology formed around the economic imperialism discussed in Chapter Two. This ideology had a fairly broad appeal and was especially influential in policymaking circles. It was not, however, universally accepted in its entirety as a legitimate basis for national policy, even among avowed imperialists. There were rival imperialist ideologies, the most important of which, the idea-set that is denoted *Lebensraum* in this study, was in many respects an outgrowth of migrationist colonialism. To differentiate the ideology that emerged out of economic imperialism from others, I shall employ the term *Weltpolitik* on the grounds that the people in Wilhelmian Germany who used the word most consistently and carefully meant by it approximately what is meant here. This usage may create some confusion because *Weltpolitik* was actually employed in a variety of ideological contexts, but it is the word that comes closest in real historical terms to denoting the ideology that is the subject of this chapter.

What was *Weltpolitik?* We can begin with Bülow's pronouncement on the subject in his autobiography:

> In the course of the [Reichstag] debate of 27 March 1900, I explained, in response to the Center Party deputy Gröber who had asked me for an authentic interpretation of the word Weltpolitik, that I understood by Weltpolitik merely the support and advancement of the tasks that have grown out of the expansion of our industry, our trade, the labor-power, activity, and intelligence of our people. We had no intention of conducting an aggressive policy of expansion. We wanted only to protect the vital interests that we had acquired, in the natural course of events, throughout the world.[2]

As we shall see, one should not take Bülow's statement of peaceful intent entirely at face value. Nor, for that matter, is there any reason to accept Bülow's rather vague definition of *Weltpolitik* as completely authoritative. He did not invent the ideological aggregation to which he was referring and he did not consistently adhere to it either in politics or in policymaking. Nevertheless, Bülow does make it clear, in general, what he understands by the term and what he expects his audience to understand by it: a foreign policy worldwide in scope, aimed at the protection and expansion of the external connections of the German industrial economy. There is nothing in Bülow's statement about agriculture, nothing about peasant settlement abroad, nothing about protecting the foundations of German culture against the perils of industrialization and modernity. *Weltpolitik* was, first and foremost, external policy in support of German commerce and the industrial sector.

We shall be concerned here with two sets of questions: first, who were the bearers of *Weltpolitik* and why did they develop the *Weltpolitik* ideology; second, what was the structure of *Weltpolitik* and what functions did it perform in Wilhelmian politics? The answers to the second set of questions depend to a considerable extent on the answers to the first set.

The *Weltpolitiker*

Before we discuss the identities and the social backgrounds of the *Weltpolitiker,* it is necessary to make some distinctions. In the first place, we must distinguish between the relatively small number of people who publicly expounded *Weltpolitik* at length and attempted to put it into practice and the much larger and more heterogeneous "audience" of the ideology. We shall be more concerned with the former than the latter. Second, among the *Weltpolitiker* proper (the expounders and practitioners), we must distinguish, primarily on the basis of occupational categories, between those whose individual and group outlooks strongly informed the structure of *Weltpolitik* and those who employed, publicized, and (in some cases) contributed to the development of *Weltpolitik* without imposing specific group interests on it. This is a crucial difference. The *Welt-*

politiker came from a narrow range of occupational backgrounds: journalists, academics involved in politics, professional politicians, and bureaucrats in both government and business. The bureaucrats were the main shapers of *Weltpolitik* after 1890 and the ones whose outlook the ideology primarily reflected. The others were not unimportant: not only did they represent *Weltpolitik* to the public, but they also interacted with bureaucratic *Weltpolitiker* in extending the elements of the ideology, revealing its nuances, and connecting it to other ideological aggregations. But *Weltpolitik* was not distinctively an ideology of journalists, academics, and politicians. Indeed, the public exponents of practically all Wilhelmian ideologies belonged to these three categories. It was the bureaucrats who were the main creative force behind *Weltpolitik,* and it is the bureaucrats who are the major focus of this part of the chapter. We shall return to the other groups later, especially in Chapter Seven when the legitimation and dissemination of imperialist ideologies are considered.

A third distinction is chronological—in some senses, generational. *Weltpolitik* was formulated in the 1890s by a fairly small number of men— mostly Foreign Office personnel selectively taking some of their cues from the journalists, entrepreneurs, and propagandists who had trumpeted economic imperialism in the 1880s. But as *Weltpolitik*'s popularity spread (especially within the occupational categories noted) and as the original *Weltpolitiker* recruited younger adherents within their own organizations, a younger generation of *Weltpolitiker* appeared in the late 1890s and thereafter. The younger generation accepted essentially the same notion of *Weltpolitik* as their predecessors, but they accepted it perhaps a little more uncritically. By the time of the First World War, *Weltpolitik* had become thoroughly institutionalized in the Foreign Office, the Colonial Office, the *Deutsche Bank,* and similar organizations directly concerned with foreign and imperial policy. Strong, often dominant, *Weltpolitik* parties existed in all of these organizations, parties that particularly attracted newly appointed personnel.[3]

A final distinction is between what we might call core and peripheral *Weltpolitiker.* We shall see the distinction most clearly among the *Weltpolitiker* of the Foreign Office, but it applies also to other groups, especially journalists. The core *Weltpolitiker* were those strongly identified with the ideology they professed, both out of conviction and as a means by which they sought to advance their careers. Peripheral *Weltpolitiker* accepted part or all of the ideology for any number of reasons (not excluding conviction), but they did not entirely identify themselves with it. Peripheral *Weltpolitiker* typically cast their public views of national policy in terms of *Weltpolitik* when it was politically expedient for them to do so, but they felt no compunction about adopting other frameworks under other circumstances.

A substantial part of the ideological innovation of the Wilhelmian era flowed from the political activities of government officials and their salaried counterparts in big business, but of all the recognizable ideologies of the Second Reich, *Weltpolitik* probably came closest to providing an effective connection between government and business bureaucracies. This connection can be described in at least three ways: in terms of the general needs of the government and business sectors for consensus in German society and politics, in terms of the needs of bureaucrats in government and business for a jointly shared ideology, and in terms of the political requirements of specific organizations.

Weltpolitik explicitly linked the making of external policy to the advancement of Germany as a modern industrial society. It could therefore be used at the level of interest-group politics to connect the government and big-business sectors of German society to each other. *Weltpolitik* justified the role and special position in national decision making of each of the two sectors in terms of the needs and social importance of the other and, by extension, of the German nation as a whole. The Foreign Office and Colonial Office could, for example, argue on the basis of *Weltpolitik* for a freer hand in making policy and for larger budgets because an expansion of their activities was vital to the economy. Business organizations could claim support and special consideration from the state, not simply through the argument that what was good for them was good for Germany, but also because *Weltpolitik* accorded great importance to close cooperation between government and business in planning and executing Germany's economic expansion. Using arguments based on *Weltpolitik,* business spokespersons could claim that, because they had to bear the major costs of the economic penetration of new overseas markets for the benefit of the whole German economy, they had a right to a voice in making national policy with respect to those markets and a right also to government assistance in protecting their investments.[4]

In one sense, the fact that many of *Weltpolitik*'s most important exponents were government officials and employees of organized business represents a classic integration of interests for the purpose of influencing politics. One of the reasons *Weltpolitik* grew out of economic imperialism in the early 1890s was the fact that government officials added their own point of view to an idea-set that was already popular in the business community. But it was not simply as representatives of the interests of the organizations to which they belonged that *Weltpolitiker* adopted the language and the framework of thought of their imperialist ideology. The fundamental idea that formed the bridge between business and government bureaucracies was the notion that rational control could be exerted over the process of economic, and thus of social and political, modernization. Control over modernization was not intended to retard or redirect it but rather to encourage the process with the smallest possible amount of waste, lost time, and social dislocation. *Weltpolitik* was manifestly an ideology of modernity, constructed at a time in which radically antimodern ideologies were becoming increasingly important in German politics. Indeed, to some extent the development of *Weltpolitik* may have been a reaction to the emergence of radical conservatism in the 1880s and 1890s.[5]

Weltpolitik affirmed the values of science, reason, and progress—the watchwords of Victorian optimism that were also the watchwords of the government and industrial bureaucracies that had emerged in Germany in the course of modernization. *Weltpolitik,* in other words, codified some of the values jointly shared by two elite groups as a consequence of their roles in society and attempted to legitimate those values by relating them to the advancement of Germany's economic well-being.

The first comprehensive formulations of *Weltpolitik* ideology were put together by protégés of the coterie of senior government officials who engineered Bismarck's fall in 1890. To the inheritance of economic imperialism they added considerations that were peculiarly their own, many of them derived from the political circumstances in which the governments of the 1890s found themselves. During the 1890s, the government *Weltpolitiker* were to be found primarily (although not exclusively) in the Foreign Office and in its administrative stepdaughter, the Colonial Department. Even in the early twentieth century, when the *Weltpolitik* ideology had spread widely in the government and business communities and had obtained an extensive public following, the Foreign and Colonial offices remained the primary bastions of *Weltpolitik* thinking and the points at which the consensus-building and policymaking functions of *Weltpolitik* converged.[6]

The original core of *Weltpolitiker* in the immediate post-Bismarckian Foreign Office can be fairly readily identified, as can many of their successors in the Foreign Office proper, the colonial administration, and other departments. But even when *Weltpolitik* had become the dominant fashion for junior officials in the foreign policy field, the *Weltpolitiker* were far from alone in the offices on the Wilhelmstrasse. Many senior Foreign Office personnel held to the traditional priorities of Bismarckian diplomacy and refused to give precedence to economic imperialist assumptions. Even more important were the peripheral *Weltpolitiker,* among whom some of the most important figures in the Foreign Office might be counted.[7]

The core *Weltpolitik* group in the Foreign Office during the Caprivi era (1890–94) included many of the members of the ministry's Political Department who were suddenly promoted or raised to prominence in the wake of Bismarck's fall. Most of these people were (at least in 1890–91) allies of Friedrich von Holstein, the *éminence grise* of the Foreign Office. Prominent among them was Paul Kayser, the head of the new Colonial Department, whose memoranda to Chancellor Leo von Caprivi appear to have been the first comprehensive treatments of foreign and colonial policy couched in terms of *Weltpolitik* to have been taken seriously at the highest levels of government. Other *Weltpolitiker* were the new foreign secretary, Baron Adolf von Marschall von Bieberstein, and, somewhat more peripherally, the later foreign secretary, Alfred von Kiderlen-Wächter, who was a counselor in the Political Department from 1888 to 1894. This group shared somewhat similar views on policy with another group headed by

Karl Göring, chief of Caprivi's chancery office and a former counselor in the Foreign Office's legal department. The Göring group appears to have merged with the *Weltpolitiker* by the end of the decade. Heinrich von Kusserow, a senior official who had been important during the seizure of the colonial empire, was certainly ideologically associated with the *Weltpolitiker,* but he was dismissed from the service in 1891 and seems to have played little part in policymaking for the preceding few years. Of the successors of the core *Weltpolitik* group who entered the Foreign Office during the 1890s, we shall pay particular attention here and in succeeding chapters to two who became foreign secretaries toward the end of the First World War: Richard von Kühlmann (foreign secretary, 1917–18) and Wilhelm Solf (colonial secretary, 1912–18; foreign secretary, 1918–19).[8]

Among the Foreign Office's peripheral *Weltpolitiker* in the 1890s, the most important were clearly Holstein and Bülow. They and a large part of the generation of officers to which they belonged never really adjusted their thinking about policy from the Bismarckian mode to that proclaimed by *Weltpolitik.* They fundamentally viewed international relations within the traditional framework of security, balance of power, and alliance politics. But Holstein and Bülow, especially the latter, fully understood the domestic political advantages of expressing national policy in the language of *Weltpolitik:* it was a way of attracting support from business and from the largely middle-class group that made up much of *Weltpolitik*'s wider audience. Moreover, practically any intellectual framework for conceiving foreign policy requires some means of identifying the national interest—the objectives for which policy is conducted. Bülow, Holstein, and others like them simply included the economic objectives emphasized by *Weltpolitik* alongside the more traditional ones enshrined in the conventions of European diplomacy. In part, this was a genuine result of their recognition that industrialization had changed Germany and had required certain readjustments in the criteria of successful policy. When political circumstances—both foreign and domestic—appeared to be appropriate, as they were during the late 1890s, Bülow turned strongly toward *Weltpolitik* with a perfectly good conscience. When they were not appropriate, as for example during his courtship of the agrarians in domestic politics and of Russia in diplomacy just after 1900, he moved temporarily away from *Weltpolitik* with just as good a conscience.[9]

Weltpolitik and the more traditional view of foreign policy were not entirely incompatible. No *Weltpolitiker* (in the Foreign Office, at any rate) ever claimed that the balance of power in Europe or the structure of international alliances did not matter. Few Wilhelmian officials, no matter how conventional in their outlook, considered the national objectives sought by the *Weltpolitiker* to be pointless. It was a matter rather of emphasis, both in identifying the most important long-range goals of policy and in assessing what was most desirable among the objectives that might practically be obtained from, for example, the manipulation of a short-term diplomatic crisis.[10]

Weltpolitik ensconced itself in certain other departments of government as well. It became a fixture in the chancellor's own office because of the Chancery's close personal connection with the Foreign Office. It also became extremely prominent in the navy, in part because of the navy's need for an ideology to justify its expansion into a major military force. We shall examine this aspect of *Weltpolitik* shortly. Admiral Tirpitz provides, to an extent, an example of a peripheral *Weltpolitiker:* one who often used, and presumably believed in, *Weltpolitik* arguments but who subordinated *Weltpolitik* to his prime concern, which was to build a battle fleet second to none.[11]

There were also many people in all branches of government, including William II himself, who were attracted simply by the novelty of an active imperialist policy rivalling that of Britain. This was one of *Weltpolitik*'s main drawing-cards with public opinion in general and one of the reasons that the advocates of alternative views of imperialism quickly adopted pieces of *Weltpolitik* for their own use. William's imperialist thinking and that of his immediate entourage was probably most heavily influenced by *Weltpolitik*. But in this as in other things, the Kaiser was inconstant. At different times he also cast his views in terms of Bismarckian power balances, Darwinian racial struggles, and *Lebensraum*.[12]

To return to the Foreign Office's core *Weltpolitiker,* there were a number of common elements in their backgrounds that, if not so pervasive as to justify a collective biography here, must at least be discussed as influences on the structure of the ideology and as clues to its political function. One of these elements was a modest deviation in social origins from the norms of the snobbish, aristocratic Foreign Office. Marschall and Kayser were both lawyers who had entered the diplomatic service after previous careers. Kayser entered in 1885, not long before his appointment as head of the Colonial Department. Marschall's first appointment in the diplomatic service came in 1890 when, surprisingly, he was named foreign secretary. In an organization dominated by Prussian Junkers, the *Weltpolitiker* were often bourgeois, from families without long traditions of government service. Many were non-Prussians. Kiderlen, for example, was a Württemberger; Marschall was from Baden. Kayser was an assimiliated Jew, one of only five to be appointed to the German diplomatic service before 1914. He owed his appointment mainly to the sponsorship of William II who, in his social-conscience phase during the late 1880s, had made use of Kayser's expertise in social insurance and labor law. Kayser was considered an interloper in the Foreign Office, both because of his "irregular" background and because of his aggressive and obvious ambition. In other words, most of the early *Weltpolitiker* were, in a mild sense, outsiders—not the least reason being (in all cases except Kiderlen's) because of their lack of expertise and regular training in diplomacy.[13]

Among the later *Weltpolitiker,* this was not invariably true. Albrecht Freiherr von Rechenberg, governor of East Africa (1906–12) and an important secondary figure in the Foreign Office during World War I, happened more or less by accident into various policy controversies during his career in which he became a prime spokesman for *Weltpolitik*. Rechenberg was an aristocrat, a career diplomat, the son of a diplomat, and a Prussian. He was also a Catholic and an active member of the Center Party, but these counted as relatively minor deviations.[14] Richard Kühlmann, although he was the son of a businessman, had impeccable manners and social connections. He married a daughter of Baron von Stumm, the Saar mining magnate, and he owed his initial appointment to the personal intervention of Chancellor Hohenlohe-Schillingsfürst, a friend of his family.[15] Nevertheless, even among the later official *Weltpolitiker,* there was a tendency toward deviation from departmental norms. *Weltpolitik* was perhaps strongest in the divisions of the Foreign Office outside the prestigious Political Department, as well as in the Colonial Office and Chancery—both spin-offs of the Foreign Office whose personnel tended to be middle class and had questionable career prospects.[16]

One might be tempted to explain *Weltpolitik* as a collective response by resentful "outsiders" to the social obstacles that faced them in their careers. This would be an exaggeration, and it would moreover obscure some of the actual functions of *Weltpolitik* in bureaucratic politics. The official *Weltpolitiker*—even Kayser—were not alienated men nursing grudges or seeking psychological compensation. Instead, many of them (people like Kühlmann, of course, excepted) were men who had, for lack of prestige and external support, to succeed in their careers on their own. Contrary to familiar myths, advancement under such circumstances does not always depend solely on the display of superior ability and acumen; it can also involve a strategy of advancement that allows the individual to project a favorable image within his department—a gimmick, if one wishes. Rising bureaucrats without protection from above need a means of distinguishing themselves from their competitors. Equally important, rising officials need some sort of ideological bond to link themselves to the cohort that will be one of the means of their advancement because promotion at the higher levels tends to be accorded to groups of contemporaries who have informally united around some person or policy position.

Thus, in the politics of the government bureaucracy, *Weltpolitik* was, among other things, an ideological structure with which officials in several different departments, in need of an engine to pull their careers along, could identify themselves. Although based on previous economic imperialist ideas (and therefore not "revolutionary"), *Weltpolitik* gave the appearance of novelty. It projected modernity and progress and a new way of doing things, both in the economy and in foreign relations. It was put together at the time of Bismarck's fall; to a considerable extent, it represented the desire of many officials raised in rank by that event to dissociate themselves somewhat from the practices and assumptions of their former master. It was nothing if not grandiose in scope and conception and, for that reason, an extremely attractive instrument for advancement and intragovernment group identification. Even in the case of the early official *Weltpolitiker* who was most an outsider—Paul Kayser—there is little evidence that his adoption of an extended economic imperialist ideology represented a rejection of the values of a social order that excluded him. Kayser was genuinely taken with economic imperialism and with the possibility of linking it to broader social concerns. We shall see in Chapter Six that he was interested in using *Weltpolitik* to gain support for increased departmental appropriations. But it is also clear that *Weltpolitik* gave him an identity in a bureaucratic structure—the Reich government and the Foreign Office—in which he was not liked and in which he might easily have been ignored.[17] Kayser and most of the other advocates of *Weltpolitik* represented their new ideology as an extension or updating of the accepted values of their departments—as reforms in thinking and policy that would make government more effective rather than alter it radically.

To make government more effective at doing what? Ultimately, as I have already indicated, at controlling the process of economic and social modernization and its effects. As was the case with most imperialist ideologies in the late nineteenth century, the link between external expansion and domestic social problems was of key importance to the ideological structure of *Weltpolitik* and to its political functioning. The particular approach of the *Weltpolitiker* rested on the belief that continued economic and social progress in the direction already taken in Europe, if it were rationally planned and controlled, would solve most existing social problems. It emphasized the need for active intervention by planning authorities, but within a context the general outlines of which were determined by the process of industrialization.[18] In some senses, then, the *Weltpolitiker* adopted the worldview of the technocrat as their ideological motif. One must be careful, however, about the use of the term *technocrat* to refer to officials or businessmen at the turn of the century. Very few important *Weltpolitiker,* whether in government or in business, were technically trained engineers or scientists.[19] Essentially, they were bureaucrats and managers who wagered their careers on being identified with the "rationalization" of government and business, in close but ill-defined connection with "science." Their self-presentation as advocates of "scientific" administration was, in the Wilhelmian period, more significant than their actual qualifications, which was one of the reasons they frequently required legitimation of their ideas by bona fide social scientists.

Just as *Weltpolitik*'s strongest initial appeal was to the new, self-consciously "technocratic" group in government, so too it appealed immediately to their analogs in business: the emerging class of educated managers within the bureaucracies of the large industrial and banking complexes and in the business-interest associations. The most prominent business *Weltpolitiker* between 1890 and 1914 were almost all leading members of the bureaucratic, managerial elite: Albert Ballin, Walther Rathenau, Bernhard Dernburg, Karl Helfferich, Arthur Gwinner. These were men who had risen within the *economic* bureaucracies of Germany, not on the basis of family ownership of their business but because of ability, sometimes because of the help of benefactors, and most especially because of their successful use in bureaucratic politics of the images they had created of themselves as rational, scientific modernizers and reformers.[20]

The connection that grew up between these business "technocrats" and their government counterparts, a connection symbolized by the eventual government careers of Rathenau and Dernburg and by the oscillation of Helfferich throughout his life between business and government, was a highly complex one. It was not simply a manifestation of a general similarity in occupation between two sets of functionaries. More than that, the connection was also based on similarities between the positions of the two groups *within* their respective bureaucracies, shared attitudes about the greater social responsibilities of business and government that came to constitute the technocrat's legitimating ideology, and the similar needs of individuals in plotting their strategies of career advancement. These similarities led the two groups to seek each other out as informal allies and preferred associates, and to subscribe to many of the same ideological structures—those which, like *Weltpolitik,* were compatible with their outlooks and career patterns and that could also be used to advance the interests of the organizations to which they belonged.

Bernhard Dernburg (1865–1937; colonial director and secretary, 1906–10) provides an example of the business-technocrat *Weltpolitiker.*[21] Dernburg had no training in science or engineering, but he rose, in the 1880s and 1890s, within the hierarchy of the *Deutsche Bank*'s industrial-financial complex as an advocate of scientific, technical solutions to economic and management problems—a reputation that he took with him into government in 1906. While head of the colonial administration, he similarly tried to build a public image of Dernburgian "scientific colonialism."

Dernburg was fully conscious of the relationship between his ideological position and his career. In his draft autobiography, he explains that he rose in the *Deutsche Bank,* despite the fact that he had no particular "protectors," by virtue of his technocratic reputation and his ability to reorganize faltering enterprises efficiently.[22] He also perceived a direct link between the business and government sides of his career: "I believe that I protected and enhanced much that was valuable to the German people, not only in the *Deutsche Bank,* but also later during my service with the *Darmstädter Bank* [of which he was briefly head], and I also reckon my activity as first minister of the German colonies in the same category."[23]

It is instructive to note that Dernburg did not become a conscious exponent of *Weltpolitik* until the prospect of holding public office arose. When it did, however, he rapidly adopted the entire structure of *Weltpolitik* ideology. The reason for this was that Dernburg, like many of his similarly placed business associates, subscribed to a set of ideas about the value of modernity and about the efficacy of rational social and economic planning that was incorporated within *Weltpolitik*. When it became necessary to concern himself with imperial policy, Dernburg turned, almost without being conscious of it, to the set of ideas about such policy that was most closely akin to his own views on other subjects.

Certain other possible affinities between business and government *Weltpolitiker* also present themselves. For example, Jews (more often people of Jewish descent) were prominent in each group—Kayser and eventually Dernburg among the officials and Rathenau, Ballin, and (again) Dernburg among the businessmen. However, although this point did not go unremarked among *Weltpolitik*'s imperialist critics, it is also true that the vast majority of identifiable *Weltpolitiker* were not Jews. If a connection is to be found here, it probably lies in the fact that Jewishness was one of the characteristics that started some members of the technocratic elites with a handicap on the career track and caused them to turn to new images and ideologies as means of catching up.

Thus far, we have considered the social basis of *Weltpolitik* primarily from the standpoint of the careers of certain types of individuals. But the organizations to which they belonged also strongly influenced the acceptance and development of *Weltpolitik*. The Reich government of the Caprivi era needed a basis for policymaking and, more important, an ideological means of creating sufficient consensus in the Reichstag, within segments of the social elite, and in the country as a whole to allow it to govern.[24] The ideas that made up *Weltpolitik* offered the prospect of filling those needs. We have already seen how various business groups picked up economic imperialism in the 1880s as a means of advancing their general political interests as well as achieving specific economic goals. These motives did not cease to operate in the 1890s. On the contrary, it became increasingly necessary for businesses and business organizations of all sorts—especially those dependent on the direction of public policy—to find ideological justifications for the specific national policies they were pushing. Many business leaders also believed that they required ideological grounding for a broad popular consensus in favor of business because of the growing size of the SPD and the labor movement on the left and the growing political effectiveness of anti-industrial conservatism on the right.[25] The need to find ideological underpinnings for business in politics was accentuated by consciousness of the fragmentation of society and the political system, the multiplication of interest groups within the business community itself, and the collapse of the fragile alliance between heavy industry and East Elbian Junker agriculture which had existed fitfully between 1879 and the late 1880s.

The senior officials of different businesses and business-interest organizations—responding to their own particular perceived situations or sometimes simply to the outlooks of their most important directors—took many different approaches to the problem of consensus creation and ideological integration. In the 1890s, the mining magnate, Baron von Stumm, turned his extensive press machine into a vehicle for a straightforward, rather brutal, free-enterprise attack on all sources of opposition to big business. The CDI and the metals lobby, after trying approaches similar to that of Stumm, rather hesitantly moved around the turn of the century to a kind of social paternalism. Part of the metals industry, led after 1909 by the Krupp concern's own "technocratic" director, Alfred Hugenberg, turned to the kind of broad-gauged radical conservatism represented by the Pan-German League. But the leaders of several industries, especially the light, export/import-dependent ones—those closely involved with the colonialism of the early 1880s as well as those that were not well represented in organizations like the CDI—tended to look to the expansionary ideology of *Weltpolitik* as a tool in politics during the 1890s.[26] We shall return to the question of why they did so later in this chapter.

It was not, of course, either government officials or business managers who publicized the *Weltpolitik* ideology outside of their own rather narrow circles after 1890, however much they may have been responsible for its formulation and many of its political uses. The publicizing of *Weltpolitik* was the work primarily of journalists, academics, and politicians—the last group active mainly in the Reichstag. As we have seen, it is difficult to identify a particular correlation between the social backgrounds of members of the journalistic profession and the content of *Weltpolitik,* as opposed to any other ideology prominent in Wilhelmian Germany. However, certain features of the backgrounds of some of the most prominent imperial journalists are of interest in the context of this study. Many of them (including Paul Rohrbach, perhaps the most famous of their number) were people with academic qualifications who had not been able to find employment traditionally compatible with those qualifications.[27] They tended to be talented and ambitious men without secure social and financial underpinnings who wanted to use political journalism to find a permanent audience and to attach themselves to a major political and economic interest. They generally adopted ideologies that were identified with groups whose support they wanted to attract in order to advance their own careers. These factors had a certain amount to do with the role of journalists in propagating and legitimating imperialist ideologies. This role, and the parallel roles of academics, will be discussed in Chapter Seven.

Party politicians and prominent figures in nonparty political organizations such as the Colonial Society also, of course, affected the formulation of *Weltpolitik,* as they did the other ideologies of imperialism. Practicing politicians were the people who could most clearly perceive the problem of political fragmentation and the practical difficulties of consensus building in an increasingly complex society. They were both the principal employers of ideologies in public and among the principal initiators of the ideological output of journalists, writers, and social scientists. Again, however, the circumstance of being a politician, although it could make individuals receptive to ideologies that might be used for support aggregation, did not in itself predispose them to any particular ideology.

Their backgrounds, previous ideological exposure, and—above all—the requirements of the political organizations to which they belonged would do that. Moreover, although the professional politician, as an occupational category, was emerging in Germany during the Wilhelmian period, most full-time politicians depended for their positions and (if they were not self-supporting) their incomes on extrapolitical organizations.[28] Thus it turned out that the politicians who most consistently advocated *Weltpolitik* in the public arena after 1890 were, in fact, members of one of the groups already indicated as providing the fundamental support base for *Weltpolitik:* government officials and business functionaries. Gustav Stresemann, for example, started his political career as a salaried lobbyist for a Saxon light-industrial interest organization and went on from there to the Reichstag.[29]

The process by which *Weltpolitik* emerged from the connection of economic imperialism to other sets of ideas purporting to deal with a wider range of social phenomena was thus somewhat diffuse. There was no one main formulator of *Weltpolitik*. The key impetus to the formation of *Weltpolitik* appears to have come from the adoption of a set of policy guidelines that incorporated economic imperialist ideas by the senior officials of the Foreign Office during the year or two after Bismarck's fall from power in 1890. These guidelines, formulated mainly by the official *Weltpolitiker* discussed earlier, were then widely taken up by business interests and political organizations that generally supported the Caprivi regime during the furious disputes over the government's policies that raged in the early 1890s.[30] To understand why all of this should have happened, it is necessary to consider in some detail the elements of the *Weltpolitik* ideology as it presented itself after 1890. The discussion that follows is not based on any one presentation of *Weltpolitik* thinking. It is rather a composite, drawn from a large number of sources and concentrating on the items most frequently featured in those sources.

The Structure of *Weltpolitik*

We have already seen that the preexisting idea of economic imperialism was the conceptual core of *Weltpolitik;* the rest of the ideology was made up of elements essentially developed from, or attached to, the core. Although economic imperialism was in no sense a legitimate economic theory in itself, it was constructed from bits and pieces of economic theories and from rather superficial theoretical statements of common attitudes toward the present and future of the industrial economy.

The central economic conception of *Weltpolitik* has sometimes been labelled neomercantilism.[31] In terms of the actual content of the ideology, this implied analogy to the major economic theories of the late seventeenth and early eighteenth centuries is largely specious. In terms of the overall goals of economic policy, it makes some sense. Both early mercantilism and late ninteenth-century economic imperialism emphasized the rational management of the economy as a means of controlling the broader social environment. This is important not only for classifying the kinds of economic thinking contained in *Weltpolitik*, but also for explaining a significant part of its appeal as an ideology: the suggestion, so attractive in periods of rapid economic change, that seemingly blind, irresistible social forces can be controlled or, at least, directed without drastic, revolutionary action.

Weltpolitik proposed to afford the German people the direction of their collective destiny by giving control over Germany's external economic relations to the nation's government and business-leadership structures, each operating in close conjunction with the other under the guidance of experts. Control was to be established in a number of ways, of which two were the most important: the creation of protected markets and investment areas outside Germany's borders and the attainment of secure external supplies of raw materials at regulated prices. The earlier versions of economic imperialism had more heavily emphasized the former, reflecting the tendency toward depression on the world's markets and the high degree of international economic competition in the late 1870s and 1880s. *Weltpolitik* maintained this emphasis in the early 1890s. Under the generally expansionary and inflationary conditions that prevailed after 1896, the second (raw materials) aspect assumed larger proportions than it previously had.

The economic imperialists of the 1870s and 1880s had enunciated a number of ideas about foreign markets that remained part of the rhetoric of *Weltpolitik* down to the First World War and beyond, although not all of them were taken with equal seriousness as guides to policy. One of these was the idea of the reserve market, which many historians have regarded (probably incorrectly) as the heart of German economic imperialism. Actually, most evidence seems to indicate that, except perhaps during the 1880s, much more complex sets of ideas were more influential in government and business circles.[32]

Briefly, the idea of reserve markets was that certain large, underdeveloped areas of the world could be maintained by Germany as protected future markets for German-manufactured products, which would be used in the event of overproduction and a depression caused by an international glut. Should a depression occur, these areas (either formal colonies or informally dependent regions in Africa and Asia) could be brought on line, as it were, as consumers of Germany's excess production—in other words, as dumping grounds. German exporters in these areas could, if necessary, be protected against foreign competition. Such countercyclical economic exploitation would thus reverse tendencies toward depression and unemployment in German industry.[33]

The reserve-market idea is an inherently improbable one in its simplest form. How, exactly, could the inhabitants of, let us say, a tropical colony be forced to buy what they had not bought before? With what were they supposed to buy it? A limited amount of coercion along such lines might be possible, but, clearly, not enough to perform the major economic tasks that the concept involved. Reserve markets might sound attractive in the heat of a political debate on colonial expansion, especially in the middle of a depression, but by the 1890s the manifest inadequacy of the idea had led to its subsumption within a much more complex theoretical structure that explained the importance to Germany of controlled foreign markets. The foundation of the structure was a view of the relationship between peripheral areas of the world economy and the central industrial ones in the process of economic *development*. We are, in fact, dealing with one of the direct ancestors of modern development theory.

As was true of later theories, the central feature of the development element of *Weltpolitik* was capital and its investment abroad. In highly simplified terms, the argument went something like this: to prosper and to perform all of the functions of social amelioration assigned to it, German industry required a continuous expansion of its markets as well as secure possession of the ones that it already had.[34] That is to say, the aggregate demand that German industry satisfied needed to grow. Only constant growth could provide stable levels of profit and employment in a world economy tending increasingly toward mechanization and competition. Growth was also necessary because the ultimate purpose of industrialization was not stability, but improvement in standards of living and real-wage levels. Domestic-wage increases were supposed, however, to *follow* increases in demand, not to precede or cause them—hence the need for external-demand growth. In addition, the capitalist economy was subject to periodic downturns. A constant expansion of demand and markets, especially if expansion occurred in areas of the world not as immediately subject to the effects of industrial depressions as western Europe, would help to prevent the irregularities that led to depressions in the first place.[35] Moreover, a vigilant German government could use ongoing projects of economic development as means of counteracting cyclical downturns. The prospect of a depression could be met, for example, by increasing the pace of railway building in German East Africa—which was supposed to stimulate the growth of the East African economy and consumer market. Thus it was not so much reserve markets that were important to *Weltpolitik* as it was the identification and control of external areas for ongoing investment and market development.

The concept of investment was crucial. According to the received wisdom that was uncritically incorporated into *Weltpolitik,* Germany's rapid industrialization in the second half of the nineteenth century had left her extremely short of investment capital. It was, nevertheless, absolutely essential that German business maintain a high rate of investment abroad because only through investment could the kind of market expansion that was required for the health of the industrial economy be assured. Only through specifically German investment could Germany be assured of access to the future markets that she needed. It was thus both a matter of individual profit and of patriotism that German business invest abroad, despite limited capital resources.[36] Because foreign investments ran high risks from the competition of non-German investors trying to take them over and because German investors lacked the capital reserves necessary to fend off such attacks, active diplomatic and financial support from the government was absolutely vital.

Here one sees rather clearly a case of the special pleading of interest groups being converted by means of the *Weltpolitik* ideology into an argument based on the general good. There *were,* of course, constraints on the availability of investment capital in Germany at the turn of the century, but such constraints exist in all economies. Weaknesses in the internal structure of German investment were matched by important strengths—especially the existence of the huge financial-industrial conglomerates surrounding the major investment banks. It is not really clear that Germany was notably short of capital in any absolute sense. Nevertheless, economic commentators and apologists for German business continually made this claim, and the *Weltpolitiker* (and modern historians) believed them.[37]

Why should the business community claim the existence of a capital shortage? In part, it reflected one of the more curious aspects of German investment psychology before 1914: its extreme timidity. In the course of rapid industrialization and the swift bureaucratization of German finance, the large banks developed a set of highly conservative attitudes toward investment that strongly influenced the newer generations of financial managers in the Wilhelmian era.[38] Perhaps because of the higher degree of bureaucratization in German finance, those who ran the main banking houses of Germany tended to take fewer risks, to insist on a higher degree of financial security for new projects, and to seek more government protection than did their American, British, and French counterparts. Within this attitudinal and behavioral pattern, it was not so much the *realities* of capital availability in Germany that led to the claim that Germany lacked capital as it was the fact that any risk at all was believed to require extremely heavy capital backing and income guarantees.

But attitudes were not the only reason for the inclusion of the capital-availability argument. It was also an almost-ideal way for businesses investing abroad to justify a great deal of (free) government assistance in their enterprises. In the more spectacular cases, such as the Baghdad Railway, the capital-availablility argument was a linchpin of a complex justification for massive subsidies and investment guarantees given by the German and Turkish governments to the *Deutsche Bank* and its associates.[39] There were many other cases that displayed the same pattern on a more modest scale.

The idea of economic *colonialism* was adapted to fit within the framework of *Weltpolitik*—mainly by the senior officials of the colonial administration and the spokespersons of colonial businesses. Colonial policy was to be tied to the central processes of market expansion and investment. Opinions among *Weltpolitiker* differed as to the means and tempo to be employed in colonial development. The Colonial Economic Committee (KWK), an autonomous branch of the Colonial Society largely supported by the textile industry, espoused the highly unrealistic view that Germany's existing colonial empire could be rapidly transformed into her main overseas trading partner.[40] The professional colonial adminstration, after about 1905, tended to advocate the slow, peasant-centered policy of development pursued in the successful colony of Togo.[41] But for the most part, *Weltpolitiker* shared the same fundamental conception of the role of colonies. Colonies existed as adjuncts to German industry. They assisted in the betterment of German society as a whole—but indirectly, through the assistance that they supposedly afforded to the domestic industrial sector. Colonies were supposed to provide locations for secure, profitable investment, investment that would create markets for German products, revenue for German carriers, raw materials for German industry, and secure returns on capital.[42] They were also to be points of economic and political entry into larger marketing areas, over which varying degrees of informal control could be exercised. Thus the German naval colony of Kiaochow in China was viewed as the center of the German-dominated, but not directly ruled, Shantung peninsula, with its major extractive industries.

In the decade before the outbreak of the First World War, the concept of economic colonialism within the framework of *Weltpolitik* developed, especially in official circles, into a grandiose scheme for a German colonial empire stretching across central Africa. Even in the *Mittelafrika* plan, however, the original structure of economic colonialism remained intact. We shall discuss the origins of the *Mittelafrika* idea in Chapter Six, in the context of colonial development policy and colonial politics. Briefly, however, the plan envisioned a belt of territories encompassing the Congo basin that would be either directly or indirectly under German control. The real economic center in terms of profitability would be the Belgian Congo, especially the copper-mining region of Katanga in the south.[44] The Congo would either be acquired directly from Belgium (by cession or purchase) or else recognized as a German sphere of influence through special privileges that would be granted the German government and through a guaranteed predominance of German capital. The Congo region would be attached, economically and perhaps politically, to the German colonies of Cameroon and German East Africa. The latter colonies would, after years of financial insolvency, finally become economically profitable by participating in a coherent economic structure connected with German industry and finance. Cameroon would be expanded (as it was in 1911) to connect with the Congo River and parts of the Portugese African colonies would be added (either by direct annexation or indirect economic and political control) to "flesh out" *Mittelafrika*. All of this would be done through international arrangements in which the French and (especially) the British would receive compensations, which the *Weltpolitiker* believed would be acceptable to them.

The main purpose of *Mittelafrika* was to effect—but on a larger scale and in an area (the Belgian Congo) with proven economic potential— policies derived from the *Weltpolitik* ideology that had been put into practice with comparatively poor results in the existing German colonies.[45] Within the German colonial administration, the tenets of economic colonialism had been modified through confrontations with reality, but even here, the general outlines of the ideology remained the same up to the First World War. One of the most striking features of *Mittelafrika*, as with similar imperialist projects within the scope of *Weltpolitik*, was the extent to which *Weltpolitik* could continue to influence policymaking in the face of empirical evidence that it was really not a very good guide to policy. The reason that it could do so, of course, was that it worked much better (within limits) as an ideology in domestic German politics. Failure, especially when it took place in colonies that were, by their very nature, "displaced" from the German political scene, could be explained away— especially by arguing that Germany had not yet tried hard enough or that Germany had been stuck with an inadequate colonial empire in the 1880s.[46] Schemes like *Mittelafrika,* in part, represented responses to years of apparent failure for economic colonialism.

Plans for developing *Mittelafrika* generally followed those that had been established earlier for German East Africa. The region would be gradually developed through investment programs that would be carefully coordinated by the government and the participating German banks.[47] Foreign capital would be involved also, but predominance and overall control would be exercised by the German participants. The extension of railroads, wage labor, and peasant farming for markets would gradually tie the population of the region to the German economy, thereby increasing the demand for German goods, producing a safe return on investments, and encouraging the further input of private capital. Careful planning would ensure steady economic modernization and the minimum of disruption to African societies consistent with the kinds of changes that would "really" benefit the Africans, whether they appreciated the benefits or not. *Mittelafrika* would become a functioning part of a worldwide trading and financial network centering on Germany—one of perhaps three or four that most *Weltpolitiker* believed were in the process of emerging in the late nineteenth and early twentieth centuries.[48]

Expanding markets and insuring the profitability and effectiveness of investment, whether in colonies or elsewhere, were not purely matters of economics. The inhabitants of the regions slated to be economically integrated with Germany had, if necessary, to alter their behavior patterns and their cultures in order to perform their economic roles. This was an important part of all nineteenth-century European concepts of economic imperialism; the German *Weltpolitiker* added almost nothing original here, borrowing most of their ideas from British theory and practice. In the colonies, various policies were tried, most of them consistent with the overall ends of *Weltpolitik* but often the subjects of intense dispute among

Weltpolitiker. In most colonies, it was believed necessary to extend the range of the cash economy to increase the real purchasing power of the indigenous population and to provide wage-labor for the enterprises established by European investment.[49] Regulations were passed requiring that taxes be paid only in cash or in highly onerous forms of labor service. The colonial authorities also organized development schemes that were supposed simultaneously to increase production for export and enhance indigenous demand for imported products. In Togo, central and southern East Africa, and Samoa, government programs encouraged the emergence of an economy of independent peasant farmers producing for export and closely tied to world trade. In northern East Africa, parts of Cameroon, and Southwest Africa, Africans were "encouraged" (often by force) to become wage laborers on plantations and in mines—in other words, to become an African proletariat.

The actual success of these policies was, on the whole, fairly modest up to the beginning of the First World War—undoubtedly, had Germany kept her colonies, the impingement of the world economy would have had some of the intended effects in the long run. More important from our standpoint were the violent disputes over native policy that arose not only between the German colonial authorities and the indigenous peoples of the colonies (resulting in major resistance such as the Maji Maji rebellion in East Africa), but also within the ranks of the *Weltpolitiker.*[50] On the whole, *Weltpolitiker* who were connected with trading or missionary interests and therefore had some stake in maintaining existing indigenous social structures as long as possible favored the peasant-development model. Those with interests in plantation agriculture or mining favored the proletarian model. The German colonial service, as it developed after 1900, was split on the issue, but the majority appear to have supported the peasant approach. In this case, *Weltpolitik* and economic imperialism could provide no guidance for policy as applied to colonial realities and could not overcome the real difference in interests that divided groups of *Weltpolitiker* from each other. On the whole, however, with the exception of some of the plantation owners in East Africa, all of these groups combined to oppose the idea of large-scale settlement of German small farmers in the colonies, which was the alternative to the *Weltpolitik* style of colonialism advanced as part of the *Lebensraum* ideological set.

Other modes of encouraging changes in culture and behavior were also, of course, advocated and practiced in the German colonies—especially education, on which a great deal of thought but comparatively few revenues were expended. These approaches, however, and other details of Germany's colonial experience do not directly concern us here.

It must be emphasized that *Weltpolitik* was not primarily a colonial ideology, although it had a colonial element. Colonies had their functions, but on the whole most *Weltpolitiker* did not think of colonies as the main instruments for attaining Germany's economic and social goals. The largest part of the process of market expansion and investment—indeed, the largest share of practically all aspects of the economic imperialism of *Weltpolitik*—was to be undertaken in places under varying degrees of *informal* German control.[51] Again, the model of British imperialism, as it was understood by the *Weltpolitiker,* was paramount. Britain's strength and prosperity were held to derive from the connection between her domestic industrial economy and a worldwide periphery of markets, investment areas, and sources of industrial raw materials—some of which were directly ruled colonies, but most of which were not. The colonies were useful for exploiting regions where political order had to be externally imposed or where there was a danger that rival powers would exclude the British. The colonies also provided self-supporting military bases and points of entry into larger marketing areas, but, with the possible exception of India, they were not the real foundation of British imperialism. The real foundation lay in the connection between British industry and the marketing areas in other countries that, because of cultural affinities, heavy British investment, or the influence of British naval power, gave preferential treatment to the British. Britain possessed, in essence, a worldwide informal empire that maintained her economy, even in the face of competition from more efficient producers such as Germany. Germany needed a similar arrangement. Because Germany could not afford the time to let such an arrangement emerge gradually and because the British would not willingly let it appear unless they saw an advantage in doing so, the German government was going to have to take the lead, with the cooperation of German business.[52]

In such areas as South America, the Near East, and China, where Germany would have to seek her share of expanding markets but where (according to the *Weltpolitiker*) formal colonies would be an expensive nuisance, the German government should exert its power to secure special status for planned programs of German investment that would, in turn, create markets for German industry. Again, the Baghdad Railway provides the clearest example of the *Weltpolitik* ideal: an investment program financially secured and guaranteed to German investors and backed politically by their government, the arrangements worked out by the German Foreign Office and the *Deutsche Bank* through the exercise of German influence in Turkey. Arrangements of this sort need not be disadvantageous to non-German parties. In most cases, benefit would be derived by both sides. Nor would the participation of foreign capital be excluded. *Weltpolitiker* were far too convinced of the inadequacy of German capital reserves to want that, and they had considerable experience, both in the German colonies and elsewhere, of the potential of joint German-British, German-French, and German-Belgian investment projects.[53] The point was to use the intervention of the German government to ensure that overall direction would be in the hands of the German participants, that the largest share of the profits and market-expansion advantages would go to the Germans, and, in general, that the areas of major German investment would come to be tied primarily to the

German, not the British, French, Belgian, or American economies. In terms of recent models of economic development, what the *Weltpolitiker* had in mind was the establishment of a classic center-periphery relationship between Germany and a substantial part of the underdeveloped world.

A number of important implications for other aspects of government policymaking flowed from these central economic concepts of *Weltpolitik,* implications that became integral parts of the ideology as a whole. For example, many of the arguments for the expansion of the German navy at the turn of the century derived from economic imperialism. Up to the latter part of the 1890s, German traditions of economic imperialism had been firmly tied to the idea of a strong navy, which was visualized as a cruiser force that could be deployed around the world to overawe recalcitrant foreign governments and gain economic advantages for German merchants. A program of expansion along these lines had, however, never managed to pass the Reichstag. Admiral Tirpitz secured major augmentations of the fleet in the famous naval laws of 1898 and 1900 in part through a masterly use of the ideology of *Weltpolitik* as it had been developed after 1890. Tirpitz wanted to construct, not a multitude of long-distance cruisers, but a new fleet of heavily armored battleships that could counter the British battle fleet in the North Sea. One of the reasons that Tirpitz got what he wanted (besides the fact that he organized the most effective public relations campaign in pre-Nazi German history) was that he translated his aim into the terms of *Weltpolitik* and thus managed to rally the support of *Weltpolitiker* in business and politics.[54] The new German battle fleet would confront Britain with a choice between attempting to maintain her naval superiority in the face of a determined German naval expansion program, thus heightening the risk of war with Germany, or seeking accommodation and partnership with Germany on a worldwide basis. According to Tirpitz and his propagandists, fleet building would force Britain to take the second option—to recognize Germany as a coequal power in the world and to enter into a comprehensive diplomatic arrangement with the Reich.

There is good evidence that Tirpitz himself never wholly believed all of this. Even if he did, he could hardly have been more disastrously wrong about the consequences of the policies that he advocated. The important point for our purposes, however, is that Tirpitz and his supporters hit on a highly significant feature of *Weltpolitik* as an extended aggregate ideology: a particular view of Britain's role in Germany's future as a great power, and a characteristic (and wholly incorrect) set of predictions about British reactions to the emergence of Germany as an imperialistic state. In the general scheme of *Weltpolitik,* the attitude of Great Britain was absolutely crucial to Germany's success. Britain, as the preeminent imperial power and as the major source of the world's investment capital, was the only European country presently in a position to interfere seriously with the *Weltpolitikers'* plans outside of Europe. Most *Weltpolitiker* envisioned Germany's eventual imperial "periphery" as Germany's share after a division of much of the underdeveloped world's economic resources and marketing areas with Britain. Both countries would benefit in the long run from thus cooperating to protect themselves against the competition of the great continental economic powers of the future: the United States and Russia.[55] The only problem was in getting the British to understand their own best interests.

The *Weltpolitikers'* aim of cooperation with Britain underlay many important German diplomatic initiatives, from the Anglo-German treaty of 1890 covering Heligoland and Zanzibar to the 1912–14 negotiations on naval arms reduction and imperial revision—initiatives that, in terms of the larger aims of the Germans, always failed. The reasons they failed are laid out with admirable clarity by Paul Kennedy, but many of them come down to this: that neither the British government nor the British public reacted to Germany's various calls for equality in the way that *Weltpolitik* claimed they would.[56] Proposals for cooperative imperial ventures and massive divisions (e.g., of Portugal's African colonies) never got very far because few British politicians and interest groups could see the need to take on an imperial partner to share what Britain already had—a partner whose politics were regarded as ideologically unsound by many Britishers and as unstable by most. There *were* important British politicians who at various times favored some sort of permanent understanding with Germany. Joseph Chamberlain held this view perhaps more consistently than anyone else, and even Lord Salisbury was occasionally tempted. But hardly anyone in England favored the kind of essentially one-sided change in relations that the *Weltpolitiker* convinced themselves was the only reasonable course for Britain. It would involve, at the very least, a voluntary loss of prestige that no British party or government could accept.

Nowhere do the debilitating effects of an inaccurate ideology and the particular deficiencies of *Weltpolitik* appear more clearly than in the *Weltpolitikers'* expectations about Britain. Even though the British did not live up to these expectations and gave every imaginable kind of evidence that they never would, most advocates of *Weltpolitik* before 1914, instead of reconsidering the validity of their basic notions, sought additional and often more dangerous means of bringing about what they predicted. The failure of amicable advances toward Britain in 1890 and 1898, for example, induced most *Weltpolitiker* to support Tirpitz's way of bringing the British to their senses, which had the perfectly predictable effect of heightening anti-German feeling at all levels of British society and initiating a disastrous naval arms race.[57]

The *Weltpolitikers'* emphasis on the relationship with Great Britain grew not only out of the specific structure of their ideology, but also out of the role that Britain played as an image and a model in their system of social perceptions. The image presented by Britain to educated Germans at the turn of the century appears to have been closely correlated with individuals' outlooks on their own society. To a great many conservatives, Britain symbolized nearly all that was wrong with the modern world: industrialization, the destruction of the traditional agrarian social order, crass materialism, and so forth.[58] Britain was not only an external political threat to Germany, she was also a cultural threat—the threat of modernity to tradition. People who thought along these lines were, on the whole, not well disposed to the idea of accommodation with Britain on any grounds.

Most *Weltpolitiker* responded to a different and more complex image of Britain. Britain, although a threat on the international scene, symbolized a great deal of what they wanted Germany and the Germans to be. The era in which Germans had much to admire in the progressiveness of British science and industry was largely over by 1900. Instead, what the *Weltpolitiker* saw in the British example was a connected set of political, social, and psychological attributes, the adoption of which in Germany would be highly desirable. Britain had successfully, so they thought, "modernized" her society.[59] That is, she had developed a political system capable of integrating the diverse forces unleashed by industrialization into a functioning, peaceful, and legitimate community of interests and aims. The British social system, despite the conflicts that inevitably arose within it, was, according to the *Weltpolitiker,* remarkably free of the kind of fragmentation, regionalism, and class exclusiveness that they perceived in their own society. Unlike the extreme conservatives and enthusiasts of the *Volk,* who claimed that with industrialization the British had lost whatever national culture they possessed, the *Weltpolitiker* tended to believe that the English had done a better job than any other nationality in reconciling modernity with timeless cultural and social values. A great deal of British success was due to the possession of an overseas empire. The creation and maintenance of that empire had required the British, regardless of class and economic interest, to rally at crucial times behind their country's foreign policy and to perceive the reality of a common national interest. It had bred in the British a set of behavior patterns and attitudes—duty, moderation, and an innate sense of superiority—that lay at the core of Britain's successful adaptation to the modern world. These traits of British society and of the British as individuals were also the reason that Britain was still the strongest imperial power.

Much of this was, of course, a result of taking British self-adulation and Kipling's stories at face value and of projecting on a major rival ideal qualities structured in terms of one's own system of beliefs. On the other hand, the German anglophiles were not entirely off the mark. Regardless of their exaggerations and credulity, they had focused on an area of social action in which Britain was, in fact, well ahead of Germany: the development of means, both structural and ideological, of overcoming political fragmentation. Some, like Max Weber, realized that parliamentary democracy had something to do with it.[60] Others, such as Paul Rohrbach, were not so sure.[61] But *Weltpolitiker,* whether or not they were political liberals, almost universally drew the conclusion from the British case that one of the main solutions to fragmentation was imperialism.

It is interesting to note that much the same thing happened in the opposite direction. In the 1890s and just after the turn of the century, various groups in British politics—groups that more or less corresponded within British society to the *Weltpolitiker* in Germany—consciously held out the image of German efficiency, rational planning, and acceptance of an interventionist government as a model for Britain.[62] British national efficiency enthusiasts such as Lord Rosebery and Sidney and Beatrice Webb were, in essence, using Germany in the same way that the *Weltpolitiker* used Britain: as an example for political action made up partly of real and partly of fictitious images—an example that had particular effect because the desirable qualities it represented were those of a serious economic and political rival that was dangerous precisely because it possessed those qualities. As in Germany, so in Britain the proponents of this kind of outlook were conscious both of their own very real admiration for the national rival and of the consensus-building effects of playing to public fears of a potential enemy.

To return to the more strictly economic aspects of *Weltpolitik,* there were a number of additional elements of the ideology that require some consideration. Besides the aims of market expansion and investment security, *Weltpolitik* also encompassed the idea of imperialism as a means of securing supplies of raw materials for German industry and, in some versions, of foodstuffs for the German population. Although this concept had been noted during the colonial propaganda campaigns of the 1880s, it had not been heavily featured. It appeared mainly as the reverse side of the export offensive idea: expanding overseas markets would, of necessity, supply a steadily increasing stream of overseas raw materials to Germany—a matter of interest particularly to import-dependent industries such as cotton manufacturing, whose leaders were worried about the effects of Germany's 1879 tariffs on their costs.[63] Under the conditions of recurring deflation and depression that existed up to the mid-1890s, most business people interested themselves more in the problems of selling manufactured goods than in purchasing material factors of production, and the ideologists of imperialism played to that interest. With the onset of inflation and expansionary economic conditions in the mid-1890s, however, the situation changed. *Weltpolitiker* in Germany, like imperialists elsewhere, began trumpeting the dangers of industry's growing dependence on foreign supplies of materials and of the attendant growing deficit in the foreign balance of payments.[64]

Undoubtedly, both dependence and the payments deficit were sources of genuine worry. But the frequently expressed fear that the machinations of the British or some other economic rival might (short of war) cut Germany off from the sources of materials on which her industry depended was highly unrealistic and not, apparently, taken very seriously by most *Weltpolitiker.*[65] The actual roots of the concern for raw materials that was incorporated into *Weltpolitik* were much more subtle and complex.

The main impetus to the new emphasis on the raw materials aspect of

Weltpolitik in the 1890s was not a real threat to actual availability but rather inflation, coupled with structural changes in the world's primary-goods market—as these were perceived by the leaders of new organizations founded in the 1890s to represent German light industry. These organizations, especially the *Bund der Industriellen* (BdI) and the Colonial Economic Committee (KWK), were among the most active proponents of *Weltpolitik* and economic imperialism.[66] We may take the KWK and its connections to the cotton industry as an example.

The KWK was started as a result of rising raw cotton prices experienced by the cotton industry in the second half of the 1890s. Although the organization became loosely connected to the Colonial Society, it was always largely autonomous and its orientation always primarily toward cotton. The president of the KWK was Karl Supf, the owner of a cotton mill and an active imperialist of the *Weltpolitiker* school. The main, underlying objective of the KWK was to push for government action to curb price rises in raw cotton through the conduct of a comprehensive program of colonial development within the general framework of *Weltpolitik*.

The KWK and the spokespersons of the cotton industry gave a structural—indeed, a conspiratorial—explanation for the inflation in cotton prices at the turn of the century. It was an explanation that, for the most part, left out of its account the general post-1896 inflation of prices throughout the world and the inflationary pressures generated by overall business expansion. The KWK (like its British counterpart, the Cotton Producer's Association, with which the KWK cooperated closely) blamed the raw cotton inflation on big speculators in the United States who had occasionally cornered the cotton market in that country, on the appearance of the American cotton growers' associations, and on the control exerted over the Egyptian cotton crop by British and French banks. These and other factors created monopolistic tendencies in the cotton market, leading to high prices but reduced production.[67] Because they were structural factors resulting from specific actions by a few individuals and institutions, they could be controlled and altered. Because they threatened the economic well-being of the industrial countries (the interests of the cotton producers writ large), they *should* be controlled or altered, either through joint action by the German and British governments or by separate, but parallel, policies.

On one level, the KWK and *Weltpolitiker* who agreed with its position argued that the German government (ideally with British help) should put pressure on the governments of countries in which businesses were "conspiring" to raise cotton prices and restrict the cotton supply. In the likely event that these efforts should fail in the short run, Germany should use the tools provided by economic imperialism to increase the world's cotton supply (thus lessening the tendency toward monopoly) and to derive as much of Germany's own cotton as possible from sources that could be controlled by the German government.[68] Friendly Near Eastern countries such as Turkey should be encouraged to grow more cotton and to seek German investment to improve cotton technology. In Germany's own colonies, government and private enterprise should cooperate to set up cotton-growing projects, "scientifically" directed and on a very large scale. To this end, the KWK sponsored a wide range of agricultural research in the African colonies and a number of pilot projects for the introduction of new crops—not just cotton, although cotton remained the KWK's main interest. The financially impoverished colonial administration cooperated closely with the KWK on these matters, and the activities of the KWK were continually held up by *Weltpolitiker* in the government and the Reichstag as models of what could be accomplished (and not just in colonial development) if government and industry worked together to solve national problems.[69]

The most spectacular of the KWK's projects was its attempt, in the years immediately after 1900, to turn the colony of Togo into a major cotton producer on a foundation of peasant agriculture.[70] Despite the fact that the Colonial Department strongly supported the scheme by attempting to restructure the society of southern Togo, the plan ultimately failed. On the whole, the KWK had more success with projects that did not concern cotton, because considerations of cotton production invariably brought into play the most inaccurate and ill-conceived aspects of the KWK's ideological approach.

The problem with the KWK's strategy for cotton was that it was based on a faulty analysis, especially in its tendency (typical of explanations founded on ideologies) to focus on structural changes and the actions of "villains" in raising prices. Structural factors existed, but on the whole raw cotton prices merely followed the patterns of almost all primary goods at the turn of the century, rising because of high demand. The existing areas of major cotton production eventually responded to increased demand by raising production. Their response, together with occasional sharp downturns in prices, made new, marginal producers like Togo economically uncompetitive.

In a *political* sense, however, the KWK enjoyed considerable success. Although it never achieved wide public attention, its reputation in official and business circles was very high—partly because of the real excellence of much of the research that the KWK sponsored.[71] Equally important, however, the KWK was able to tie the interests of the cotton industry and related sectors of the economy into a program of action highly compatible with *Weltpolitik*—so compatible, in fact, that it became *part* of *Weltpolitik*. Using the structural theory of primary-goods inflation together with somewhat less sophisticated arguments about the political need for economic self-sufficiency, the KWK was able to wield great influence, not only over colonial policy, but also over aspects of foreign policy that concerned the cotton industry.

In 1907, for example, the newly appointed Colonial Secretary, Bernhard Dernburg, framed his view of colonial development around notions derived in large part from KWK propaganda. Dernburg went to the extent of believing that, as Supf claimed, properly developed colonies could supply most of Germany's raw materials needs and also solve her balance of payments problem.[72] Dernburg eventually backed off from such optimism, but even then the KWK was able to use Dernburg as an advocate within the German government of joint Anglo-German action to lower raw cotton prices.[73] Thus in the case of this particular aspect of *Weltpolitik,* we can see an idea-set of limited empirical accuracy acquiring importance because of its connection to a broader composite ideology, permitting at least the partial realization of the aims of an interest group, and affecting the framework of thought within which policy was made.

Another aspect of *Weltpolitik* that requires attention is the idea of the central European economic union—a notion that had been connected to German economic imperialism ever since the time of List. The concept is generally known by the name it acquired from the writings of Friedrich Naumann during the First World War: *Mitteleuropa.* The development of the concept after 1890 is made somewhat confusing by the fact that there were two distinct versions of *Mitteleuropa* simultaneously in vogue: one, which evolved directly out of the older economic imperialist idea, became an integral part of *Weltpolitik;* the other, a later, vaguely defined concept, was loosely attached to the *Lebensraum* ideological complex.[74] The latter will be discussed in Chapter Five.

The *Mitteleuropa* associated with *Weltpolitik* corresponded fairly closely to List's original idea of an organized and protected system of economic exchanges between an industrial Germany and an agricultural periphery in central and eastern Europe. The advantages of such a union for Germany would be largely the same as those of a successful policy of *Weltpolitik* as a whole: the acquisition of control over the economy; the protection of industrial jobs, profits, and investments against foreign competition; and the securing of raw materials—all, if necessary, at the expense of large-scale German agriculture. Agriculture would become the function of Germany's continental trading partners.[75] *Mitteleuropa* was in some respects merely the form that *Weltpolitik* took when it was applied to Germany's continental environs, especially in the east. It did not, however, start out in the 1890s quite that way.

As we have seen, the idea of Central European economic integration had been advanced in the 1880s as one possible goal of national policies that would benefit heavy industry, policies that had also included economic colonialism. Nothing much had come of it then. At the beginning of Caprivi's chancellorship, the idea was adopted by a group of officials within the new administration as their particular policy objective. The group overlapped the *Weltpolitiker* in the Foreign Office to some extent in membership and to a great extent in basic thinking, but its central figures were different. Chief among them was Karl Göring, the head of the Chancery Office, who exercised great influence over Caprivi. It was primarily Göring who, responding to pressure by heavy industrial organizations, designed the new tariff policy that Caprivi announced in 1891 and implemented beginning in 1892.[76]

The tariff policy was, at its most basic level, an attempt to lower German duties on agricultural imports to encourage other countries, especially Russia and Austria-Hungary, to reduce their duties on German industrial products. The abatement was to be accomplished, not through a comprehensive, unilateral reduction of German tariff schedules but rather through the renegotiation of commercial treaties with the countries in question when they came up for renewal. The major heavy-industry organizations, especially the CDI, had become extremely interested in such a policy by the late 1880s. With the temporary reversal of depressed conditions in industry during those years and the growing awareness of Germany's competitive edge over rival producers in many areas of manufacturing, industrialists became less concerned about protecting their domestic markets and more concerned with opening up new ones—of which the most promising were those of eastern and central Europe. At the same time, their uneasy political alliance with East Elbian agriculture, which produced the tariff of 1879, had to a large extent broken down. As a result, organized big business strongly favored Caprivi's initiative—at least at the start.[77]

By and large, the *Weltpolitiker* in and out of government also favored the Caprivi tariff policy. Caprivi and Karl Göring for their part were by no means opposed to the worldwide economic aims of the *Weltpolitiker*. Caprivi, it is true, thought little of formal colonies, but his main objection was to the idea of extensive colonial settlement. Although he believed that people such as Kayser went a little overboard in their enthusiasm for *Weltpolitik,* in general he agreed that government action was needed to expand Germany's economic links both eastward in Europe and overseas.[78]

One of the main reasons that the *Weltpolitiker* and the low-tariff group in the Caprivi government were able to cooperate with each other was that the reasoning that underlay their positions was practically identical. The key to economic success and social peace for Germany was held to be the rationally planned expansion of the industrial sector. People such as Karl Göring emphasized the continental implications of this sort of thinking and people such as Kayser pushed for an overseas concentration, but neither group believed that policy should be exclusively limited to one direction or the other. The logic of the Caprivi tariff policy went, in fact, well beyond the immediate needs or aims of heavy industry. It was constructed and defended in public as a means of creating the integrated, German-dominated system of exchanges in Europe that List and his successors had recommended. An overseas economic empire, both formal and informal, was an important complement to such a system. Similarly, because the Listean idea of European economic integration was a long-standing part of the economic imperialism from which they were developing *Weltpolitik,* the official *Weltpolitiker* of the Caprivi era regarded the tariff policy as a complement to their own efforts. Indeed, the *Mitteleuropa* idea merged rather quickly in the 1890s into the broader *Weltpolitik* ideology to become one of its elements. From the ideological standpoint then, it is not entirely correct to speak, as some historians have, of a decisive change in German diplomatic goals in 1890 or in 1897 away from a continental orientation and toward *Weltpolitik* and of a reversal in 1912–14.[79] The adherents of *Weltpolitik* (as the term is defined here) accepted *both* continental *and* overseas objectives and visualized them as part of the same ideological structure. They argued among themselves about the specific direction to emphasize at a particular moment, but this did not prejudice their overall consensus about the need in the long run to pursue all of the aims of *Weltpolitik*.

The Caprivi tariff had several different aspects. It was, among other things, a response to demands by heavy industry for assistance in entering new markets; it was also one move in an attempt to reverse the growing diplomatic estrangement between Germany and Russia. From the standpoint of the politics of German imperialism, it can be seen as an effort to link national policy to a broad framework of economic and social ideas— a framework the proponents of the policy believed would simultaneously guide effective government action and create consensus among an array of different social groups. The tariff initiatives, interpreted to the "modern" segments of the country's social elite and eventually to the public at large through the media of *Mitteleuropa* and *Weltpolitik*, were intended to demonstrate that the government was alive to the need to plan for Germany's economic future and to reduce the level of social tension by maintaining prosperity. The Caprivi tariff initiative was expected to engender support for the government among manufacturing interests, among "modern-thinking" elements of the public at large, and among industrial workers concerned about jobs and wages.[80]

However, the tariff policy, in fact, did not have its intended political effect. It aroused a storm of protest from Junker agricultural interests and from the conservative parties. The debate in the Reichstag over the Caprivi policy soon became the most bitter and divisive issue of Wilhelmian political history: the conflict between the adherents of industrialism and the agrarians.[81] It was the occasion for the formation of fragmentary interest groups such as the *Bund der Landwirte* and for the general radicalization of German conservatism. And in the end, the advocates of lower tariffs lost. In 1902, the government of Chancellor von Bülow, pursuing its continuing aim of *Sammlungspolitik* (a politics of integration), passed through the Reichstag a new, higher agricultural tariff schedule—a move that was accepted by the same heavy industrial lobbies that had pushed for lower tariffs twelve years previously.

The significance of the relationship between *Weltpolitik* and the Caprivi tariff will be discussed at greater length in Chapter Six. The important point is that many of the apparent advantages of *Weltpolitik* as a creator of consensus behind the government and big business were obviated by the fact that *Weltpolitik* came to be identified with the attitudes that lay behind the lowering of tariffs. The opponents of tariff reduction therefore attacked all the ideological structures associated with the Caprivi tariff, including *Weltpolitik*. To attack *Weltpolitik* imperialism was, in essence, to attack the tariff policy, and vice versa. And (as we shall see in the next chapter), the agrarians in their assault had the willing cooperation of the proponents of *Lebensraum*.

Social Imperialism and Liberal Imperialism

Before turning to *Lebensraum*, it is necessary to refer briefly to two concepts widely employed by historians attempting to explain *Weltpolitik:* social imperialism and liberal imperialism. It was pointed out in previous chapters that the ideological characteristics used by Wehler and others to define social imperialism were part of practically all forms of imperialism in European politics—in Britain and France as well as Germany.[82] Both *Weltpolitik* and *Lebensraum* featured the argument that active imperialism would reduce the subversive tendencies of the working class, although their explanations of how this would happen differed considerably. The *Weltpolitiker* claimed that the job security and rising prosperity resulting from successful economic imperialism would undercut the appeal of the Socialists and help to reconcile the workers to the capitalist order, especially if expansion were associated with a rational, progressive social policy at home. This argument was, however, only one part of *Weltpolitik,* certainly not its defining element, any more than its equivalent in the *Lebensraum* aggregation defined *Lebensraum*.[83] Social imperialism was nonetheless important to *Weltpolitik*. Not only did it provide one set of reasons for the necessity of economic imperialism, but it was also essential to the *Weltpolitikers'* view of the consensus-building function of their ideology. Many of them actually believed that *Weltpolitik* would attract wide support among workers. Even more important was the expectation that *Weltpolitik* and its advocates would elicit support from members of the *upper* and *middle* classes if the latter thought that *Weltpolitik* could indeed pacify the proletariat.[84] In other words, the social imperialist aspect of *Weltpolitik* was (like other elements of the ideology) partly directed toward dealing with the complexities of political and social fragmentation as well as the spectre of worker/bourgeois class conflict.

Liberal imperialism is difficult to define in Germany because of the ambiguities inherent in German liberalism itself.[85] It is sufficient for the present to note that, although many important *Weltpolitiker* were self-conscious liberals (especially the leaders of *Weltpolitik* opinion during World War I), many others were not. Karl Helfferich, for example, was as orthodox a *Weltpolitiker* as one can imagine, but he was also an enemy of most of the ideas that passed for liberalism in Germany. *Weltpolitik* was decidedly not simply a liberal version of German imperialism. It had many links to liberalism, most especially the fact that both shared, on the whole, a positive view of material progress and modernity. But it was entirely possible to be a modernist and to oppose liberalism—witness the views of such people as Helfferich, Tirpitz, and Wilhelm von Kardorff.[86]

If the term *liberal imperialism* is to be used at all in the German context, it should probably be applied quite narrowly to people such as Max Weber and Friedrich Naumann: *Weltpolitiker* who attempted to construct an integrated imperialist ideology going beyond *Weltpolitik* as a support for a program of domestic social and political reform. The activities of these people will be examined in Chapter Seven.

In this chapter, we have examined *Weltpolitik* from the standpoint of the interests of its proponents and from the standpoint of its intellectual content. *Weltpolitik* was a classic aggregate ideology, formed from the accretion of a wide variety of ideas around a central core of economic imperialism. The constitutent ideas represented both the perceived interests and the collective outlooks of several different social groups, among whom bureaucrats in government and industry predominated. *Weltpolitik* performed many political functions, in addition to creating an appealing—if often self-contradictory and ultimately disastrous—framework for constructing foreign and imperial policy. *Weltpolitik* encouraged and justified close cooperation between government and business, especially on matters of external investment. It provided an attractive format for presenting many different policy initiatives of varying provenance to the Reichstag and to the public in general: fleet building, colonial improvement, and tariff reduction among others. It was especially useful as a device for career enhancement within bureaucratic organizations. *Weltpolitik* owed its broad appeal and much of its political effectiveness to its identification with science, modernity, rationality, and planning as well as to the image it presented of a Germany that could rival Britain as an imperial power and as a successful modern society. The modernist, proindustrial attitudes associated with *Weltpolitik* were also, however, the main reasons that the ideology could not ultimately be used to create consistent national consensus. For *Weltpolitik* had a rival, an aggregation of imperialist ideas that, although sharing some of *Weltpolitik*'s elements, specifically rejected many of its modernist associations. We shall turn to the rival ideology in the next chapter.

CHAPTER FIVE

Lebensraum

Weltpolitik's major rival was a composite ideology put together mainly in the 1890s through the combination of migrationist colonialism and a number of other ideological entities, with many of which migrationism was already vaguely associated. This new ideology had no particular name at the time—and none has been given to it by historians. We could call it "conservative imperialism" or "radical conservative imperialism" because of the way it was used in politics. Such a name, however, would convey an incorrect impression that its referent was merely a particular imperialist manifestation of a broadly defined, coherent conservative ideology. As we shall see, it is probably more accurate to see it as one of a number of parallel ideologies manifesting, one way or another, resentments against aspects of the modern world—ideologies that intersected but that were not effectively integrated with one another before 1918. These ideologies were employed by many political groups— mainly conservative ones—as instruments of consensus creation and attempted political integration. Some other name for *Weltpolitik*'s rival must therefore be found.

In this study, an anachronism—*Lebensraum*—will denote the alternative imperialist ideological aggregation. The degree of anachronism is not severe. Although the inventor of the term, the noted geographer Friedrich Ratzel, popularized it only after the turn of the century and ostensibly only in the context of his biological theories, *Lebensraum* came to be widely employed in imperialist literature after World War I to refer essentially to the set of expansionary political ideas that we shall discuss. Moreover, Ratzel himself was an advocate of what we shall call *Lebensraum* imperialism; his scientific theories were closely connected to his political ideas and activities.[1] Because no more appropriate name presents itself, we shall use *Lebensraum*.

The Elements of *Lebensraum*

Just as economic imperialism constituted the central core of *Weltpolitik,* so migrationist colonialism, as it emerged from the colonial movement of the

1880s, originally provided the key element of *Lebensraum.* Migrationist colonialism did not, however, dominate *Lebensraum* to the extent that economic imperialism dominated *Weltpolitik.* For one thing, the idea-content of migrationist colonialism was a good deal more circumscribed than was that of economic imperialism; for another, *Lebensraum* was formed from the conjuncture of several limited ideologies of which migrationist colonialism was only the least diffuse and marginally most central to the aggregation that emerged. In the long run, in fact, extensions of migrationist thinking became more important within the overall structure of *Lebensraum* than migrationist colonialism itself.

Nevertheless, it was migrationist colonialism, with its proven (or assumed) appeal to the urban and rural middle classes, its conservative implications, and the prominence it attained during the colonial enthusiasm of the 1880s that attracted the attention of many politicians and publicists in the early 1890s as a potential central element in a larger aggregate conservative ideology. We shall shortly examine the process of ideological aggregation in one of the most important organizations that participated in the construction of *Lebensraum:* the Pan-German League. In general, what the formulators of *Lebensraum* did was to attach to the existing migrationist ideology a number of ideological constructions (especially agrarianism), many of which possessed some of the same social and intellectual roots as migrationist colonialism.

The attachment of these additional elements to migrationism did not prevent their continued existence as autonomous ideological entities. Agrarianism, for example, not only contributed a substantial amount to the structure of *Lebensraum;* in the 1890s, it simultaneously became the nucleus of a separate ideology, radical agrarianism, that was widely employed by conservative political organizations.[2] *Lebensraum,* radical agrarianism, and a number of other new aggregate ideologies were therefore in some senses parallel and related structures with similar histories and political uses, sharing some of the same intellectual elements and appealing to similar (but not identical) segments of the German public. Altogether, these parallel aggregate ideologies constituted the phenomenon of "new" (or "radical") conservatism in the early Wlhelmian era.

The new forms of conservative ideology that appeared in German politics during the Wilhelmian era have bedeviled historians for years, both because their relationship to Naziism (although obviously important) is not clear and because they appear to be a confusing welter of ideas, some congruent, some wildly inconsistent. Attempts to fit them all into a single category on the basis of their intellectual content have not been successful. Not all of the tendencies of the new conservatism were *völkisch* or entirely antimodern, although many of them were.[3] "Illiberalism" fairly indicates the overt opposition to liberal stereotypes that characterized practically all of these tendencies, but it obscures the liberal origins of much of the new conservatism and the lack of consistency among the stereotypes of liberalism taken under attack.[4] Even *radical nationalism* and *radical conservatism* (the terms used for convenience most often in this study) have little analytical value because of the vagueness of the word *radical*.[5] It will not do, either, simply to dismiss the whole phenomenon as "irrationality" in politics, as an atavistic response to modernity. There was irrationality aplenty in the new conservative ideologies, but it took the general form shared to greater or lesser degrees by all aggregate ideologies: contradictions between inconsistent aims and ideas incorporated within the same intellectual structure. This general characteristic was derived from the uses for which the ideologies were constructed, especially the creation of consensus and the aggregation of political support.

We are left then with a structural characterization of radical conservatism: a plethora of related aggregate ideologies resulting from attempts in the late nineteenth and early twentieth centuries to create a broad-ranging, fundamentally conservative consensus and to build support for political organizations. The motives that lay behind these attempts were as varied as the motives of any sort of political action: the beliefs of individuals in the rightness of some, if not all, of the ideas that they propounded; the narrow aims of economic-interest groups and the wider ones of social classes; personal ambitions; fear of socialism or of social change. None of the attempts was completely successful before the First World War, and no efforts to integrate the various ideologies that made up radical conservatism succeeded before that time either. But altogether the radical conservative ideologies constituted an important new force in politics. Also, because some of these ideologies took on lives of their own and engendered widespread belief, they became even more important influences on national policy after 1914. Among these, *Lebensraum* was particularly important because it provided one of the most effective available means of linking together inconsistent elements in radical conservatism.

We have already examined the origins of the migrationist element in *Lebensraum,* but to understand its function within the larger ideological aggregation it is necessary first to consider another important constituent: agrarianism. Migrationist colonialism had, of course, contained agrarian elements since its beginnings. In the 1880s and 1890s, a number of politicians and publicists organized several of the disparate strands of romantic agrarianism into a functional aggregate ideology widely employed in conservative politics. The most important period of ideological aggregation took place in the wake of the Caprivi tariff policies of the early 1890s, as groups such as the *Bund der Landwirte* and the conservative parties attempted to rally popular suppport against a pro-industrial policy by making reference to an ideology that was explicitly anti-industrial and anti-modern. Even before that time, however, the need of western German farmers for a coherent ideological expression and the potential of agrarian ideas for assembling support from social groups whose only significant similarity in outlook was an animus against modernity had led to substantial development toward an agrarian ideology.[6] *Lebensraum* was thus influenced by agrarianism in two ways: by the romantic agrarian thread that ran through the migrationist colonialism of the Bismarckian era and by the full-scale aggregate ideology of agrarianism that was in the process of forming at the time that *Lebensraum* itself was being constructed.

By the early 1890s, ideological agrarianism was presented in many different ways, from sophisticated examinations of the past and current state of agriculture by important economists such as Adolf Wagner and Max Sering to highly emotional descriptive contrasts between the urban and rural environments in popular periodicals.[7] Although there existed several varieties of agrarianism, most versions focused strongly on the romantic image of the small peasant farm and the society built around it that had been the central element of agrarianism in the past. The reason for this was fairly obvious, both to employers of the ideology and to their critics: an ideology that openly advanced the interests of big Junker and pseudo-Junker agriculture would appear to be merely self-serving rhetoric and would therefore have little efficacy in advancing the public campaign against the Caprivi tariffs. However, one that focused on the need of the peasant farmer for protection could attract support from many different segments of society.[8] For small-scale peasant agriculture was as much as anything else a symbol—a symbol of preindustrial society, of all that was threatened by modernity and industrialization. The images of peasant agrarianism could appeal not only to the small farmers themselves as well as to other residents of agricultural districts, but also to urban dwellers of many different social classes: artisans, shopkeepers, members of the *Gelehrtenstand*. Even industrialists could subscribe to agrarian ideas in response to their own feelings of guilt about damages, real and imagined, that industrialization had done to German society; even Junker landowners, who were, because of the innovations they had introduced into eastern grain agriculture and their increasing use of seasonal Polish labor, primarily responsible for the decline of peasant agriculture in eastern Prussia, could identify with romanticized, peasant-oriented agrarianism as a set of symbols of their outlook on the world. Romantic agrarianism was often used in politics to justify proposed policies that would primarily benefit groups other than small farmers. There were also, however, a great many sincere believers in agrarianism at all levels of society—including many of the very people who were using agrarianism for their own purposes.[9]

One of the most important aspects of popular, peasant-centered romantic agrarianism that found its way into *Lebensraum* was its array of political implications, implications based on the assumption that peasants were naturally free and virtuous.[10] The traditional peasant farmer of agrarian mythology was a free man (or, in Prussia, free at least since the Stein reforms). His personal freedom had been, in part, a product of his economic freedom. He was not a subsistence agriculturalist, but he was not a slave of the market or of capital either; the market was a convenience, not an all-consuming nexus. The independence of the peasant had made him politically and intellectually free in the "true" sense of the word.

That is, he accepted the existing structure of social and political order out of free choice and not by compulsion because he was in a position to realize that stability benefitted all and that rash innovation usually promoted strife. Although these idealized peasants accepted the necessity of a hierarchical society and of deference to social betters, they were willing nonetheless to defend themselves against the tyranny of governments and elites who presumed too much on the peasant's habitual sense of order. The threat that modernity (usually identified with industrialization and urbanization) posed to the economic independence of the peasantry thus endangered their "responsible" independence of political behavior, to the detriment of the entire German nation.

Agrarianism incorporated a catalog of virtues that were held to inhere in the character of small farmers. Peasant farmers had a stronger and more direct connection with nature than almost any other social type, yet they were not simply nature's untamed children.[11] Their whole life consisted of an interaction between ingenuity and will on the one hand and the forces of nature—both predictable and unpredictable—on the other. The idea that farmers achieved, through effort, a balance among natural forces gave the agrarian image part of its appeal to people with little first hand experience of actual agriculture. The forces present in the advanced industrial economy could be represented as analogous to the forces of nature; the peasants' mode of controlling them, or at least adapting to them, could be viewed as an ideal for all of society. Direct contact with nature (by which was meant, more or less, the nonurban outdoor environment) was essential to the agrarians' views of the political virtues of the peasantry. The varied experiences that resulted from such contact made small farmers "well-rounded" persons, gave them a common-sense sagacity and an ability to judge people and issues superior to that of town dwellers or wage laborers.

The political implication of all this was, of course, that peasants deserved special consideration because of the manifold benefits that they conferred on society simply by being the way they were. Such implications are commonly found in ideologies that idealize particular groups and social types.[12] In the case of peasant agrarianism, the unique political virtues of the peasantry were among the most important reasons given for the protection of agriculture, the necessary context within which the virtues developed. That this protection would also, indeed primarily, benefit capitalist Junker agriculture was simply not emphasized by the leading opponents of the Caprivi tariff policy in the 1890s. By assuming a continuity of interest between big and small agriculture and using the images of peasant agrarianism as a front, the agrarian interest could seek broad political support.[13]

The political aim of building consensus and overcoming political fragmentation is revealed in other aspects of agrarian ideology. It was argued, for example, that only those classes with traditional roots in agriculture—especially the peasantry—could correctly adjudge political issues and perceive the correct course for Germany once it was presented to them as an option. Other segments of society, including many elite groups and the political parties that represented them, could not see beyond their selfish interests. Thus one of the arguments for protecting and strengthening the peasantry was that, in so doing, Germany would partly overcome the effects of her own internal fragmentation. By implication and association, political organizations that advocated peasant agrarianism, especially if they were not composed of peasants, could represent themselves as being above the conflict of special interests, regardless of whatever else they advocated.[14]

Agrarians had other arguments for protecting small-unit agriculture and the society and economy built atop it. There was the argument from cultural nostalgia: that peasant society retained the forms of the good old days before modernity had destroyed for most people the affective bonds that had given them a comfortable place in the world. In the late nineteenth century, this view was being sanctioned by an increasing body of academic and social scientific literature.[15] Not only did it enhance the utility of agrarianism as a set of counterimages to modernist and industrialist ones, but it also lent support to schemes for reestablishing agricultural communities in places in which peasant farming was in danger.

Agrarianism could also be easily related to the various *völkisch* ideological movements that attracted wide public attention in the latter part of the 1890s. The evocation of nostalgic social and economic images by *völkisch* and agrarian propagandists alike and the general agreement among them that the true embodiment of the *Volk* was the peasantry led to a notable overlap between the two ideological trends.[16] Agrarianism also encompassed a connection to more utilitarian forms of nationalism in, for example, the argument that a strong German peasantry was needed for national defense because the sons of small farmers made the best soldiers. They supposedly accepted discipline better and their minds were not cluttered with deviant political views sprung from city life. Their lives close to nature made them healthier and tougher than town dwellers, and they were instinctively more patriotic. The fact that the actual experience of the army with its conscripts went somewhat contrary to the myth of the peasant soldier did not prevent the same adages about the peasantry as the foundation of national defense from being repeated right down to the Nazi period.[17]

One of the most interesting characteristics of post-1890 agrarianism—a characteristic it shared with other radical conservative ideologies—was its evident connection to various traditions of liberalism. This is a serious complication for historians because agrarianism was commonly used during and after the Wilhelmian era to attack liberal ideas and liberal organizations. Nevertheless, the connections are quite apparent. Many of the leading proponents of agrarianism were former liberals and some of them remained important members of the National Liberal party.[18] Many of the notions associated with agrarianism were originally linked to liberalism: the defense of the ordinary man against the elites, the emphasis on the political utility of common sense, the vaguely Jeffersonian ideals implicit in the ideology. Moreover, although migrationist colonialism had arisen primarily from very moderate strains of administrative liberalism earlier in the century, the liberal connections of agrarianism were to the left, democratic, or populist tradition—the tradition of Gustav von Struve, Friedrich Hecker, and Rudolf Virchow. It was this tradition that was supposed to have acquired for the National Liberal and Progressive parties the bulk of their rural electoral support up to the 1880s. The addition of a strong new element of agrarianism to migrationist colonialism during the creation of the *Lebensraum* ideology in the 1890s implicitly meant a strong addition of populism as well.[19]

From the standpoint of political function, the important point about the populist element in agrarianism (and thus in *Lebensraum*) was precisely its separation from its original liberal context. Left liberalism had included not just images of a valuable, virtuous, and threatened peasantry but also a prescription for political action to protect the lower classes, agrarian and otherwise—that is, the establishment of a truly representative political system based on a broad or universal franchise. Taken out of this context and placed in one that included a specific attack on the liberal idea of representative government, populism could be used as a means of rallying the support of nonelite segments of society for elite-dominated institutions such as the conservative parties, without, at the same time, threatening actual elite interests. Thus Junker members of the *Bund der Landwirte* could safely accept an agrarian populist program in the knowledge that, although the program might contain criticisms of their own class and its economic interests, it did not contain among its aims any effective means of ensuring that these criticisms would result in action—that is, the diminution of the real political power of the elite.[20]

To be sure, in order to be politically effective, the Wilhelmian agrarian ideology had to include some goals or action items. The ones most commonly suggested were legislation to protect small farmers from foreclosure, policies of making additional land available to real or would-be *Bauern*, and schemes for government-backed, low-interest loans to farmers. A great many of the formulators and defenders of agrarianism—people such as the academics Max Sering, Adolf Wagner, and Friedrich Ratzel—sincerely believed in the efficacy of these ideas. Many of them also believed that liberalism, in its classical form, had sold out the interests of the peasantry and that notions of representative democracy were essentially a sham to assemble support for those who would entirely destroy traditional German society.[21] Other agrarians were perhaps more hypocritical, especially those who were practicing politicians. But in any event, the functional political importance of agrarianism remained its ability to detach the populist aspect of liberalism from its original context and to insert it into a conservative context that did not substantially threaten elite interests, that allowed agrarianism to be turned against the liberal doctrines that were used to justify proposed political actions that really did threaten the Prussian agrarian elite (electoral reform, free trade, etc.), and that shored up the agrarian elite's position on issues such as its opposition to the Caprivi tariff policy.

Or, at least, this was *supposed* to be the political utility of agrarianism. There were, however, problems with its employment in real politics, one of which was that the spokespersons of many conservative interests were leery of the apparent radicalism implicit in agrarianism—the very thing that made it potentially useful. The introduction of radical agrarianism into conservative politics during the dispute over the Caprivi tariff was one of the sources of the persistent splits in conservative and anti-Caprivi ranks. Futhermore, the radical agrarian position was most forcefully stated by academic figures such as Adolf Wagner—people who were highly suspect to many political conservatives (especially industrialists) as self-proclaimed social reformers ("socialists of the chair.")[22] On the face of it, this was not much of a difficulty because the industrial interest was ostensibly the enemy of the conservative agrarian movement. However, a great many conservatives sympathetic to the agrarian interest realized that the long-term future of Junkerdom and big agriculture in Germany depended on working out an accommodation with the politically conservative part of the nation's industrial and financial leadership and on continuing the process of coopting that leadership—a process that had been going on for some time. The radical veneer of 1890s agrarianism, although it gave the ideology a large part of its political utility, also tended to disqualify it from being an ideology of integration within the German social and political elite.[23]

This was one of the reasons that *Lebensraum* became an important element of Wilhelmian politics. *Lebensraum* featured the idea of displacing the "radical" effects of agrarianism to locations where they would not pose even a hypothetical problem for established interests. In settlement colonies in Africa or South America, in the "internal" colonies that became an essential feature of the *Lebensraum* aggregation, in "colonies" for German settlers to be acquired in eastern Europe, the peasant (and many other useful but threatened social types) could be preserved and strengthened, thus protecting the foundations of German culture. In calls for such forms of colonialism, the values implicit in the agrarian ideology could be affirmed without serious danger of contradiction. Conservatives could argue that settlers in Southwest Africa should be given a strong voice in the affairs of the colony to protect themselves, and thus the advantages to Germany they manifested, against big-business interests. At the same time, they could deny the desirability of democratization in Germany.[24] Spokespersons for Junker agriculture, much of which by the 1890s depended on seasonal Polish labor, could display their real or supposed sympathy for the peasant farmers being driven out of East Elbian agriculture by Polish labor by publicly favoring *Lebensraum*-style settlement projects, both abroad and in Germany, and still continue to employ Polish seasonal workers. In other words, although *Lebensraum* was not formed simply as an adjunct to agrarianism and although it contained a great many other elements besides migrationist colonialism and romantic agrarianism, its connection with agrarianism went well beyond parallel origins and specific borrowings. *Lebensraum* provided a means by which conservatives identified with the agricultural interest could resolve the political difficulties that arose in the use of agrarianism as a support-building ideology. By the same token, *Lebensraum*'s association with agrarianism allowed groups with specific imperialist interests to muster support from a broad range of conservative organizations.

Ideas that were essentially extensions of migrationist thinking became increasingly important parts of the *Lebensraum* ideological aggregation in the course of the 1890s and after 1900. The notions of internal colonization and territorial annexation in eastern Europe to settle masses of German small farmers had appeal in themselves, once the assumptions of *Lebensraum* were accepted. But the factors that primarily brought these ideas close to the forefront of political imaginations by the time of the First World War emerged from the political circumstances in which *Lebensraum* was used.

Agrarianism displaced by migrationist colonialism to real or projected colonies did not exhaust the range of elements that were linked together by the ideologues of *Lebensraum* in the 1890s. It was entirely natural that racist and *völkisch* ideas so prevalent on the political right should have been associated with *Lebensraum* as well. *Völkisch* ideology helped to define one of the dimensions of the cultural entity—*Deutschtum*—that *Lebensraum* imperialism was supposed to protect and enhance. Racism, of course, served to justify the seizure of territories from "racially inferior" non-Germans and non-Europeans. Racist and *völkisch* arguments also constituted important elements of Social Darwinist presentations of *Lebensraum*. They were not, however, really central features of the *Lebensraum* aggregation. Furthermore, there were significant and readily apparent contradictions between the materialist, biological foundations of racism and the cultural idealism inherent in much *völkisch* ideology.[25] It took until the 1920s for a clearly effective integration of these tendencies to appear within the framework of *Lebensraum*. Racism and *völkisch* ideology—the latter in the guise of notions of cultural superiority—will be examined in Chapter Seven as part of a discussion of the legitimation of imperialist ideologies.

It should be noted that, although *Lebensraum* developed in the same political and ideological setting that engendered Wilhelmian political anti-semitism and although some of the leading advocates of *Lebensraum* were personally anti-Semitic, anti-Semitism had relatively little significance in the ideology's overall structure—at least until the time of the Nazis. Political employers of *Lebensraum* occasionally hinted, to be sure, at connections between Jewish business interests and government policies of colonial development for the benefit of industry, but, on the whole, the organizations most closely identified with *Lebensraum,* groups such as the Pan-German League and the right wing of the Colonial Society, avoided overt anti-Semitic statements. The Pan-Germans turned toward anit-Semitism only after Heinrich Class became the League's leader in 1908, and even then the new ideological direction had little effect on the League's version of imperialism.[26]

There was not, in fact, much reason for overt anti-Semitism in *Lebensraum* ideology during the Wilhelmian period. Anti-Semitism was useful for political organizations that wished to attack the evils of capitalism and economic modernity without alienating potential capitalist support. They could blame, not modernization and capitalism per se for what was wrong with society, but the Jewish perversion of those phenomena. Anti-Semitism could also be used to muster middle- and working-class support for organizations whose other aims had little relevance to the majority of voters.[27] But the *Lebensraum* aggregation featured alternative means of accomplishing the same ends. *Lebensraum* effected the trick of disparaging aspects of modernity without threatening modernity's beneficiaries by displacing the images of traditional society to colonial settings. It used the radical aura of its populist agrarian element to attempt to rally broad nonelite support. An emphasis on anti-Semitism was largely superfluous, and it involved the danger of multiplying the contradictions already present in *Lebensraum*.

Lebensraum, like practically all other European imperialist ideologies, heavily featured nationalism—that is, the identification of national survival as the prime criterion of policy and thus the major source of legitimacy of the proposals that the employers of the ideology advanced. So prevalent was the nationalist element in all forms of imperialism that nationalism itself can hardly be regarded as *individually* characteristic of any of them—certainly not as a means of distinguishing *Lebensraum* from *Weltpolitik*. In practice, the essence of nationality that imperialism was supposed to protect and enhance was defined in terms of the other elements of an imperialist ideological aggregation. Thus the national interest protected by *Weltpolitik* was largely an industrial one: markets and sources of raw materials, thus jobs and profits. *Lebensraum*'s nationalism, on the other hand, tended much more to be defined in terms of *Deutschtum*.[28] As we shall see, overt nationalism did play a potentially important role in justifying the integration of ideas conventionally regarded as inconsistent. The overriding requirements of the German nation when faced by foreign enemies could be cited as reasons, for example, for protecting the interests of German industrial producers abroad, even though these same producers were presumably the people most responsible for the damage done by industrialization in Germany. *Lebensraum* had, if it was to be effective in politics, to be accommodated to real industrial interests, and nationalism provided a convenient means of doing so.

Included within *Lebensraum* as it emerged from the 1890s were a number of other elements that closely resembled populist or romantic agrarianism in origin, structure, and political function. As was the case with agrarianism, these elements were often the post-1890 manifestations of more limited ideologies that had already left their traces in migrationist colonialism. For example, *Lebensraum* easily encompassed the antimodernist ideas included in the programs of the national master artisans' organizations of the 1880s.[29] Master artisans, journeymen, and apprentices were held up as proper subjects for social protection for much the same reasons that the agrarians gave for protecting the peasant: the possession of traditional virtues that defined the culture of Germany, and political utility. At least as much as agrarianism, the artisanal ideology derived a significant part of its origins from a genuine expression of social conservatism on the part of the group that provided its central images; like agrarianism, the ideology could be employed by external political organizations both to garner the support of the master artisans and to provide striking images useful in building a general conservative consensus. *Lebensraum* held out the prospect of protecting the traditional artisanal segments of society by creating opportunities for them in colonial settings—opportunities that were becoming increasingly scarce in Germany itself. The same thing could be said for small entrepreneurs, for academically qualified but unemployed members of the intelligentsia, and for impecunious sons of the nobility. All could be accommodated and could prosper in the circumstances of a settlement colony, defended from the invidious effects of industrialization.[30]

As is obvious from this brief summary, *Lebensraum* had a strong and overt social imperialist aspect, but it was a different one from that of *Weltpolitik*. Although *Weltpolitik* claimed the capacity of averting social conflict and solving social problems by bolstering the industrial economy, *Lebensraum* identified itself with the defense of traditional German society against the assault of industrialization. To be sure, *Lebensraum*'s solution to the industrialization problem and its attendant "social question" was on the whole a moderate one when compared with many others proposed on the right: social and cultural protection through geographic displacement.[31] As we shall see in Chapter Seven, a few of the same ideas of social reform could be accommodated within both *Lebensraum* and *Weltpolitik*. But the images and idea-sets that made up the two ideologies were in most respects quite different, and so also were the ways in which they could be used as instruments of social and political integration. They do not give the impression of being different aspects of the same "plot" to deflect the energies of a discontented working class. They appear instead as different approaches to the problem of political consensus building.

The fact that *Lebensraum,* although it disparaged industrialization and modernity generally, nevertheless accepted the importance of an industrial and commercial sector in the economy was one of the reasons that it was more commonly adopted by organizations seeking to link the "old" and "new" elites than by socially and economically reactionary groups.

Lebensraum imperialism was, for example, fundamental to the program of the Pan-German League but not that of the *Bund der Landwirte*. *Lebensraum* must certainly not be understood as a direct reflection of the outlook of the agrarian elite but rather as a collection of ideas and images, some of them derived from the attitudes of the self-consciously "declining" classes and some of them not, put together for the purpose of overcoming political fragmentation.[32]

At the same time, the ability of *Lebensraum* to appeal to the interests and outlooks of people with favorable attitudes toward modernity was distinctly limited by at least two factors. First, *Lebensraum* was rather loosely constructed as an ideology and full of obvious inconsistencies that could easily be spotted by people not inclined to accept its assumptions uncritically. For example, the phenomenon around which migrationist thinking was structured—massive emigration—came to an end in the 1890s, causing the notion of an "overcrowded" Germany to lose its tenuous hold on economic and social reality. Proposals for solving Germany's problems by settlement colonization were therefore, in this as in many other ways, manifestly out of touch with the real world. Many critics among the *Weltpolitiker,* the left liberals, and the socialists pointed this out.[33] Until the majority of the German public could be brought to accept the assumptions on which *Lebensraum* was based—for example, through the socialization of the post-1890 generations of children through "patriotic" instruction in school—*Lebensraum* remained vulnerable.

The second major limit to the political effectiveness of *Lebensraum* was the convention widely accepted in German politics at the turn of the century (a convention reinforced by the dispute over the Caprivi tariff policy) that an agrarian political orientation must necessarily oppose an industrial one. *Lebensraum* was naturally aligned in the public mind with agrarianism and with rather more reactionary conservatism than it actually embodied. No matter how hard, for example, the propagandists of the Pan-German League tried they could not before 1908 or so convince substantial numbers of business leaders that a foreign and imperial policy framed along the lines of *Lebensraum* was consistent with the active (indeed, hyperactive) promotion of German economic interests abroad that the Pan-Germans also advocated.[34] The Pan-Germans constantly attempted to connect *Lebensraum,* if not to *Weltpolitik* as defined here, at least to the images of economic imperialism. But until just before the First World War, they were unable to do so in a manner convincing to those who accepted the basic assumptions incorporated into *Weltpolitik.*

Lebensraum and the Pan-German League

The nature, political uses, and evolution of *Lebensraum* can best be illustrated by reference to its functions in the programs of specific organizations. Several possibilities present themselves as examples, including the Colonial Society, the two conservative parties, and the National Liberal party—all of which at one time or another adopted imperialist stances based on *Lebensraum*. In none of these cases, however, was *Lebensraum* consistently central to the organization's platform. As we shall see in Chapter Six, the Free Conservatives adopted a *Lebensraum* posture on colonial issues almost entirely for immediate, opportunistic political reasons. The radical conservative pro-*Lebensraum* group in the National Liberal party, at whose instance the National Liberals sometimes took *Lebensraum* positions, was matched by equally solid blocs of *Weltpolitiker*.[35]

The Colonial Society (DKG) is a promising candidate, for its national and local meetings and its publications were among the most important places where *Lebensraum* ideas were developed and enunciated. The colonial elements of *Lebensraum* had been part of the platform of the DKG since its founding in 1887, and it was always at least formally sympathetic to most of the rest of the *Lebensraum* credo. The DKG had, however, a place for almost any ideological viewpoint that could be used to attract support for its main objective: the expansion of Germany's colonial undertaking. Throughout its existence, with the possible exception of the period of the First World War, most of the DKG's leaders were in fact *Weltpolitiker*. However, their conception of the DKG as a point around which all nationalist forces could gather to defend German colonialism caused them to espouse all appropriate viewpoints. Although some very active local chapters (e.g., Berlin-Charlottenburg) were self-consciously oriented toward *Weltpolitik,* others (especially Meiningen and the main Berlin branch) were militantly committed to settlement colonialism and to *Lebensraum*. As a result, the DKG was never able to follow a consistent political or ideological line, except under very unusual circumstances (such as the "Hottentot election" campaign of January 1907). Certainly, the DKG never before 1914 succeeded in intellectually integrating the two major thrusts of imperialist ideology, and as an organization it seldom tried.[36]

Many of the leading adherents of *Lebensraum* in the DKG and in the parties were also active members of the Pan-German League, the organization that came closest to treating *Lebensraum* as its central program element and that most consistently indicated in its platform and public statements the direction in which *Lebensraum* was developing. For these reasons, we shall concentrate on the Pan-Germans here.

The Pan-German League was created in 1894 as the successor to a number of smaller nationalist organizations that had been founded and had pursued short chaotic careers between 1886 and 1893. Of these, the most important was the General German League, an organization established in 1891 ostensibly to protest the 1890 treaty with Britain over Zanzibar and Heligoland.[37] It is somewhat difficult to characterize the long-term intentions of the founders of the Pan-German movement because they varied considerably. The founders all appear to have agreed, however, on the necessity of using nationalism and especially imperialism as the core of an attempt to create national political consensus. It was this central *political* motivation that lay at the heart of the Pan-German phenomenon down to the First World War, much more so than the varied and often inconsistent positions on specific issues taken by the league and its ideologically diverse local chapters. As recent students of the Wilhelmian nationalist societies have indicated, the Pan-Germans and similar groups did have a distinctively violent, hysterical political style. But the style was a direct consequence of the main political purpose that the nationalist organizations were intended to serve: the assembly of political support and the creation of consensus. Imperialism, especially *Lebensraum* imperialism, came to play a vital role in the performance of this function.[38]

Some of the pre-1894 Pan-Germans (e.g., the young conservative ideologue Alfred Hugenberg and the Free Conservative politician Otto Arendt) believed that what Germany needed was an extraparty political organization that could propagate an ideological line around which could rally large segments of the country's social elite and a majority of the "responsible" members of the public—in other words, the middle classes in general, the peasantry and perhaps the more patriotic and "intelligent" segments of the working class. This extrapartisan aim was similar to that which had underlain the formation of the *Kolonialverein* in 1882 and the DKG in 1887 as well as the intentions of the founders of most of the other nationalist organizations such as the Navy League, the *Ostmarkverein*, and the Imperial League Against Social Democracy. All of these groups wished to stand apart from the parties, to "educate" the public, and to convince most Germans that the interests of the nation took precedence over class, religion, locality, and occupational-interest group.[39] The main difference was that although other organizations had a specific focus—the colonial empire, the navy, eastern settlement, and so on—the Pan-Germans wanted to create a general national consensus by linking a broad cross-section of interests and ideologies together into a single program. The consensus thus created would make it easier for the regular parties of the center and right, especially the Free Conservatives and the National Liberals (to one or the other of which most of the founders of the Pan-German movement belonged), to make common cause with each other and to establish a center of power in the Reichstag. Such a coalition could set a firm political course for the government, deal effectively with pressing social and economic problems and the threat of socialism, fill the void in foreign policy direction left by Bismarck's fall, and, in general, end the supposed "chaos" of German politics. These aims make it clear why people with quite varied political opinions on other matters were attracted to the Pan-Germans, at least at the start. The movement's main immediate and conscious objective was to overcome the effects of political fragmentation, something about which people as different as Max Weber and Ernst Hasse could agree. Their disagreements about what was to be done thereafter could be played down for the time being in the hope that ways could be found ultimately of accommodating all segments of Pan-German opinion.[40]

Others clearly wanted to do more. Carl Peters, who was involved in the formation of at least two of the early Pan-German organizations and was widely touted as a potential leader of any such movement, expected that a successful Pan-German organization would rapidly evolve into a real imperialist political party. This party, possibly incorporating the Free Conservatives, would crush all the other parties at the next Reichstag elections and assume the direction of the nation's destiny. Peters took part together with the journalist Wilhelm Schroeder-Poggelow and the Free Conservative leader Wilhelm von Kardorff in an abortive attempt to create such a party in 1892–93.[41] Even in the case of the National Party, however, the basic idea was similar to that of the other Pan-Germans: the construction of a national consensus, primarily through the use of imperialism, that would make the political system work. Like the other Pan-Germans, the "National Party" group were by no means agreed about what the new party was supposed to do after acquiring power.

The central ideological role of imperialism is evident in the programs of the early Pan-German organizations. These programs, however, were strikingly lacking in ideological coherence, as though their authors were surveying the spectrum of existing ideologies to find a combination of ideas that would express their own attitudes, afford consensus among themselves and the social groups to which they belonged, and aggregate wide public support. From the standpoint of this study, what is most interesting is the relatively minor role played by the constituent ideas of *Lebensraum* in the pre-1894 Pan-German programs as compared to the program of the later Pan-German League.

There was certainly no immediately obvious reason for the Pan-Germans to feature *Lebensraum* heavily. One of the original Pan-Germans, Schroeder-Poggelow, was, in fact, one of the early journalistic influences on the formation of *Weltpolitik,* and others, including Kardorff and Peters, privately accepted most of the tenets of *Weltpolitik.* Other Pan-Germans such as Ernst Hasse and the geographer Friedrich Ratzel had earlier committed themselves to migrationist colonialism, and Alfred Hugenberg had recently written his dissertation on inner colonization in northwestern Germany and in 1894 became a Prussian civil servant attached to the Settlement Commission in Posen. But hardly any of the latter group entirely rejected the economic imperialist thinking that went into *Weltpolitik.* Although the leadership segment of the Pan-Germans came from diverse social backgrounds, these were not notably different from the backgrounds of the early *Weltpolitiker.* Few tenured government officials, it is true, identified themselves with the Pan-Germans, but Alfred Hugenberg and many of his associates in the eastern settlement movement were civil servants for varying periods of time. One of the early backers of the Pan-Germans was the *Deutsche Bank* director Georg von Siemens, whose background and general social outlook were not terribly different from those of Arthur Gwinner, his pro-*Weltpolitik* successor as chief of the *Deutsche Bank*'s foreign investment section.[42] It was not at all clear before about 1894 that the Pan-Germans would not focus primarily on an ideology of economic imperialism; even afterwards, they constantly attempted to attach broadly stated economic imperialist ideas to their program, with mixed results.

If we look at the draft program of the General German League drawn up by Hugenberg and others in 1891, we can see the flexible, tentative, and somewhat incoherent character of early Pan-German thinking and the absence of a clearly delineated *Lebensraum* ideology.[43] The featured theme is the need for action and unity to overcome various dangers to *Deutschtum*. The first of the dangers is the inflow of Slavic people into the eastern provinces of Prussia that threatens the region with a loss of German speech and culture and endangers all of Germany by eliminating the economic basis for a vigorous peasantry. Second, there is the narrowing of Germany's "economic territory," a vague term that appears to refer to the area in which German capital can be invested without fear of foreign competition. There are also the dangers emanating from the ending of Germany's hopes for a great colonial empire in Africa because of the 1890 treaty and the government's unwillingness to push for imperial expansion. There is the international threat of the Russians and the "Anglo-Saxons." Finally, there are the ominous (but not very exactly described) constrictions that Germany has recently experienced on her necessary "cultural development." The program calls for a truly "national" policy conducted by a government that is decisively committed to the real interests of the German people and that would confront each of these dangers directly.

The 1891 program is, at best, a list of complaints without clear indications of what is to be done about them or even what the connections between them are. The attempt to deal with agrarian issues by confusing them with the nationalities question in the Prussian east (an important later Pan-German ploy) is much in evidence, but inner colonization is not much emphasized, despite the fact that Hugenberg was considered an expert on the subject. The Pan-Germans would later lay more stress on inner colonization, usually attached to the idea of the Polish "threat," and then extend it to encompass external annexation. "Economic territory" is loosely related to traditions of economic imperialism but is much too unspecific to be connected effectively to any particular imperialist view. The colonial statement is even vaguer, probably indicating nothing more than Hugenberg's belief that the government's acquiescence in the 1890 treaty offered an opportunity for embarrassing Caprivi and his entourage.[44] The closest that the program comes to an explicit link to migrationist colonialism and to the later ideology of *Lebensraum* is in the part about cultural development. Satisfactory cultural development for Germany's rapidly growing population required, by implication, an increasingly large area of the world's surface to provide the material basis of German culture: the suggestion of a connection, but little more.

By 1894, with the formation of the Pan-German League and with, at least, the temporary abandonment of the idea of constructing a party out of the Pan-German movement, a much more coherent program had been agreed on—one which emphasized the *Lebensraum* ideological aggregation. Some of the original backers of the Pan-German idea from the ranks of business, politics, and academia who had the greatest intellectual affinity to modernism and industry had distanced themselves from the movement, mainly because of doubts about the ability of a Pan-German organization to overcome ideological splits within itself.[45] This left the field to others more thoroughly committed to radical conservative ideas and to the notion of creating political consensus through an imperialist ideology built around migrationist colonialism and its agrarian connections.

The leaders of the Pan-German League after 1894 tended to be people outside the leadership strata of the existing parties and business-interest groups. The most important leader was Ernst Hasse, a professor at the University of Leipzig and a social scientist with a sound, if not first-rate, reputation in the field of economic statistics. Hasse was a fairly typical example of the politically involved German academic.[46] He had been very active in the early colonial movement, consistently arguing for a migrationist direction as opposed to one based on economic colonialism. He had also participated in the affairs of the early Pan-German organizations, although not originally as a member of the inner circle of leaders. His election to the presidency first of the General German League in 1893 and then of the Pan-German League in 1894 resulted, in part, from the Pan-Germans' recognized need for regular leadership by someone of standing outside politics who was capable of devoting a great deal of time to the role and, in part, from the general withdrawal of direct interest in the movement by many of its founders among the business and political elite. Hasse proved to be an effective organizer, establishing a structure of local chapters on the model of the Colonial Society and starting a regular publication, the *Alldeutsche Blätter,* under the editorship of his like-thinking vice president, Ernst Lehr. Both Hasse and Lehr added to their political stature by getting themselves elected to the Reichstag in 1898 as National Liberals.

The official program of the Pan-German League adopted in 1894 and modified thereafter manifested both the new direction in the movement's leadership and the political circumstances facing an organization with the league's aims. The most significant way in which these factors were reflected was in the prominence given to *Lebensraum,* which emerges as a superficially coherent aggregate ideology in the Pan-German platform.

Although the 1894 program touched on a wide range of national issues, it concentrated on two main topics: what to do about Polish immigration into eastern Prussia and how to promote German settlement colonies abroad. These remained central features of Pan-German ideology continuously down to the First World War—a framework to which other items were, with greater or lesser degrees of coherence, attached as political circumstances dictated.[47] The two main thrusts were explicitly related to one another as aspects of the protection of *Deutschtum,* of German culture and nationality. Both were based on preexisting ideological developments embodied in the programs of particular pressure organizations. Both, moreover, encompassed the crucial connection between migrationist colonialism and romantic agrarianism. The migrationist aspect came naturally to people like Hasse with previous experience in the colonial movement. From 1894 onward, the Pan-Germans' annual program always contained several heavily featured items referring to the need to expand German settlement in the overseas colonies, to acquire additional colonies, to afford support to settlers, and to protect them against policies solely benefitting big business. This direct continuity with the tradition of migrationist colonialism was maintained into the twentieth century, despite the actual end of large-scale emigration. Whenever possible, the Pan-Germans tried to ignore this unfortunate intrusion of reality into their world of ideology, arguing that at most a lull had occurred in the cycles of emigration.[48]

But the theory of migrationist colonialism had never depended on mere numbers. Like their migrationist predecessors, the Pan-Germans emphasized the dangers to German culture, personality, social structure, economic well-being, and military defense inherent in industrialization and argued that overseas colonies were needed to maintain for German society the advantages of possessing a small-unit agricultural component. In dilations on the colonial theme outside the rubric of the league's platform, however, they were much more explicit than the pre-1880 migrationists about the nature of the society and culture that the colonies were supposed to advance. In this, they showed the strong influence of agrarianism and other populist ideologies on the original migrationist pattern and the political motives that gave these ideologies such influence.

According to the Pan-Germans and the *Lebensraum* wing of the Colonial Society, the individual settler-farmer, with his family, his community, and his non-European employees, was the ideal foundation for a "new" national German character. The traditional German small farmer, although admirable in himself and well worth protecting, was hemmed in, both physically and spiritually, in Germany. Overpopulation on the land, the turning of agriculture into a big business, the flood of competing Polish labor, the restrictions of a bureaucratic political system, and, most especially, the lack of career alternatives to farming besides those provided by spiritually deadening industrial employment—all were factors that made it necessary for Germany to have a new outlet for the energy with which traditional German culture endowed its bearers. Colonial settlers would not just re-create traditional peasant village life but, having internalized that life in the course of their upbringing, they were supposed to develop it further under less restrictive conditions in the colonies. Colonial settlers would transform the small farmer's spirit of independence into an ethos of self-reliance (modeled on the myth of the American frontier) and command (through the supervision of "lesser" races). The settlers would form communities bound together by "true" feelings of racial and cultural affinity, without the bureaucratic oppression present in Germany. Under colonial conditions, the settlers would prosper and become significant trading partners for Germany—thus increasing her economic security in a dangerous world.[49]

The *political* function of migrationist colonialism in Pan-German *Lebensraum* was mainly that it permitted its employers to make the criticisms of modernity and industrial society associated with populist agrarianism—criticisms with which people such as Hasse and Lehr sincerely agreed—without significantly threatening any elite group whose support the Pan-Germans wanted. The migrationist element in *Lebensraum* provided concrete proposals for action (somewhat lacking in earlier Pan-German programs), but it displaced the proposed actions to colonies beyond the seas.

Although Hasse firmly believed in the efficacy of settlement colonies as a means of preserving and extending the valuable aspects of traditional German culture, he understood that colonial settlement was not by itself a sufficient real solution to the problems of industrialization. But it *was* one of a number of things that could be done; orienting a political campaign around it might help to create the political circumstances in which other, more complex solutions could be accomplished.[50] An emphasis on migrationist colonialism might also help the Pan-Germans avoid the most serious of all the political problems facing them: the tendency to be caught on one side or the other of an issue that split their potential supporters. The dispute over the Caprivi tariff policy, for example, was the last thing that the Pan-Germans needed, even though it provided a link to the agricultural interest when the league attacked the government on other grounds. As long as the interests of heavy industry were aligned with Caprivi's policy (which they were up until Johannes Miquel's efforts to create a *Sammlung* of industry and agriculture in the late 1890s), statements of the league in favor of agricultural tariffs would alienate big-business support. They would also alienate antitariff and anti-Junker Pan-Germans such as Max Weber. On the other hand, support for Caprivi's policies would turn the wrath of the *Bund der Landwirte* against the league and devalue the Pan-Germans' claims to conservatism. It is no wonder that Hasse avoided taking a position on the tariffs for as long as possible, emphasizing instead agrarian ideas in an imperialist setting. Even so, he was eventually forced by the polarization of politics to express a moderate acceptance of the idea of high agricultural duties, at which point Max Weber and several others resigned from the league.[51] Migrationist colonialism, in short, was an important part of the Pan-Germans' program not only because its leaders believed in it, but even more because they needed it as an instrument for building consensus and combatting fragmentation.

The Pan-Germans used the migrationist element of their program in a number of interesting ways. By displacing agrarianism to colonies, they could paint an optimistic picture of the future of the German farmer, not the defensive, desperate one presented by many conservatives. A positive, optimistic image probably made a better impression on urban middle-class people, who were more important targets of Pan-German propaganda than the rural peasants to whom the normal defensive agrarian line might be expected to appeal. Moreover, the image of the colonial frontiersman was a flexible one. Hearkening again to the myth of the American frontier, Pan-Germans and other settlement enthusiasts pointed out that not just peasants, but also middle-class people from many walks of life could become colonial farmers as they responded to the urge to free themselves from the "unnatural" restrictions inherent in industrial society. Urban workers could also be "reclaimed" in a healthier and culturally superior colonial environment.[52] This approach presumably appealed to the imaginations of young middle and working-class men brought up on the novels of Karl May and James Fenimore Cooper. Of course, even had the real opportunities for settlement in Germany's colonies or in more informal German settlements in South America been better than they were, only a small proportion of these people would ever have actually become colonial settlers, but their ability to *imagine* the circumstances of an idealized colonial life was what was important from a political standpoint. Among other things, it created a favorable attitude toward other items that might be included with migrationist colonialism as part of the same ideological set.[53]

But migrationist colonialism was not enough by itself to serve as the sole focus of a national political movement. Substantial segments of Germany's social elite the Pan-Germans had to attract to achieve their self-proclaimed political aims, and even some of the members of the league, were simply not very interested in the colonies or in colonialism. The depth of general public interest in the subject was easy to exaggerate as well. The colonial enthusiasm of the 1880s had greatly impressed politicians at the time, but it had dissipated as a practical political force by the latter part of the decade. It took the Pan-Germans and the other nationalist organizations, strongly aided by the navy and by radical conservative schoolteachers, many years after 1890 to spread imperialist assumptions widely among the public at large.[54] Organized interest groups, especially conservative ones with an affinity to the league and its assumptions, wanted the Pan-Germans to pronounce themselves on matters other than colonies—which, of course, multiplied the risks of offending potential constituents.[55] This political dilemma helps to explain the other main element of the 1894 Pan-German program—the proposals for dealing with the Polish "threat" in East Elbia—and the strongly antigovernment bias these proposals, and indeed the whole thrust of Pan-German ideology, bore for the rest of the league's existence.

Hasse and most of the other leading members of the Pan-German League were genuinely concerned about the extent to which the population of the eastern provinces of Prussia was becoming ethnically Polish instead of German. The "polonization" of the German east had been an issue for some time and had been the subject of Prussian legislation in

1886. During the 1890s, it became the prime focus of attention for several nationalist political organizations, especially the *Ostmarkverein*. Although, of course, the replacement of German peasants with Polish agricultural workers in the east attracted the attention of *völkisch* ideologues, it was also a matter of concern to a great many others, including Max Weber who did his first important empirical research on the subject.[56]

The nationalities question in the east provided a rich field for Pan-German propagandizing and consensus building. *Deutschtum* was clearly threatened there in every sense: militarily by the evolution of a potentially "disloyal" minority into a majority in some districts; culturally, by the displacement of native German culture by an "inferior" Slavic one; and socially and economically, by the destruction of the independent peasantry, who were supposedly being driven out of the region by Polish immigrants. The last point, of course, afforded a direct connection to the migrationist and agrarian elements in *Lebensraum*. The threat to German peasant society was widely considered to be the crux of the entire problem, one on which other groups such as the *Ostmarkverein* also concentrated. But it also held political dangers. The inflow of Poles was mainly due to their employment as seasonal labor by German estate owners. What was driving out the German small farmers, as Weber discovered in the course of his study, were the facts that their farms were noncompetitive and that they could no longer eke out their incomes with part-time employment on the large estates. In other words, Junker agriculture and its attempts to stave off collapse by employing cheaper Polish labor was a cause of the difficulties of the East Elbian peasant.[57] A sincerely radical response to the problem would necessarily involve limitations on the economic activities of the larger landowners, ranging from a prohibition of Polish seasonal labor to the outright expropriation of big estates and their redistribution to peasant farmers. Such an approach, however, would obviously have split the agrarian movement in the midst of its war against the Caprivi tariff reduction, demonstrating graphically the lack of coincidence between the interests of great and small agriculture. If the Pan-Germans or any other group were to demonstrate their "radical" credentials in this way, they would earn the enmity of the agrarian elite without much compensating gain elsewhere.

Hasse and many of the Pan-German radicals were tempted. Especially during Hasse's period of leadership, the league encompassed quite a broad spectrum of political opinion, especially on eastern and social questions. Hasse included references both to immigration prohibitions and to expropriation in several authoritative league statements in the later 1890s, although in somewhat muted form. In the end, Hasse and the rest of the league's leadership had to bow to the political imperative of consensus creation—hence the league's overwhelming emphasis on the *cultural* aspect of the Polish threat.[58] The Pan-Germans called for vigorous government action to "Germanize" eastern Prussia: to insist on the use only of

German in schools and courts of law; to alter the culture of the Poles, especially the Polish children, already present in the area; to give preferential treatment to people of proven German culture; and so forth. This sort of cultural engineering boded continual annoyance to Germany's Polish citizens, but it had really little to offer in the way of a solution to the problems of peasant agriculture in the east. As Weber and others recognized, it represented a deliberate attempt to seem radical without really insisting on effective action to do anything that would split a potential nationalist consensus.[59]

The ploy obviously did not convince everyone, although because it directed attention toward a disliked minority, it could tap the sources of chauvinism found in any multiethnic and multidenominational society. To extend its effect and, presumably, also to deflect attention away from the equivocation that the Pan-Germans' compromise "radicalism" on eastern questions embodied, the league couched its pronouncements primarily in the form of a vigorous—indeed, a vicious—attack on the "softness" of the Prussian government in dealing with the problem. The Pan-Germans accused the government of not enforcing the spirit of early resettlement legislation, of not pushing Polish expropriation harder, of being, in fact, the "polonizer" of the Prussian east by permitting the spread of Polish language and culture there.[60]

This posture of opposition to the government was typical of the Pan-German movement throughout its existence. It was partly the result of a certain amount of genuine radicalism and resentment of the closed circles wielding authority in Germany on the part of some of the league's leaders, often compounded by disappointments they had experienced in their own careers. But the adversary role of the Pan-Germans vis-à-vis the government was primarily a consequence of their aim of aggregating support and building broad consensus. Positive statements of specific Pan-German intentions inevitably offended some important group or other, but blaming the government for not carrying out national goals identified by the Pan-Germans as obvious and patriotic, especially goals government leaders had accepted as valid in some form, directed attention away from the most obvious sources of fragmentation within the Pan-Germans' projected national consensus and toward inadequacies in an entity that was even more prone to exacerbate fissiparous tendencies: the government. By attacking the government on grounds related but not identical to those of the protectionist agrarians, the Pan-Germans could hope for agrarian cooperation. In fact, the very nature of the Pan-German League's political intentions and its position in politics prevented it ever from supporting a government for any length of time before 1917. Other nationalist organizations such as the Colonial Society and the Navy League were capable of extended cooperation with the government because of their more limited immediate objectives; the very breadth of the Pan-Germans' aims precluded cooperation.[61]

This tendency, often expressed in almost hysterical terms, extended to imperialism as well. The Pan-German League's normal position on government colonial and imperial policy was that the government was not being vigorous or forceful enough in the defense of Germany's interests abroad. By preference, these interests were described in terms of *Lebensraum:* Germany needed additional colonies because the ones she already had were, many of them, unsuitable for European settlement. The league also criticized the government's lack of support for the relatively few Germans who actually did settle as farmers in Africa.[62]

But the Pan-Germans did not limit themselves to critiques of policy based on *Lebensraum*. Increasingly after 1894, they emphasized Germany's need to obtain an economic place in the sun, although this aspect of their program never had the centrality, coherence, or continuity of the migrationist-agrarian ideological linkage. The Pan-Germans' version of economic imperialism followed the negative pattern of much of their other propaganda. It was often used as a vehicle for criticizing the government and the foreign policy establishment for their assumption that "we can only conduct world policy through an understanding with Britain."[63] Britain and the other major powers were represented as implacable foes of Germany, impelled by Darwinian imperatives to prevent Germany from taking its rightful place in the world. German traders, investors, and exporters operating outside Germany had therefore to be protected vigorously against the many threats that they faced. Cooperation, as the *Weltpolitiker* proposed, was simply a sellout of German interests.

The Pan-Germans' use of economic imperialism was partly an attempt to cash in on the imagery of *Weltpolitik* and its potential appeal to the leaders of German business while arguing that an effective economic imperialist policy could be conducted only by a truly national-minded government. The word *"Weltpolitik"* itself became a standard part of the league's vocabulary, but only in its broadest sense of crude economic imperialism and Germany's self-assertion in the world. It was, in fact, rather difficult to reconcile with the *Lebensraum* element in the Pan-Germans' program. When obvious conflicts arose, *Lebensraum* and settlement colonialism usually won out.[64] Pan-Germans tried to justify the inconsistency of complaining about industrial society at home while seeking its security and expansion through imperialism by emphasizing Germany's military need for a strong industrial base and by insisting that it was essential, for security and national purposes, that Germany not let herself be pushed around for any reason abroad. In fact, however, the Pan-Germans made few serious efforts to create a coherent, integrated imperialist ideology until almost the time of the First World War. Economic imperialist notions were tenuously attached to the *Lebensraum* core of Pan-German ideology, but not consistently or convincingly. The idea of a Germany economically threatened abroad was mainly used to insert the Pan-German League into the naval building issue at the end of the 1890s, to criticize the government, and to attempt to extend the appeal of the league. There is not much evidence that the Pan-Germans' version of economic imperialism made many inroads into the support base of the *Weltpolitik* ideology until after about 1908.[65]

To return to the eastern nationalities question, the Pan-German attack on the government for inadequate performance of its tasks and for its softness on the matter of Polish culture, although a relatively safe course to take so as not to offend anybody but the German Poles, the government, and the Center party, did not present the kind of positive image most conducive to political success. It also did not satisfy either the league's membership or its leaders. In the twenty years after 1894 therefore, the Pan-Germans adopted a series of additional aims with respect to eastern Prussia and eventually eastern Europe, aims built on the ideological foundations of migrationist colonialism and agrarianism but carried to new lengths. The most important of these were the ideas of inner colonization and eastern territorial annexation.

The notion of inner colonization was not new in the late 1890s when the Pan-Germans adopted it. It had been suggested half a century before by Friedrich List and had reappeared several times since then, especially in the 1880s when the Prussian government commenced its policy of making "unused" land and some of the property of large Polish landowners available for occupation by German farmers.[66] This was supposed to encourage German peasants to settle in the eastern region, thus counteracting the effects of Polish immigration. In fact, however, the government's policy had not had the desired effect. Peasants still left the east, and new small farmers did not take their places. The main beneficiaries were middle-class people wanting to set up as pseudo-Junker landlords and using this opportunity (and financing schemes established under government supervision) in order to do so.

As a result of rising public interest in the question and the growth of radical agrarianism after 1890, serveral pressure organizations were founded that took the resettlement of the eastern provinces as their theme. The *Ostmarkverein* (H-K-T Society) was probably the most important of these, but many other groups were founded before 1914 to push for inner colonization. There was even a small, not-very-effective organization on the left committed to the resettlement of urban workers on the land and to substantial land expropriation from German as well as Polish owners of large estates.[67] The major academic advocate of inner colonization was Max Sering, a professor of economics at the University of Berlin and, in 1912, one of the founders of the influential Society for the Advancement of Inner Colonization.[68] The essence of Sering's version of inner colonization, which was generally followed by the Pan-German League, was the explicit application of migrationist colonialism to the Prussian east.

Sering and the Pan-Germans argued that the government needed to extend drastically its policy of land expropriation in the east and to provide substantially larger loans on easier terms than before so that real or potential small farmers could actually afford to take part in the program. Most important, German resettlement should be more highly organized, featuring the establishment of planned settlments of German farmers as the centers of a small-unit agricultural system functioning on a colonial basis. The network of colonies that Sering envisioned would restore the profitability of small-unit agriculture in the east and stem the tide of Polish immigration. At the same time, these inner colonies would develop in their inhabitants the same qualities that overseas colonies were supposed to foster, thus creating a new social type with deep roots in the German cultural tradition. Some supporters of inner colonization argued that the advantages of such a program lay mainly in its cultural effects and in its contribution to national security, which would be worth the expense, even though the settlements might not actually pay for themselves.[69] Sering and apparently Hasse believed, however, that small-scale agriculture had greater economic potential than extensive grain agriculture in the region. If properly organized and directed, successful settlement colonies ought ultimately to transform eastern Prussia.

Advocating inner colonization afforded the Pan-Germans distinct political advantages. Inner colonization linked the widely shared emotions generated by the ethnic changes in the east and the whole array of antimodernist ideas represented by the image of the beleaguered small farmer to a program for action. Like settlement colonies overseas, the appeal of Sering's eastern colonies could be generalized by pointing out that they would provide opportunities for other threatened groups, including small entrepreneurs and artisans. Furthermore, the supposed "problems" of the eastern provinces were of much more immediate concern than those of overseas colonies to a greater number of people because they were closer to home. But this was also one of the sources of difficulty in using inner colonization in politics. It lacked the factor of geographic displacement that was one of the great advantages of migrationist colonialism. The absence of effective displacement, in turn, brought to light two further difficulties.

The first was that the whole idea did not correspond very well to the realities of the situation in East Elbia. There was little indication of an overwhelming interest among Germans elsewhere in "returning to the land" themselves and the small farmers already there wanted protection and enhanced government financial assistance, not colonies.[70] In arguing that small-unit agriculture could actually succeed, Sering was probably right in abstract terms, but success for the internal colonies depended on their ability to compete with the larger grain estates of the Prussian agricultural elite as well as the diversification of their production. Such colonies, even presuming the unlikely event that farmers, factory workers, and young *Kleinbürger* could be enticed to them in large numbers, could not succeed unless they were protected both from foreign competition and from their Junker neighbors and unless they could be established on substantial amounts of first-rate land—land that probably could only be acquired by expropriating existing Junker estates.

And this, of course, was the root of the second, the political difficulty involved in the advocacy of inner colonization or any other notion of real agrarian reform. If Sering or the Pan-Germans had seriously called for actual expropriation of estates and a radically new socioeconomic constitution for the German east, they would have guaranteed a break with the agrarian elite and called down on themselves the wrath of the *Bund der Landwirte* and the Conservatives. While this would have pleased some of the league's real radicals such as Theodor Reismann-Grone and nationalist liberals such as Max Weber and although it might have increased the Pan-Germans' appeal among small farmers and the urban middle classes, it would have driven a wedge into the fissure already present within the bloc of social groups that most Pan-Germans saw as the foundation of an integrated national polity. In the end, the leadership decided that the costs were too high. Hasse, as we have seen, by the end of the 1890s was downplaying anti-Junker ideas, concentrating on cultural policies and calling for German colonial settlement mainly on land expropriated from Poles. Even Sering, whose arguments in favor of the economic viability of small-unit agriculture should have led him to emphasize the expropriation of the Junker estates, followed much the same line as the Pan-Germans.[71] Inner colonization remained part of the program of the Pan-German League and a constituent element of *Lebensraum* down to the time of Hitler, but it could not become the central focus of the ideology for the largely political reasons just noted.

The political problems posed by the advocacy of inner colonization help to account for the appearance in Pan-German political writing of the idea of territorial annexation in Eastern Europe. This idea, of course, also possessed a long pedigree and had been widely discussed during the 1848 revolution, but in the Bismarckian era the notion had languished.[72] It revived in the 1890s at the time of the growth of the Franco-Russian entente, particularly among the imperialist writers and journalists associated with the Pan-Germans.

The Pan-German League did not officialy come out for the annexation of additional territory to the Reich until the First World War began, but the idea was increasingly an informal part of the ideological repertory of members of the league from about the mid-1890s and came to be widely associated with radical conservatism.[73]

The structure of the annexationist argument as presented by Friedrich von Bernhardi and other radical conservative publicists before the war is quite familiar in the light of its ideological antecedents. Because the economic modernization of Germany is, regretably, irreversible and necessary for military security, something has to be done to guarantee the continued integrity of the material and social bases of German culture. That culture, by definition, cannot be grounded in an industrial economy. Insufficient space is available in Germany to recreate "traditional" culture and society on a foundation of peasant agriculture. Although the overseas colonies are a useful supplement to the Reich's territory in this respect, they are presently too small and too hemmed in to have much effect on the totality of German society. Hence arises the need to acquire lands adjacent to Germany, especially in Poland and the Baltic area, which are "historically" Germany's frontier territories anyway. Colonies of German farmers should be established there.[74]

Annexationism was, in other words, essentially migrationist colonialism projected spatially into eastern Europe and temporally into the future. And it was clear what the precondition of that future was: a major war. Whether the war came because of Germany's need for additional farming land or for other reasons, one of the main *results* of a successful European war should be large-scale annexations in the east.[75]

Annexationism had many political advantages over inner colonization as an element of a general imperialist consensus ideology. Because it displaced the agricultural colonies to places beyond Germany's borders, it posed less of a threat than inner colonization to organized interests in Germany. If the proposals of the annexationists were carried out, Junker grain estates in Prussia could continue to operate as before—indeed, they could grow. Annexation of some of the areas of eastern Europe from which grain producers' most significant competition came would bring the economies of those areas under direct German political control—presumably providing the means of protecting Junker interests. Equally important, annexationist imperialism could be conceptually connected to a form of *economic* imperialism that might make the whole package acceptable to big-business interests. The key to this last connection was the *Lebensraum* version of *Mitteleuropa.*

Around 1900, a version of the idea of central and eastern European economic integration alternative to the one included in *Weltpolitik* was developed by a number of conservative social scientists, especially the economist Julius Wolf, and it was rapidly adopted by political organizations on the right that were attempting to transcend the political split between agrarians and industrialists.[76] The Pan-Germans took it up immediately. Bülow's government in the years just after 1900, seeking to create a *Sammlung* that included the Junker agrarians, also adopted some aspects of the alternative *Mitteleuropa* and employed them, publicly at least, as a basis for official policy on continental economic integration.[77]

The *Lebensraum* version of *Mitteleuropa* emphasized economic integration as a vehicle through which heavy industry's products could penetrate central and eastern European markets while, at the same time, German grain agriculture could be protected, not by tariffs as much as by production and distribution agreements negotiated through the economic union. It was not clear why either Austria-Hungary or Russia, the main targets of such proposals, should agree to such a union—unlike the case with the *Weltpolitik* version, which sacrificed Prussian grain agriculture to them. In fact, Austria-Hungary consistently rejected plans for economic integration structured in this way, plans that were put forward by a succession of German governments after 1900 in attempts to prove to the Junkers that the government had their interests at heart. Annexationism and the conservative version of *Mitteleropa,* however, reinforced one another as elements of the *Lebensraum* ideology because annexation provided a putative means of effectuating German control over eastern European agriculture and because the most obvious way to put annexation into practice—a major war, presumably against Russia with Austria-Hungary as a depen-

dent German ally—would also solve the problem of how to elicit acceptance for an economic union unfavorable to the interests of most of its
members except Germany. We shall return to this point in considering the
Lebensraum ideology during the First World War.

Annexationism and the *Lebensraum* version of central European economic integration became increasingly important elements of Pan-German
ideology in the years immediately preceding the First World War.[78] This
tendency was closely related, although not identical, to a growing emphasis
within the political right on Germany's need to strengthen her strategic
position on the European continent rather than overseas. Some of the
factors underlying the shift on strategy were only tangential to the content
and political functions of *Lebensraum*. Among these factors were the efforts of the army to reacquire its dominance over defense appropriations
after the navy's triumphs in 1898 and 1900, which led to army attempts to
mobilize conservative support behind a continental military strategy that
necessarily emphasized the army's role. Also, it has been suggested that
the growth of interest in a continental as opposed to an overseas policy on
the radical right from about 1905 onward resulted partly from the takeover
of effective control of the navalist movement by Tirpitz and by conservative big business, which drove radical nationalists like General August
Keim and Theodor Reismann-Grone into the camp of the continental
strategists.[79] In any event, *Lebensraum* ideas focused on Europe rather
than overseas colonies were certainly excellent means by which the advocates of continental primacy could justify their positions.

The new direction in strategic thinking created yet another split within
the Pan-German League, exemplified in 1905 in a debate at the Pan-German *Verbandstag* between Reismann-Grone (now a continentalist) and
ex-colonial governor Eduard von Liebert (who favored an overseas emphasis.) But this split clearly took place within a context of agreement on
the outlines of *Lebensraum*. As Reismann-Grone put it, a successful continental policy was a prerequisite for a successful overseas policy. Reismann-
Grone and Liebert, both of whom had continually insisted on the need to
include Germany's industrial interests in a larger pattern of imperialism,
gave priority nevertheless to the migrationist and agrarian aims of *Lebensraum,* whether conducted primarily in Europe or overseas.[80]

The tendency to emphasize annexationism and Central European integration within the context of *Lebensraum* became very strong after Heinrich Class assumed leadership of the Pan-German League in 1908 and
especially during the attempt by Class, Hugenberg, and others to integrate the political right in the face of the SPD's electoral success in 1912.
Class, in particular, hoped to make the Pan-Germans the vital link in an
aggregation of organized Junker agriculture, heavy industry, the conservative parties, and several newly formed general organizations claiming to
represent the *Mittelstand*. Under the circumstances of the period, the
ability of the elements of the Pan-Germans' *Lebensraum* ideology to tap
sources of popular resentment against modernity and against the political
and social elite and, at the same time, offer apparent advantages to a

broad spectrum of that elite gave Class considerably more political influence than Hasse and Lehr had ever exercised.

Class used the notion of eastern European economic integration as a way of encouraging reconciliation between the agrarian and industrial elites. Annexationism, even if not officially and formally acknowledged as an aim of the Pan-Germans, provided through the writings of propagandists associated with the league a series of forceful images useful in the search for popular support, especially within the *Mittelstand.* By projecting the colonial solution to the problems of economic modernization—as seen from a radical conservative standpoint—onto an eastern Europe conquered through a "necessary" and victorious war, it was possible to paint a picture of an ideal German society of the future, complete with small farmers, artisans, retailers, and so on, unthreatened by industry, capitalism, and the Junkers—all in a newly occupied living space to the east.[81] This was an image of immense potential appeal, especially in a Germany in which the likelihood of major war was being discussed more and more constantly. Thus annexationism grew in importance as part of the *Lebensraum* ideological set not merely (or even mainly) because of real interests that conservative elite groups had in massive territorial acquisition for economic purposes, but also because of the important political role that such acquisition played in establishing a popular image for German conservatism.

There were many other ideas and concepts that came to be attached to the aggregate ideology of *Lebensraum* in the years between 1890 and 1914 within both the program of the Pan-German League and those of other organizations sharing similar goals. The idea of linking *ausland* Germans culturally and politically to the Reich, for example, was something that the colonial movement had advocated since its foundation and that the Pan-Germans largely borrowed from the Colonial Society. This and most of the other elements of *Lebensraum,* however, performed political functions similar to those already discussed.[82]

By the time the First World War began, *Lebensraum* had been a fully articulated imperialist ideology for two decades. There had been changes in the distribution of some of its emphases in the propaganda of organizations such as the Pan-German League (e.g., from its overseas to its continental aspects), but, in most respects, it took the same general form that it had in the 1890s. It had taken that form largely in response to the requirements of German politics as perceived by its formulators, and it had survived mainly because of its apparent utility in the politics of conservative consensus building. Moreover by 1914, it had clearly acquired a firm place in German political culture and in the process of political socialization. This occurred despite the fact that *Lebensraum* was manifestly full of inaccuracies and inconsistencies when applied to any other aspect of social reality than the narrowly political one within which it had evolved.

CHAPTER SIX

Imperialist Ideologies in Conflict, 1890–1914

Thus far, we have examined *Weltpolitik* and *Lebensraum* separately, from the standpoint of their development into functioning composite ideologies of imperialism in the Wilhelmian era. We have noted points at which the two ideologies contradicted each other and points at which they overlapped, and we have also noted that they developed in the 1890s in connection with distinctly different arrays of political ideas and organizations. For the most part, however, we have considered them apart from one another.

In reality, the two ideologies and their proponents constantly interacted and frequently clashed over a wide variety of issues. Because this is not a comprehensive study of German imperialism, we shall not examine all of the important controversies of imperialist politics. A few examples will suffice to make the point that, contrary to the hopes of many of those who turned to imperialism in the late nineteenth century as a tool of political integration, it turned out to be a means to only a limited degree of consensus. The imperialist ideologies, both separately and together, could attract broad public attention and could strongly influence discussions of policy. *Weltpolitik,* in particular, created a framework of assumptions that greatly affected government decision making. But neither ideology by itself formed the basis of a political appeal that could continuously tie together the support of more than a minority of the elements of the German political system.

The reasons for the political failure of Wilhelmian imperialist ideology were complex. One of the most important, however, was its inherently bifurcated nature and the fact that its two main varieties were employed individually by groups that often contended over issues that had little to do with imperialism. The marshalling of one variety of imperialism behind a political initiative brought with it, as often as not, opposition from the adherents of the other. Still, the political difficulties of using imperialism for consensus building were not always immediately apparent. By 1914, the imperialist ideologies had succeeded in influencing the thinking of a generation of Germans, and the temptation to use these ideologies in politics was often almost overwhelming. Many of the politicians who made imperialist statements but were not specialists in imperialist issues were probably not entirely aware of the distinction between the ideologies or of the dangers involved in becoming identified with one of them. For short-term political purposes, the partial consensus available through adherence to one or the other of the ideological lines was often enough to achieve a group's aims. Admiral Tirpitz, as we have seen, played astutely on elements of *Weltpolitik* to assemble support for his basic goal of fleet building. But not even Tirpitz could, in the long run, maintain a working consensus through an imperialist appeal.

Dozens of public political issues in the Wilhelmian period could be discussed in terms of conflict between the major imperalist ideologies—questions arising over naval expansion, colonial acquisition, foreign policy, central European economic integration, and so forth. We have touched on some of these in previous chapters. Here we shall consider two examples of issues that brought out different aspects of imperialist politics and major incompatibilities between the imperialist ideologies: conflicts over colonial development policy and the issues concerning territorial expansion in Africa implicit in the Moroccan crisis of 1911. The first was a complex and continuous (if somewhat secondary) source of political conflict; the second illustrates the long-term ideological background to the kind of fierce, crisis-laden, but short-lived, controversy that was highly characteristic of German imperialist politics. Because our main concern is with imperialist ideology per se, we shall pay little attention to overtly anti-imperialist positions on these issues.

Colonial Development Policy

Although questions of colonial development seldom became really major political issues in Wilhelmian Germany, they did tend to last for long periods and to engender bitter controversy. Considerably more time and effort were expended on the politics of development by the government, the Reichstag, the parties, and the extraparty organizations than one might expect, considering the paltry sizes of the appropriations involved and the minor economic importance of the German colonies. The reasons for the attention to colonial development lay partly in the nature of Reichstag politics and partly in the roles of the colonies in the structures of the major imperialist ideologies.

One of the few political weapons available to the Reichstag and its parties vis-à-vis the Reich government was a minute review of the national budget. In the budget-review process, the parties could publicize their positions on issues and could, if some of them cooperated with each other, obtain concessions from the government on matters often quite unrelated to the subjects of their criticism. The colonial budget was particularly useful as an object of attack and scrutiny. Because the colonies were not financially self-supporting, their administrations were heavily dependent on Reichstag-approved subsidies. In the 1890s, the government was forced by the Reichstag to accept particularly detailed examination of the colonial budget as a quid pro quo for the subsidies.[1] At the same time, the colonial appropriation was sufficiently unimportant (unlike, say, the army appropriation) so that a government was not likely to make a major issue out of a conflict with the Reichstag majority over it. An exception to this occurred in December 1906 when Bülow dissolved the Reichstag over the house's failure to pass a supplementary colonial appropriation. Parties that took an anti-imperialist line, expecially the Social Democrats, particularly liked to focus on the colonial budget. Budget items could be easily linked to cases of official misbehavior and colonial atrocities that attracted widespread public attention. The other parties also used the colonial budget hearings to make their points, and organizations such as the Colonial Society and the Pan-German League devoted considerable attention to them.[2]

The most important new items of colonial expenditure were usually projects that the government had proposed for the economic development of the colonies. Because colonial development was conceived and, more important, had to be defended in terms of the colonies' role in larger schemes of imperialism, disputes over proposed development almost automatically brought the imperialist ideologies into play, not infrequently against each other. Such disputes demonstrate not only the differences between the ideologies, but also the nature of the ideologies' connections with the networks of interest groups and organizations that employed them.

When a separate and largely autonomous department was established within the Foreign Office in 1890 to run German's newly acquired colonial empire in Africa and the Pacific, it was placed under the leadership of Paul Kayser. We have already met Kayser as one of the early official formulators of *Weltpolitik*. He had come to office on the coattails of the bureaucratic group that had pushed for Bismarck's dismissal in 1890—the same group among whom the official version of *Weltpolitik* first gained currency.[3] To Kayser fell the task of organizing the administrative structure of the colonial empire on a permanent basis. He also had to undertake the more difficult job of formulating an economic-development policy for the colonies with the double aim of making them financially solvent and removing the stigma of failure that had attached itself to the first half-decade of German colonial rule.

In putting together his policy, Kayser responded to practical political considerations and to his own personal views of what German colonialism meant. Both led him to frame and defend the policy explicitly within the context of *Weltpolitik*. In practical terms, Kayser needed to elicit economic support for colonial development (and, indirectly, political support for the new Colonial Department) from as wide a range of interested groups as he could. German banks and financial houses had shown themselves to be, on the whole, unwilling to risk more than token amounts of money on the colonies. Most of the Reichstag parties—imperialist rhetoric aside—hesitated to help much in the way of direct appropriations. The other Reich departments considered the Colonial Department a sideshow, and the Caprivi government gave the colonies a low budgetary priority.[4] Among other things, Kayser had recourse to *Weltpolitik* in its consensus-building aspect to correct this state of affairs. It is also more than likely that Kayser believed sincerely in most of the central tenets of *Weltpolitik*—particularly the idea that social peace and economic progress for all classes depended on the orderly, successful, and rapid development of industry and that the main role of the colonies lay in facilitating industrial development.[5]

Kayser represented his development policy as an extension of these ideas. The resources of the colonies as producers of industrial raw materials and as markets were to be developed as quickly as possible. To that end, the Colonial Department offered concessions of land and privileges to private business consortia willing to invest extensively in particular colonies.[6] The companies did not even have to be German, although they did, in theory, have to accept a certain amount of direction from the German government. The most important of the companies receiving concessions under this policy in the 1890s were, in fact, foreign backed. The two main concession companies in Southwest Africa were both satellites of the Rhodes interest, and the most successful of the companies that specialized in Cameroon rubber, the *Gesellschaft Süd-Kamerun,* was funded by Belgian and German investors.[7]

Kayser's concession companies were not supposed to perform the same functions as the chartered companies that Bismarck had established in several of the colonies in the 1880s. Bismarck had wanted the chartered companies to relieve the government of almost all responsibility for development and administration.[8] His plan had failed. Kayser, on the other hand, intended that government and big business, working together, would establish comprehensive programs for colonial development. The government would guarantee monopoly rights to the concessionaires and provide ancillary political services. (In many cases, these included disguised forms of forced labor.) The concession companies would provide that most necessary of all prerequisites for colonial development: capital. They would also organize the specific projects that would make the colonies profitable.[9]

In the area of planning, Kayser created the *Kolonialrat* (Colonial Council), an appointed board advisory to the colonial director that included representatives of the bureaucracy, colonialist organizations, and businesses with colonial interests.[10] The *Kolonialrat* was intended to be both a means of coordinating overall development policy and a way to encourage further colonial investment by German business. It would perform the latter function by assuring potential investors that their concerns would be felt in the policymaking process. The government would still, where necessary (as in East Africa), arrange major construction projects such as railways, but, even in those cases, the actual construction would be undertaken by German companies founded for the purpose. Funding would come through bonds with interest guaranteed by the Reich government.

All of the major elements of Kayser's program were explicable in terms of *Weltpolitik:* the idea of colonies as secure investment areas where the participation of foreign capital would not be threatening to Germany; the concept of colonies as dependent markets and sources of raw materials; the view that an increase in colonial business, by expanding German industry and protecting it from cyclical economic fluctuations, would ultimately increase prosperity for all classes of the German population; the idea that close cooperation between government and business on imperial matters was the key to rationalizing the process of economic change. Kayser himself and the defenders of his policy (both within the government and outside) used every part of the *Weltpolitik* argument that they could to drum up support among other government departments, among business interests, and among the Reichstag parties that had announced themselves as favoring colonialism.[11] Kayser's policy remained that of the Colonial Department even after he left office in 1896. On the whole, up until the late 1890s, the Colonial Department succeeded in maintaining widespread acceptance of the policy by the ideological means it had adopted.

Unfortunately, three major problems with Kayser's policy had emerged by the end of the decade. One, perhaps the least important in a political sense, was that it did not work. Businesses did not eagerly line up at Kayser's office door to seek concessions, as Kayser had expected. Rational assessments of potential profitability led most big investment institutions to continue to avoid the German colonies, except for token contributions. Most of the companies that did obtain concessions, with the exception of the *Gesellschaft Süd-Kamerun* and the Otavi Mining and Railroad Company of Southwest Africa (the latter backed by the giant *Diskonto-Gesellschaft* bank), invested only a fraction of their theoretical capital in their concession areas and simply waited for the values of their land holdings to rise or for the government to stimulate the colonial economies through subsidized development projects. It was hard to justify the concession program, although the Colonial Department tried to do so by using references to *Weltpolitik* ideology long after its failure had become apparent.[12]

The second difficulty arose from the use that the left opposition in the Reichstag made of scandals stemming directly from the concession policy's implementation. Particularly in Cameroon, the establishment of plantation enterprises in the middle 1890s had elicited substantial resistance from local peoples. The advent of the *Gesellschaft Süd-Kamerun* had led the administration of the colony, under the governorship of the enthusiastic and extremely violent *Weltpolitiker,* Jesko von Puttkamer, to prepare the ground for the company's rubber operations by mounting small military expeditions to "recruit" labor.[13] Inevitably, these policies produced many cases of violence and brutality. They also made it appear after 1900 that Cameroon was following in the path of King Leopold's Congo, which was by then acquiring the evil reputation in Europe that it so richly deserved. Because the exposure of colonial scandals was one of the means by which the Social Democrats and left liberals attracted attention to their negative view of colonialism and also to the rest of their programs, the Colonial Department found its whole concession policy under attack from the left in the Reichstag.[14] Also, because Puttkamer's policies aroused the opposition of missionary societies in Cameroon, the concession policy as a whole (not just in Cameroon) came under assault from missionaries and humanitarian imperialists. The latter, whose position we shall examine in Chapter Seven, adhered generally to the lines of the *Weltpolitik* ideology. Their attack on the concession policy meant that a segment of the *Weltpolitiker* had turned against a program based on *Weltpolitik*. Both the emerging professional colonial service and the small trader interest in the African colonies had also, by 1900, begun to have second thoughts about concessions, which led to a further crack in the ranks of the *Weltpolitiker*.[15]

But neither practical failure nor fragmentation among *Weltpolitiker* led to the abandonment of the program. What did the concession policy in was a series of attacks from the adherents of *Lebensraum*. In the early 1890s, complaints that Kayser's policy neglected the importance of settling German farmers in the colonies (especially Southwest Africa) had led Kayser to permit the establishment of the *Siedlungsgesellschaft für Südwest-afrika*—a company that was supposed to sponsor farming and ranching settlement in *Südwest*.[16] The *Siedlungsgesellschaft*, although supported by the Colonial Society and by public subscription, never amounted to very much. It was enough, however, for several years to allay possible objections by *Lebensraum* adherents that the concession policy benefitted big business at the expense of the "real" purpose of colonization: settlement. For the most part, even the Pan-German League and the most *Lebensraum*-oriented segments of the Colonial Society originally accepted the concession policy as a necessity for economic development. In addition, some of the leaders of both organizations had financial interests in the concessions.[17]

At the end of the 1890s, however, this tolerance for a *Weltpolitik*-inspired development policy rapidly dissolved. To some extent, the occasion arose from conflicts over the application of policy within the colonies themselves, especially conflicts in East and Southwest Africa that were at first only tangentially related to the subject matter of the imperialist ideologies.

In all colonies, political conflicts inevitably arose among the various European interests present: the government, traders, settlers, companies, and so on. In Southwest Africa in the late 1890s and at the turn of the century and in German East Africa during the next few years, the principal conflict (other than the basic one between Europeans and Africans) was between the government and the white farmer interests.[18] In Southwest Africa, the few hundred small farmers (actually, ranchers with huge acreage but small herds and profits) demanded a high level of government support. They desperately needed larger and better watered tracts of grazing land and additional breeding stock for their cattle herds. The former necessitated expensive irrigation projects, and both needs implied the dispossessing of the indigenous Herero and Nama peoples, a task that could only be performed by the government. Although the colonial authorities moved a certain distance to support them, setting in motion the process that would lead to the terrible Herero and Nama wars of the period 1904–7, the settlers were correct in perceiving that most colonial officials disapproved of them. The policies that the authorities were most interested in effectuating were those that would attract big capital to the colony and facilitate *Südwest's* development as an outpost of German industry.[19] The Colonial Department and its representatives in Southwest Africa refused many other settler demands such as cheap loans for prospective farmers and a subsidized educational system. For the most part, colonial officials tended to view the settlers as obstructions in the path of rational economic development and native policy. Although the settlers generally viewed the concession companies as opponents and more successful competitors for government support, they originally directed their main objections against the bureaucracy.

By themselves, of course, the Southwest African settlers would have been practically helpless against the colonial administration. They were not by themselves, however. They had representatives of their interests in Germany, mostly journalists and politicians looking for an issue with which to attract public attention. These began in the late 1890s to publicize the settlers' "plight," using the *Lebensraum* ideology as the framework for their complaints. Their attack focused, however, not so much on the colonial administration itself as on the administration's concession policy.[20] With almost incredible alacrity, major parties and political organizations took up the issue. By 1905, the concession policy was dead, abandoned by the Colonial Department under general assault from the political right and without support from a substantial part of the *Weltpolitiker*.

How did this happen? The key lies in the relationship of Southwest African settlement to the *Lebensraum* ideology. From the time of the seizure of the colonial empire in the 1880s, Southwest Africa, with its extensive grazing lands and supposedly temperate climate, had been fixed on by advocates of migrationist colonialism as the most likely of the colonies to support a large population of independent German farmers.[21] In truth, the similarity between the actual settlements that began to appear in Southwest Africa in the 1890s and the migrationist ideal was not very great. A large proportion of the early settlers were Boer immigrants or discharged members of the colonial military, not German farmers or artisans seeking a better life. Their farms were ranches large in area but sparse in grass, water, and livestock. Little of traditional German agricultural practice was useful there. Many settlers eked out precarious existences through small-scale trading with the Herero and Nama. But, at least, the Southwest African settlers came closer to the migrationist image than did many of the farmers and plantation operators of the northeastern highlands of German East Africa, who also used the *Lebensraum* ideology to seek political support in Germany.[22] Whatever the realities, Southwest Africa was the potential model colony of the *Lebensraum* enthusiasts, and this was what gave the settler interest its handle.

As we have seen, the migrationist image of the colonial settler had become, in the course of the tariff dispute of the 1890s, closely related to that of the idealized German peasant farmer of the agrarians and connected also to the symbolism of popular anti-industrialism. By identifying the Southwest African settlers with the images incorporated into the *Lebensraum* ideology, spokespersons for the settlers could appeal for the support of the powerful conservative alliance that was being put together to uphold the agrarian end in the tariff dispute: the *Bund der Landwirte,* the conservative parties, and so on. Reciprocally, the adherents of the agrarian interest could seek wider support for their own position among imperially minded people not particularly disposed toward high tariffs by emphasizing the ideological connection of agrarianism to *Lebensraum*. Political organizations such as the Pan-German League took full advantage of an issue that could be represented as symbolizing a major problem of German society (the dominance of national policy by selfish business interests) and that could be resolved by properly directed political action.

The Pan-German League also had quite specific reasons for taking up the cause of the Southwest African farmers and turning it into an attack on colonial concessions. The settlers' position was couched largely in the same ideological terms as the most central parts of the Pan-German platform and was easy to adopt. To maintain credibility as many of its original members turned away from it in the later 1890s, the league needed major issues that allowed it to apply its ideology and attract attention. The Pan-Germans had jumped early on the fleet-building bandwagon and had hoped that the naval issue would become exclusively their own, but Tirpitz had chosen to put his support mainly behind the more specialized Naval League.[23] In 1899 and 1900, the Pan-Germans needed another issue, and Southwest African settlement (expanded later to include the demands of plantation operators and farmers in East Africa) was the best thing that came along. It was essential, however, that the issue be formulated primarily in terms of opposition to the concessions and only secondarily to the government because only through identifying the concession companies with the big-business bogey of the agrarians could the necessary link to the protariff and supposedly anti-industrial right be made.

The Pan-Germans were not the only group to adopt an anticoncession stance at the turn of the century, although they and pro-*Lebensraum* local sections of the Colonial Society, in essence, orchestrated the ensuing publicity campaign. Hasse and Lehr harped on the question and forced a reluctant Colonial Society leadership to permit open discussion of it in the DKG's organs. When the issue had been given sufficient publicity, Hasse and Lehr brought it before the Reichstag, using debates over appropriations for colonial development as the means to give force to their criticisms.[24]

Hasse's argument, repeated by many other publicists, revolved around the identification of the Southwest African and East African settlers as the exemplars of the frontier small farmer and artisan whom the tradition of migrationist colonialism held to be so necessary for Germany's future and assistance to whom ought to be the key point of all colonial development policy.[25] Germany needed more colonial settlement and could only achieve it if proper conditions for settlement were established in the colonies. The Southwest African concession companies, representing high finance and big business in their most objectionable (and international) form, demanded special privileges that diverted all forms of government action to supporting them and that led to the establishment of a colonial climate in which settlement colonialism could not survive. The Colonial Department's policy was sacrificing a vital national interest to the promotion of the selfish pursuit of profit. Economic expansion was not objectionable in itself, but it needed to be directed so as not to run counter to the common good—in this case, a common good defined by the *Lebensraum* ideology. Hasse also made the connection to the agrarian position on tariffs explicit: the same capitalist industrial interests that were ruining society in Germany were doing the same thing to colonial settlement, one of the possible sources of Germany's salvation.

The general anticoncession line was put into a relatively radical-sounding form as a populist, anti-industrial, and anticapitalist attack on the existing order. However much Hasse may have thought that he was genuinely defending popular interests against special ones, however, the nature of the Pan-German attack actually followed the general outlines of the Pan-Germans' radical conservatism that were described in Chapter Five. That is, except for the concession companies themselves, no one really stood to be seriously hurt if the anticoncession movement got what it wanted—and, in fact, most of the proposals that were put forward called for a ban on any *future* concessions rather than a revocation of the existing ones. What was fundamentally wrong with the concessions, according to their opponents, was that they were *speculative* capitalist ventures rather than just capitalist ones.[26] Speculation was of course one of the classic bogeys of both the political left and right at the turn of the century—a concept so vaguely defined that it could be applied to almost any business enterprise that one happened to dislike, but in such a way that it implied a distinction between bad capitalist enterprises that were speculative and good ones that were not. Speculators sought profit not by legitimate innovation and responsible increases in productivity, but by financial manipulations that Hasse and many others believed to be the cause of economic depressions. Speculation was widely represented as the result of English and "international" Jewish meddling in the German economy (and, of course, the concession policy was easily associated with that particular constellation.) By concentrating their fire on the speculative nature of concessions, the Pan-Germans could still appear in a good light to supposedly responsible, right-thinking, self-consciously *German* big business.

One of the reasons for the ultimate success of the anticoncession movement was that the Free Conservative party quickly supported it. This occurred despite the fact that many of the leading Free Conservative politicians had earlier backed the concession policy, possessed direct links to concessionary investors, and tended, on the whole, to think about colonial policy in terms of *Weltpolitik* rather than *Lebensraum*.[27] This turning of the most staunchly imperialistic section of the Reichstag away from the concession policy appears to have resulted largely from the Pan-Germans' successful attachment of the settler interest to the *Lebensraum* ideology and the further attachment of both to the agrarian position on the tariff issue. The Free Conservatives, despite the association of many of their leaders with business and finance, had taken the agrarian side on the tariff issue—partly because many of them (including Otto Arendt) were genuine agrarians, partly not to offend Junker opinion, and partly as a means of widening their rather narrow support base.[28] They had added several populist, radical conservative elements to the political platform in the early and middle 1890s for similar reasons. By the late 1890s, the Free Conservatives had publicly associated themselves with a whole range of ideas and political images, including romantic peasant agrarianism and opposition to unbridled speculative big business, that were also generally associated with *Lebensraum* and with the agrarian antitariff movement. When the Pan-Germans succeeded in representing the concession policy as a manifestation of naked international capitalism doing its worst, the Free Conservative leaders Kardorff and Arendt had no option but to come out against concessions. Their alternatives had been eliminated by their previous ideological choices.

It is not necessary to go into the details of the Colonial Department's gradual surrender, between 1903 and 1905, to the snowballing attack on the concessions.[29] The important point is that the Department's initial attempt to build a colonial development policy around Weltpolitik failed in at least two ways. Partly because of *Weltpolitik*'s deficiencies as a guide to policy, the concession scheme itself foundered in implementation. Because of the relative economic insignificance of the German colonies and the government's minimal investment in them, however, this failure was probably of little importance. More significant was the ideological and political failure of *Weltpolitik,* in the form of the concession policy, to create consensus in favor of an expanded role for the Colonial Department and in favor of the department's efforts at colonial development. In the long run, not only did *Weltpolitik* prove not to be the integrative force that Kayser had hoped (because *Weltpolitiker* split on elements of his policy), but also the very act of adopting *Weltpolitik* connected the concession policy to a set of positions on general issues that eventually placed the policy among the objects of attack by powerful political forces. Even this might not have been fatal if German imperialist ideology had not been inherently dichotomous. It required the existence of the *Lebensraum* ideological set—its presence in the minds of people like Hasse and its general acceptance by large numbers of German imperialists—to connect the interests of a handful of unsuccessful Southwest African ranchers with the supposed plight of traditional German society under the onslaught of economic modernization and thus with the agrarian movement.

Even as the advocates of concessions were fighting their losing struggle, a new approach to colonial development was taking shape among *Weltpolitiker* on the permanent staffs of the Colonial Department and the colonial administrations. The new approach found its prime expression in a series of railroad-building projects advanced, mainly for East Africa, after 1900. As we have seen, according to the theory of economic development implicit in *Weltpolitik,* railways were the key capital investments that would serve both as catalysts and as regulators of socioeconomic modernization in the areas through which they passed. Whereas Kayser had envisioned a cooperative effort between government and industry in planning such development, with perhaps the majority of the responsibility falling on the latter, the post-1900 attitude heavily emphasized the government's leading role.[30] This approach reflected the Colonial Department's actual experience with private investment, recognition of the political liabilities of Kayser's policy, and the growing self-awareness and self-confidence of the emerging colonial bureaucracy. Under the new system, private companies would construct the railroads and take advantage of the resulting economic growth, but the Colonial Department would plan the total process of economic development, lay out the routes of the railways, and, most important, seek the interest guarantees from the Reichstag that would permit the contractors to assemble the necessary capital. The whole scheme was another variation on the theme of *Weltpolitik*. Thus when the Colonial Department made its first attempt to obtain Reichstag backing for massive East African railway construction under the new scheme in 1901, it used practically every element of the existing Weltpolitik ideology to support its case.[31]

The government's 1901 budget request to the Reichstag included items for interest guarantees for two East African railroads: a *Zentralbahn* across the middle of the colony to the lakes region, and a *Nordbahn,* an extension of an earlier attempt to connect the Indian Ocean coast to the northern highlands of Usambara. The *Zentralbahn* was the centerpiece of the total project; the *Nordbahn* was pushed mainly to appease the small number of white settlers and plantation operators in Usambara and their supporters in the colonial movement.[32]

Despite the Colonial Department's best publicity efforts and the almost universal support of imperialists of all stripes (including the Pan-Germans), the 1901 attempt failed miserably. The efforts of the nationalist and imperialist organizations to help the project through the Reichstag were severely hampered by the disunity among them caused by, among other things, the concession issue. Anticolonialists in the SPD and Center parties and among the left liberals jumped at the chance to attack the large expense that the project might represent. Most important, the Conservatives and the *Bund der Landwirte* withheld their support. They chose to include the railroad project in the same category of legislation as further naval building: programs of minimal benefit to the landed interest for which they would, in general, vote only in return for a guarantee that agricultural tariffs would be revised upward. It was reasonable enough for the agrarians to regard the project in this light because it was advertised, as fleet expansion was, in terms of *Weltpolitik*. In other words, most of the Colonial Department's scheme was quashed because it became connected, through the ideology used to formulate and defend it, to a category of proposed actions that made it an object of exploitation by a segment of the political right. The department did get part of the *Nordbahn* extension, largely because the existence of the settler interest in Usambara gave the *Nordbahn* at least a flavor of *Lebensraum* to offset the identification of the overall program with *Weltpolitik*.

By 1903, when the Colonial Department tried again, the tariff question had been partly settled by the 1902 upward tariff revision, but the *Bund der Landwirt* was still militantly attempting to raise tariffs even further. Opposition to the railway scheme among the center and the left liberals had been stilled by emphasizing the advantages of the *Zentralbahn* as a development tool and by portraying the *Zentralbahn* itself as the focus of the project and an example of applied *Weltpolitik*. On the other hand, and partly as a result of the way the *Zentralbahn* was advertised, a new pattern of opposition that would become a central feature of East African politics also emerged in 1903. Plantation operators and European small farmers in Usambara, anxious that the major development effort be placed behind the *Nordbahn,* had managed to convince the Pan-Germans and many of the same publicists and journalists who had taken up the cause of the Southwest African settlers that East African settlers were also real live representatives of the migrationist colonial ideal.[33] The desire of the few hundred Usambara planters for cheap transportation was again in 1903 represented as an issue vital to the future of Germany, as defined by the *Lebensraum* ideology. The question of East African development was thus transformed into a classic conflict of *Lebensraum* versus *Weltpolitik*. A coalition of parties and fragments of parties formed in the Reichstag and turned down the *Zentralbahn,* funding instead another extension of the *Nordbahn*.[34] Again, the Colonial Department had used *Weltpolitik* to create a limited degree of consensus behind its policy, only to discover that the very use of that ideology evoked its rival—*Lebens-raum*—with devastating effectiveness.

Did anyone learn a lesson from all this? Only in part. Between 1904 and 1907, the German colonial empire was shaken to its foundations by the Maji Maji rebellion in East Africa and by the Herero and Nama wars in Südwest. The colonial administration was criticized by imperialists and anti-imperialists alike, and the conduct of operations in Southwest Africa was turned over to the army. Development projects lost precedence to the necessity of countering the threat, both in Africa and in German politics, to the very existence of the empire and the Colonial Department. In any case, it was entirely clear that survival and future development projects in large measure both depended on creating a public image that would overwhelm particular interest groups and disarm *Lebensraum*-oriented opposition. It happened that in 1906, for reasons largely unrelated to the troubles of the colonial empire, Chancellor von Bülow was searching for a means of creating a wide-ranging and permanent basis of support in the Reichstag and decided that imperialism, especially colonialist imperialism, might be part of the answer. The needs of the Colonial Department and the *Sammlungspolitik* of Bülow together led to the appointment of the banker Bernhard Dernburg as colonial director in 1906 and his transformation into the state secretary of an independent Colonial Office in 1907.[35]

Dernburg's qualifications for the job consisted partly of his reputation for dynamic business leadership as a rescuer of foundering projects backed by the *Deutsche Bank* and as an unorthodox head of the *Darmstädter Bank* and partly of the multisided image that he could project. To the public at large, he was represented as a symbol of the government's commitment to making the colonial empire live up to its promise. Dernburg supposedly brought with him the ability and the vigor that the Colonial Department required at its helm. He was the first big-business manager to make it to the top ranks of the national government and could claim the support of all levels of the business community. He had connections with the left liberals without being far beyond the ideological range of the National Liberals and Free Conservatives. Also, although Dernburg was a baptized Christian, he came from a distinguished Jewish family; his appointment represented a gesture toward Jewish assimilation. He seemed to have what both Bülow and the colonial administration, for rather different reasons, needed in 1906. What he did not have was any expertise in colonial affairs.

The reform program that Dernburg introduced and publicized in 1906–7 has been discussed at some length in other studies and need not be detailed here. Although in its original formulation it showed little acquaintance on Dernburg's part with the realities of colonial development, it was clearly structured with careful attention to the realities of imperialist politics.[36] The general framework of the program came from *Weltpolitik,* not only because most of Dernburg's official advisors in the colonial administration subscribed to the ideology, but also because of the close connection between *Weltpolitik* and Dernburg's outlook as a manager and technocrat. The colonies had to be made productive adjuncts to German industry as markets, sources of raw materials, and investment areas. Massive development projects had to be undertaken, planned, and guaranteed by the government but financed and carried through by German business. The quality of colonial administrative personnel had to be raised, especially in the area of scientific and technical training, to permit them to direct the colonial development effort. In general, the colonial empire should provide as many of the raw materials needed by German industry as possible to free Germany from the tyranny of the monopolistic iinternational market. Most of Dernburg's early program was, of course, unoriginal, but Dernburg managed to put all of these old ideas together as a new "reform" package, replete with striking images of the future of Germany's colonies, that could be used as the basis of a large-scale public campaign. Dernburg said forcefully the things that the leaders of the Colonial Society and other imperialist organizations wanted to hear. In addition, at the start of his term in office, Dernburg also said the things that the settlers, their supporters, and *Lebensraum* imperialists wanted to hear. German agricultural settlement needed to be increased and the government had to back up the settlers in Southwest Africa and reduce the red tape that impeded their economic success, and so forth.[37] In his effort to touch as many political bases as possible, Dernburg criticised earlier policies because of their lack of attention to the needs of the settlers. Even in 1906 and early 1907, however, it was clear that Dernburg found the *Weltpolitik* policy framework most congenial and that he tended to emphasize elements from *Weltpolitik* in his public pronouncements.

He was given plenty of opportunity for such pronouncements. After Bülow had attempted unsuccessfully (through Dernburg) to appease critics of the colonial administration in the Center and Social Democratic Reichstag delegations, he decided in December 1906 that their criticism could be turned to his own political advantage. Bülow maneuvered the Center and the SPD into defeating a supplement to the colonial budget.[38] He then immediately dissolved the Reichstag and called new elections, making the future of the colonial empire and Germany's world aspirations the key issue of the subsequent electoral campaign. Bülow assigned Dernburg the job of organizing an electoral campaign and a coalition of progovernment parties. Dernburg rose to the task with alacrity and efficiency. His reform program for the colonies became the centerpiece of the campaign. The Colonial Society, the Pan-German League, a large variety of other patriotic nationalist organizations, the Conservative, Free Conservative, and National Liberal parties, and one of the two left-liberal parties jumped on the government's imperialist bandwagon. For the first time, the Reich government, through the use of a colonial issue and all forms of imperialist ideology, appeared to have the whip hand in electoral politics and to be building a strong basis of partisan support.

But a great deal more was going on in December 1906 and January

1907 than a nationalist-imperialist electoral campaign orchestrated by Bülow's government, whatever Bülow and Dernburg might have thought. Practically every political organization that had ever taken a proimperialist posture of any kind saw in the election an opportunity to increase its access to power. Self-conceived radicals in the Pan-German League, the Navy League, the Imperial League against Social Democracy—people such as Theodor Reismann-Grone, Eduard von Liebert, and General Keim—found the moment particularly opportune to reassert themselves in organizations that they believed to have become too accommodating to the "establishment," which included Bülow's government. Among many politicians on the right, it appeared that the lost opportunities of the Caprivi era might have appeared again—especially the opportunity to create a national front against the forces of socialism, liberalism, uncontrolled economic change, or whatever else one's own particular devil happened to be. These were the people who responded to Bülow and Dernburg's call—not because they thought much of Bülow, the dandified, opportunistic diplomat, or Dernburg, the "Jewish" capitalist, but because they smelled power. Dernburg may have thought he was managing an electoral campaign; in fact, it was imperialist activists in the Colonial Society, the Pan-German League, and kindred organizations who put out the publicity and arranged the meetings Dernburg addressed. The radical imperialists, in fact, quickly got out of control, advocating an expansionary policy far more aggressive than anything the government had in mind. They also elected a few of their number to the Reichstag in 1907. These new delegates, regardless of formal party affiliation, thought of themselves as an imperialist party, and, unlike Dernburg, they thought of colonies and imperialism mainly in terms of *Lebensraum.*[39]

The election of January 1907 semed to be a smashing success for Bülow and Dernburg. The Center and SPD did poorly, the coalition partners well, and the new, informal "imperialist party" seemed at first a source of support for the government. But Bülow's hopes were relatively quickly shattered. To the extent that the party coalition he had helped to create functioned at all, it worked to control Bülow's actions rather than to give him the political initiative. Moreover, in the not-very-long run, the new Reichstag imperialist group turned out to be a highly vocal opposition, demanding both a more aggressive foreign policy and a colonial policy based on *Lebensraum.* Eventually, these same people were to form part of the attempt to create a "national opposition" against Bülow and his successor, Bethmann Hollweg. But, in the short term (at least to the end of 1907), Dernburg was able to take advantage of his sudden popularity and the burst of imperialist enthusiasm engendered by the election to put a substantial number of reform projects into effect.

Most of Dernburg's reforms were conceptually connected to one another. He proposed the reorganization of the central establishment of the Colonial Office, a "regularization" of the bureaucratic status of the colonial service, and an expansion of facilities for the training of colonial personnel in the technical fields appropriate to their jobs. All of these Dernburg effected by the time he left office in 1910, both by pushing reforms through the Reichstag and by enlisting an unprecedented level of business suppport for such projects as the Colonial Institute in Hamburg—the cornerstone of Dernburg's scheme for improving the training of officials and building their contacts with their opposite numbers in business bureaucracies.[40] But these reforms were all conceived as adjuncts to the main thrust of colonial policy: the economic development of the colonies as part of a grand scheme of economic imperialism.

Dernburg's actual program for colonial development, as opposed to the vague and overblown plan around which he had built the electoral campaign, was formulated after consultations within the Colonial Office and with business- and *Weltpolitik*-oriented colonial interest groups such as the KWK. The final shape of the plan took form after Dernburg's much-publicized inspection tour of East Africa during the second half of 1907. In East Africa, Dernburg was strongly influenced by the governor, Albrecht von Rechenberg. Rechenberg was a staunch advocate of *Weltpolitik*, economic imperialism, and integrated planning for African peasant agricultural development centering around railroad construction. He pushed hard for the reactivation of the *Zentralbahn* scheme as the first priority in development policy, in opposition to the settler and plantation interest in Usambara, which wanted the alternative *Nordbahn*. Dernburg came away from East Africa with an enhanced appreciation for the difficulties of colonial development as well as for the capacities of colonial officials, a bias in favor of African peasant agricultural development rather than white settlement, and, most important, a conviction that the route to economic advancement lay along the track of the *Zentralbahn*. When he returned to Germany, he publicly announced an expanded development program more or less along the lines of the pre-1905 schemes of the Colonial Department, in which the East African *Zentralbahn* was the first order of business. Using the reserves of his popularity, he put the *Zentralbahn* and other secondary items through the Reichstag.[41]

In successfully pushing the *Zentralbahn,* however, Dernburg engendered the same sort of opposition that had defeated the scheme in 1903. The East African settlers complained and *Lebensraum*-oriented imperialists backed them up. Dernburg's popularity and the general enthusiasm for colonial development reduced the effectiveness of the imperialist opposition. Its underlying strength was, however, considerable, both because of the ideological connections of *Lebensraum* to other forms of radical conservatism and because of the new imperialist group in the Reichstag. Dernburg had his way over the *Zentralbahn,* but in getting it he had come out firmly on the side of *Weltpolitik* and against some of the most fundamental tenets of *Lebensraum* ideology. The consequences of the split with the *Lebensraum* group became clear in 1908 when diamonds were discovered in Southwest Africa. The settler interest and many of the leading publicists of German colonialism campaigned strenuously for the expropriation of the diamond fields by a settler-dominated Southwest African government or, at least, for a policy of directing a large proportion of the profits toward the support of settlement.[42] Such a policy would, it was claimed, make migrationist colonialism actually work as it was supposed to do. Dernburg, however, arguing in *Weltpolitik* fashion that the function of the colony was to support industry, ordered that the majority of the diamond profits were to go to the company in whose concession the diamonds had been found and that all diamonds were to be marketed under the supervision of a board representing the Colonial Office and big financial establishments. By the end of 1908, Dernburg had become the soul of *Weltpolitik* and thus an object of hatred and attack for those who held to *Lebensraum*.. This circumstance, although it turned Dernburg into the hero of the colonial reformers, developers, and officials, greatly limited his effectiveness in the Reichstag and in public politics.[43] The temporary consensus among imperialists formed in early 1907 had collapsed entirely.

The diamond issue and other controversies surrounding Dernburg illustrate, among other things, the growing importance of the imperialist ideologies as elements of politics in their own rights. A great deal of the motivation behind some of the earlier conflicts over colonial development could be explained as the result of conscious selection of particular imperialist ideologies by interest groups for ulterior economic and political purposes. By the Dernburg era, a colonial policy based on *Weltpolitik* was the only kind conceivable to most (although not all) colonial authorities. The ideology had, in essence, become internalized by the colonial bureaucracy.[44] The proclamation of an exclusively *Weltpolitik*-oriented policy, on the other hand, triggered a genuine negative response in the minds of politicians and colonialists conditioned by past controversies to view colonial policy in terms of *Lebensraum*. There continued, of course, to be specifically interested parties to colonial disputes. The settlers and plantation owners in East Africa, for example, had clear economic reasons for opposing Dernburg's development schemes and substituting their own. But they would have gotten nowhere if they had not been able to rely on the knee-jerk reaction to the Colonial Office's policy by the *Lebensraum* imperialists.[45] Also, organizations such as the Pan-German League needed issues such as the East African railroad question to keep in the public eye, and politicians in the Conservative, Free Conservative, and National Liberal parties could make good use of an issue that allowed them to take a radical-conservative position supposedly popular with the *Mittelstand* groups to which they were attempting to appeal. But, again, the key to the usefulness of this sort of issue was the internalization, the uncritical acceptance of *Lebensraum* and its connections to radical-conservative antimodernism on the part of many political participants.

Dernburg eventually resigned in 1910, in part because he realized that he no longer had the political strength to push significant colonial legislation through the Reichstag. He was replaced by his former undersecretary, Friedrich Lindequist. Lindequist had been given his previous job because he was the colonial administration's token *Lebensraum* enthusiast. It appears that his appointment was partly a gesture toward *Lebensraum* sentiment and a sign of the government's recognition of the new strength of radical conservatism.[46] Lindequist attempted, with the support of settlement-oriented colonialists, to redirect colonial policy along the lines of migrationist colonialism and *Lebensraum.* In doing so, he attracted considerable opposition from economic imperialists both within and outside the colonial service, and he started an acrimonious dispute with Governor Rechenberg over railroad and labor policy in East Africa. Lindequist's administration also provided the impetus that drove together rather disparate missionary, humanitarian, commercial, and administrative groups—all oriented toward *Weltpolitik* and a more humane native policy than Lindequist (or Dernburg, for that matter) had envisioned. This humanitarian movement, exploited by the SPD, the left liberals, and the democratic wing of the Center, eventually produced a minor political crisis in 1914 and a government declaration of indigenous rights in the colonies.[47] In other words, the bifurcated nature of imperialist ideology produced just as many problems for *Lebensraum*-style policy initiatives as it did for ones derived from *Weltpolitik.*

By 1914, however, Lindequist was out of office, having resigned at the end of 1911 over an issue that, although it was connected to economic development and the dichotomy between *Weltpolitik* and *Lebensraum,* takes us into the world of diplomacy and prewar German foreign policy: the resolution of the Moroccan crisis of 1911.

Mittelafrika and the Second Moroccan Crisis

The diplomatic and domestic political crisis that arose over the German claim to a share in the partition of Morocco in 1911 is one of the most frequently studied of the conflicts in international relations that immediately preceded the First World War.[48] We shall examine it here from the standpoint of the light it sheds on the political roles of the imperialist ideologies.

By the turn of the century, it had become clear to German observers that France and Spain, especially the former, were moving steadily to turn their informal paramountcy over Morocco into direct imperial control. German commercial interests in Morocco—especially the Mannesmann investment firm, which had moved heavily into Moroccan mining—started a publicity campaign just after 1900 to pressure the German government into intervening in Morrocco—ideally to establish a German protectorate to match the projected French and Spanish ones; more practically to obtain guarantees of the continued openness of Morocco to German investment after a French takeover.[49] the German Moroccan interest enlisted some support from other business groups and from the Colonial Society and Pan-German League, primarily using arguments from *Weltpolitik.* Morocco was portrayed as a major future investment area, the site of a growing consumer market, and a place that could, with proper development, become a prime source of industrial raw materials. The general agreement among imperialists that a stake in Morocco or some equivalent compensation would be worth striving for was one of the reasons that the Bülow government in 1904 made its famous decision to enunciate a German deisre to "protect" the country. Even more important, however, there appear to have been largely diplomatic aims, particularly Bülow's wish to create a colonial issue that would entangle Britain and France on opposite sides and thereby head off tendencies toward international cooperation between the two powers.

The details of the first Moroccan crisis of 1904–6 and Germany's failure to accomplish all her diplomatic purposes do not concern us here.[50] The important point is that, although the main public explanation that was given for the utility of a German Morocco was couched in terms of *Weltpolitik,* both the government and the groups with a specific stake in Morocco had invoked the *Lebensraum* ideological set during the crisis to mobilize the whole of German imperialist sentiment behind them. Organizations such as the Pan-German League responded with their usual eagerness when their particular chord was struck. By the time that the crisis was temporarily resolved through an international agreement in 1906, Morocco was regularly being described in the right radical press as an ideal settlement colony for German small farmers.[51] The form in which the crisis was resolved—recognition of French predominance in most of Morocco, with safeguards for the investments of other nations—had been a face-saving withdrawal for Germany from an untenable diplomatic position, but it did nothing to satisfy the *Lebensraum*-oriented radical conservatives who had been attracted to the issue. To them, it seemed as though the government had once again retreated on a question of imperial expansion.

Having been set off in 1904–6, the Pan-Germans and other *Lebensraum* enthusiasts continued afterward to harp on the possibilities of Morocco for German agricultural settlement. The idea served as a useful basis for criticism of the Bülow regime from the radical right because the government had largely backed off from the question. Official opinion after 1906 generally held that Morocco would cost more to acquire and defend than it would be worth in terms of the benefits of overseas empire as depicted by *Weltpolitik.* Although the Mannesmann interest continued to push for German intervention, most *Weltpolitiker* in business generally played down the potential of Morocco as a German possession in itself.[52] By 1911, Morocco was firmly lodged in the *Lebensraum,* not the *Weltpolitik,* ideological aggregation.

The German government reopened the Moroccan issue in 1911, not because of the role that Morocco had come to play in *Lebensraum* nor even primarily because of the continued pressure from investors to intervene to protect German concerns, although the second element had some effect. The 1911 initiative resulted mainly from the widespread growth of interest among government and business *Weltpolitiker* in German expansion in central Africa—in other words, in the concept of *Mittelafrika* discussed in Chapter Four.[53]

German plans for expansion in central Africa were not new in 1906–11. Ever since the establishment of the colonies of Cameroon and German East Africa, the possibility of linking them by acquiring part or all of the Congo basin had been discussed by imperialists, although not always very seriously within the government. Regardless of how genuine the desire to gain the economic benefits of central Africa originally was in the highest government circles, the idea of redrawing colonial boundaries had had substantial official appeal as a means of reaching the general imperial understanding with Britain that was a major goal of *Weltpolitik*. Friedrich von Holstein, for example, was not particularly impressed with *Mittelafrika* as a goal of policy in itself, but he was willing to pursue it if the negotiations about it would permanently improve relations with Britain.[54] This possibility had arisen twice: during the negotiations over the Anglo-German treaty of 1890 and during the discussions between the two countries that led to an abortive treaty concerning the Portuguese colonies in 1898.[55] In the latter case, the question of dividing up the Portuguese colonies in the event of Portugal's bankruptcy together with general considerations of Germany's role in southern and central Africa had led to substantial lobbying for particular acquisitions by businesses with interests in the region and to pressure from the nationalist organizations for an aggressive stand. The circumstance of having to develop some sort of policy about what part of the Portuguese colonies to demand led Foreign Office personnel to lay out potential acquisitions defined in terms of *Weltpolitik*. The effort turned out to be an entirely theoretical one when, after the conclusion of a treaty of partition to go into effect when Portugal defaulted on her financial obligations, Britain turned around and guaranteed those obligations through further loans and through a secret agreement with Portugal.

As enterprises such as the *Gesellschaft Süd-Kamerun* and the East African *Zentralbahn* were proposed or implemented after 1900, the outlines of an actual German economic interest in central Africa emerged—an interest that was consistent with the ideas of *Weltpolitik* and usually thought of in terms of *Weltpolitik*. This led German officials periodically to dust off and consult the 1898 treaty, which was theoretically still valid. For the most part, the growth of this interest should *not* be understood as the development of specific investment aims by particular businesses that had persuaded the government to convert their private aims into national ones. Major financial institutions such as the *Deutsche Bank* and some of the private investment banks did, indeed, seriously consider the encouragement of a national policy that would lead to their domination of various enterprises such as the copper mining of Katanga in the Congo, for example. German investors had money in a great many of the extractive and transportation enterprises in the Congo and in adjacent colonies, just as Belgian investors were heavily involved in German Cameroon. But in the policymaking process leading to the 1911 crisis, these connections between German business and central Africa appear to have been factors that provided a bridge between *Weltpolitik* ideology and economic reality in Africa rather than particularly strong sources of motivation.[56]

The actual formulation of a comprehensive policy encompassing plans for German trans-African economic development, diplomatic moves to acquire preeminence in central Africa, and the vitally important element of gaining British concurrence with such expansion took place mainly within the Foreign and Colonial offices among the most *Weltpolitik*-oriented of senior officials. Like-thinking business officials, especially in the *Deutsche Bank* and many of the firms whose leaders would shortly form the *Hansa-Bund,* were also apparently consulted, although, for the most part, it was the government agencies that sought private investment in likely areas for expansion rather than the other way round—that is, major businesses once having invested in those areas then seeking government support.[57] The emergence of *Mittelafrika* marks a new stage in the career of *Weltpolitik*—one in which *Weltpolitik* has clearly taken on an autonomous life of its own as a force in politics and policymaking. Of course, the successful establishment of formal or informal German hegemony in central Africa would be a major internal political coup and would have the effect of taking the force out of radical conservative criticism of the government; but, in the surviving documentation concerning the policy decisions leading to the *Mittelafrika* initiative, the move is almost always treated as something that would be highly beneficial in its own terms—that is, in terms of *Weltpolitik.*[58] It would secure an important region for future economic development complementary with existing plans for Germany's present colonies, and its accomplishment would both encourage and require the kind of general accommodation with Britain that was one of the major goals of *Weltpolitik.* These were the kinds of consideration that led Dernburg, during his last year or two in office, to concentrate increasing amounts of his attention on the international context of colonial development and expansion, especially on the evolving scheme for *Mittelafrika.*

As far as one can tell, at no time before the First World War did the Foreign and Colonial offices ever draw up a "final" plan for *Mittelafrika* or settle on a specific model of what the political structure of a German Central Africa would be once it was constructed. *Mittelafrika* could be made up of formal or informal dependencies, and the shape of German hegemony would depend on the course taken in negotiations with the other imperial powers.[59] The general *economic* form of *Mittelafrika*—that of an integrated production, marketing, and investment area dependent on the German industrial economy—was more clearly delineated. It was derived from *Weltpolitik,* partly by projecting the thinking that lay behind the individual development schemes in colonies such as East Africa onto a continent-wide stage. Some of the motivation that lay behind *Mittel-afrika* may well have been a reaction to the difficulties that the smaller scale development programs had experienced in getting through the Reichstag and to the generally less-than-satisfactory results that had been obtained from those that actually had been implemented. Instead of reconsidering the whole framework of assumptions on which development policy was based, the official *Weltpolitiker* elaborated the same ideas on a more grandiose scale, arguing that what had not worked in limited schemes would work in greater ones.[60] Also, because of the huge areas theoretically covered by the scheme, it was conceptually possible to resolve differences between interest groups and between colonial ideologies by claiming that *all* could be accommodated within *Mittelafrika*. The supporters of *Mittelafrika* were almost right. *Lebensraum* imperialists *did* like the idea; in fact, they stole it for themselves as soon as it attracted public attention in 1911.[61] But the general form of the official *Mittelafrika*, which connected it with the *Weltpolitik* idea, and the way the government chose in 1911 to go about putting it into effect guaranteed that the broaching of the idea in the context of the second Moroccan crisis would create division rather than unity among imperialists.

Despite the fact that *Mittelafrika* contained almost all of the faulty assumptions and unreasonable expectations that characterized *Weltpolitik* as a whole, and despite the further fact that the concept left a great deal to be desired in terms of clarity of definition, it was not the question of the scheme's practicality as a policy aim that attracted the most attention from officials in the Foreign and Colonial offices. They concentrated, instead, on the diplomatic means to be employed in its implementation. This concentration resulted partly from the immense diplomatic obstacles that existed to achieving a German Central Africa and partly from the importance within the conceptual system of the *Weltpolitiker* of achieving a "special relationship" with Britain.[62] Bülow's insistence on the *prior* existence of such a relationship was probably one of the things that kept him from adopting *Mittelafrika* as an immediate policy aim. Dernburg, on the other hand, together with Foreign Office personnel such as Kiderlen-Wächter and Richard von Kühlmann, argued that an approach to Britain over colonial gains for both countries in Africa would help to produce the needed comprehensive understanding between the two powers.[63] They did not, however, make much headway against Bülow's caution and against the general lack of interest in the idea on the part of the navy and the treasury. When Bülow fell from power in 1909 and was replaced by Theobald von Bethmann Hollweg, the *Weltpolitiker* in government and business gained a political chief who was generally sympathetic to their outlook, but they were still without effective momentum in shaping national policy.

The situation changed in 1910 with the appointment of Kiderlen-Wächter as Foreign Secretary. Kiderlen was an active and ambitious bureaucratic politician, a strong advocate of *Weltpolitik,* and a proponent of

Mittelafrika.[64] The expectations of those who favored initiatives in the direction of *Mittelafrika* focused on Kiderlen, in part because the Colonial Office had come under the control of Lindequist who, although not opposed to expansion in central Africa, conceived of it primarily in terms of accretions of settlement land and was not, in any case, a member of the established coterie of *Weltpolitiker*. Kiderlen did not disappoint. He made central African expansion a prime objective of foreign policy, and he set about effectively organizing an approach that he thought would ultimately yield the kind of expansion the *Weltpolitiker* wanted.

Kiderlen's appointment and policy initiatives resulted from the complex political circumstances of the early years of Bethmann Hollweg's chancellorship.[65] The Bethmann government was faced with at least as difficult a problem of fragmentation as Bülow's had been, a problem that strongly influenced the making of policy. The breakup of the Bülow bloc in the Reichstag and the formation of a cartel of conservative parties and the Center party meant that the government was no closer than its predecessor to the creation of a cooperative legislative coalition. Quite the contrary. The question of financial reform and imposing an income tax had had to be raised by a government desparately in need of revenues to keep up the arms race. The threat of financial reform drove the conservative bloc into a posture of opposition, or at least of wary distrust of Bethmann. The left—liberal and Social Democratic—was recovering rapidly from its defeat in 1907 and was demanding political and economic reform. Outside of party politics, attempts were underway to create broad economic interest groups with particular ideological appeals: on the moderate left, the *Hansa-Bund*, representing shipping and banking interests closely connected to Dernburgian *Weltpolitik*; on the right, the growing informal connection of heavy industry with radical nationalist organizations, including the Pan-Germans. The latter connection strongly featured *Lebensraum* imperialism in its public pronouncements, and much of the pressure that it put on Bethmann's government took the form of criticism of the government's "weakness" in securing Germany's rightful place as an imperial power. The fragmented state of politics also gave the Kaiser continued opportunities to intervene in the making of policy.

Kiderlen was chosen to be foreign secretary in order to gain a success in foreign affairs that would give the political initiative to the government. Kiderlen was one of the acknowledged leaders of the *Weltpolitiker* circle in the Foreign Office. It was a measure of the extent to which *Weltpolitik* had permeated the middle ranks of the ministry and had become the criterion by which much of the public judged the success of foreign policy that the most active of the *Weltpolitiker* should have made foreign secretary at a time when the Foreign Office was under attack for its supposed lack of direction. On the one hand, Kiderlen's penchant for extreme statements and for vigorous, not to say vulgar and violent, pronouncements on foreign policy made it seem that he might appeal to Pan-German-style imperialists; on the other hand, his subscription to *Weltpolitik* and his generally good reputation among leading bankers, shippers, and some industrialists made him acceptable to them as well.[66] Kiderlen quickly acquired the largest share of influence on the making of foreign policy. One of the areas that he selected as the scene of the spectacular success expected of him was *Mittelafrika*.

Kiderlen had to proceed carefully. An open move to take over the Belgian Congo or other areas would undoubtedly be met by resistance, and it was clear from early approaches to Britain on the subject of cooperative, joint expansion that the British were more concerned about maintaining their existinig alignment with France than with accommodating Germany.[67] The way Kiderlen decided to achieve his aims—both a step toward *Mittelafrika* and ultimately a realignment of Britain with Germany—was to create a crisis that would have to be solved through serious negotiations and without reservations among the various parties. The first stages in the construction of *Mittelafrika* would be taken through Germany's pursuit of compensation in the resolution of the crisis, and the general understanding achieved with Britain (and possibly France) in the aftermath of the crisis would be the means by which the rest of *Mittelafrika* would appear. This brought Kiderlen back to Morocco.[68]

By 1911, it was clear that France intended to turn Morocco into an outright dependency in the near future. Although various German business interests in Morocco considered themselves threatened by this change, much of the responsible opinion in the government held that Germany should not advance a counterclaim to Morocco, at least with the intention of actually acquiring a German colony there.[69] Nevertheless, Kiderlen sought and received the chancellor's and emperor's concurrence with the dispatch of a gunboat to Morocco to symbolize German interest in what was going on there. He did so partly to ensure the continued integrity of German investments in the country, partly in the hope that Britain and France would split over their responses, and partly with the aim of projecting a vigorous image for the Bethmann government for domestic political consumption. But what Kiderlen mainly wanted was to precipitate the crisis that he believed was necessary for achieving significant German expansion elsewhere, preferably in central Africa. The crisis would force the other powers to give Germany compensation for recognition of France's paramountcy in most of Morocco. Even before the crisis commenced in the summer of 1911, Kiderlen apparently had a fairly clear idea of the minimal compensation he wanted: the largest part of the French Congo—the area that separated Cameroon from the Congo River and from the Belgian Congo. This would be consistent with plans for developing the interior of Cameroon, and more important, it would make the German colonies on both coasts of Africa contiguous with the Belgian colony, the main object of German designs and a necessary component of an economically coherent *Mittelafrika*. The aim of cooperation with Britain and France in imperial expansion would also be served, although indirectly. Once the resolution of the Moroccan crisis had put the machinery in motion, so the *Weltpolitiker* argued, Britain especially could be brought into a wider set of agreements that would not only give Germany most of the Belgian Congo and part of the Portuguese territories, but would also constitute British recognition of German coequality and imperial partnership in the world.[70]

One of Kiderlen's problems was that he could not make his priorities public at the time that he manufactured the issue. To obtain compensation in central Africa for renouncing Morocco, the German government had to make at least a pretense that it was serious about Morocco to begin with. Otherwise, neither the British and French governments nor public opinion in those countries would be convinced of the need to compensate Germany. His main bargaining counter was the assertion that if Germany did not receive satisfaction, German public opinion would "force" Germany into war. Because the British and French foreign offices would suspect a bluff, Kiderlen's greatest hope of success lay in creating conditions in which it was not at all unlikely that war would result from a rejection of the German initiative.

It was here that imperialist ideology entered strongly into the picture. Morocco, as we have seen, had since 1906 become primarily an element of radical conservative, *Lebensraum*-style imperialist thinking. The Pan-German League and other organizations on the far right had stridently and continually demanded German action on Morocco (along with every other front in the cold war of bloc diplomacy).[71] Morocco was portrayed as the ideal future settlement colony for German farmers, the kind of acquisition that would actually allow the realization of the migrationist colonial vision. By taking up the cause of Germany's interests in Morocco, Kiderlen would apparently not only be responding to the demands of the radical right, but also be mobilizing an impressive array of political organizations able to represent themselves as the voice of popular imperialist opinion. Kiderlen could then seek compensation from the other powers as a means of satisfying a public mood over which he had no control. Because Kiderlen was fairly sure that the general idea of *Mittelafrika* would appeal to the Pan-Germans and much of the rest of the radical right, he believed that when the final resolution of the conflict revealed a substantial expansion for Germany in central Africa, the *Lebensraum* interest would be satisfied. *Mittelafrika* would accommodate all ideological lines, even though its logic was patently that of *Weltpolitik*. Even before the crisis, Kiderlen had held discussions with Class of the Pan-German League, pressing the advantages both of Morocco and of *Mittelafrika*.[72]

To an extent, Kiderlen's plans worked out as he had predicted. The German initiative in Morocco met a more united Anglo-French front than he had hoped, which meant that he had to think in terms of the lower end of the scale of demands that he had envisioned, but this was not a decisive setback. The nationalist and imperialist press, the Colonial Society, the Pan-Germans, all responded as Kiderlen had wished, allowing him to go into secret negotiations with the British and French with an adequate weight of bellicose "public opinion" behind him.[73] The other powers satisfied Kiderlen's minimal aims for compensation. When the results of the international negotiations were leaked in the fall of 1911, it was clear that Germany, in return for acknowledging French control of Morocco, had received guarantees for her economic interests and a large expansion of Cameroon to incorporate most of the French Congo. By his own lights and those of *Weltpolitik,* Kiderlen had been successful.

Almost immediately, however, things went wrong for Kiderlen and the *Weltpolitiker,* mostly because of the assumptions that underlay the Moroccan policy and that they had derived from their ideological framework. As soon as the terms of the Moroccan treaty became public, an outcry arose from the *Lebensraum* imperialists on the radical right.[74] Germany's acquiescence was labelled a sellout of her most fundamental interests. The Pan-Germans announced that Morocco was far more valuable than the French Congo, mainly because it could be settled with hundreds of thousands of Germans, and that the expansion of Cameroon did nothing for Germany's settlement posture. As to the advantages of "New Cameroon" as an opening to further African expansion, *Lebensraum* imperialists (justifiably) asked to be shown *Mittelafrika* in being and (unjustifiably) claimed that Germany had a "right" *both* to Morocco *and* to an immense central African empire. Kiderlen and the *Weltpolitiker,* in other words, had overestimated the capacity of the mere promise of *Mittelafrika* to satisfy *Lebensraum* enthusiasts and had underestimated the commitment of groups such as the Pan-Germans to the spirit of migrationist colonialism and the *Lebensraum* ideology.

While the right-radical press was having a fieldday lambasting the government, Lindequist, the colonial secretary, decided to resign in protest against the treaty that ended the crisis.[75] Lindequist, as an imperialist ardently and publicly committed to *Lebensraum,* had been led by Kiderlen to believe that Morocco really *was* the object of Germany's gambit. When events proved otherwise, Lindequist resigned, both to separate himself from a policy of which he disapproved and to express his displeasure at being misled by his colleagues.

By the end of 1911, the government had been able to recover its domestic political initiative to a certain extent. It pulled strings within the Colonial Society and in the press, and it mobilized the *Weltpolitiker* by explaining the supposed gains Germany had made in terms of *Weltpolitik* and *Mittelafrika.* The government was, of course, forced to go public with *Mittelafrika,* staging a substantial propaganda campaign for the idea that extended down to the start of the World War.[76] *Mittelafrika,* whatever its defects as a basis for policy planning, was sufficiently impressive that the idea attracted widespread public attention and was almost immediately taken over as a policy aim by some of the very groups, such as the Pan-Germans, that had attacked Kiderlen's Moroccan policies. To these groups, the considerations inherent in *Lebensraum* were still paramount (thus justifying their position on the 1911 crisis), but the apparent advantages to Germany of having a supposedly secure source of tropical raw materials in event of war seemed to make central African expansion a worthwhile aim if it did not interfere with goals of higher priority.[77] Nevertheless, the attack on the sellout of 1911 clearly tied the hands of the government in diplomacy during the ensuing years. It could never again afford to brave a repetition of such an assault, which had a severely restrictive effect on the range of options open to it in diplomacy.

Although the *Weltpolitikers'* strategy had clearly backfired on them in terms of domestic German politics, it was possible to argue, at least as late as the time of Kiderlen's sudden death in 1912, that the larger imperial and diplomatic aims of Kiderlen's policy were succeeding. Plans were worked out with the *Deutsche Bank* and other investors for systematic penetration of the Congo region and its environs.[78] The British government, moreover, appeared to be genuinely interested in reviving secret negotiations over colonial and naval issues. The interest seemed to stem directly from the experience of the Moroccan crisis. The German Foreign and Colonial offices, working closely together and strongly dominated by *Weltpolitiker,* explored several avenues of imperial accommodation with Britain in 1912 and subsequent years, efforts that resulted in the Haldane mission of February 1912 and in the attempt in 1914 to negotiate a comprehensive agreement to end the naval arms race and to rearrange colonial spheres of influence.[79]

Unfortunately, even in the imperial and diplomatic sphere, Kiderlen's initiative turned out ultimately to have been a failure. The reasons for its failure were again partly bound up with its ideological context. For one thing, the economic essence of the *Mittelafrika* scheme, built as it was on excessively optimistic thinking derived from *Weltpolitik,* did not, in the few years remaining before the First World War, work itself out as expected. The actual economic benefits of the expansion of Cameroon were limited, to say the least. The increased German economic presence in the Belgian Congo and the Portuguese colonies yielded few immediate results. Even in the long run, it is unlikely that a German-dominated *Mittelafrika* would have delivered to Germany anything like the economic benefits its proponents had claimed it would.[80]

In the end, the promising rapprochement with Britain proved fruitless as well. The British government was clearly willing to consider at least some imperial readjustments as the price of peace between 1912 and 1914. But the official *Weltpolitiker* directly concerned with colonial negotiations with the British during those years—men such as Colonial Secretary Solf and Richard von Kühlmann in the London embassy—greatly exaggerated in their own minds the extent to which the British would or could accept a full-scale, *Weltpolitik*-style division of spheres of influence throughout the world.[81] The mind-set of the *Weltpolitiker* led them to envision and push for a cooperative imperial arrangement with Britain that no British government could have presented to British public opinion and for which there was only very limited support among British policy-makers. As they had for twenty years, the *Weltpolitiker* willfully misunderstood the political setting in which they were operating, constantly attempting to enlarge a limited area of agreement with the British Foreign Office into a grandiose reshaping of imperial alliances. In so doing, they courted rejection.[82]

On one point, however, *Weltpolitiker* such as Solf, Kühlmann, and the shipping magnate Albert Ballin, were in close accord with British policymakers after 1911: that was that understanding between the two countries depended on ending the naval arms race. If doing so meant acknowledging British naval superiority, most official *Weltpolitiker* were willing to accept this condition, partly in the hope that the British would reciprocate with imperial concessions. *Weltpolitiker* such as Solf and Ballin had by 1911 lost faith in Tirpitz and the battle fleet. Naval building had not produced the results Tirpitz had promised, and it heightened the danger of war. During the negotiations with Britain in 1912 and 1914, opinion in the German Foreign Office favored naval limitations in return for imperial agreements, especially in central Africa.[83]

The initiatives taken toward Britain on the naval question were frustrated, however, by Tirpitz's success in rallying the support of the Kaiser and most of the groups attempting at the time to form a conservative, imperialist coalition.[84] The factors involved in Tirpitz's success were many, but one of the most important was the backing of *Lebensraum* imperialists such as Class and Hugenberg. This was not primarily due to the tendency among imperialists in the years just before the outbreak of World War I to emphasize continental as opposed to overseas expansion. Class, Hugenberg, and many other adherents of *Lebensraum* advocated *Mittelafrika* and aggressive overseas imperialism, although increasingly as matters of secondary priority to continental dominance. Continentalism need not, ostensibly, have ruled out a naval understanding to achieve British neutrality, which would have been useful in forwarding German continental expansion. Rather, the *Lebensraum* ideological set, with all of its geographic aims, required hostility to England as Germany's main potential enemy. *Lebensraum* acted as one of the central ideological elements of the attempt to create consensus on the political right to head off the Social Democrats and possible government-sponsored reforms. The effort by the Foreign Office to push accommodation with Britain, because it implied a rejection of *Lebensraum* imperialism in favor of *Weltpolitik* and because it could easily be represented as yet another German "surrender," had to be attacked by the Pan-Germans, by Hugenberg's Cartel of the Productive Classes, and by the whole range of organizations groping toward conservative integration before the war. Tirpitz was in an ideal position to take advantage of the situation.

The frustration felt by the *Weltpolitik* group in the Foreign Office, with their inability to get Germany seriously to seek accommodation with Britain on naval limitations and imperial arrangements, was manifest in their decision to make their views public in a celebrated anonymous 1913 pamphlet, *Deutsche Weltpolitik und kein Krieg.*[85] This pamphlet, although often ascribed to Kühlmann, was not, in fact, written by him. But it did articulate the ideas of the coterie in the Foreign and Colonial offices who thought as he did. Germany should make an obvious effort to reduce sources of tension with the other powers, partly by military and naval reductions, but, most especially, by making it clear that Germany's imperial aims were centered on *Mittelafrika* rather than eastern Europe. The most pressing sources of tension in Europe in 1913 were in the Balkans, and any attempt to defuse them would be useful.

The Kühlmann group's advocacy of overseas as opposed to continental imperialism should not be taken to mean that there was a clear split between those *Weltpolitiker* favoring *Mitteleuropa* and those pushing *Mittelafrika*. Kühlmann and his group favored both areas of expansion, as practically all *Weltpolitiker* always had. The overseas emphasis was an expedient to be employed because of existing diplomatic circumstances in order to achieve some of the fundamental aims of *Weltpolitik*. *Weltpolitiker* who favored continued emphasis on central European integration and economic domination—such as Walther Rathenau—did so because they believed that the European objectives could be practically achieved in the near future and that the necessary arrangement with Britain could be accomplished without giving up these objectives even temporarily.[86] At no point did Rathenau abjure *Mittelafrika* as a policy aim. In either case, one of the main reasons for advocating policies (whether continental or overseas) based on *Weltpolitik* was to combat the apparent tendency toward integration on the far right, a tendency that revolved, in part, around a connection between *Lebensraum* and opposition to domestic political reform.

The distinction between the *Weltpolitik* and *Lebensraum* forms of imperialism remained politically the most important one that divided imperialists as Bethmann's government was drawn into the series of crises that produced the First World War in 1914. Before we pursue the career of Germany's dichotomous imperialism into the war years, however, we must look at various related efforts to legitimate the imperialist ideologies and to overcome the differences between them. These efforts had been going on since the 1890s and, although not successful before the First World War, nevertheless had important effects on the later history of German imperialism.

CHAPTER SEVEN

Legitimation and Integration in Wilhelmian Imperialism, 1890–1914

The Legitimation of German Imperialism

Legitimation is part of the essence of an ideology, as we saw in Chapter One. All political ideologies contain devices for legitimating the ideas, images, and proposals for action of which they are composed. Under certain circumstances, the employment of an ideology in politics appears to require special efforts at legitimating the ideology as a whole by relating it to structures of ideas that can lay claim to a transcendental, universal validity. Under the conditions of fragmented politics in the late nineteenth and early twentieth centuries, imperialists in many countries felt obliged to legitimate their ideological systems in this general way, probably to be able to compete with rival ideologies.

Attempts at general legitimation of the German imperialist ideologies are of interest here for several reasons. In the first place, they have often been confused by historians with the ideologies themselves. Thus, for example, German imperialism in its ideological aspect is sometimes portrayed as a specialized form of social Darwinism (or at least a product of it), whereas, in fact, the use of a crude Darwinian mode of expression was a means by which some proponents of both major imperialist ideologies claimed scientific validity, and thus legitimacy, for the ideological sets to which they subscribed.[1] Second, attempts to legitimate the German imperialist ideologies in universal terms before the First World War played a considerable role in shaping the use of imperialism by postwar radical-conservatives—especially the Nazis—as a means of support aggregation and as a framework for policy. Finally, some of the most significant efforts to reconcile *Lebensraum* with *Weltpolitik* grew out of comprehensive attempts to legitimate the major German imperialist ideologies. For this reason, we shall deal with legitimation in the first part of the present chapter and then turn to ideological integration.

The key task in the legitimation of extensive ideological structures is to show that they are somehow grounded in a set of universal relationships that are thought by the intended audience of the ideology to be right (in the broad sense of "just") and to constitute an accurate model of reality. In the vocabulary of Chapter One, an ideology, to be regarded as legitimate, must be shown to conduce to the general good of the community. The connection to the general good should be demonstrated by means apparently outside the structure of the ideology itself so as to counter in advance the accusation that the ideology is being justified by a disguised tautology. An ideology that can be successfully legitimated in this way possesses an important advantage in the competition for public support and a powerful means over time of eliciting belief among those in a position to make policy.

Very roughly, there were three major ways in which Western imperialists attempted to legitimate their favorite ideologies in the late nineteenth and early twentieth centuries: through reference to political necessity raised to the level of historical "law" (*Realpolitik, Staatsräson,* manifest destiny); through the attachment of imperialism to moral and ethical imperatives ("humanitarian" imperialism); and through reference to science. These categories were by no means mutually exclusive, and all three approaches were taken in almost every major imperialist country.

Representing the actions proposed by an ideology as extensions of a transcendental *raison d'état* is, of course, a common means of legitimation. It can be employed with practically any contemplated policy. Both *Weltpolitiker* and *Lebensraum* imperialists commonly included in their comprehensive statements of projected expansionary aims justifications based on the assumption that overseas or continental possessions were a political necessity for Germany because they would make her stronger in the competition among states. Such arguments were often tied, circularly, to demands for greater German strength so as to acquire more possessions. Indeed, the circularity of this kind of approach was a little too obvious and gave socialist and left-liberal critics opportunities for highly effective attack.[2] A common variation placed this sort of argument in a pseudolegal and historical context. Germany was held to be somehow "entitled" to overseas possessions as a consequence of her emergence as a unified, powerful nation because all the other major nations had them. History, by delaying German unification, had started Germany with a severe handicap; therefore history obligated the other powers to make room for a German empire.[3]

In Britain, nineteenth-century imperialism had been profoundly influenced by the attempts to legitimate it through reference to the moral obligation of the English to spread civilization throughout the world, to stamp out the slave trade, and so forth. Humanitarian imperialism, although not absent in Germany, was considerably less significant there either as an influence or as a means of legitimation. Germany possessed only a pale reflection of Britain's enormous, interconnected network of moral-improvement organizations supported by industrial money and middle-class Nonconformist and Evangelical voters, organizations that made British humanitarianism such an important political force. There *were* German missionary and antislavery societies, and it was possible to interest them in imperial matters (the colonial movement of the 1880s tried, in part, to represent itself as an antislavery movement), but they were small and normally exercised only limited influence on politics.[4] German imperialists such as Friedrich Naumann, who toyed with the idea of creating a comprehensive humanitarian movement emphasizing both domestic moral and social reform and overseas imperialism as part of the same ideological package, were not, as their counterparts in Britain were, attempting to extend an already-existing political force for change into the area of overseas policy. They were rather hoping that the imperial emphasis would help to *create* a new reformist political force at home— one that currently existed only in a highly attenuated form.[5] Other imperialists who used humanitarian arguments, people such as Friedrich Fabri, did so in a more limited way—that is, as a means of justifying imperial expansion through showing the social and moral benefits it would achieve for Germans at home and for prospective colonial subjects overseas.[6]

Humanitarian imperialism, although weak in comparison to its British counterpart, did have some effect. It created a basis on which missionary societies operating in the German colonies could appeal for financial support. It also provided an ideological means by which missionary societies such as the Baseler mission in Cameroon, which took seriously their roles as "protectors" and "educators" of non-European colonial subjects, could resist government policies harmful to themselves and the peoples among whom they worked.[7] Humanitarian imperialism, with its dual character of advocating the moral, social, and economic "advancement" of colonial peoples and simultaneously attempting to protect them from excessive exploitation, often fitted in with the interests of German businesses engaged in direct trade with African producers. Palm-oil traders in West Africa, for instance, generally favored gradual Westernization of their trading partners—Westernization of the sort provided by missionary schools—but they opposed rapid economic transformation that would destroy traditional social forms and proletarianize colonial peoples because such changes would destroy the basis of their trade.[8] On the other hand, the relationship between humanitarian imperialism and the advocacy of socioeconomic change also created unresolvable contradictions within humanitarian groups over questions of development policy—indeed, over the basic question of the reasons for having a colonial policy at all. Humanitarians committed to "civilizing" non-European peoples could not ultimately avoid giving some support to coercive development programs (e.g., in Togo and East Africa).[9] At the same time, they found it difficult to withstand social imperialist arguments for the exploitation of colonial peoples based on the material advantages that such exploitation supposedly brought to the poorer classes of German society at home. For the most part, humanitarian imperialists subscribed to the general ideas of *Weltpolitik,* although, in terms of specific colonial development policy, they tended toward the group of *Weltpolitiker* who favored the development of indigenous peasant economies rather than toward those who favored the rapid creation of a colonial wage-labor force.[10]

Between about 1908 and 1914, there emerged a small but vocal colonial reform movement made up about equally of Dernburg-style *Weltpolitiker* and humanitarian imperialists. The movement—led by figures such as the missionary anthropologist Diedrich Westermann, the West African merchant and missionary society director J. K. von Vietor, and the former colonial official and entrepreneur Ernst Vohsen—centered its activities around Vohsen's journal, the *Koloniale Rundschau.*[11] The movement (as we have seen) was driven to action in 1910–11 by Lindequist's policies in the Colonial Office and kept up its efforts thereafter. Although its members also wanted a general return to Dernburg's policies of administrative and economic reform, they focused their public activities on native policy, criticizing the government for inadequate protection of indigenous peoples from exploitation and for insufficient expenditures on health and education in the colonies. This direction reflected both the concern of the missionary interest for precisely these matters and a calculation on the part of the movement's leaders that a clear humanitarian direction would appeal to the emerging left-liberal and socialist powerbloc in the Reichstag, especially after the election of 1912. The leaders were correct. As a means of attacking the equally apparent conservative bloc that also formed in the Reichstag after 1912—a bloc strongly committed to *Lebensraum,* white colonial settlement, and therefore antinative policies—the left-liberals, the Center, and the SPD forced the government in 1914 to issue a declaration of the rights of colonial subjects and the government's obligations to them.[12] Whether the declaration would, in fact, have meant anything if Germany had not lost her colonies shortly afterward is difficult to say, but humanitarianism did have at least this much effect, in the end, on German imperialism.

From the standpoint of the long-term history of German expansionism, the third major means of legitimating imperialism—the appeal to science—was the most important. The nineteenth and early twentieth centuries were an age of science in terms of consensus politics, as they were in so many other ways. Political ideas that could be identified with science could attain popularity and legitimacy on the basis of that identification. On the other hand, science and technical progress were commonly identified with economic and social change. People who perceived themselves as endangered by change could react negatively to the same identification.[13] Thus, although the legitimation of an ideology through science held great promise as a means of support aggregation, it also posed the danger of connecting an ideology with one side in one of the most fundamental conflicts of attitudes in German society. It is not therefore surprising that science tended to be brought into play before the last quarter of the nineteenth century in Germany mainly on behalf of ideological constructs already closely identified with change and modernity: liberalism, socialism, and more limited ideologies such as economic imperialism. Politicians and publicists attempting to bridge gaps in the ideological structure of German politics after about 1875 had to be especially careful about how they employed science as a means of legitimation. This is one of the reasons that, in the case of imperialism, the task of finding an effective scientific justification tended to be connected directly with the attempt to integrate the fundamental imperialist ideologies. It also required the employment of a variety of science that, on the one hand, did not automaticallly appear to line up on the side of technological change but, on the other hand, did not automatically appear to oppose it either.

Scientific legitimation required the participation of certified academics—especially in Germany with its high esteem for academic credentials. The emergence in the late nineteenth century of new social sciences, largely but not entirely in an academic setting, and the simultaneous appearance of a class of academically qualified social scientists and theoreticians with a journalistic bent provided the means by which the legitimation of the imperialist ideologies could occur. To a considerable extent, the social scientific disciplines of economics, political science, sociology, and even anthropology appeared in Germany in close connection with the sides taken in major political and social debates.[14] At the same time, the tendency of the German university system to produce more qualified academics than it could absorb drove a substantial number of university-trained young men into journalism in the last years of the century. The structure of the German academic profession also tended to push young scholars, especially those in fields that gave them a presumptive right to pronounce authoritatively on social questions, into journalism early in their careers, mainly as means of supplementing their incomes during the long wait for fully salaried positions. Even some of the most successful social scientists (e.g., Max Weber and Friedrich Ratzel) went into political journalism in their twenties for this reason and maintained their journalistic activities throughout their lives.[15]

The advent of the Darwinian mode of analysis and expression—the best-known case of the impingement of science on imperialist ideology in the nineteenth century—was mainly the work of people who combined academic and journalistic careers. Before the 1880s, Darwinism tended to be identified with political radicalism and with the consciously materialistic advocates of technological "progress." In the 1880s and 1890s, however, as need arose among political organizations in all areas of the political spectrum to find new ideological approaches to consensus building, new Darwinian formulations of social, political, and economic questions were attempted by journalists trying to put conservative ideas forward in a popular way.[16] Darwinian ideas proved to be sufficiently flexible when takjen out of a strictly biological sphere that they could be employed to express almost any ideological position. But they were especially useful when it became necessary to defend the privileges of particular classes, the aggressive behavior of one's own nation against others, or the "necessity" of economic exploitation. In the area of imperialist propaganda, although Darwinian formulations originally came most easily to economic imperialists with their generally favorable views of modernity and change, some of the early *Lebensraum* advocates also employed Darwinian ideas. Wilhelm Hübbe-Schleiden was one of the first colonialists in the 1880s to cast his arguments in favor of imperial expansion in explicitly Darwinian form, just as he was one of the first radical-consevative propagandists to attempt to link distrust of the direction of socioeconomic change with an acceptance of the need for radical political action to redirect it.[17] Hübbe-Schleiden's Darwinism, however, did not seriously affect the nature of the migrationist arguments that he advanced.

Darwinism was, however, only one form (although a very common one) in which reputedly scientific theory affected the formulation of imperialist ideology. For an important example of the complexities of the relationship between science and imperialism, we can examine the work of Friedrich Ratzel (1844–1904). Ratzel was the originator of the term *Lebensraum*. Although he employed it as the key concept of a biological theory, Ratzel's *Lebensraum* and the *Lebensraum* imperialist ideology were in fact closely connected.

During the latter part of his career, Ratzel was a professor at the University of Leipzig and Germany's best-known geographer.[18] He was also a leading journalist, having moved into journalism in the late 1860s when he had been unable to find an academic job after taking his doctorate in zoology. Ratzel's interest in geography, a brand-new academic field, like many of his interests in politics, arose directly from his work as a journalist and travel correspondent in the 1870s. Ratzel's initial concern about the problem of emigration and his partiality toward popular romantic agrarianism (Ratzel worked up agrarianism into a highly sentimental idealization of rural life) appear, however, to have been derived from Ratzel's early social background as a member of a lower middle-class family in southwestern Germany. The *Auswanderung* was a stock topic of discussion in the rural villages in which Ratzel grew to adulthood. He went through an early infatuation with liberalism; along with much of the rest of his generation, he also experienced an emotional conversion to German nationalism at the time of the Franco-Prussian War.

To these basic ingredients of Ratzel's background were added his training in science and his early career in journalism. In the late 1860s, Ratzel became an adherent and popularizer of Darwinism. His scientific notions remained Darwinian in a great many senses throughout his career, although he later criticised some parts of the Darwinian corpus of ideas and attempted to modify others. Darwinism certainly influenced his thinking in the 1870s when he obtained his first academic appointments in geography and began to do theoretical work in a large number of different fields within his primary discipline, continuing his journalistic work all the while.

In the 1880s and 1890s, Ratzel developed a series of theories about the relationship between biological species and their physical environments that, despite serious flaws, became highly influential. The theories culminated in Ratzel's concept of *Lebensraum*. Briefly, Ratzel argued that human (and nonhuman) social phenomena are the results of complex adaptations over time to a physical environment and that Darwinian natural selection takes place within an overwhelmingly important spatial context. In human society, both the state and culture (the sum of beliefs, language, social practices and material equipment common to an identifiable group of people) are primarily adaptations to geographic circumstances.[19]

This kind of determinism was, in its essentials, not particularly new, although Ratzel's explanation that the "laws" of change and adaptation are a complex set of probabilities had a modern, relativistic ring to it. What was new was Ratzel's emphasis on species *migration* as the most significant factor in social adaptation and, with respect to human society, cultural change. Species did not just adapt to a present environment (often, in the case of humans, interacting with it to change it). They also, if they adapted successfully to one location, spread naturally to others, requiring further adaptations. Among humans, it was this constant movement of peoples, with its concomitant diffusion of cultural traits and the creation of new ones through cultural integration and adaptation, that was the real engine of history.[20]

For present purposes, the important point about Ratzel's idea of migration is that it was directly connected with his adherence to migrationist colonialism. Ratzel possessed many links to the colonial movement. His first important academic mentor had been the zoologist, Moritz Wagner, who had proposed to modify Darwinian theory in the 1860s by adding to it a "law of migration": this held that the degree of trait differentiation within a species was proportional to the spatial separation of its members. Ratzel realized that Wagner's "law" was incorrect, but he acknowledged that it was the main starting point for his own work. Even before Wagner had attained prominence as a biological theorist, he had been a leading propagandist of migrationist colonialism and a proponent of settlement schemes for Central America. Wagner's biological theories were to a considerable extent projections of arguments that he had already developed to justify a colonial solution to the problem of the *Auswanderung*. When Ratzel absorbed Wagner's influence, he was in fact absorbing migrationist colonialism into his scientific outlook.[21]

During the 1870s and 1880s , Ratzel devoted much of his attention as a geographer and journalist to the phenomenon of migration. At the same time, he involved himself deeply in the budding colonial movement as a publicist and a founding member of *Kolonialverein* and the Colonial Society. Although originally Ratzel followed the economic imperialist line of the early colonial movement quite closely, when he was criticized for this in the mid-1880s by Ernst Hasse, he came out strongly for migrationist priorities in colonial policy. He remained committed to migrationist colonialism for the rest of his life.[22] Ratzel's involvement in disputes about particular colonial issues motivated some of his most important scientific work: for example, when he attempted to demonstrate the adaptability of European populations to tropical climates in order to counter the opinions of the liberal anticolonial pathologist Rudolf Virchow.[23] At the same time, Ratzel's general theories of migration began to conform more and more closely to migrationist colonial thinking, especially with respect to the prime implication of Ratzel's later theory of *Lebensraum*: that a *Volk* must constantly expand the amount of space it occupies to survive and prosper.

The other major ingredient in Ratzel's thinking that led to his theory of *Lebensraum* was romantic, peasant-oriented agrarianism. This element comes out strongly in Ratzel's autobiographical writings and also in his theoretical work.[24] Ratzel did not think that just any form of migration could satisfy a people's need for expanded living space. Conquests were historically unimportant unless accompanied by "colonization," which Ratzel defined very specifically as the taking over of agricultural land for direct, small-unit farming by the new occupiers. The key to a people's or a state's success lay in its ability to expand its living space and adapt to the requirements of farming new land while maintaining its connection to the land through peasant agriculture. "The simpler and more immediate the relationship of the State to its land," Ratzel wrote, "the sounder at that time is its life and growth."[25] Conquerors and occupiers who did not undertake direct peasant agriculture were swallowed up, culturally and genetically, by the indigenous people. Even commerce, which Ratzel valued highly, did not have the cultural or historical significance of what Ratzel called "colonization."

Ratzel's growing emphasis on the concept of agricultural primacy in social and cultural change was probably influenced by political questions of the 1880s and 1890s. We have already seen how the apologists of Junker agriculture and the conservative parties used the peasant-agrarian idea as a means of generalizing their argument for protection, especially during the tariff debates of the 1890s. Ratzel's involvement was more indirect than that of many apologists for agriculture and rural peasant society. He had no particular liking for Junkers as a social class or as a political elite. But Ratzel was a relatively prominent member of the National Liberal party and an important participant in the National Liberals' ongoing debate about the party's ideological direction. He took the position that the National Liberals must direct their appeal toward the "little people" threatened by economic change but unwilling to be accounted as proletarians: peasant farmers, artisans, shopkeepers—strata of society from which Ratzel himself sprang. Adopting a policy of agrarianism tied to advocacy of policies of protecting traditionally "valuable" classes would allow the National Liberals to speak for and to these groups and produce a firm basis of electoral support. Ratzel's agrarianism therefore followed essentially the lines of development taken by the *Lebensraum* imperialists discussed in Chapter Five. It was reinforced by the popularity of agrarian ideas in academic circles at the end of the century. Ratzel tended to subscribe to current academic fashions.[26]

By the 1890s, the matrix of Ratzel's thinking about both political and scientific matters closely resembled the structure of the *Lebensraum* imperialist ideology—not simply because Ratzel thought about imperial issues in terms of *Lebensraum,* but also because his entire process of intellectual formation had followed a pattern similar to that which produced *Lebensraum.* Thus, when he attempted in the late 1890s to create a grand synthesis of his thought explaining all aspects of nature, ideology and science were thoroughly fused in his mind. In his various statements of the theory that he called *Lebensraum,* including a famous essay with that title published in 1901, the political implications of the theory were readily apparent beneath its overtly scientific surface.[27] Ratzel, whatever his intentions, had created a means of legitimating an imperialist ideology through science.

Ratzel advanced his concept of *Lebensraum* as a set of rules applying to, and confirmed by, all of nature. Migration was a natural characteristic of all living species, a behavioral manifestation of the need of a species for additional living space. The nature of the interaction of a species with new living space and the kind of competition experienced in trying to take it over determined the social forms of the species. As he had previously, Ratzel called the manner in which a species successfully occupied new space "colonization." After citing numerous examples of this process throughout nature, Ratzel turned, sometimes directly and sometimes by implication, to humans. Here his units were, as they had usually been in his earlier work, "peoples" (*Völker*).[28]

Ratzel used his customary peasant-agrarian definition of human "colonization." His treatment of the relationship between humankind and nature had grown increasingly mystical through the years, but its implication for, among other things, the tariff debate was entirely clear: industrialization at the expense of agriculture would in the long run be disastrous for Germany. It would destroy the foundations of German culture and the German character, which lay in the peasant's relationship to the soil and to nature in general. Therefore the agricultural sector, especially the peasant agricultural sector, had to be fostered and protected. Ratzel had created a scientific basis for standard radical agrarianism.[29]

Ratzel turned to migrationist colonialism both to demonstrate a way in which traditional agrarian society might be protected and to show how it might be possible to reconcile that society with the need for trade and manufacturing. The process of industrialization at home might be controlled and restrained, but it could not, Ratzel argued, be turned back.[30] Germany therefore had to create compensations, partly by such means as bringing a rural environment into the industrial city but mainly by occupying new living space abroad and ensuring its development through "colonization" (defined in Ratzel's peculiar sense). Ratzel, like many others attracted to *Lebensraum* imperialism, suggested, in essence, a "displacement" solution to the controversy over industrial policy and to Germany's major social problems.

In his theory of *Lebensraum* therefore, Ratzel replicated the basic tenets of the ideology of *Lebensraum* and conferred on them the legitimacy of science. At the same time, Ratzel emphasized that once the primacy of the *Lebensraum* worldview was accepted as scientifically correct, an important place could be found for industrial concerns and for the ideas of economic imperialism. Ratzel, in fact, strongly supported naval building, the protection of German economic interests abroad, and central European economic integration (in its more conservative formulation).[31] As long as agrarian settlement and the protection of traditional values were given priority in policymaking, it would be possible to define a vital role in society for the modern industrial sector. Ratzel did not do so systematically, but he influenced a large number of others who later attempted to reconcile modernity and tradition by linking imperialist ideologies.

Ratzel was not the only person who, consciously or unconsciously, attempted to legitimate an imperialist ideology through science before 1914, nor was this kind of activity confined to the advocates of *Lebensraum*. We have already seen that Dernburg deliberately conceived and publicized his reforms in the colonial administration as "scientific colonialism." This catchword clearly focused the main thrust of *Weltpolitik*: the attempt to create the means of rational control of the social and economic environment to afford orderly progress. The term *scientific colonialism* was taken perfectly seriously by Dernburg, the colonial bureaucracy, and most *Weltpolitiker* as an accurate description of correct imperial policy.[32] But Dernburg, the post-Dernburgian reformers, and such imperialist theorists as Walther Rathenau, Moritz Bonn, and Karl Helfferich also employed "scientific colonialism" as a slogan designed to rally a portion of public opinion behind the general set of policy aims that they favored. They were, in essence, seeking approval by claiming that their proposals were not only scientifically legitimate but in some way "science" exemplified.

In all imperialist countries in the late nineteenth century, notions of the *racial* and *cultural* superiority of Europeans—in particular one's own countrymen—were already part of general imperialist attitudes.[33] They were given "scientific" formulation with specific implications for imperialist ideologies during the decades around the turn of the century—often, but not always, using an explicitly Darwinian mode of expression. Ideas of German racial and cultural superiority, mostly borrowed from English expressions of these ideas, were regularly employed to justify policy proposals derived from *Weltpolitik* after 1890. Wilhelm Solf, for example, based the defense of his program for government-sponsored economic and educational development in the colonies on a "scientifically" sanctioned view of the superiority of German culture of those of non-European colonial subjects and on the derived necessity of gradually adjusting indigenous colonial societies to the plainly superior German model for the benefit of all concerned.[34] The idea that the superiority of German or European culture over those of non-Europeans was scientifically demonstrable was also frequently used in *Lebensraum*–style imperialist writings.[35]

The supposedly "scientific" formulations of biological racism—the idea that certain peoples are physically and genetically superior to others— that gained currency at the end of the nineteenth and the beginning of the twentieth centuries are well known and need not be pursued in detail here. However, it is important to note that, although we normally think of notions of racial and cultural superiority as part of the same ideological package because of the prominence of both ideas in post-1918 radical conservatism, the two concepts were, in fact, not initially entirely compatible. In the late nineteenth century, it was much easier to associate conservative ideologies such as *Lebensraum* with the idea of cultural superiority than with biological racism.

Biological racism possessed a direct connection, in image at least, to Darwinism and physical science, but the "cultural sciences" were formulated, to some extent, in opposition to the more "materialistic" forms of science. Through the 1880s, Darwinism tended to be identified by many radical-conservatives, including Adolf Stoecker, as a threat to religion and one of the main dangers that modernity posed for traditional society.[36] Some early radical conservative publicists, especially Hübbe-Schleiden, had attempted to combine both notions; but it took, for the most part, until after the turn of the century for the concepts of cultural and racial superiority to become firmly associated with each other within the same general ideological set.[37] Even then, cultural concepts continued to be more compatible with expressions of *Lebensraum* ideology, especially when those expressions appeared in a scientific format.

Friedrich Ratzel, once again, can be used to illustrate the way in which science in the guise of cultural-superiority theory could be used to legitimate imperialist ideology. In the 1880s and 1890s, Ratzel laid the groundwork for what shortly became the dominant theory of ethnology in Germany: cultural diffusionism.[38] Ratzel argued on the basis of comparisons of ethnographic data that there existed a limited number of distinct cultures in the world, each of them an array of spiritual and religious ideas, social and political forms, and styles of material artifacts. Each culture predominated in a particular large geographic region. These cultural areas resulted from the diffusion of the cultural traits that comprised them from the comparatively few places in the world at which true invention had occurred. Diffusion could take place in many ways (trade, war, etc.), but the most important, according to Ratzel, was the mass migration of peoples looking for living space. Mixing of cultural traits, of course, occurred, but most cultural changes were primarily the results of the adaptation of traits to new physical environments. When two cultures confronted one another, the superior one (the one that permitted the more effective "colonization" of new land) would displace the weaker, borrowing only limited amounts from it. The force that impelled the movement of peoples—the search for living space—proceeded unavoidably from nature. The diffusion and triumph of superior cultures were simply the products of natural laws.

The applicability of this theory to the legitimation of imperialism is obvious. The acquisition of new territory and new means of national subsistence was entirely lawful behavior in a scientific sense and therefore, by extension, in the sense of "natural" morality. In principle, the idea of cultural diffusion could be employed in connection with either major imperialist ideology. Diedrich Westermann, for instance, used it in conjunction with *Weltpolitik*.[39] But diffusionism's special affinity with *Lebensraum* can be seen in the theory's use of the concept of living space, in Ratzel's insistence on migration as the main engine of diffusion, and in the essentially conservative, agrarian view of technological change that made diffusionism consistent with the ideological array to which the *Lebensraum* ideology belonged. In his treatment of diffusion, Ratzel again left a place for the kind of technological change associated with industrialization, but only within a framework that recognized the primacy of peasant agriculture and the cultural traits to which it was connected. Ratzel furthermore downgraded the importance of biological race in the process of cultural diffusion, arguing that there were no pure races and that biological groups inevitably mixed in the course of migration. Superiority could be effectively defined only in terms of collections of cultural traits, not in terms of genetic ones.[40]

By the time of the First World War, Ratzel and dozens of other scientists and scholars had produced a considerable body of theory that could be, and regularly was, employed to legitimate German imperialism in general and the ideologies of *Lebensraum* and *Weltpolitik* in particular.[41] Many of them, again including Ratzel, had in the process constructed means by which an integration of elements of *Lebensraum* and *Weltpolitik* could be advanced, although they had not done much in the way of exploiting them. It must be remembered that people like Ratzel were primarily social scientists and academics. Although many of them participated in politics and, consciously or unconsciously, connected their theoretical work to their political interests, they still (for the most part) sincerely believed that what they were doing was primarily science. Only a few of them, together with some journalists influenced by their work, turned themselves consciously to the task of employing science in ideological integration before the First World War.

Attempts at Integration in Imperialist Ideology

Most of the efforts made before 1914 to bridge the gaps between the major German imperialist ideologies failed in a practical sense. Some of them, however, did profoundly affect the framework and vocabulary of imperialist discourse and to some extent laid the groundwork for the integration of ideologies that occurred after the First World War. Not all of these attempts were undertaken by social scientists, but the kinds of scientific legitimation of imperialism that we have just discussed were extremely important in the creation of structures of ideological integration.[42]

Friedrich von Berhardi, a retired general and radical-conservative publicist of the immediate pre-World War I years, provides an example of a nonacademic who approached the problem of imperialist ideological integration from the *Lebensraum* side. In his notorious 1912 book *Deutschland und der nächste Krieg* ("Germany and the Next War"), Bernhardi used what he proclaimed to be the very high probability of a coming major European war to create a generalized framework for aggressive German imperialism.[43] Bernhardi starts with an extreme and highly simplistic Darwinian conception. The essence of life itself is the struggle among individuals and among groups. Those best equipped in the struggle of life will win and propagate themselves; the losers will go to the wall. At the highest level of struggle, anything that a *Volk* does to win in its perpetual struggle with other *Völker* is legitimate according to the laws of nature. People and nations have a "right" and a "duty" to go to war.[44] The strength of the German *Volk,* the basis of its power in its inevitable struggles with others, resides to a large extent in the presence in the population of people following traditional occupations—especially peasant farmers. Because these groups are under pressure for land and for a socioeconomic setting in which to maintain themselves, the major goal of the upcoming war should be to acquire a great deal of additional agricultural territory. As it is, Bernhardi continues, many of the socially and culturally most valuable Germans have been lost to Germany through emigration because "the German Reich possesses no colonial land in which its growing population can pursue remunerative employment and a German existence."[45] The present colonies are manifestly inadequate; although future overseas expansion may produce some of the necessary space, most of it will have to be seized in eastern Europe.[46]

To this fairly straightforward and brutally aggressive *Lebensraum*-style presentation with its Darwinian gloss for legitimation, Bernhardi adds a number of arguments about the racial and cultural superiority of Germans. On the whole, he is more comfortable with cultural factors. His concept of *Deutschtum*—the essence of Germanness, which gives the German people its peculiar strengths and constitutes that which Germans must protect and expand—is basically a cultural entity in the fundamental tradition of *Lebensraum. Deutschtum* depends heavily on peasant agriculture and the possession and expansion of agricultural land. Bernhardi's attempts to link *Deutschtum* to biological race are halfhearted; he does not have a fully articulated concept of the connection between *Blut* and *Boden* that would be so important to radical conservatism later.[47]

From a basis in modernized *Lebensraum,* Bernhardi attempts an explicit connection with *Weltpolitik.* According to Bernhardi, a large, efficient, and expanding industrial sector and a financial structure capable of massive capital accumulation are also vital necessities for Germany in the coming war. Science, munitions, and money are obviously essential ingredients of modern warfare. Rather than accepting this solely as an unfortunate necessity, Bernhardi takes the opportunity to glory in the superiority of German industry, technology, and science as testimony to the genius of the German *Volk*.[48] Modernity—in the form of democracy, crass materialism, inattention to duty—and the dominance of international capital is still very much an evil to Bernhardi. He separates these things, however, from the products of change that flow from German intelligence and that allow a people to survive and triumph in the modern world.

Even if the demands of industry create hardship for some important categories of the *Volk,* the hardship must be borne as a duty of a people always potentially at war. In particular, the industrial working class must be reconciled to their lot for the time being, in the expectation that a victorious Germany will acquire the space and other benefits that will allow the worker's lot to be relieved. All efforts must be bent toward obtaining for Germany "a share of the dominion of the world far beyond her current sphere of influence," by which Bernhardi means *both* sufficient farming land for an increasing population of small independent farmers *and* secure markets and sources of raw materials.[49] The latter are needed not only to bolster industry, but also (and more importantly) to provide the material basis of military strength. In other words, the circumstances of impending war, legitimated by a crude Darwinian argument, provide the framework within which Bernhardi attempts to integrate *Lebensraum* and *Weltpolitik*. Specifically, Bernhardi advocates that a victorious war be utilized to acquire settlement space primarily in eastern Europe. Expanded overseas colonies could also take settlers. But by and large Bernhardi argues for extra-European expansion on the grounds of a hyperbolic *Weltpolitik*: Germany should aim at economic autarky, with control of almost all of her markets and sources of raw materials.[50] Colonies are primarily instruments for creating autarky. As with Ratzel (and Bernhardi uses a great many of Ratzel's ideas), considerations of *Weltpolitik* are important, but they are integrated with *Lebensraum* as subordinate concerns.

Bernhardi was only one of many publicists on the *Lebensraum*-oriented right who attempted to combine elements of the major imperialist ideologies in the years immediately before the First World War. His efforts can be seen as part of the rather confused process of conservative political integration that resulted from the resurgence of Social Democracy and reformist liberalism during the period.[51] Bernhardi's ideological approach resembled that of the Pan-German leadership under Class. Bernhardi organized his presentation partly around an appeal to radical conservatives, emphasizing the protection of *Kleinbürger,* farmers, and artisans against the various forces arrayed before them. At the same time, by casting his radical conservatism in terms of *Lebensraum* imperialism and by employing a hierarchy of policy values that placed agrarian interests and the maintenance of social order at the top, Bernhardi could hope to attract the support of the agrarian elite. The addition of elements from *Weltpolitik* was clearly intended to appeal to the segment of public opinion that responded to economic imperialism. More important, the *Weltpolitik* elements were supposed to provide an ideological framework within which as large as possible an assortment of big-business interests could be accommodated—subject, of course, to the primacy accorded by *Lebensraum* to agriculture and an updated version of traditional peasant and artisanal society. The international threat to *Deutschtum* was the cement that was supposed to hold the sections of Bernhardi's ideological edifice together. The whole structure was supposed to serve as an ideological platform for an integrated conservative political movement that would attract the adherence of many different elite interests and the support of a majority of the public.

As it turned out, neither Bernhardi nor his radical-conservative associates were able to construct a truly effective composite imperialist ideology. For one thing, most *Weltpolitiker* were unwilling to accept either the priorities in national policy that Bernhardi put forward or their obvious consequences.[52] For another, the various segments of the German political and economic elite continued, certainly up to 1914, to be sufficiently fragmented in ideological outlook that rather blatant attempts at integration such as Bernhardi's could not convince their audiences to give up critical scrutiny of ideological elements of which they traditionally disapproved. Thus the leadership of the National Liberal party, although opposing the colonial reform movement of 1914 as part of a general policy of cooperation with the overtly conservative parties, could not bring itself to do so on the basis of a *Lebensraum*-centered argument.[53] The right-radicals' version of economic imperialism, with its overblown rhetoric and lack of a coherent theoretical basis, could hardly appeal to people who had thought for over twenty years about the future structure of Germany's overseas economic relations along lines determined almost exclusively by the assumptions embedded in *Weltpolitik*. Only the conditions created by the First World War could make Bernhardi's thinking appear credible to serious *Weltpolitiker*.

Other figures, far more capable and distinguished than Bernhardi, attempted at various times to construct an integrated imperialist ideology working from the *Weltpolitik* side. The most important of these were either academics such as Max Weber or publicists with strong academic connections and credentials like Friedrich Naumann and Paul Rohrbach. Where Bernhardi used the threat of war as the means of tying together the disparate elements of imperialist ideology, the *Weltpolitik*-style integrators (although they did not ignore the international threat) tended to emphasize *reform* as the unifying concept. That is, they represented an aggressive expansionary policy as either the means of accomplishing needed political and social reforms at home or as the necessary result of effective reform or (most often) both at the same time. "Reform" is a particularly appealing central motif around which to construct an aggregate ideology. Its definition, even in specific cases, can be quite vague, thus providing a means of apparently accommodating within a single program the interests of very different groups. The idea of reform as systematic political action to make things better has a certain appeal just in itself. On the other hand, the advocacy of reform implies a much more explicit commitment to action than many other possible ideological positions, which means that a reformist group has to attempt to deliver on its promises fairly quickly if it is to keep its credibility. Under these circumstances, reform groups often find it difficult to avoid fragmentation and failure; their focus on immediate programs of action makes the existence of differences in conceptions of "reform" in the minds of their adherents appear quickly and clearly. Problems experienced in the 1890s in attempting to establish political reform movements with largely domestic goals were probably among the reasons that people like Weber and Naumann turned to imperialism in connection with reform. They sought to use the ideological displacement that imperialism afforded to generate agreement with the domestic reformist aims they had previously advocated. Although some of them, especially Naumann, remained optimistic about the potential of a broad-gauged reformist imperialism to affect German politics and, through politics, the nature of German society, others, including Weber, quickly realized that imperialism could not perform the consensus-building functions that they had hoped it would. Weber, in particular, retreated from the attempt to create an integrated imperialist ideology and became instead, after about 1900, a fairly orthodox *Weltpolitiker*.[54]

Weber, Naumann, and many of the other academic imperialists of the 1890s and the turn of the century moved toward imperialism partly as a result of their participation in academic-dominated organizations that combined the idea of scientific social investigation with the intention of effecting social reform. The most important of these was the *Verein für Sozialpolitik* (VSP), a society formed by Gustav Schmoller and other economists in the 1870s to promote the discussion and investigation of the social question and to attempt to establish a consensus on its solution among the educated elite of Germany. Although Weber and Naumann belonged to other, more overtly political organizations as well, the members of those organizations also tended to evince the attitudes characteristic of the VSP: that the social problems created by economic change were susceptible to rational solution through the structuring of national policy around programs defined by social science; that such policies could be initiated if a consensus about their objectives could be created among the academic elite, which would then influence the national and state governments, the political parties, and the educated classes in general; and that most of the basis for action was already present in the broad agreement among academic social scientists about the nature of modern social problems.[55]

In fact, most of these assumptions were incorrect, as Weber eventually realized. The formation of policy around proposals derived from social science turned out to be a most difficult political task. On the whole, academic reformers vastly exaggerated their own influence, mistaking the desire of political leaders for legitimation through association with science for a real commitment to rational, scientifically based politics. Most of all, they overestimated the extent of existing consensus among social scientists themselves in the late nineteenth century. Economists, who were the mainstay of the VSP, split readily into warring groups over the policy implications of their research, even on the rare occasions on which they agreed about the actual nature of the questions with which they were dealing. Their divisions usually reflected the general lines of conflict in German politics as a whole, for example, on the question of the tariff.[56]

The need for a program that would cut across the political lines that divided academics was one of the reasons many *Sozialpolitiker* looked to imperialism as a major part of an effective reform movement in the 1890s. Weber, in particular, was probably encouraged by what he had seen as the apparent success of the early Pan-German League in bringing together the leaders of different political groups and economic interests around a program of national self-assertion and imperialism.[57] Even more important, however, was the role that imperialism was supposed to play in dealing with a problem that almost all of the academic social reformers recognized as the paramount obstacle to any kind of rational change: the fragmentation of German politics. The large number of competing interest groups, the chaotic structure of national government, the persistence of outmoded hierarchical conceptions of class, and the spread of ideologies such as Marxism, which emphasized class conflict, all of these made it immensely difficult to take more than a few steps in the direction of needed social reform.[58] The manifold problems of social disunity and lack of national political consensus had to be solved, at least in part, before effective reform could occur; manifest steps toward consensus, should they be seen to issue in significant improvements in German politics and society, would generate even more consensus once they were widely perceived. A program based around imperial expansion with a heavy dose of nationalist rhetoric thrown in might provide the necessary impetus.

This was the argument that Max Weber made in his most famous imperialist statement, his Freiburg inaugural address in 1895, which briefly became a kind of political manifesto for liberal, nationalist academic reformers.[59] Weber called for an aggressive, expansionary nationalism as the key feature of all German policy and politics. He laid down as the explicit criterion for desirable national policy neither morality nor consonance with political theory but rather the needs of the German nation—which he defined largely in terms of military security and the economic goals of *Weltpolitik*. These needs could be met only when all classes, parties, interest groups, and political organizations identified themselves fully with the nation's interests. Domestic social and political reforms could also be achieved through such consensus. More important, internal reform, or at least a start in that direction, was necessary to create the consensus needed for the achievement of external goals. Aggressive imperialism was thus the reciprocal of domestic reform. Weber clearly understood the tautological nature of this argument.[60] What he was trying to do was to use it to create the affective, psychological basis for overcoming fragmentation. Weber hoped that the kinds of shared emotions that could be coordinated through imperialist politics could be directed to domestic political purposes under the guidance of the intellectual elite.

The specific proposals that Weber made both for liberal political reform and for imperial policy were actually neither very extensive nor very original. Weber's main "reform" objective was the clear assignment of political responsibility to specific institutions and state officials who would be answerable to the Reichstag as a representative parliamentary body. By "imperialism," Weber essentially meant *Weltpolitik*: the securing of markets, raw materials, and investment areas by political action and the assertion, through the building and exercise of naval power, of Germany's coequality with Britain in the world as well as her "right" to an equal share of the world's economic resources. Both Weber's liberalism and his imperialism were formulated in a very broad way, with something for everybody (except the objects of Weber's most intense dislike: the Junkers and the Hohenzollerns).[61]

Because of the political aims of his imperialism and probably also because of his experience with the Pan-German League, Weber attached ideological elements associated with *Lebensraum* to his relatively orthodox *Weltpolitik*. He did *not* advocate overseas settlement colonialism. His use of the *Lebensraum* approach can be seen instead in the extreme violence and bellicosity of his imperialist pronouncements in the mid-1890s and in his advocacy of internal colonization in eastern Germany. Weber had undertaken a classic study of East Elbian agriculture and migration in the early 1890s. His version of internal colonization was similar to Sering's in some ways, except that Weber took a radically anti-Junker line on land expropriation and, unlike Sering, believed small-scale German farming in the east would be economically unsuccessful in the foreseeable future. The reasons for supporting it were political, not economic: to reduce Junker power, to create national consensus behind a kind of frontier settlement policy, and to reverse the tide of polonization in the east.[62] As we shall see, during the First World War Weber became an opponent of massive annexations in eastern Europe, not because he was opposed to the idea of peasant settlement but because he approached imperialist questions mainly from the standpoint of *Weltpolitik*—in which such settlement could play, at most, a minor role.

The importance and effects of Weber's advocacy of imperialism in the 1890s have been somewhat exaggerated by Wolfgang Mommsen, among others.[63] The claim that Weber's imperialist ideas were original will not stand the test of comparison with other pronouncements in the German imperialist tradition. What he attempted to do was to *combine* already-existing elements of imperialist ideology into a single package; even in this, he had been preceded (in a sense) by the Pan-Germans. Weber made his attempt at ideological integration in a context legitimated by social science and directed toward social reform, but there is little evidence that his version of imperialism had very much long-lasting influence on the government, the parties, or the majority of imperialists. Weber himself appears to have realized this; he tended to back away from imperialist politics from the late 1890s onward. On the other hand, Mommsen rightly points out that Weber's inaugural address did strongly influence a number of other politically minded intellectuals who maintained the effort to create a reformist imperialism with considerably greater perseverance than Weber himself did. Of these, the most important was Friedrich Naumann.

Naumann, a theologian who had turned to social questions and thence to politics and journalism in the late 1880s, advanced a broad program of liberal and humanitarian reform based largely on the concept of reconciliation among social classes. In the various organizations with which he was associated during his long career—the Evangelical Socialists, the VSP, the left-liberal parties—he advocated the adoption of highly eclectic ideologies that would facilitate social reconciliation. In his most famous political tract, *Demokratie und Kaisertum* (1900), for example, Naumann attempted to reconcile radical democracy with the authoritarian principles of monarchical government.[64] In Weber's concept of imperialism in the mid-1890s, Naumann thought he perceived an ideal instrument of political integration. For several years thereafter, Naumann heavily emphasized imperial questions in his reformist periodical *Die Hilfe*.[65] Although during the First World War Naumann would attain notoriety as an advocate of central European economic integration and as an opponent of massive direct territorial annexations by Germany, much of his prewar effort in imperialist politics was directed toward integrating *Weltpolitik* with emigrationist colonialism and *Lebensraum* within a general framework of political reform.

Like most of Naumann's other projects, his imperialism was a practical failure.[66] Although it attracted attention among academics and liberal intellectuals, it could not be translated into political success for Naumann or for any of the political groups in which he was influential. He was not a very good political organizer, and he was mistrusted by professional politicians of all stripes outside the narrow range of reformist-progressives— by far the weakest group in Wilhelmian politics. Nor could Naumann overcome his greatest deficiency: his inability to direct his political message to any group other than the educated upper middle class. Naumann did not even produce a comprehensive imperialist statement, although he strongly influenced someone who did—the journalist Paul Rohrbach. We shall examine Rohrbach's imperialism at some length here both as an illustration of the kind of integrative ideological approach taken by Naumann, Weber, and a host of others and because Rohrbach was probably the most popular German imperialist writer of the first quarter of the twentieth century. His writings, although they had only limited practical effect before 1914, became an important part of the corpus of imperialist thinking in the 1920s and 1930s.

We have already met Rohrbach on several occasions.[67] His books are often cited by modern historians of German imperialism, which is perhaps one of the reasons that historians tend to exaggerate the unity of German imperialist ideology.[68] Rohrbach, like Naumann, consciously attempted to bridge the gaps in German imperialism and to create an integrated ideology from the elements of *Weltpolitik* and *Lebensraum.*

Born a Russian subject of German extraction, Rohrbach moved to Germany to pursue (unsuccessfully) an academic career in theology. He came under Naumann's influence in the 1890s. Naumann, among other things, encouraged him to take up journalism, in which he made a name for himself as the popularizer of the Baghdad Railway as an imperial issue in the full spirit of *Weltpolitik.* This led to Rohrbach's appointment as a government settlement commissioner in Southwest Africa, where he took part in the suppression of the Herero rebellion and became a staunch supporter of settler interests. When Rohrbach went back to journalism in 1905 (partly with Naumann's assistance), he had developed an eclectic view of Germany's imperial destiny based partly on his own experience and partly on Naumann's idea of imperialism as a means of social reconciliation.[69] He quickly became one of Germany's most prominent journalists.

In his most comprehensive ideological statement, his 1912 book *Der deutsche Gedanke in der Welt,* Rohrbach begins by establishing a legitimating connection to the German academic tradition: he posits as the fundamental tension in the modern world the conflict between materialism and idealism, a tension to which he refers throughout the book but does not describe consistently.[70] He comes down, in consonance with the conventions of turn-of-the-century German academia, on the side of idealism. Any discussion of Germany's present and future must concern the German Idea, an ethical concept that is supposedly the central concern of the book. In fact, Rohrbach can now take practically any position he wishes and defend it by calling it part of the German Idea—which turns out to be a compilation of bits and pieces taken from preexisting imperialist ideologies and academic social criticism. In this way, Rohrbach can employ conventionally contradictory ideas and imply that there is an underlyiing consistency among them. He can also use overtly materialistic arguments, yet claim that he shuns materialism with its connotations of change, revolution, and modernity.

Rohrbach claims that the government and most of the political parties and interest groups have failed to recognize the overwhelming importance of the German Idea. It is the historical duty of the Germans, as a virtuous people who have developed an important and distinctive culture, to put their cultural stamp on the world through the impress of the German Idea. But such a stamp can only be affixed by a country with power, and a country can only have power if it expands its boundaries in an economic and military sense as well as in a cultural one. "The German Idea can thrive and expand if its material bases—that is, the number of Germans, the economic welfare of Germany, the mass and extent of world-economic relationships serviceable to German economic life—are continually extended."[71] In the end, Rohrbach gets back rather quickly to the material factors that he has, pro forma, abjured at the start. Unlike Weber, both Naumann and Rohrbach claim that imperialism is based on broadly conceived ethical considerations, but in Rohrbach's work these are extremely transparent.

When Rohrbach writes of the "material bases" of the expanding German Idea, he means largely what the *Weltpolitiker* did: a widening cooperative marketing and investment area that will protect and be dominated by the German industrial economy. He throws in, however, the standard clichés of *Lebensraum*: not only must the number of Germans grow, but they must also maintain virtues that are characteristically German. In this way, Rohrbach attempts to create an ideological basis for the amalgamation of *Lebensraum* and *Weltpolitik*.[72]

To cement the connection, Rohrbach turns to the external threat of England. The future of the German Idea depends, he says, on maintaining German strength and unity (in all senses), for the English will not voluntarily allow a coequal in the world.[73] Rohrbach's analysis of Germany's relations with England is also recognizably taken from *Weltpolitik*: that is, Germany does not aspire to replace Britain as the dominant nation, but she wants Britain to acknowledge her equality in power and cultural impress—and in a substantial way. Although Rohrbach does not fully spell out what that way is, enough clues are given so that the *Weltpolitiker* will read it as a division of areas of economic dominance throughout the world, an agreement to share control of the balance of power, and an alliance. The English, he argues, do not want to do this. Therefore they must be faced with a strong united Germany that will be in a position to tell them either to agree or to fight. Elsewhere, Rohrbach gives a somewhat broader statement of the risk theory attributed to Tirpitz: Germany must be militarily strong enough, on land and especially on sea, that the British will make the correct decision when Rohrbach's alternatives are posed to them. Rohrbach, in fact, contradicts himself here, although the contradiction is not immediately obvious. On the one hand, Germany is supposed to be strong enough that she can deal with Britain whichever way the latter goes—which implies military superiority. On the other hand, Rohrbach indicates elsewhere, in keeping with the *Weltpolitiker*'s version of the risk theory, that Germany should not aim at military superiority or necessarily even parity, but only enough power to make the alternative of war a less satisfactory one to the British than recognizing Germany's importance. Rohrbach waxes indignant at one point about claims in the British press that Germany is seeking total dominance, yet his own statements in other sections can logically imply nothing else.[74]

Rohrbach summarizes the international aspect of his argument with the statement that "the fate of Germany is England," and he organizes the rest of his book very loosely around the question of whether or not Germany will be able to maintain itself against Britain.[75] The formal basis of his criticism of things that he does not like about German society is the extent to which they detract from Germany's ability to stand up to Britain, and his main justification for reform is that it will allow Germany to compete better with Britain. Rohrbach has thus managed to cover most of the necessary preliminary ideological bases; he has let the *Weltpolitiker* know that, despite some criticism, he is essentially one of them; he has used most of the *Lebensraum* vocabulary and some *Lebensraum* ideas; he has introduced a connection to academic social reform; and he has established an external threat as the supposed motive for national integration.

Rohrbach then proceeds to explain why Germany is not coming up to scratch in its competition with England. First, because of emigration, Germany has permanently lost 12 to 15 million of its people to America.[76] More important is the threat to *Deutschtum* posed by internal disunity in Germany. Here is the main theme of Rohrbach's politics: social and political fragmentation and what to do about it. Overcoming fragmentation should be the major aim of German policy. Disunity includes religious and regional division, but it also encompasses the selfish, narrow class interests of various social strata, including the industrial and agrarian elites, the self-indulgent bourgeoisie, and the working class. The class system is a major defect of German society. It can, however, be overcome by the development of *Gemeinschaftsgefühl* among the German people as a whole, by the impressment on them of a National Idea to which they can feel an emotional attchment.[77] He contends simultaneously that the lack of common national feeling is the result of social disunity and that the way to reduce disunity is to increase national feeling.

Thus, according to Rohrbach, the external threat of Britain can be used to promote unity. The English, he maintains, are powerful because they possess a highly developed national feeling shared by all classes. It is not entirely clear to what Rohrbach is referring, but he seems to be thinking of English feelings of personal superiority over other peoples, a constant source of irritation and envy to a great many Germans. He wants to see the same thing in Germans and believes that colonies could be useful in developing it. In the colonies, Germans could acquire the habit of mastering "inferior" peoples (for those peoples' own good, of course). This would put the petty differences between groups in Germany into perspective and create an attitudinal basis for common action. Rohrbach was, in fact, a violent racist—a factor that must be taken into account when considering the liberal or democratic elements of his thinking. His colonial "democracy" was actually an equality among members of a master race.[78]

Among the many points that Rohrbach makes, we should note particularly his continual return to the economic imperialism of *Weltpolitik* as the general framework for policy, his insistence on developing an ethic of group feeling and self-sacrifice among the nonelite segments of the population as well as a sense of responsibility among Germany's leaders, and his portrayal of Germany's overseas colonies as a means of attaining both economic and noneconomic goals. *Weltpolitik* and *Lebensraum* could be reconciled by emphasizing *Weltpolitik* in Germany's noncolonial foreign relations and *Lebensraum* in her actual existing colonies. Thus in the colonies, European settlement is to be encouraged wherever physically possible—but *not* because of population pressure.[79] Rohrbach admits that emigration is no longer a problem. Indeed Germany has become an importer of labor, which has increased the problems of internal disunity. A reduction of the rate of population increase in Germany, if it occurred, would become a major source of difficulty because it would make the other forms of expansion impossible. In other words, Rohrbach has implicitly recognized the logical bankruptcy of migrationism and has exactly reversed its traditional priorities: rather than population expansion justifying overseas colonial expansion, projected overseas expansion justifies efforts to increase population.

Rohrbach defends white settlement colonialism and the absolute local priority of settlers' interests in two ways. First, he argues that white colonies are economically more valuable to Germany than are other colonies, on the basis of British experience and his own inveterate racism: "A Canadian or Australian signifies economically forty times as much as a Hindu, and yet how far the countries of the negroes in Africa are from the powers of production and consumption even of India!"[80] Economic rationality dictates that wherever white enterprise is possible in Africa, it be encouraged at the expense of native African economic acivity.

Rohrbach's second justification for settler priority comes straight from the tradition of migrationist colonialism: it is in Africa, in the frontier existence and constant struggles of settler life, that the social and personal characteristics needed for Germany's greater world struggle will be nurtured. According to him, the new frontier personality as revealed so far is not noted for "fineness of culture" or for a liberal spirit in dealing with indigenous peoples, but these deficiencies will eventually be made up. Frontier life in the colonies will develop the individual self-reliance that lies at the heart of any true community: each member, acting as an individual, is bound by the necessities of the frontier condition to assist his neighbors and to sympathize with their problems. *Lebensraum* in the colonies thus will serve as a foundation for social reform that will eventually spread back to Germany.[81]

In the last analysis, Rohrbach failed as Naumann had done. Naumann, whose aim encompassed the creation of a new popular ideology and a new national political movement, was almost bound to fail without the backing of highly organized political structures. Rohrbach's aims were more modest: to use his journalistic popularity to make a political career for himself so that he would be accepted in the inner councils of government and could influence policy. In fact, however, although some of his books sold well and were widely discussed, he seems not to have had anything like the impact on the government or the parties that he wanted. Some of his letters to high officials before World War I are almost pathetic in their ingratiating tone, and they appear to have been ignored, except for polite acknowlegements.[82] During the First World War, he volunteered his services to the government as a publicist and a go-between with Russian minority groups. Here again, although the wartime situation led officials and politicians to take him more seriously, his overall importance was not great.[83]

The failures of Naumann and Rohrbach can be attributed to a number of causes, some of which can be explained in terms of the general framework of this study. Their attempts to created imperialist ideologies with broad-ranging appeal foundered on the fact that the divisions between the individual ideologies that they tried to link were too well known to be papered across without a good deal more preparation than they were able to undertake. *Weltpolitiker,* for example, could appreciate the general scheme of Rohrbach's imperialism, but they could not accept his espousal of the settler position on colonial policy. Contradictions are an inherent part of ideologies, but they must not be *perceived* as contradictions within the framework of current political thought; the major contradictions in Rohrbach's and Naumann's approaches lay right at the points of known conflict between familiar, antithetical imperialist views. Neither Rohrbach nor Naumann, to do them credit, was able to bring himself to employ the full range of devices available for reconciling divergent ideological elements—such as the overt anti-semitism to which the radical right increasingly turned. But even radical nationalists such as Bernhardi and Heinrich Class had little more success before 1914 in creating a really effective imperialist ideology out of the different strains of German imperialism.

An even more important reason for the failure of these and other attempts at ideological integration in German imperialism before 1914 was that they were not, for the most part, tied to the activities of a political organization large enough, well enough structured and led, or sufficiently acquainted with the techniques of modern mass propaganda to make an aggregation of contradictory ideological elements work as part of a single program. Such organizations were appearing, especially on the radical right, in the years just prior to the outbreak of the war. If Dankwart Guratzsch is correct, the prototype was the informal network of institutions, individuals, and journalistic media that Alfred Hugenberg was constructing around an ideology that included *Lebensraum.*[84] But the notion that ideological innovation must be matched by innovations in technique and organization to create even partial consensus in a modern political system was only in its infancy in Germany in 1914. Postwar groups, especially the National Socialists, were more successful at creating and selling an integrated imperialist ideology partly because they possessed the technical means of presenting it without revealing its internal contradictions. Another reason that imperialist ideological integration was easier and more rewarding for the Nazis than it had been for Rohrbach, Naumann, and Bernhardi was that the Nazis could take advantage of radically altered political and ideological conditions created by World War I. We shall turn to these next.

CHAPTER EIGHT

The First World War

The relationship between pre-1914 imperialism and German policy during the First World War has been one of the main topics of research and dispute in German history at least since the work of Fritz Fischer in the 1950s and 1960s. The nature of the questions asked and the sides to the controversies associated with those questions have varied somewhat, reflecting the constant change that has occurred in historians' approaches to the Wilhelmian period. The arguments in the 1960s over Fischer's work revolved around the question of continuity. Did German war-aims policy after 1914 manifest a continuity with prewar German imperialism, as Fischer argued, or was it a short-term response to the peculiar conditions of total war?[1] More recently, attention has been focused on the relationship between expansionist policy in wartime and the structure of German politics. To what extent was German war-aims imperialism a reflection of the economic needs of elite groups, particularly the directors of heavy industry? To what extent was it a product of the consolidation of the various German elite classes to prevent democratization, the triumph of socialism, and revolution?[2] Common to almost all approaches has been the question of the responsibility of imperialism, German imperialism in particular, for the outbreak of the war.

The last question does not directly concern us here, but the others touch on matters of great importance to this study: the problems of ideological continuity and development from the prewar period down to the Nazi era. That is to say, we must investigate not only the aspects of prewar imperialist thought and action that manifested themselves in recognizably similar form between 1914 and 1918, but also the ways in which German imperialist ideology changed during the war and the factors that caused the changes. We must also concern ourselves with the effects that changes in the structure of politics had on imperialism, and vice versa. The task is complicated by the fact that, although most modern students of German imperialism have assumed an underlying unity in thought and intention among imperialists, we have developed thus far a picture of an ideologically dichotomous imperialism. Indeed, one of the main elements of continuity that we shall examine between prewar imperialism and war aims after 1914 is the persistence of the *differences* between *Weltpolitiker* and *Lebensraum* imperialists. Among other things, we shall recast the pre-Fischer distinction between the annexationist and antiannexationist war-aims positions into the terms of the continuous split in imperialist ideology presented in the earlier chapters: annexationists advocated war aims developed in large parts from *Lebensraum,* so-called antiannexationists were in favor, not of abjuring territorial gains, but of defining them in the context of *Weltpolitik.*[3] Yet important steps were taken during the war toward the creation of an integrated imperialist ideology—steps taken mainly from the *Lebensraum* side in consequence of important alterations in the structure and conduct of German politics in wartime and of the massive shocks the war administered to German society. These, too, must be explained in the terms of the overall study.

Before we proceed to the specific careers of the imperialist ideologies in wartime, it would be useful to say a few words in general about the effects of the war, and also of its loss by Germany, on the political environment in which the ideologies operated. In the first place, the circumstances of all-out war had the effect in practically all the major participant countries of making the specific subject matter of imperialist ideologies seem more vital and real to the average citizen than had been the case before. At the same time, these circumstances dissolved, temporarily at least, many of the logical and common-sense restraints on the efficacy of imperialism as a builder of consensus that had been present in popular political culture before the war.[4] Thus, for example, extreme autarkic versions of economic imperialism that had gained only limited currency before the war seemed more plausible under circumstances of blockade, shortages, and rationing. The ideal of complete autarky as a peacetime condition to be attained through a successful war was, in fact, no more practical after 1914 than it had been before, but it seemed to be. That imperialist ideas tended to be accepted more uncritically during wartime than before was due partly to the stress produced among the European populations by very real threats to their national and personal survival. It was also, however, partly the result of increasingly well-organized propaganda operations by governments seeking to maintain social control and by national political organizations attempting to use the psychological conditions created by the war to elicit consensus. Both the need to orchestrate public opinion and the opportunities that the war presented for doing so encouraged—in Germany as elsewhere—major changes in the conduct of public political appeals and a wholesale modernization of propaganda techniques.[5] The war, in other words, produced in Germany both a mental climate and some of the technical means required to make large-scale composite ideologies, including *Lebensraum, Weltpolitik,* and hybrids of the two, more effective means of support aggregation, despite the inherent inconsistencies that these ideolo-

gies contained. The effectiveness of imperialist ideologies in particular
was enhanced by the war because they focused overtly on the factors
uppermost in people's minds in wartime: power, security, and the relationships between international conflict, national prosperity, and individual survival.

In the second place, although the onset of peace in most countries
might have been expected to "normalize" the national mental climate if
not turn back the advances that had been made in the techniques of
consensus creation, this was not the case in defeated Germany. Defeat
meant that the German government did not have to try to make long-
range policy for newly acquired territories and thus endure the hard
confrontations with reality that ultimately weakened imperialism as a
political force in Britain and France. (The problems experienced merely
in making policy for occupied lands in 1918 make it clear that a German
victory would have created even more difficulties.) Furthermore, the circumstances of defeat, the Army's "stab-in-the-back" theory, the continuance of the Allied blockade after the Armistice, the mere fact of losing
after four years of propaganda devoted to what would happen after the
inevitable victory—all contributed to a widespread feeling that the war
had not, in fact, ended but had rather entered a dormant stage to Germany's present disadvantage. The encouragement of this attitude was, of
course, a major aim of a great many postwar nationalist political organizations, not only because their leaders believed it to be correct, but also
because it helped to maintain the sort of mental climate in which extensive, inconsistent, aggregate political ideologies might continue to be effective at consensus building. Although in reality the war completed the
process of destroying the traditional preindustrial society that lay at the
heart of the *Lebensraum* imperialists' vision, the political circumstances
of the war and of its loss made *Lebensraum* potentially more effective
than ever as a political entity—*if* it could be combined convincingly with
elements generally associated with *Weltpolitik*.

We must pass now from these generalities to the actual histories of the
German imperialist ideologies in wartime. We shall start with *Weltpolitik*,
which constituted the intellectual framework for government war-aims
planning during the first years of the war and which rapidly also became
part of the ideological program of a liberal-reformist political bloc that,
although largely defeated during the war, reemerged during the Weimar
Republic.

Weltpolitik and War Aims

The continuity that Fischer emphasizes between prewar German foreign
policy and imperialist thinking, on the one hand, and official war-aims
planning, on the other hand, resided largely in *Weltpolitik*. The first
tentative draft of a war-aims position produced by Chancellor von Bethmann Hollweg's office after the outbreak of hostilities in 1914 was the

famous "September Program." Fischer describes this program as "the essential basis of Germany's war aims right up to the end of the war"; it contained an admirable summary of the practical aims of *Weltpolitik* in the immediate prewar years.[6] To these aims were added a number of specific items reflecting particular military and heavy-industrial interests. Conspicuously absent was any substantial reference to the traditional central concerns of *Lebensraum:* colonial expansion for purposes of settlement, eastward expansion of Germany's borders to accommodate German peasant farms, expansion as a limiting response to economic change.

A key feature of the September Program, as it was of practically all efforts by the Chancery and Foreign Office to produce a general war-aims plan, was the central European economic union—a concept that gained a popular nickname, *Mitteleuropa,* when a relatively restrained version of it was publicized by Friedrich Naumann in his famous book with that title in 1915.[7] Naumann's proposals and most of the presentations of the *Mitteleuropa* idea *emanating from government offices* during the first years of the war—including the September Program—followed the same general lines as economic imperialist formulations of the idea back to the time of List.[8] The economic union would rest on a grand division of labor in which Germany would act as the industrial center, technological innovator, and source of capital and overall direction. Each of the peripheral component regions would specialize in a particular range of production, especially of primary and agricultural goods; at the same time, each would act as a secure investment area for German capital. The union would protect its members from excessive competition and permit capital to be invested more economically and rationally; fear that investments would be taken over by foreign rivals would be eliminated. Although Germany would be the main obvious beneficiary of such a system, most of its proponents argued that it would have manifold positive advantages for its other members as well, especially Austria-Hungary. *Mitteleuropa* was represented in its broadest terms both before and during the war by Walther Rathenau as a necessary concomitant to the next stage of capitalist economic development—a structure that would protect a major sector of the world's economy against the shocks of international business fluctuations and provide a framework within which the system of rational economic management that was the hallmark of advanced corporate capitalism could be extended to the national and regional economies.[9] The adherence of countries such as the Netherlands and perhaps France to the union would also bring in their colonies, which would be vital adjuncts to the whole scheme.

The different *Weltpolitik*-style versions of *Mitteleuropa* varied with respect to the proposed composition of the economic union. The September Program, drawn up in the glow of Germany's first offensive and before the consequences of the Marne had become clear, cast *Mitteleuropa*'s net broadly: the union was to include Germany, France, Belgium, Holland, Denmark, Austria-Hungary, a Poland detached from Russia, and possibly Italy, Sweden, and Norway.[10] Although the members were to be theoretically equal, Germany was, in fact, to dominate the union politically. Some of the members would be forced to join as a result of the war; the others would have no alternative to joining except economic suicide once the central apparatus of the union was constructed. Naumann, on the other hand, writing for public consumption some months later, after quick victory had become an illusion, concentrated on what had always been the minimal core of the projected union: the creation of a common market between Germany and Austria-Hungary, with which countries immediately adjacent to the members would voluntarily seek to associate themselves.[11] Except for the presumed detachment of Poland and other territories from Russia, the September Program left eastern war aims for future discussion. However, most official and unofficial formulations of the *Weltpolitik* version of *Mitteleuropa* called explicitly for the inclusion of substantial areas of the Russian Empire.[12]

Practically nothing in the official versions of *Mitteleuropa* at the start of the war made any notable provision for the protection of the the preindustrial social order. This was a crucial distinction that must be grasped between the *Weltpolitik*-type *Mitteleuropa* of the September Program, the official planning documents, and the Naumann scheme, on the one hand, and the proposals for central European union put forward by the Pan-German League and the plethora of radical-conservative nationalist war-aims commentators, on the other hand. The logical consequence of the *Weltpolitik* version of *Mitteleuropa* was the economic annihilation of the Junkers. The economic union would be constructed to promote the exchange of German manufactured products for foreign primary and agricultural goods, and it could only work if large-scale German grain agriculture were deprived of its protection. Large landowners and small farmers in Germany could only survive in such a system if they were able to specialize in particular items that foreign competitors could not produce as cheaply and that could find markets in adjacent German cities. Even with the substantial improvements that were taking place in the German intensive-agriculture sector, clearly a large part of German agriculture—including the Junker part—would have to be sacrificed. When Rechenberg, the former colonial governor, attempted to defend the central European economic union in 1917, he was not able to disguise this fundamental consequence behind appeals to the greater aggregate good that the union would do for the German economy as a whole and to the desirability of competition as an encouragement to technological modernization in agriculture.[13] Some *Weltpolitiker,* including Rechenberg, perceived the necessary results of *Mitteleuropa* for German agriculture with regret; others anticipated the results with equanimity or even a certain amount of glee because of the irreparable damage that would be done to the Junkers.[14]

The absence of protection for preindustrial classes from the official *Weltpolitik* version of *Mitteleuropa* before 1917 does not mean that the idea was without a social imperialist aspect. Many of its most important proponents, inside and outside the government, continued to see the central European union both as a means of heading off future economic crises that might lead to revolution and as the kind of policy that would keep the leadership of the political reform movement in Germany in the hands of moderate liberals with government connections—and out of the hands of the radicals and socialists.[15] *Weltpolitik,* as a comprehensive imperialist political ideology, had always had the same general social imperialist characteristics. These had been strongly accentuated in the writings of reformers such as Weber and Naumann before the war and were now placed by them in a wartime context.

Mitteleuropa was not the only element of the *Weltpolitikers'* view of war aims, although it was probably the most important one. In the September Program and in the surviving documentation on later official war-aims planning, *Mittelafrika* was also strongly featured. Again, versions of *Mittelafrika* varied, depending on the government department or organization that was drawing up its shopping list for overseas acquisitions. On the whole, conceptions of *Mittelafrika* formulated within the government tended to become more grandiose as the war went on. During the last year-and-a-half of the war, most of the advocates of extensive African acquisition were calling for essentially the same thing: practically all of the continent from the Sahara down to South Africa, with the addition of Morocco and some sort of control over the Suez Canal. This had been what the Colonial Society and the Pan-German League had demanded from 1914 on.[16] Toward the beginning of the war, however, most intra-government conceptions of *Mittelafrika* were considerably more modest and more closely tied to analyses of the economic utility of additional colonial possessions—utility as assessed in terms of the framework of *Weltpolitik.*

The views of *Mittelafrika* contained in early Colonial Office planning documents and in Wilhelm Solf's correspondence were essentially the same as those propounded in *Weltpolitik* circles between 1911 and 1914: a large swath of land across central Africa connecting most of the existing German African colonies and centering around a German-controlled Congo.[17] To this central core, various other territories could be added as the fortunes of war and negotiation and as the interests of the navy, investment banks, and similar groups dictated. The mere acquisition of territory for its own sake was generally eschewed before 1917. Although Solf ruled out exchanges of territory, he did not insist on depriving France and Britain of *all* their colonies.[18] Despite the extent of territorial and economic gains for Germany incorporated within the government's conception of *Mittelafrika,* the scheme was thus not originally limitless. The loss of this sense of limitation in colonial war-aims planning, which ironically occurred after most of Germany's actual colonies had been seized, was connected to a general movement in government policymaking away from *Weltpolitik* during the latter stages of the war.

Mitteleuropa and *Mittelafrika* did not exhaust the war aims actively

propounded within the context of *Weltpolitik.* The question of annexing
territories bordering on Germany to east and west, especially defensible
regions in the former and industrial and mining areas in the latter, was
thoroughly discussed—in large part because of pressure from the military
and the various industrial organizations.[19] Serious disputes arose between
government departments over the nature of gains to be insisted on in
peace negotiations, for example, between the Navy and the Colonial
Office over which islands in the Atlantic, Pacific, and Indian Ocean to
demand as naval bases.[20] On the whole, however, within the policymaking realms of the government before 1917, the language and the intellectual framework of *Weltpolitik* were employed almost universally in war-
aims discussions. Largely absent from serious consideration were notions
of territorial expansion in eastern Europe for purposes of peasant settlement and of the acquisition of settlement colonies abroad.

The overwhelming influence of the *Weltpolitik* ideology can be seen not
only in planning for *what* would be acquired by Germany as a result of a
victorious war, but also about *how* it would be acquired. In wartime as in
peacetime, the fixation of the *Weltpolitiker* on the role of Britain in
international affairs and in Germany's future was highly apparent, and it
had a great deal to do with the positions taken by most official *Weltpolitiker* on one of the most important policy issues of the war: the necessity
or desirability of a negotiated peace.

Weltpolitiker such as Solf and Kühlmann, like Bethmann Hollweg himself, saw the eventual outcome of the war not as total world domination
by Germany but rather as the final establishment of an intercontinental
sphere of influence for Germany resting on *Mitteleuropa* and
Mittelafrika—an idea held over from pre-war *Weltpolitik.* Other such
areas would also exist, one "belonging" to the United States, one to
Russia (unless Russia were successfully dismembered as Rohrbach,
among others, advocated), and one to Great Britain—the still-extensive
remnants of her empire. Because most analysts within the Foreign Office
and Chancery believed it unlikely that Britain could be driven totally to
her knees the way France and Russia might be, it was clear that the
establishment of the German sphere of influence would have to result
from negotiations primarily with Britain.[21] Such negotiations would require a willingness by Germany and Britain to tolerate each other as
imperial powers, indeed, to cooperate with one another after the peace in
much the same way that the *Weltpolitiker* had anticipated before the
outbreak of hostilities.

France and Russia might be treated in different ways, depending on the
military situation; the possibility of negotiating with them was frequently
considered, especially during periods in which the war was going badly
for them. Occupied areas like Belgium and small neutrals such as Holland
would be treated as it appeared to be convenient for Germany. But
negotiation with Britain was a sine qua non. Britain was to be forced to
acknowledge German equality and guarantee German security in much

the same way that she was supposed to have done before the war, once Germany had displayed to Britain her own best interests.[22] The British would lose a few colonies and their naval preponderance, but they might even acquire some benefit from the settlement because their economic security would probably not be seriously impaired, their empire would be left essentially intact, and they might be able to rely on German support against the growing economic threat of the United States in the future. Now that war had demonstrated to the British upper classes the need to align with Germany, Britain would eventually come to the negotiating table. Germany had, however, to refrain from too-outrageous public demands for war booty lest the convinced Germanophobes in Britain (such as Winston Churchill) rally public opinion against a negotiated peace.[23]

As they had done before the war, the *Weltpolitiker* took a highly unrealistic view of British politics and social structure, one that was by 1914–18, in essence, built into their ideology. No matter how tough-minded they tried to be toward Britain and no matter how genuine their animus toward the country they considered to be their country's betrayer, the outlines of the traditional *Weltpolitik* view of Britain still held firm under the stress of war. Even Bethmann Hollweg—who in following his policy of hewing to the diagonal in politics, never fully identified with the *Weltpolitiker* surrounding him and, in 1915, seriously considered seeking a separate peace with Russia to prosecute the war in the west more vigorously—largely conceived of policy toward Britain within the framework of the *Weltpolitikers'* illusions about how the British governing class would react to pressure from Germany.[24] Neither he nor most *Weltpolitiker* understood until quite late that the British simply would not accept German "equality" in the world on the terms of *Weltpolitik,* terms that involved so many advantages for Germany that "equality" could easily be interpreted from the British point of view as "superiority." The British would not accept such terms, at any rate, without being much more severely hurt by the war than they had been by 1917. Although the *Weltpolitiker* did not wholly realize it, this meant that the wartime policies conceived in terms of *Weltpolitik* were doomed to failure. The very nature of the peace conditions that *Weltpolitik* led the government to demand made it next to impossible to bring about peace by the means (negotiation with Britain) that most *Weltpolitiker* favored.

There was, of course, a great deal more to the process of making war-aims policy between 1914 and 1917 than has been discussed here. There were severe disputes between individuals and departments in the government. Even among people whose general conceptions of imperial and war-aims policy fit comfortably into the framework of *Weltpolitik,* there were great differences with respect to the immediate ends of policy and the ways to bring about a successful end to the war. These differences and the evolution of the war-aims positions of the various government departments have been ably described by Fischer and others.[25] The point to be made is that official war-aims discussions up to 1917, and to a considerable extent thereafter, strongly reflected a continuity with the prewar *Weltpolitik* ideology as a framework for analysis and planning. On the other hand, it must also be recognized that *Weltpolitik* was not limited to official circles any more than it had been before the war, that not all government officials accepted its dictates in framing policy positions, and that there existed a strong and growing tendency in the nonadministrative sphere of German politics to advance war-aims positions based, not on *Weltpolitik,* but on an expanded conception of *Lebensraum.* Before considering *Weltpolitik* outside the inner realms of government, it is first necessary to turn to *Lebensraum.*

Lebensraum at War

Despite its questionable internal logic and the weak connections of its formal elements to external social reality, *Lebensraum* imperialism had reached the beginning of the First World War as a still-viable political ideology. Its constituent ideas and images still captured the attentions of people with a grudge against the direction of socioeconomic change, thereby offering means of aggregating such people's support and mobilizing them for political action. This was significant because of the attempts of business and agrarian-interest groups and the center-right parties to broaden their electoral stength by appealing to the new general peasant and *Mittelstand* organizations. The *Bund der Industrieller* and the *Hansa-bund* had made substantial progress, using a moderate liberal approach, toward attracting the organized *Mittelstand.* One of the responses of the CDI, the Cartel of the Productive Classes, and the conservative parties as they groped toward coalescence was to emphasize the appropriate parts of *Lebensraum:* the need to protect the peasantry and artisanal classes through settlement colonialism and inner colonization.[26] This use of *Lebensraum* was already characteristic of radical conservative groups such as the Pan-Germans, which claimed to protect "little people" against the forces of change but which were coming under the control of elite interests as represented by the CDI and the conservative parties.[27] We saw in Chapter Five the ways in which *Lebensraum* could be adapted for these purposes and in Chapter Seven how, partly through the addition of economic imperialist elements strongly featured in *Weltpolitik,* it could be rendered non-threatening to both big business and big agriculture.

But *Lebensraum* was not simply an ideology of integration between part of the German political and economic elite, on the one hand, and a segment of conservative middle and lower middle-class opinion on the other. It also became an ideology of integration among elements of the elite itself—especially those elements that stood to the right on questions of political reform. That is to say, it became part of a political program, espousal of which put the leadership of a large segment of German industry, big Prussian agriculture, and a number of parties, politicians, and interest groups into the same loosely organized political camp. This camp, already forming before the war, was after 1914 increasingly estranged from Bethmann's government, increasingly friendly toward the idea of military rule, and increasingly antagonistic toward the *Weltpolitiker* over questions such as massive territorial annexation, a negotiated peace, and the resumption of unrestricted submarine warfare.

What did groups as diverse as the CDI, the conservative parties, a large part of the leadership of the National Liberal and Center parties, and the *Bund der Landwirte* have in common? In the first place (as we saw in the previous chapter), they shared an aversion to political reform in Germany together with a real fear of incipient working class revolution.[28] This was, of course, partly the result of a common perception of increasing social conflict on the part of an elite that considered itself threatened on all sides. It was also, to some extent, the product of a very real tendency toward cultural and familial amalgamation between the business and agricultural aristocracies that some have called "feudalization."[29] But why should these groups have required an imperialist ideology to cement their connection—especially an imperialist ideology that had in the past contained undertones of resentment against big agriculture and outright hostility toward big business? For one thing, they needed a common means of rallying support outside the recognized social elite on grounds that linked the continuance of their power to the fulfillment of a mission vitally important to the German people. The idea of protecting and extending traditional German culture and reconciling it with the material circumstances of the modern world through imperialism provided such a means. In this respect, the elements of the anti-big–business and anti-big–agriculture sentiment in *Lebensraum* were very useful. They reduced the appearance of self-interest on the part of the elite groups advocating *Lebensraum* policies; in fact, by 1914, *Lebensraum* no longer contained policy aims that constituted a real threat to any important elite interest. Very few alternative ideological structures available to organizations attempting to bridge the gaps among the segments of the German upper classes possessed this advantage.

Lebensraum was an important elite integrative force in other ways. The images of which it was composed and the policy proposals to which it was linked had, by 1914, become a permanent, self-sustaining ideological entity, widely accepted as an important form of active conservatism in Germany. The images of *Lebensraum* were generally not reactionary ones; they did not involve an intention of turning back the historical clock. Such forms of conservatism were often self-defeating in politics, branding their proponents as members of the lunatic right.[30] Usually, *Lebensraum* manifested itself as a means through which the old social order could be adapted to new conditions. If properly presented, it was the kind of ideological set that could appeal to all sorts of people who regarded themselves as "responsible" conservatives, whether they were business owners, professionals, army officers, or Junker agriculturalists. By displacing the theoretical location of its proposed actions to external geo-

graphic areas, *Lebensraum* was able to play to commonalities in the cognitive framework of a large part of the German upper and upper middle
classes without arousing their mutual antagonisms over interests closer to
home. The inadequacies of *Lebensraum*'s logic and its depiction of current social reality were no great handicap in this respect. The general
tenets of *Lebensraum* were legitimated, after all, by endorsements from
leading scholars. And the very fact that the world represented by *Lebensraum* was not, in most senses, a real one made it that much easier for
members of different segments of the German elite to hold common
ground on imperial questions, thus creating a structure of cooperation
that would be extended to other issues as well.

It must be remembered that, despite tendencies toward sociocultural
integration and shared antipathies toward socialism and reform, even the
conservatives in the German social elite were still, in 1914, deeply divided. Divisions over economic interests played their part: differences
between agrarians and industrialists, differences about the incidence of
the increased taxation that most people knew to be necessary, and so
forth.[31] Also, there still existed no single organization that could legitimately claim, as for example the British Connservative Party could, to
represent practically all parts of the social and economic elite and that
could effectively compromise their interests. At least as important as
these "real" or structural factors, however, was the fact that intellectual
and ideological aggregations to which the various segments of the elite
could conscientiously subscribe were still relatively few in number and
still underdeveloped. Such aggregations were forming, built of diverse
materials such as racism, anti-semitism, and several versions of nationalism, but, for the most part in 1914, only their outlines were clear and
their connections to effective political organizations were tenuous.[32]
Under these circumstances, *Lebensraum* was an extremely attractive
ideological foundation for an aggregate conservative ideology for the reasons already given. It was still not, however, wholly ideal as of 1914
because of limitations in its appeal to business and bureaucratic interests.
It would become more so under wartime conditions as the process of
ideological integration with elements of *Weltpolitik* continued.

The lead in ideological integration from the *Lebensraum* side had been
taken by the Pan-Germans, by publicists such as Bernhardi, and by figures such as Hugenberg at the juncture between elite big-business interests and radical conservatism. To these people, the war presented an
opportunity not just to realize some of the overt aims of *Lebensraum,* but
also to build a conservative public consensus around an expanded *Lebensraum*—a consensus that could be used as an instrument of elite political
integration, as a means of bending government policy in a conservative
direction, and as a means of discrediting attempts to reform the Prussian
and German political structures.

These intentions and the continuity in the *Lebensraum*-based attempt to
accomplish them can be seem in the memorandum drawn up by Heinrich

Class in September 1914 as an elaboration of the Pan-German League's position on war aims.[33] The memorandum was later expanded by Class, printed in December 1914 for wide "private" circulation within the government and among organized interest groups, and finally issued to the public in 1917. It is worthwhile to discuss Class's memorandum at some length for a number of reasons. The memorandum shows the process of ideological integration on the imperialist right at work. It set the standard for an entire genre of similar conservative, *Lebensraum*-oriented war-aims proposals over the next several years. It is also, by reputation at least, a well-known document in the literature on German war aims, having been cited as significant evidence by Fritz Fischer in both of his major books.[34] This last point makes an examination of the memorandum in the context of the present study especially interesting, for the summary and analysis that Fischer gives of it focus on items that, with allowances for differences in detail, Class's presentation shares with the major early official compilations of war aims—particularly Bethmann Hollweg's September Program. In fact, what Fischer has concentrated on are the elements in Class's approach that display Class's intention of creating an integrated imperialism in the midst of war. Fischer has paid much less attention to the segments of the memorandum that come directly from the *Lebensraum* tradition, that are fundamentally different from the official war-aims line, and that are— as far as one can tell from the structure of the presentation and the amount of attention given to them—the most important elements of Class's argument. Seen in the light of the present study, the Class memorandum, rather than manifesting an elite consensus on war aims, instead represents an attempt to *create* consensus through an imperialism still basically grounded in *Lebensraum*.

To Class, the goal of German policy is the permanent dissolution of all threats to the security of the nation, both external and internal. External threats are to be met by weakening Germany's foes for all time. In his discussion of the reasons behind his specific policy recommendations, however, he concentrates heavily on the internal factors. Following the pattern of Pan-German argumentation since the 1890s, Class sees the overcoming of fragmentation and the creation of national unity as the most important of Germany's immediate internal needs. They can be achieved by building on the national sentiment aroused by the war and by official action against "internationalist" elements in politics, both liberal and Socialist, and against "foreign" bodies in the German state.[35] The very first focus of Class's war-aims declaration therefore constitutes a link to a domestic political intention: the reduction of fragmentation and the building of consensus.

Equally important in the long run is vigorous action to guarantee the "physical and ethical health" of the German people, particularly against the debilitating effects of urbanization and industrialization. The war provides a golden opportunity for accomplishing this end as well, through a policy of "inner colonization," which Class explicitly describes as the massive settlement of German peasant farmers on large areas of agricultural land to be annexed in eastern Europe and on Germany's western borders.[36] Class discourses at length on this point, which is the underlying argument beneath many, indeed most, of the specific proposals for European annexations that he makes thereafter. It is an aspect of Class's imperialistic thinking that flows directly from the tradition of *Lebensraum* and migrationist colonialism, and it is a logical consequence of the process of evolution in Pan-German ideology that was summarized in Chapter Five. It is also fundamentally alien to the rationale behind the expansionary aims of the September Program and the other *Weltpolitik*-derived official war-aims proposals. Class does present as a subsidiary justification for extensive annexation and settlement the notion that areas in Europe acquired for their economic value to Germany can only be effectively held if they are occupied by a German population and cleared of a majority of their native inhabitants, but this is a sidelight to his basic argument for annexation.[37]

Class's specific policy recommendations with respect to Germany's gains from the war are therefore different from those of the government, not just in the much larger scale of territorial acquisitions envisioned (as Fischer implies), but also in the overt ideological structure that is used to explain *why* the annexations should be made. This, and not the question of annexation in itself, differentiated the imperialists of Class's persuasion from people such as Solf, Bethmann, Max Weber, and Bernhard Dernburg. It was not so much annexationists against antiannexationists as it was proponents of a modified *Lebensraum* imperialism against *Weltpolitiker*.

Class proposes extensive additions to German territory both in the east and the west. In the east, Russia must be reduced to its size in the era of Peter the Great.[38] Germany must annex the Baltic provinces and a large part of Poland, with the rest of Poland (including accretions from Russia proper) becoming an autonomous state with a Hapsburg monarch but under actual German control. The annexed lands must be cleared of most of their present inhabitants and settled with German farmers, mostly war veterans and urban workers. The Polish population will be transferred to the new Polish state, and the Jews will be sent to a special Jewish state carved out of Russia or established in the midst of the Turkish Empire.[39] It should be noted that these aims, although in the mainstream of conservative wartime proposals in most respects, tend toward the radical end of them. That is, there is little consideration given to the idea of a peace that will prop up the Tsarist regime in Russia as a potential ally for Hohenzollern authoritarianism. There is no suggestion, as there was in some other *Lebensraum*-based war-aims propaganda, that annexed lands in the east be feudalized with a Slavic serf class under a German aristocracy and *Bauernstand*.[40] The Pan-Germans had never gone in much for such explicit reactionary nostalgia, which had limited public appeal and limited attraction for the league's radical element and for the business groups whose support the league's leadership continually sought. Class insists on the clearing of resident native populations from annexed lands and emphasizes the usual Pan-German "antipolonization" theme in a cultural sense. Yet he also advocates the importation of temporary or seasonal foreign labor into the annexed territories (and by implication into Germany itself) to make the agricultural economy work.[41] In other words, Class is not really offering a solution at all to the problems of German peasant agriculture as they had been identified two decades before by Max Weber. He is including in his plans for the new territories a labor system that will permit the perpetuation of the large grain estates and that will create the same pressures toward the dissolution of German peasant agriculture that had been at work in East Elbia at the end of the nineteenth century. The fact then that Class fixes the Pan-German proposals firmly in the context of the "modernizing" wing of radical conservatism does not mean that he represents a tendency that threatens the Junkers or the rest of the traditional elite. What one sees here is an example of the kind of ideological elite integration and support aggregation that the league had been attempting for years.

The same sort of thing can be seen in many of Class's other proposals. Like most of the *Lebensraum*-oriented proponents of war-aims positions, Class includes a call for *Mitteleuropa* as a central feature of any peace settlement in the east.[42] We have already seen that well before the war the *Lebensraum* ideological set had come to encompass a version of *Mitteleuropa*—one that was substantially different from the *Weltpolitik* version that resurfaced during the war in the September Program and in Naumann's book. Class's brief reference to *Mitteleuropa* falls into the *Lebensraum* tradition. It is vaguely defined, especially in terms of the economic function that it is supposed to serve. In general, Class views *Mitteleuropa* as a means of securing the raw materials of German industry and as a protected marketing area—by implication, not simply for manufacturing, but also for German agriculture. As we saw previously, this was the key difference from the *Weltpolitik* version, which primarily sought to benefit German industry at the expense of agriculture. The only way that the extra-German regions of *Mitteleuropa* could function as part of an integrated marketing and investment system would have been if they could have sold their agricultural products freely in the industrial areas. This was precisely what the leaders of German agriculture did not want, and it was what the *Lebensraum* version of *Mitteleuropa* avoided beneath its nonspecific references to reorganizing the central European economy.

Even in the *Lebensraum* version, however, the idea of a central European economic union could appeal to the directors of certain heavy industries, particularly the metals industry, that had been partly excluded from the Russian and Austro-Hungarian markets by tariffs and could anticipate an increase in demand from a German-controlled *Mitteleuropa*, regardless of how it was structured.[43] Like many other elements of war-aims proposals made by Class and his political associates, such a system could only operate under circumstances in which Germany possessed total power of coercion over the other members of the union so that they could not object to being forced to buy German industrial products without receiving new German agricultural markets in return. This, in turn, implied the destruction not only of Russian power in eastern Europe, but also (to all intents and purposes) that of Austria-Hungary. Even then, close examination of the economics of the concept did not bode well for its practical implementation.

The Pan-German *Mitteleuropa* proposals must be seen mainly as attempts to use an expanded imperialist ideology in the guise of a war-aims recommendation as a means of creating political consensus among important elite groups. Because of the prevalence of the general concept and vocabulary of *Mitteleuropa* among the various groups that subscribed to *Weltpolitik,* it was possible to attract support from some *Weltpolitiker* who did not examine the implications of the *Lebensraum* version carefully or who thought that once the principle of economic union was accepted, economic realities would cause a modification in the direction of *Weltpolitik* (which is essentially what happened when a German-Austrian customs union was finally negotiated in 1918).[44] The attraction of Class's *Mitteleuropa* was especially notable among a particular group of *Weltpolitiker:* those such as Gustav Stresemann directly associated with the business interest organizations that had competed with the CDI before the war (the BdI and *Hansa-Bund*) and those (also like Stresemann) associated with the National Liberal Party.[45] These organizations and the majority of their leaders had every reason to attempt to find common cause, at least in some respects, with the CDI and the conservative agrarian elite. Although liberals of Stresemann's sort favored a limited degree of political reform, they were afraid of a socialist revolution brought on by wartime conditions and were anxious to join hands with any group that would help to prevent it. Also, in the making of wartime and postwar policies, no economic or political group—especially those like the BdI and the National Liberals whose degree of influence on policy before the war had been relatively small—could afford to be without links to the political heavyweights or to continue grudge matches with them. Concurrence on war aims such as a vaguely defined concept of *Mitteleuropa,* the annexation of industrial and mining areas in France and Belgium, and *Mittelafrika* was a most effective means of building these links, one that was appreciated by Class and most other conservative politicians almost as soon as the war began. Thus Stresemann—although a classic *Weltpolitiker* of the Dernburg school before 1914 who would revert to largely the same habits of thinking under different circumstances after 1918—often allied himself during the war with the advocates of extensive annexations, settlement, and total victory.[46] Stresemann also maintained his connections with the *Weltpolitiker* in government and in his own party, of course. Under the fluid circumstances of wartime politics, one could never tell which constellation of power was going to dominate the scene.

Similarly, the BdI and many of the leaders of the financial community came out publicly for extensive annexationist war aims in common with the CDI, although they tended to avoid references to peasant settlement and other favorite *Lebensraum* notions.[47]

Class also included substantial western annexations in his recommendations—much greater ones than Bethmann or most other government officials were envisioning in 1914–15, although not out of line with many of the aims seriously considered within the government as the political force of right-wing consensus expanded thereafter.[48] All of Belgium was to be annexed, together with large areas of eastern and northern France. This was to be done partly to secure sources of raw materials such as coal, partly to guarantee German control over competing industries and port areas, and partly to give Germany a permanent strategic advantage over future foes. Much of the annexed territory was, however, to be cleared of its population and settled with German farmers. In this last respect, once again, Class's proposals differed fundamentally from even the most extreme war-aims positions expressed in terms of traditional *Weltpolitik*. The specific annexations that Class recommended were, many of them, ones that were also recommended individually by the military or by business organizations such as the CDI for their own particular reasons (e.g., the desire of heavy industry to secure direct control over the mines of French Alsace.)[49] In a sense, these, too, indicate Class's and the Pan-Germans' desire to include within their program something for everybody of political importance, to use ideology in a wartime setting to create an elite consensus with broad popular support and to make the fortunes of the league and its leaders.

Class's approach to colonial war aims is extremely interesting as a stage in the development of *Lebensraum* culminating in Nazi expansionism.[50] In Class's memorandum, one sees the completion of the tendency for the logic of migrationist colonialism to be transfered almost entirely to proposed settlements in Europe rather than overseas, a tendency that was noticeable before the war in, for example, Bernhardi's writings. Class demands massive colonial acquisitions, particularly in Africa—acquisitions that are much larger than any of the official African war-aims proposals advanced prior to 1917.[51] He also refers to colonial settlement and the need to expand the opportunities available to current colonial settlers. But the obligatory nod toward migrationist colonialism is rendered purely in passing; it is not emphasized and, unlike settlement in Europe, has little to do with the structure and logic of Class's African war aims. Class explicitly calls for *Mittelafrika*, as the Pan-German League had done since 1912. It is to be the central feature of a much larger African empire that will incorporate the northern two thirds of the continent. The southern third, minus, presumably, German Southwest Africa, will be turned over to a pro-German South African Boer state.

There is in Class's version of *Mittelafrika* the same looseness in logic and argument and the same limitlessness that had been characteristic of prewar Pan-German presentations of both central European and central African union. Class devotes little space to defining *Mittelafrika* and practically none to serious considerations of which African areas could be most profitably employed as supports to German industry and which could not. In essence, he implies, Germany will take it all, regardless of expense or utility. It is difficult to avoid the suspicion that Class, for all of the Pan-Germans' rhetoric about Germany's need for additional colonies, does not give this part of his program the attention that he gives the European elements. He seems to be more interested in the effect of making an extreme demand than in the content of the demand.

The overseas empire that Class advocates is needed mainly to supply German industry with raw materials, particularly in the event of a future war. As Bernhardi had done, Class thus encompasses his version of economic imperialism within the structure of highly generalized strategic thinking that allows him to avoid dealing with hard questions of the economic utility of new territories. The African war aims have become, in Class's rendering, not so much a continuation of the migrationist tendency in traditional *Lebensraum* but rather a crude attempt at ideological integration by employing a concept (*Mittelafrika*) drawn from the structure of *Weltpolitik* and by making broad references to the raw material needs of industry.

There is, however, one echo of traditional *Lebensraum*-type colonialism in addition to the pro forma mention of agricultural settlement colonies. Class argues that overseas colonies are especially useful as fields of endeavor for the "free professions" whose practitioners are vital components of a viable German culture but who are experiencing difficulties in the face of industrialization.[52] Colonies would create opportunities for these people that the then-current German economy could not provide at home. Whether Class is referring to the liberal professions or to master artisans he is clearly using a characteristic *Lebensraum* appeal to those who considered themselves "professionals": the displacement of the response to the social threat of change into overseas colonies. For the most part, however, Class shows the extent to which *Lebensraum* imperialism had come to focus on continental Europe and, at least in the outlook of the most important organizations employing radical-conservative political ideologies, had relegated colonial expansion to the function of creating a bridge—if not to *Weltpolitik* exactly, then to the groups to whom *Weltpolitik* might reasonably appeal.

One further point about Class's position paper requires consideration: his attitudes toward Britain and her major allies. Unlike the government and the *Weltpolitiker* in general, Class clearly did not contemplate a peace negotiated with Britain or anybody else on grounds other than the total defeat of Germany's enemies—or in the case of Britain, as total a defeat as Germany could manage. The kinds of gains that Class proposed could not be acquired in any other way. Although people such as Bethmann, Solf, and Kühlmann struggled to find a basis for negotiation with Britain in which British interests would, at least, be considered, Class wanted a peace dictated to an exhausted Britain whose allies had been overrun, a peace that would eliminate a large portion of the British empire, provide for German strategic advantage in the form of a German occupation of practically the entire coast opposite southeastern England, and guarantee German naval superiority.[53] The postwar world was not to be made up of equal spheres of influence but rather to be dominated by an all-powerful Germany. It is in Class's proposals and the similar positions taken by other organizations of the radical right (and after the summer of 1917, by the German government) that we see an actual conscious intention to grasp for exclusive world power.[54]

Much of the political debate over the question of a "peace of understanding," like that over the resumption of unrestricted submarine warfare, revolved around these fundamental differences in perception. Given their war-aims position, Class and his associates and the whole political movement that organized itself around the same viewpoint could hardly demand anything less than total victory. Given their assumptions (or illusions, if one wishes) about the possibility of ultimate imperial cooperation with Britain, the *Weltpolitiker* in government and academia tended until very late in World War I to emphasize a negotiated peace and to claim that all of Germany's significant goals could be achieved by such a means—making the prolongation of the war to achieve the ends of the *Lebensraum* advocates appear a needless waste of lives and resources.[55]

Both sides—Class together with the myriad of conservatives who followed the general lines of his presentation of war aims, and the supposedly antiannexationist advocates of a "peace of understanding"—saw each other's positions in terms of fundamental differences on questions of internal German politics. Both used their different war-aims positions and the implications about the means of ending the war that flowed from those positions as ways of rallying support for their stances on domestic politics—especially the question of political reform in Prussia and the Reich. Class and those who thought as he did linked the need to achieve the external goals of *Lebensraum* imperialism with the need to build national unity and prevent liberal reform at home. Class in particular used this connection in his continuing struggle against the tendencies of the Bethmann government to compromise with the advocates of political liberalization who had pressed strongly since 1912 for the abolition of the three-class voting system in Prussia.[56] By setting forth a war-aims program formulated in terms of *Lebensraum,* a program different from that of the government in certain important respects and compared with which a *Weltpolitik* policy could be made to look like a compromise of Germany's basic interests, Class, the Pan-Germans, and a wide variety of conservatives could make the government appear weak and inadequate. They could then represent government-sponsored reforms as part of the same tendency toward a sellout of Germany's basic interests. *Lebensraum* war aims thus provided both a means of achieving a conservative consensus of

important elite groups with a fair shot at popular support and a specific
method of asserting conservative control over the Bethmann government.

These developments, which began with the start of the war, manifested
themselves in pressure on the Bethmann government from the Pan-Germans and Hugenberg's various alliances of business interests to declare
itself publicly in favor of *Lebensraum*-style war aims. The pressure inten-
sified as 1914 passed into 1915. Bethmann was not, of course, about to
cave in to demands that he and his advisors believed to be foolish and
that were clearly intended to embarrass the government. His reaction was
therefore primarily negative—a denial of most of the *Lebensraum* interpretation of war aims and an attempt to prosecute Class for publishing his
war-aims position in defiance of a government ban on publications that
might assist enemy propaganda—which Pan-German pronouncements
certainly did.[57]

On the other hand, Bethmann's normal procedure of tracing the diagonal between competing political forces precluded an outright rejection of
the entire *Lebensraum* position. Furthermore, although *Weltpolitik* thinking predominated in the Foreign Office and among Bethmann's main
advisors, there existed important pockets of *Lebensraum* imperialism
within the government. The formulation of Polish policy especially was
strongly influenced by a connection of officials in various ministries that
had formed during the Bülow years and that had firm links to Hugenberg's conservative political network.[58] Friedrich von Schwerin, a senior
official of the Prussian Interior Ministry, was well known as a proponent
of inner colonization and territorial annexation. Schwerin had been a
friend of Hugenberg for years and was also closely associated with Max
Sering and ex-Colonial Secretary Lindequist in the inner colonization
movement. Bethmann's undersecretary in the Chancery, to whom he had
entrusted the conduct of Polish affairs, was Arnold von Wahnschaffe,
whose association with Hugenberg, Schwerin, and inner colonization
went back to the turn of the century. Although Wahnschaffe was not
committed to *Lebensraum* imperialism as a general proposition, he certainly leaned in that direction with respect to Polish policy.

Under the circumstances, both as a gesture to a certain body of opinion
among his subordinates and as a means of reconciling the conservative
Lebensraum imperialists, Bethmann in 1914 empowered Wahnschaffe to
begin planning the future of Poland on the understanding that some
population movement and frontier "rectification" would be necessary on
the Polish border after the war. The official designated by Wahnschaffe
to do the actual initial planning was, however, ex-Colonial Governor
Rechenberg, a prominent *Weltpolitiker* with Polish expertise. It seems
that the whole process was, in part, an attempt by Bethmann to hold out
a carrot to *Lebensraum* opinion by using the Wahnschaffe–Hugenberg
connection to formulate policy in the particular, limited case of the Polish
border but to circumscribe the result by approving the appointment of a
Weltpolitiker to do the work. The result was a compromise, the border-

strip idea.[59] According to Rechenberg's plan, Poland would be an independent state under informal German control. Parts of the current Polish–German border would be straightened out for defense purposes (in Germany's favor), and, from this area and its immediate hinterland, part of the Polish population would be removed to Poland and replaced by German peasants. It was a scheme to which, in outline, both *Weltpolitiker* and *Lebensraum* imperialists could subscribe. The same sort of scheme would later be extended into the German-occupied Baltic provinces as a means of deriving policy from the clash of political forces in Germany. In the long run, however, Bethmann's gesture availed him little politically because no amount of local compromise could reconcile the differences between the two general imperialist ideologies or between the two political coalitions that employed them.

Weltpolitik and Reform

The appearance of the *Lebensraum* war-aims position as the ideological focus of a potential conservative consensus also provoked the emergence of a countertendency that linked *Weltpolitik*-style war aims to the advocacy of moderate political reforms, partly as a means of heading off possible revolution from the radical left or a possible seizure of power from the right. This tendency, noticeable in liberal political and academic circles in 1914, became highly organized in 1915 through the efforts of several networks of academics, journalists, business leaders, and former officials who had strong contacts with *Weltpolitiker* in the government. Among the most important participants in the movement were Bernhard Dernburg, Hans Delbrück, Max Weber and his brother Alfred, and the circle of journalists surrounding Friedrich Naumann. Most of these people had been major advocates of *Weltpolitik* before the war. They organized drives in 1915 to obtain the signatures of prominent Germans on petitions calling for negotiations to end the war based on limited gains for Germany. The same networks were among the forces behind the 1917 Reichstag Peace Resolution.[60]

The ostensible aim of the extragovernment *Weltpolitiker* was to bring about a peace speedily by assembling public support for a war-aims position to which (as it was thought) the enemy could agree—or at least to which the enemy peoples would force their governments to agree. Although in their formal summaries of their positions, the *Weltpolitiker* advocates of a "peace of understanding" implied that they were not calling for annexations or major territorial gains for Germany, their self-restraint was really obvious only when compared with the views of self-conscious annexationists such as Class. Even in his public statements, Dernburg made it clear that Germany should insist on getting from the war what was rightfully hers—this included frontier rectifications, additions to her colonial empire, and recognition of her position as a world power (within the *Weltpolitikers'* conceptual scheme of a world divided

into three or four autonomous economic structures). In their private correspondence with each other, *Weltpolitiker* such as Max Weber and Ge-
rhart von Schulze-Gävernitz indicated that even more extensive gains
would not be repugnant if they could be obtained rapidly within the
context of *Weltpolitik* and a negotiated peace.[61] Many of the standard
features of the antiannexationist position—such as an autonomous Kingdom of Poland as part of a German-dominated economic *Mitteleuropa*—
might be represented as Naumann had portrayed them, as noncoercive
measures, but they involved the stripping of a large part of Russia's
eastern provinces from her. Despite implications to the contrary, which
were intended mostly for dissemination in neutral and enemy countries,
the antiannexationist *Weltpolitiker* were not really advocating a return to
the status quo ante but rather to the situation that would have existed in
1914 had the British not been so foolish as to reject the *Weltpolitikers'*
suggestion of German–English cooperation in support of each other's
empires.

But there was a good deal more to the antiannexationist war-aims
position and the groups that advanced it than simply a desire to see a
quick end to the war and the achievement of the formal aims of *Weltpolitik*. The wartime *Weltpolitiker* went public with their arguments to rally
public support against precisely the kind of conservative connection that
Class was attempting to create with *his* version of war aims. Not only did
Weltpolitiker such as Weber and Dernburg think that the nature of Pan-
German imperialism was misguided, but they also saw it as a threat to
political order and progress in Germany. In this, they were in close agreement with many of the leading *Weltpolitiker* within the government itself,
including Solf and Rathenau.[62]

The *Weltpolitiker* argued that the kinds of proposal put forward by the
Pan-Germans and their associates were deliberately intended to prolong
the war by making negotiation impossible. Prolongation of the war would
also prolong the authoritarian emphasis in wartime government and allow
conservatives, possibly working in conjunction with the Army, to prevent
the liberalization of the political system. Liberal *Weltpolitiker* such as
Dernburg and Rathenau saw political liberalization as the most likely
means of modernizing German politics, preventing violent working-class
revolution and heading off equally violent conservative counterrevolution.[63] They also recognized the radical right's use of *Lebensraum* war
aims as a weapon against reformist tendencies in the Bethmann government. Even conservative *Weltpolitiker* such as Karl Helfferich and Hans
Delbrück—who advocated a *Weltpolitik* line mainly because they believed *Weltpolitik* to be the proper guide to foreign policy and who had
before 1914 usually opposed any association of *Weltpolitik* with constitutional change—now agreed both to the notion of limited government
reform and to the use of a public antiannexationist campaign as a means
of turning aside opposition to reform.[64] Such an approach might, under
the right circumstances, attract back into the *Weltpolitik* fold the many

people like Stresemann who had temporarily aligned themselves with radical-conservative imperialist policies. Thus *Weltpolitik,* antiannexationist war aims, and the concept of limited political reform became linked temporarily during the war—both as parts of an ideological array and as the main items of the program of a small but well-connected coterie of members of the academic, journalistic, and government elites.[65]

Weltpolitik had not been explicitly tied to constitutional reform before 1914, although it was inherently a modernizing and "progressive" ideology in general aspect and could easily be adapted, as it had been by Weber and Naumann, to reformist uses. Under wartime conditions it became closely, if temporarily, linked to reformism, and that linkage helped to determine its fate during the war. For despite their close connections with the policymaking elite in the government up to 1917, extragovernment *Weltpolitiker* were badly outmatched by the opposition. Although the antiannexationists won some small victories in the last year-and-a-half of the war, it was the *Lebensraum*-oriented conservative coalition that possessed the big guns and won the day in the course of 1917. The *Weltpolitiker,* both those in government and those outside, were forced either to retire in defeat and impotence or else to align themselves with the victors.

The Triumph of *Lebensraum* in 1917–18

The main reason for the victory of the *Lebensraum* orientation was the rapid takeover of effective political primacy by the army high command under Paul von Hindenburg and Erich Ludendorff during the first half of 1917. The takeover was initiated in January with the military's defeat of the Bethmann government on the question of resuming unrestricted submarine warfare, and it was completed by Bethmann's resignation in July. This quiet revolution was supported by the growth of the radical-conservative–*Lebensraum* consensus, and one of the revolution's main results was the increasing use of the *Lebensraum* framework as a basis for policymaking.

The tilt toward *Lebensraum* was not an inevitable consequence of growing Army political influence in itself. The image of the monolithic Prussian-army political mentality was shattered by historians some time ago.[66] Although Ludendorff always leaned ideologically toward the *Lebensraum* constellation of ideas, especially when these were placed in a strategic light by publicists such as Bernhardi and Class, he showed himself on several occasions to be willing to consider policy alternatives that fit into the *Weltpolitik* mold if these suited the army's purposes. Furthermore, a number of important senior officers were clearly members of the *Weltpolitik* camp, most notably General Max von Hoffmann, the eventual chief of the army's eastern command.[67] The Bethmann government, even while battling the army and navy over the question of submarine warfare, always gave high precedence to the demands made by the military for territorial gains couched in strategic terms, many of which were by no means incompatible with *Weltpolitik.*

The victory of *Lebensraum* (extended, Pan-German fashion, to incorporate industrial interests and a number of *Weltpolitik* concepts) in conjunction with the army's rise to supreme influence was primarily the result of a community of interest that grew up between the army high command, on the one hand, and the aggregation of conservative organizations, parties, and groups that had assembled around the annexationist war-aims position, on the other hand. Ever since the beginning of the war, relations between the army and Bethmann's civilian government had been rocky, and they became more so when the supreme command was turned over to the heroes of the eastern front, Hindenburg and Ludendorff, in 1916. Hindenburg and Ludendorff not only possessed views of politics that emphasized the preeminence of the military in wartime, but they also had the political skill and the personal popularity needed to make an effective claim for a major share of overall political power in the Reich. In late 1916, Bethmann and his closest advisors were seen increasingly by the high command as obstructions to a proper order of things in wartime Germany.[68] Fierce conflict arose over several issues, including the resumption of unrestricted submarine warfare and the possibility of government sponsorship of a limited liberal reform of the political system in Prussia (the introduction of universal manhood suffrage in elections to the Prussian Chamber of Deputies.)

The army, convinced by the navy that a full submarine blockade of Britain could bring total victory, campaigned vigorously in late 1916 to get the government to withdraw the restrictions on the use of the submarine that it had imposed in 1915 in order to prevent war with the United States. The Bethmann government, backed up by careful economic calculations done by the *Weltpolitiker* Vice Chancellor and Treasury Secretary Karl Helfferich and by the massed sentiment of almost all *Weltpolitiker,* resisted the military's importunities, arguing that a full submarine campaign would not have the effect of starving Britain out of the war and thus was not worth the risk of bringing America into it. The story of the way Hindenburg and Ludendorff, by threatening to resign over the issue, got the emperor to decide in favor of unlimited submarine warfare in January 1917 is quite familiar, as are the consequences of Bethmann Hollweg's agreement to accept the decision and to remain in office.[69] For our purposes, it is important to note that the submarine issue was directly related to the dispute over war aims and to the ideological and political split that lay behind it.

The *Weltpolitik*-oriented Bethmann government and the increasingly reformist *Weltpolitik* connection outside the government saw unlimited submarine warfare as the most immediate threat to the possibility of meaningful peace negotiations with the British and thus as a direct attack on the whole structure of their foreign policy conceptions. The *Lebensraum*-oriented conservatives, on the other hand, saw the total defeat of Britain, which the navy promised, as a necessary precondition to the kind of peace and the kind of postwar world they envisioned. The lines between the major imperialist ideological approaches were very clearly drawn on this issue, and it was entirely natural that the military, in seeking to impress its views of policy on the government and to acquire thereby a presumptive control of national policy, should find its allies in the aggregation of political groups oriented around *Lebensraum:* the conservative parties, the industrial and agrarian lobbies, and the major conservative nationalist political organizations such as the Pan-German League. The partnership was already apparent by the end of 1916; although it was probably not the key factor in the emperor's January decision, it was an element of the political situation that had to be taken into account. Both partners, the Army and the conservative connection, needed the support of the other to increase their political power, both were antagonistic to the present and possible future direction being taken by the Bethmann government, and both could easily agree on an extended *Lebensraum*-based national policy of the sort suggested by Class (and a host of others). The army's initial political success with unrestricted submarine warfare was widely taken as a success also for the conservative, annexationist, and *Lebensraum*-oriented imperialists.[70]

After January, the Bethmann government found itself increasingly compromised in its dealings with the army, the emperor, the public, and especially the Reichstag. It undertook to defend the new submarine policy and thus to take responsibility for the policy's failure and for the entry of the United States into the war. This not only alienated Bethmann from *Weltpolitik*-oriented opinion, but also brought him afoul of much of the socialist and left-liberal leadership in the Reichstag. They correctly saw the new direction in national policy as a harbinger of further authoritarianism and an obstacle to a rapid conclusion of peace, and they believed that Bethmann had to some degree sold out. As it happened, the war, with the need that it brought to reconcile as many segments of the population as possible to the war effort, had greatly enhanced the relative power of the Reichstag in politics as the only effective locus in the German political system where such reconciliation could be effected in practical political terms. Bethmann allowed himself to be dragged into a position in which he could be attacked from all sides and in which his attempts at compromise were fruitless.[71]

By the early summer, important leaders of the National Liberal, Progressive, Center, and majority SPD delegations in the Reichstag had come to the conclusion that Bethmann had to go or, at least, that the damage done by unrestricted submarine warfare, which had thus far been unsuccessful in bringing Britain to her knees, had to be undone. Furthermore, the government, which had had to accommodate increasingly to the point of view of the army and to adjust its policies wherever possible to the outlook of the conservative connection, had to be shown that a moderate-to-liberal line on policy in general could command a majority in the Reichstag. These and other factors, including the continuing campaign by *Weltpolitiker* outside the government for a "peace without annexations," led to the introduction and passage on July 19 of the famous Reichstag Peace Resolution.[72] The Peace Resolution called on the government to seek a negotiated peace with the enemy on the basis of a vaguely worded principle of territorial abstinence on both sides. It appears that most of the people who voted for the resolution, except perhaps on the extreme left, did so with the sort of mental reservations that we have already discussed when considering what the *Weltpolitiker* really meant by "no annexations."[73] Although the Peace Resolution movement hardly brought peace, it did succeed temporarily in bringing back into a political constellation oriented toward moderate liberal reform and *Weltpolitik* such parliamentary leaders as Stresemann (by now the effective leader of the National Liberals) and Erzberger—*Weltpolitiker* who had earlier in the war tended toward more extreme annexationist positions.

By the time the Peace Resolution was passed, Bethmann was no longer chancellor. He had resigned on July 13. His resignation was partly tied up with the crisis-laden politics surrounding the Peace Resolution, but it was even more the result of the squeeze placed on him by the army and conservative imperialists on one side and moderates and liberals in the Reichstag on the other.[74] The latter not only held him responsible for the submarine campaign, but also complained that he was not moving fast enough in introducing political reform in Prussia; the former resented Bethmann's attempts to curb their efforts to achieve total victory and his willingness to introduce at least some reforms in response to liberal pressure. The military wanted a more pliable civil government. Hindenburg and Ludendorff were perfectly willing to play Reichstag politics and, in essence, cooperate with the moderate left to get rid of Bethmann, but they did not want to see meaningful constitutional change in Germany. In the end, with Bethmann's resignation, the military got what it wanted. Bethmann's successor, the nonentity Georg Michaelis, did the military's bidding; Graf Georg Hertling, who followed Michaelis, found a situation in which his influence on policymaking was thoroughly constricted. Although the military continued to recognize the Reichstag's new apparent role in politics, it checked attempts to introduce real parliamentary government. By maintaining a close connection with the political right in the Reichstag and outside, a connection symbolized by alterations in the government's policies on war aims and the disposition of conquered territories, the army command managed to exercise substantial influence over the actions of the Reichstag.[75]

The task of the military was aided to some extent by the formation of the *Vaterlandspartei* in the wake of the 1917 Peace Resolution. The *Vaterlandspartei* was a conscious institutionalization of the conservative *Lebensraum* connection discussed previously. It was formally organized by the leaders of the major nationalist leagues and the conservative parties to fight future attempts by liberals to encourage a negotiated peace. It also coordinated the opposition to constitutional change and organized support for the army's role in politics.[76] The *Vaterlandspartei* had the active support of a large cross-section of the German economic and social elite; it was led by Tirpitz and by the president of the Colonial Society, the Duke of Mecklenburg. The party came close to being the kind of broadly based, conservative, nationalist, imperialist party envisioned by many of the original founders of the Pan-German League. Its program consisted of a mixture of not entirely compatible ideological elements drawn from all across the conservative political spectrum, but its most notable positions were imperialist ones. The program of the *Vaterlandspartei* with respect to war aims and the long-term goals of German foreign policy was quite similar to that put forward in Class's memorandum: *Lebensraum*, modified by the inclusion of *Mitteleuropa*, *Mittelafrika*, and substantial annexations of industrial areas in the territories of Germany's enemies. The party's emphasis on modified *Lebensraum* imperialism followed directly from the earlier use made of *Lebensraum* by Hugenberg, Class, and others attempting to create consensus among conservative groups still strongly divided between radical and traditional conservatives, between industrial and agrarian interests, between politicians of aristocratic and middle-class origins, and so on. It was not a fully integrated imperialist ideology incorporating all the major features of *Weltpolitik* and *Lebensraum*, but it was broadly enough conceived that the kind of policy that it implied, which rapidly became influential in the government also, could be adopted by former *Weltpolitiker* attempting to adapt themselves to new political circumstances between the summer of 1917 and the late summer of 1918.

The adjustment of the senior personnel in the main civil government departments to the new situation is evident in the documentation on war-aims planning in 1917. In the Colonial Office, as Solf tried to keep his job and some of his influence, war-aims planning tended increasingly to follow the extravagant lines laid down by the Pan-Germans and the Colonial Society and to break away from the previous limitations imposed by the *Weltpolitik* habit of thought and the rational consideration of concrete economic advantages to be gained from particular colonial annexations. Solf and his subordinates were now talking in terms of annexing practically all of Africa between the Sahara and South Africa, regardless of demonstrated economic utility.[77] Because all the German colonies had been seized by the end of 1917 (except for Colonel Paul von Lettow-Vorbeck's military force in the southwestern corner of German East Africa), the whole process of colonial war-aims formulation was a little unreal anyway.

The same cannot be said for eastern war-aims policy after the Bolshevik revolution in the fall of 1917, at least not initially. It was clear that victory on the eastern front was imminent and that the government would have to decide precisely what it wanted in return for the peace that the Bolsheviks were bound to seek. Late in 1917, a flurry of political activity commenced in Germany concerning the future of eastern Europe; this lasted almost until the German collapse a year later.[78] Under the pressure of having to face real problems of imperial policy as opposed to mainly hypothetical ones, German leaders displayed a wide variety of responses. Some, especially those in the Foreign Office and the army specifically charged with dealing with the Russians and their subject nationalities, moved away from ideologically determined positions to what appeared to be more pragmatic ones as they tried to comprehend the complexities of the eastern situation. This tendency was circumscribed, however, by the continued importance of imperialist ideologies in German politics and by the fact that many Germans still attempted to fit eastern policy into one or the other of the major imperialist ideologies. *Lebensraum* was, of course, particularly strong because of the central role it played in the conservative alliance in domestic politics and in the connection of the conservatives to the army. When German policy toward Russia, Poland, and the Ukraine began unravelling after the treaty of Brest-Litovsk in March 1918, the response of the main powers within the political system was not to move more strongly toward pragmatism but rather to retreat into the unreality of *Lebensraum.*

Late in 1917, however, there still appeared to be grounds for ideological compromise that would permit the Hertling government to follow a successful pragmatic course in eastern Europe. The Germans were clearly in the driver's seat and, within limits defined by geographic realities and their alliances with Austria-Hungary, Bulgaria, and Turkey, could apparently impose any settlement they wished—including one based on both *Weltpolitik* and *Lebensraum.* Moreover, the differences between *Weltpolitiker* and *Lebensraum* imperialists had never been as clear-cut on eastern war aims as they had been on other matters. Most antiannexationist *Weltpolitiker* agreed with the border-strip policy toward Poland. Many, including Paul Rohrbach and Hans Delbrück, believed that most of the Baltic provinces should be separated from Russia and come under German domination—in some areas, through annexation.[79] For their part, the conservative leaders of the *Vaterlandspartei,* both radicals like Class and more traditional conservatives, now commonly supported such measures as the dismemberment of Russia, the formation of an "independent" Kingdom of Poland (under a Habsburg ruler and informal German control), and the establishment of a German-dominated economic union in *Mitteleuropa.*[80] *Lebensraum* imperialists and *Weltpolitiker,* anxious about the consequences of continued economic privation for social order in Germany, had every reason to cooperate to create the means through which eastern Europe could be quickly exploited. *Weltpolitiker* such as Rathenau had given up hope of a negotiated peace in the west, and many *Weltpolitiker* in official positions like Solf and Kühlmann (the latter now foreign secretary) were anxious to accommodate themselves at least to some extent to the new locus of power on the right.[81]

Moreover, the smell of victory in the east had endangered a new expansiveness in the outlooks of *Weltpolitiker* and *Lebensraum* imperialists alike. Rohrbach's proposal of a grandiose *Mitteleuropa* consisting (in addition to Austria-Hungary) of German client states carved out of Russia and extending into central Asia was given some serious attention, although most official *Weltpolitiker* were a little more modest.[82] *Lebensraum* enthusiasts such as Schwerin and Lindequist envisioned whole Russian provinces turned into settlement colonies for German peasants and war veterans (a notion that appealed strongly to Ludendorff.)[83] Given an impending massive victory, there appeared to be enough to satisfy every type of imperialist. As long as Germany's immediate need for foodstuffs, raw materials, and the disengagement of troops from the east could be realized, long-term developments could be dictated at will.

Reality, of course, turned out to be much more complicated. In the first place, the apparent agreement between the different camps of imperialists was only superficial. The notion of *Mitteleuropa,* for example, meant to most *Weltpolitiker* an orderly structure of cooperating autonomous states in central and eastern Europe. The economic interests of each state would be served by membership in the union. The version of *Mitteleuropa* put forward by members of the *Vaterlandspartei* was essentially the standard *Lebensraum* version of the concept: part window dressing, intended to reconcile *Weltpolitik*-oriented opinion; part justification for a program of imposed economic exploitation that would serve practically no interests but German ones. One of the conditions of conservative consensus on *Mitteleuropa* was that external economic integration had to protect almost all sectors of German industry and agriculture, which precluded the degree of international specialization required by the *Weltpolitik* version of *Mitteleuropa* and precluded also a structure in which non-German interests could be effectively satisfied. *Lebensraum's Mitteleuropa* required the constant imposition of German will by force and the violation of most conventional notions of economic exchange. It also implied that such participants as the "independent" Kingdom of Poland and the "autonomous" Ukraine could really be nothing but German colonies. The *Lebensraum* notion of economic integration was usually justified as a foundation for German economic self-reliance or autarky in a hostile world; as critics pointed out, the expenditure of force required to maintain this kind of exploitive autarky could well become a drain on the military resources of Germany rather than a benefit.[84]

In fact, the whole set of German ideological approaches to the question of eastern Europe, when applied to the tasks of framing a workable peace treaty with Russia and organizing a satisfactory political structure for the region, was shot full of fallacies. The *Weltpolitik* version undoubtedly exaggerated the extent to which the interests of German industry were compatible with the economic interests of Germany's present and future allies.[85] Moreover, the voluntarist, cooperative approach to economic integration, which was actually applied to some extent in the Ukraine in the spring of 1918, was not likely to square with Germany's urgent need for food, raw materials, and troops in a region already damaged by war. In addition, it was not at all clear that the *Weltpolitiker* would have any more luck in solving nationality problems than the Russians had had or the allied powers would have after 1918. The *Lebensraum* approach, with its muddled concept of economic integration and its insistence on massive annexation and settlement, was bound to reduce itself to military occupation and German rule through force—which might solve the problem of local resistance to German interests but would require the use of substantial numbers of troops in the short term and would probably be unworkable in the long run. *Weltpolitik* and *Lebensraum* together were even worse. How could the cooperation of Polish, Ukrainian, Estonian, and Latvian leaders—essential for the Weltpolitik version of *Mitteleuropa*—be obtained if the German authorities announced their intention of expropriating large amounts of land for German settlement?

As it turned out, the inconsistencies in German ideological imperialism were less important than they might have been because the difficulties of effectuating even short-term pragmatic policies were insuperable. The story of how the German position on peace with Russia was determined in February and March of 1918 is familiar.[86] The harsh terms forced on the Bolsheviks at Brest-Litovsk over the objections of the Foreign Office (and part of the army command) resulted from Hindenburg and Ludendorff's insistence on the widest possible latitude for German policy in determining what was to happen in the east. One might read an element of *Lebensraum–Weltpolitik* competition here, in that Kühlmann and General von Hoffmann, the chief army negotiator, were *Weltpolitiker* while Ludendorff's *Lebensraum* propensities and connections to the radical right were well known. Because a *Lebensraum* solution to eastern problems would require that Germany be effectively unopposed there and *Weltpolitiker* hoped for cooperation—possibly even from the Bolsheviks—the army command's line was at least consistent with *Lebensraum* and inconsistent with *Weltpolitik*. It appears, however, that the primary points in dispute were differing conceptions of how best to achieve Germany's immediate aims, not ideological differences over ultimate solutions. Kühlmann and his associates were perfectly willing to work within the framework of Brest-Litovsk once the Bolsheviks had accepted it, and Ludendorff showed himself willing to entertain a wide variety of proposals—many derived from *Weltpolitik*—for eastern as well as western and overseas policy.[87] German recognition of the "socialist" *Rada* government in the Ukraine and the initial attempt in March and April of 1918 to work through it to produce the food and raw materials Germany needed followed procedures acceptable to the *Weltpolitiker*. It was only the inability of the *Rada* to meet German demands (which were in fact impossible) that led the army to turn the *Rada* out and to establish the more congenial Skoropadsky puppet dictatorship. Even this arrangement, although opposed by Rohrbach and other *Weltpolitiker,* did not outwardly contradict *Weltpolitik* imperialism. The only problem was that it failed to meet immediate German production requirements.[88]

By the summer of 1918, the army was essentially ruling the Ukraine directly and, with the help of German big business, attempting to place Ukrainian agriculture, transport, and industry under German control. Their success was at best marginal, and thousands of troops were kept away from the Western Front. Under these circumstances, Ludendorff, who had been sponsoring studies of possible German settlement in the Baltic region since 1917 and making migrationist noises to conservative politicians, now initiated serious plans for massive German settlement all the way across the Ukraine into the Transcaucasus. Friedrich Lindequist was assigned to direct the first stages of the project.[89] In this and other respects, we can see a general retreat into *Lebensraum* ideology in the face of practical adversity.

Exactly what would have happened if German rule in the east had continued and if the war had not ended on the Western Front in the fall of 1918 is difficult to say. In any event, the military collapse and the revolution changed the context in which politics and imperialism affected each other in Germany. They did not, however, fundamentally alter the structure of German imperialist ideology as it had emerged by 1918. Imperialism was still divided into two main ideological camps, one of which—*Lebensraum*—had shown a strong tendency toward conceptual expansion through appropriating ideas and vocabulary from *Weltpolitik* and had, moreover, become the integrating ideology of a powerful aggregation of political-interest groups. All the deficiencies of *Lebensraum* as a guide to policy had remained; indeed, they had been increased by the inevitable internal contradictions that the attempts to make *Lebensraum* acceptable to industrial interests brought with them. *Lebensraum* was to some extent discredited by being associated with the party of total victory in the midst of defeat, and this helped set the stage for a revival of *Weltpolitik* (in greatly altered form) during the Weimar Republic. But, on the whole, the experience of defeat caused neither major group of imperialists to reassess its basic assumptions.

CHAPTER NINE

Imperialist Ideology in the Weimar Republic

The question of continuity and discontinuity in German imperialist ideology during the period of the Weimar Republic is extremely complex. This would not be the case if it were possible to limit the discussion merely to resonances of prewar and wartime imperialist programs in party platforms during the 1920s or to the use of specific imperialist ideas by the Nazis. Unfortunately, the relationship between the standard imperialist ideologies and the interplay of groups participating in politics goes well beyond the conscious use of imperialist notions in public statements. Under the fragmented conditions of Weimar politics, the ideological heritage of imperialism found an amazing variety of political roles as different groups attempted to create consensus, frame policies, and find bases for coordinated action with other groups. Some of these roles were extremely subtle, involving as they did the recasting of imperialist ideas in a form compatible with Germany's weakened international position in the 1920s. So complex were the circumstances of imperialist and neoimperialist politics in Weimar that we can only note here in very general terms some of the more important developments in expansionary ideology during the period. In the present chapter, the Nazis will be left largely out of account. Their adoption and use of imperialist concepts will be the subject of Chapter Ten.

Continuities in *Weltpolitik*

A great many of the founders of the Weimar Republic—the people who shaped the Weimar constitution in 1919 and set the initial course of German democracy—were former *Weltpolitiker*. People such as Naumann, Dernburg, and Max Weber, whose thinking was extremely influential during the republic's formative period and who founded the German Democratic party (DDP) to be the mainstay of the new system, had been leaders of the group that had attempted to combine *Weltpolitik* with the advocacy of liberal political reform and a moderate war-aims policy dur-

ing the war.[1] Other *Weltpolitiker* who had not been so closely or permanently associated with the reformist group—especially Rathenau and
Stresemann—became important political leaders and strongly affected
the direction of Weimar foreign policy. Even such major antagonists on
questions of internal political structure and policy as Karl Helfferich and
Matthias Erzberger shared a similar imperialist ideological background in
Weltpolitik. The *Weltpolitik* habit of thought was thus deeply embedded
in the early republic through many of its chief political personnel. However, because of Germany's lack of military strength and because of the
need perceived by the republic's main supporters to achieve immediate
foreign and domestic aims that could not involve full-scale imperialism,
they tended to avoid overt references to imperialism as a national policy
goal. (The public movement for the return of the lost colonies was an
exception to which we shall turn later.) *Weltpolitik*-style thinking was
reflected primarily in conceptions of the ways in which the Versailles
treaty should be revised, in views of the kind of economic role Germany
should play in Europe and the world, and in attitudes toward the relationship between foreign policy and domestic politics.

Most of the *Weltpolitiker* who favored the republic or became reconciled to it saw the political success of a liberal democratic state, the
creation of a national consensus to overcome what seemed an appalling
problem of fragmentation, and the eventual implementation of a desirable foreign policy as inextricably bound together. Paul Rohrbach, for
example, transformed himself rapidly into a classic *Vernunftrepublikaner*
after 1918. In a prorepublican tract published in 1925, Rohrbach argued
that it was not a deep-seated belief in the universal superiority of representative democracy that led people like himself to support the republic.[2]
Instead the republic offered the best available means of overcoming the
social divisiveness and political fragmentation that were Germany's traditional political weaknesses and had always been the main obstacles to
effective policymaking. A political system constructed to involve all citizens could lessen the fragmenting influence of special interests and force
the parties to seek broader public support. A government in which responsibility was clearly defined, as it supposedly was in a parliamentary–
cabinet system, would be able to take decisive action to reconcile the
interests of the different segments of society and to create national consensus. Such a government would be able to act purposefully in achieving
Germany's main foreign policy goals: economic and military security, a
legitimate place as a participant in the world polity, and sufficient economic scope and territory to meet the needs of her people. These were to
be accomplished mainly through the revision of the Versailles treaty and
through a reconciliation with the other powers, which would only occur if
Germany were politically unified, stable, and firm without being hysteri-
cally bellicose.[3]

Such an approach, replicated in the writings of dozens of leading supporters of the republic, was obviously in many ways different from the

prewar political thinking of all but the most reform-oriented and liberal of the *Weltpolitiker,* but it was not in its main lines inconsistent with the fundamental aims and assumptions of *Weltpolitik.* Economic security; a climate favorable to modernization; an active foreign policy conducted by a strong government and aiming, if possible, at cooperation with other major powers; a reduction of internal fragmentation without recourse to violent, authoritarian means—all were themes that had been advanced by the very same people before the war in the context of *Weltpolitik.* Although they recognized the differences in the postwar environment, people like Rohrbach gave every indication that they believed that their ideological positions and their assessments of the major goals of German national policy were basically consistent over time.[4]

Even in the case of Karl Helfferich, who as a leader of the Nationalist Party (DNVP) before 1924 attacked both the structure and the policies of the republic, echoes of *Weltpolitik* recurred in his general views of the ends of German foreign policy. Real security could only be achieved if Germany regained not just her political independence, initiative, and power, but also her proper economic role as the center of a worldwide network of exchanges between an industrialized Germany and agricultural and primary-goods producers abroad. Only the possession of colonies, secure European markets, and informally protected investment areas would give the Germans what they needed as one of the world's leading peoples. Although Helfferich disagreed strenuously with Stresemann's policies of "understanding" and "fulfillment" as short-term directions in German foreign affairs, his conception of the long-range goals of German external economic policy did not fundamentally differ from that of Stresemann.[5] Both were consistent with *Weltpolitik* and both were framed within the same idiom as prewar *Weltpolitik.* Neither Helfferich nor Stresemann had much use for *Lebensraum*-style annexationism, and neither (after 1918) advocated a policy of economic autarky (i.e., attempting to create a closed economic system made up of an expanded Germany and its satellites). What they had in mind was essentially the kind of industry-oriented international economic system centering on Germany that they themselves, as *Weltpolitiker,* had urged before 1914.[6]

Despite continuities in idiom and aim, would it really be correct to describe these elements of post-1918 foreign policy thinking as *Weltpolitik* reborn? Not in the sense that Stresemann, Helfferich, or other shapers of Weimar policy consciously intended to put into effect an aggressive expansionary program through the use of warfare, nor that they were covering their "real" intentions behind more limited interim statements of goals. Attempts to demonstrate a conscious imperialist intention in the case of Stresemann, apart from his desire ultimately to "rectify" the Polish border, have conspicuously failed. Even Stresemann's Polish aims were limited to regaining territories lost to Poland under the Versailles treaty. Attempts to read the massive annexationist aims of 1917–18 into Stresemann's concept of border rectifications have also failed.[7] What one sees in the 1920s is what one would expect to see: continuities with the general categories and sets of assumptions about political, social and economic reality that had provided the framework within which *Weltpolitik* was conceived before the war. This can be detected in the overall scheme of foreign policy, especially foreign economic policy, adopted by German governments and by the Foreign Ministry during the period in which Stresemann directed external affairs (1923–29).

As we saw in Chapter Eight, Stresemann's outlook on external policy before 1918 had been essentially that of a *Weltpolitiker,* although out of political expediency he and his party had often sided with the extreme annexationists during the war. Under the conditions of postwar Germany, Stresemann, like most of the senior Foreign Ministry personnel, saw that a successful foreign policy had of necessity to deal with the immediate problems facing Germany on the international scene (Germany's exclusion from a share in international decision making, the difficulties caused by reparations, the occupation of the Ruhr in 1923) before long-range aims could be achieved or even formulated in specific terms. Germany must for the time being follow, "as hard as it is to say, a policy of opportunism."[8] Priorities were clear, especially during the crisis years of 1923–24 when Stresemann achieved his first big diplomatic successes. Neither *Weltpolitik* nor *Lebensraum* had much to do with the short-term tasks of government. On the other hand, when it came to articulating the longer range goals of foreign policy—the aims to be accomplished once Germany had gained some room to maneuver and had achieved readmittance to the "normal" structure of international politics—the general framework of *Weltpolitik* reasserted itself.

Such a framework was as natural to the chiefs of the Foreign Ministry as it was to Stresemann. It had become part of the political ethos of the department before the war, the structure of assumptions within which a great many officials had been professionally socialized, just as it had also been the ideological system within which Stresemann himself had first developed a comprehensive conception of national policy.[9] In addition, many of the considerations that had caused Stresemann to distance himself from other *Weltpolitiker* during the war had disappeared by the 1920s. For instance, although it was still important to Stresemann to stay in the army's good graces, the army no longer played the paramount role that it had toward the end of the war and was no longer in the hands of people like Ludendorff, who had been extremely sympathetic to radical conservatism and to the *Lebensraum* ideology. The army command also understood, perhaps better than anyone else, how impossible an active annexationist policy was for the moment.[10] Furthermore, Stresemann's party, the German People's Party (DVP)—essentially the National Liberals shorn of their right and left wings—emerged in the Weimar era as a rival of the much more conservative DNVP for votes and for the support of organized big business. A policy stance that tied the perceived foreign interests of large segments of big business to a framework of political and economic assumptions that gave those interests legitimacy and indicated a practical way in which they might be satisfied could, and did, give the DVP a considerable boost in its competition with the DNVP. The national lobbying organizations of light- and finished-goods industry lined up behind the DVP, and even the *Reichsverband der deutschen Industrie* (RdI), a general manufacturers' association dominated by the heavy industries that had so closely associated themselves with the far right (and *Lebensraum*) during the war, supported *both* the DNVP and the DVP—the latter partly because of the general tenor of Stresemann's foreign policy.[11]

In a larger sense, Stresemann's domestic political use of the economic implications of his foreign policy worked, at least up to 1929, to achieve his aim of reconciling the main repositories of industrial power to the republic by demonstrating that the republic, as it was currently structured, provided the most effective means of meeting the needs of the manufacturing sector. Those needs were conceived both in specific terms (the desires of particular industries for protection or for help in reentering prewar markets) and in general ones (the desire for an orderly capitalist society in which government and industry cooperated closely and in which the mass of people acted as contented employees and consumers). The needs could be legitimated most readily by a framework of ideology tied closely to the one that had previously spawned *Weltpolitik* imperialism. Essentially, the same factors that had made prewar *Weltpolitik* a reasonably effective instrument of political integration within a limited range of the German social and economic elite gave political significance also to Stresemann's foreign policy in the 1920s—especially when that policy was tied to a domestic program that also catered to the specific economic aims and ideological predilections of a great many business leaders.[12]

To Stresemann, as to all pre-war *Weltpolitiker,* the economic aspect of foreign policy was at least as important as any other, even in the short run. Under the conditions of the 1920s, Germany's underlying economic power (once the period of crisis ended in 1924) would give her the means of conducting successful international relations. "I believe," Stresemann told the executive committee of the DVP in 1925, "that the task today of every foreign minister is the employment of the international economic situation so as to construct foreign policy around the only thing that makes us still a great power: our economic strength."[13] This economic strength was to be used to achieve longer range goals, some of which bore a close resemblance to the goals of *Weltpolitik*.

Stresemann, in common with the senior personnel of the Foreign Office and the leaders of the light- and finished-goods lobby, aimed at the eventual establishment of a "free-trade" area in continental Europe as the best device for securing the permanent prosperity of the German economy.[14] France and perhaps Britain might adhere to the area, but it would be dominated economically by Germany. The main feature of the area would be a system of exchanges in central Europe between Germany as the industrial center and a periphery producing agricultural and other primary goods, consisting of Poland, Czechoslovakia, Hungary, and the Balkans. ("Free trade" was something of a euphemism because the system would display a substantial amount of structure and conscious direction.) According to this view, such an arrangement was the "natural" one for Europe, the one most likely to benefit its member nations, and the one into which the European economies were most likely to fall if left to interact "freely" among themselves. The conception was very similar to the prewar *Weltpolitik* version of *Mitteleuropa.*

The involvement of the German government in the process of constructing the free-trade area was necessary because political circumstances in the 1920s interfered with the "natural" economic evolution of central Europe. The government under Stresemann and all of his successors provided diplomatic and political assistance in dealings between German investors and other European states.[15] It also attempted to arrange treaty relations that were favorable to exporters. Here, however, Weimar governments were hampered by the fact that the agricultural lobby, supported by the heavy-industrial segment of the RdI and by the DNVP, insisted that German agriculture be protected in tariff arrangements made with Germany's eastern neighbors and that any tariff adjustments that favored finished-goods exporters be linked to adjustments that benefitted agriculture and heavy industry.[16] This constituted a recrudescence of one of the major issues of Wilhelmian political economy, and its political and diplomatic effects were similar to those that it had had in the *Kaiserreich.* The political link between heavy industry and agriculture, which the former sought primarily as a foundation for political conservatism in Germany rather than as a means of attaining specific economic ends, proved too much for any of the Weimar governments to overcome. Satisfactory comprehensive treaties with Poland and Czechoslovakia were never worked out because those countries insisted on tariff treatment of their agricultural goods in Germany similar to that which the German government sought for German industrial products abroad—a point of view that former *Weltpolitiker* like Stresemann found only too reasonable.

The aim of creating a continental free-trade area also involved considerations that impinged directly on the most important aspects of Weimar foreign policy: relations with the major powers and the revision of the Treaty of Versailles. According to Stresemann and those who thought about policy as he did, Britain and the United States could eventually be convinced not only that German economic recovery was a short-run benefit to themselves, but also that they would be similarly benefitted in the long term by trade with economically secure Germany playing its natural role as the industrial leader of Europe. The main obstacle was France.[17] France did not have the capacity to lead Europe economically or to create a functioning international economic system on her own. However, her "unnatural" political hegemony in Europe—a product of the unfortunate result of World War I—and her fear of Germany, which manifested itself in her potentially anti-German alliances with many of the very states in eastern Europe that the new model *Mitteleuropa* was supposed to encompass, could lead France to destroy Germany's chances of achieving her ultimate international economic aims. One of the many reasons therefore for Stresemann's policy of attempting to reduce French power in Europe, deflect French antagonism, and draw the United States and Britain away from France and toward the support of Germany was to accomplish a long-range economic goal closely linked to the *Weltpolitik* tradition.

The more immediate aims of the same policy were obvious: the reacquisition by Germany of complete national independence and the prevention of occurrences such as the occupation of the Ruhr. These aims took precedence over others, but they were often envisioned and defended as part of a larger policy design that included economic expansion and investment security. Indeed, one of Stresemann's stronger selling points for the policy of "understanding" among the leaders of German business was the connection that could be made between that policy and the conduct of a program of German commercial expansion overseas.[18] Even heavy industry, which put its alliance with organized agriculture ahead of other considerations when it came to tariffs, nonetheless was attracted by the implications of Stresemann's foreign policy for European economic integration. Until 1929, the idea of a loose and informal European economic network, led by Germany but closely connected to non-German overseas markets, could encompass most of the self-perceived needs of the heavy industries represented in the RdI. How such a system could be reconciled with the "need" to protect agriculture remained to be seen, but the basic concept of integration found almost universal acceptance among the leaders of business. This was, of course, useful to Stresemann as foreign minister and party leader and also useful to the republic in seeking tolerance for itself among the leaders of organized capitalism.

Stresemann's position on relations with the Soviet Union shows many obvious connections with his *Weltpolitiker* background. In a review of foreign policy that he drew up in 1923 not long after becoming foreign minister, Stresemann discussed the proper attitude for Germany to take toward Russia in terms not only of the balance of power, but also of economic considerations that come right out of the tradition of *Weltpolitik* imperialism:

> We must furthermore have a reserve territory in Russia for our overflow of intellectual and economic products. Activity in overseas countries is, for the moment, forbidden us. We must secure a new field of effort for our intelligentsia, our doctors, engineers, technicians and businesspeople. The Russian regime has thus far openly accepted these gentlemen. We must concern ourselves about the continued importation of raw materials into Germany. The most immediate cheap source of these is Russia, from which, because of the recently-concluded food products treaty, we already obtain great masses of grain and hopefully will continue to do so together with other raw materials such as hemp, flax, wood, oil, and minerals that are essential for our economy.[19]

Other resonances of *Weltpolitik* appeared in the foreign politics of the Weimar Republic. For example, the expectations of the government about the extent to which Britain (and the United States) would go in backing Germany against France or countenancing German economic expansion were clearly excessive. Wilhelm Solf, from his distant post as ambassador to Japan in the 1920s, warned his correspondents against what he regarded as the greatest weakness of the approach to a policy that he himself had shared before the war: basing too many hopes on the prospect of a future alliance with an Anglo-Saxon power.[20] Despite warnings of this sort, however, and despite the considerably more realistic view of the possibilities available in international politics that characterized Weimar in comparison with the *Kaiserreich,* the German governments of the 1920s continued to formulate policy within a framework of ideas that exaggerated the fundamental attractiveness to Britain of a permanent understanding or alliance with Germany. So deeply ingrained was this idea in German political conceptions that it was used to justify naval rebuilding during the 1928 debates on the first of the pocket battleships.[21] It even prevailed on Hitler, as we shall see.

Just as many features of Stresemann's diplomacy broke down at the time of the foreign minister's death in 1929 and during the years of economic and political crisis that followed, so also did the characteristic Weimar policy conceptions related to *Weltpolitik* lose much of their direction and effectiveness. During the depression, several leaders of heavy industry and banking began to look more favorably than they had previously done toward the extreme versions of the idea of central and eastern European economic integration—versions similar to the *Lebensraum* concept of *Mitteleuropa* that had been put forward before and during the First World War. In the radical conservative press, the coming of the depression was attended by a spate of calls for the establishment of a closed economic system in Europe, dominated and overtly controlled by Germany, within which *both* Germany industry *and* German agriculture would be protected.[22] Attached to an overseas empire, the system would be essentially autarkic. The attractiveness of this idea to business leaders and to politicians within parties closely attached to the interests of business stemmed partly from the circumstances of enhanced competition in the international economy during a time of depression, but even more from the circumstances of German politics in the late 1920s and early 1930s. To understand this development, we must turn to the career of *Lebensraum* during the Weimar Republic.

Continuity and Change in *Lebensraum* Ideology

Considering the slight connection between the conceptual base of *Lebensraum* and any sort of reality external to German politics, it may appear surprising that *Lebensraum* should not only have survived throughout the Weimar era as a viable political ideology, but also have emerged from Weimar as a major influence on national policy in the 1930s and 1940s.

To us, as to many social observers in the 1920s, the fundamental *Lebensraum* ideas of peasant agrarianism and settlement colonialism, even when brought up to date by association with economic imperialist ideas put forward within the framework of economic autarky, seem irrelevant to a modern industrial society. Why should *Lebensraum* have remained a significant part of the spectrum of political ideology in Germany?

We have already seen several of the reasons. The circumstances of a lost war and the tentative image projected by Weimar on the public mind tended to insulate ideologies such as *Lebensraum* from the effects of confrontations with empirical realities. It was easy for advocates of *Lebensraum* to argue that what made their position *seem* irrelevant was the social and political situation created by the "unnatural" 1918 revolution and the "unjust" Versailles treaty. *Lebensraum*, like other conservative ideological aggregations, could be held to indicate the proper direction for national policy once the temporary and dangerous interference of the Weimar system was ended.[23] Within such a structure of argumentation, *Lebensraum* imperialism could be quite effective as an agent of conservative consensus building.

An additional factor contributing to the continued existence and political effectiveness of *Lebensraum* was the very fact of its longevity as an ideological set and the extent to which it had been legitimated through its partial adoption by the government during the war and through its presentation as "science." Many of the ideas that justified *Lebensraum* imperialism had, for example, formally entered the processes of education and political socialization via the successive editions of Friedrich Ratzel's textbook on *"Heimatkunde,"* used in schools throughout Germany.[24] As we shall see in the discussion of geopolitics later in this chapter, newer and more effective means of legitimating *Lebensraum* as "science" had developed by the early 1920s—a factor that helped to condition at least part of the German political elite to regard policy conceptions derived from *Lebensraum* with some sympathy.

The most important reason, however, for the continued importance of *Lebensraum* in politics and for continuities in its ideological content was the fact that conservative political organizations that had adopted *Lebensraum* as an important part of their political programs remained in existence throughout the Weimar era and were joined by a host of others that similarly subscribed to *Lebensraum* ideas. *Lebensraum* had always been one of the most central, and certainly one of the most clearly defined, of the constituents of Wilhelmian radical conservatism. We have observed the manner in which political parties and interest groups adopted *Lebensraum*-oriented programs before and during the First World War. We have also examined the complex motives that led them to do so—especially the hope that *Lebensraum* imperialism would allow them to tap the sources of radical-conservative popularity without actually threatening elite interests. Once having been adopted by these parties and groups, *Lebensraum* ideas became part of their public images and part of the framework within which new program elements were improvised as needed. The utility of the expanded *Lebensraum* ideology of the First World War era in creating a conceptual basis for conservative political consensus remained apparent after the war, and the contrast between the policy implications of *Lebensraum* and the policies actually pursued by the governments of the 1920s made *Lebensraum* an especially useful part of the attack of the anti-Weimar parties on the republic.[25] Real effectiveness depended, however, on the ability of the organizations employing *Lebensraum* in public politics to expand the ideology further in some of the directions that had been taken during the war and to make it appear to be relevant to the specific concerns of important social groups in the 1920s.

Several of the organizations with which the *Lebensraum* ideological complex was traditionally associated survived more-or-less intact after 1918. One of these was the Colonial Society, which had incorporated *Lebensraum* supporters within its ranks and *Lebensraum* ideas within its program but had not succeeded before 1918 in satisfactorily integrating *Lebensraum* with the *Weltpolitik* that it also espoused. We shall examine the Colonial Society later in this chapter in the special context of German colonialism under Weimar. Continuity with the past was even stronger in the case of the Pan-German League, which had in many ways pioneered the use of *Lebensraum* as a central part of a more extensive radical-conservative program before the war. However, although the Pan-Germans continued to advocate the same sort of program as before and although they took part in a variety of organized movements on the radical right, their day as an important political force had essentially passed.[26] The idiosyncratic leadership of Heinrich Class, the inability of the league to transform itself into a mass party, and the fact that a large array of other groups—ranging from the DNVP to the nascent Nazi movement—eventually adopted practically all of the Pan-Germans' ideological positions left the league as but one among many groups calling for much the same thing: the forceful overturning by Germany of Versailles, the replacement of republican institutions by more truly "German" ones, and the acquisition of an adequate amount of living space to guarantee Germany's political security, her economic well-being, and the agrarian roots of her culture.

The first two of these program points were, of course, specific to the circumstances of Weimar as perceived on the political right, but they had pre-Weimar histories as well. The second point especially (the aim of altering the republican political structure) was directly connected to the attempt by the *Vaterlandspartei* and other conservative organizations during the war to head off the democratizing of Germany—an event which, in fact, occurred in 1918–19 through the revolution that the conservatives had feared and through the state-building actions of the very people who had advocated political reform before 1918. Republican Germany was now a fact rather than part of a frightening future. The connection of antirepublicanism to the third point, the need for sufficient geographic space and economic resources to be able to support German society, also had a long prehistory (as we have seen). *Lebensraum* imperialism conventionally justified opposition to liberal and socialist ideas by emphasizing the need for discipline, orderly acceptance of authority, and government action to protect the most important foundations of German culture. Through its links to the loose aggregation of anti-industrial, agrarian, and anti-Semitic concepts that constituted much of radical-conservative ideology in Germany, *Lebensraum* also retained its appeal as a means through which conservative groups could rally support among the varied segments of the general population that responded favorably to such concepts without, apparently, risking any elite interests of great importance.[27] The displacement function of imperialist ideology still worked in the 1920s. In fact, one of the main directions taken in the further development of *Lebensraum* in the 1920s was toward an ideological framework that gave priority to the concerns about industrialization and modernity embodied in most elements of radical-conservative ideology and simultaneously afforded an ideological justification for policies beneficial to big business.

Lebensraum imperialism, in other words, became diffused in the 1920s along almost the entire political right in Germany, both as part of the framework of social ideas with which conservatives genuinely attempted to structure their alternatives to Weimar policies and as a tool for creating popular consensus behind the varied aims of the major conservative groups. The DNVP, for example, included demands for agrarian living space and inner colonization as parts of its program.[28] The former could, of course, be interpreted merely as a basis for demanding the return of the territories taken from Germany at the end of the First World War; the latter was ostensibly a recommendation for a purely internal policy of resettling urban populations in rural areas. The logic that lay behind the living space idea, however, was such that no reasonable analysis of the concept could lead to any other conclusion than that Germany would eventually have to expand beyond her 1914 borders.[29] We have already seen how readily the inner colonization idea could be extended into a notion of territorial annexation in Europe—so much so that the term itself had come to be used during the war to refer to external expansion to acquire agricultural land. Other conservative organizations, ranging from the *Stahlhelm* to the Nazis, made similar pronouncements with similar implications.[30]

The DNVP was a heterogeneous party, both in the social composition of its leadership and in the attitudes and ideological positions of its members. It was to some extent an updated version of the old Conservative and Free Conservative parties, but it was also closely connected to radical-conservative groups such as the Pan-Germans and to conservative industrial and white-collar unions. It attempted to incorporate as many elite-interest groups as possible into its leadership segment and to make as broad a public appeal as it could, using any means of doing so consistent with the general tenor of its aims.[31] This created tensions within the party. The party leadership included a "moderate" wing of business

leaders and government officials who represented the kind of government–business establishment that many on the "radical" right claimed to
execrate. We have already seen that, although the "moderate" Karl Helfferich criticized the details of Weimar policy before his death in 1924, he
and a large part of the DNVP's old-line establishment leadership in the
early and mid-1920s shared many of Stresemann's long-range aims—especially the ones that were closely connected with the *Weltpolitik* imperialist
tradition. Helfferich and others also opposed the inclusion of blatantly
radical-conservative elements in the DNVP program, including *Lebensraum* and an open avowal of anti-Semitism.[32] Throughout most of the
1920s, the DNVP's leadership under Count Kuno von Westarp performed
a kind of balancing act between the "moderates" and the "radicals." The
latter included the Pan-Germans and other groups that advocated the
full-scale adoption by the DNVP of a program encompassing noncoopera-
tion with the Allies, immediate rearmament, *Lebensraum* imperialism,
anti-Semitism, and the protection of social classes threatened by industrialization. The eventual rise of Alfred Hugenberg to the leadership of the
party marked the triumph of the radical wing. Even before the success of
the radicals, however, the party had come to incorporate a wide variety
of radical-conservative elements into its program.[33] The party's program,
like the programs of practically all other political parties in Weimar Germany, thus represented an attempt at a compromise among the various
interest organizations, social groups, and ideological leanings that the
party attempted to incorporate.

Under these circumstances, there was considerable motivation to find
means of reconciling the different, apparently irreconcilable ideological
structures through which a would-be mass conservative organization such
as the DNVP wanted to organize its appeal. It can be argued, for instance,
that the return of establishment conservatism to an advocacy of anti-Semitism in the mid-1920s was the result not simply of a desire to attract support
from anti-Semites in competition with more radical groups, but also of a
need to reconcile the antiindustrialist, anticapitalist, antimodern elements
of radical-conservative ideology to the fact that the DNVP was backed by
industrialists and financiers and sought, among other things, to advance
the interests of the capitalist elite.[34] As in the 1890s, when the same problem arose for the conservative parties, anti-Semitism provided a convenient means of having an ideological cake and eating it too. It was possible
to argue that, although there were many problems with modern industrial
society, they could all be corrected by a truly German government with
close connections to the realities of German culture, nationality, and race.
What was fundamentally wrong with modern capitalism and industry as
they existed was that they were controlled directly or indirectly by Jews,
who were essentially cultureless and internationalist in outlook and certainly not German. A large advance in solving the ills of modern society
could be made by eliminating the influence of the Jews in Germany. This
argument was, of course, similar to ones that conservatives in search of

working-class votes made about socialists and Communists: that the aspirations of the working class were, many of them, entirely legitimate and would be satisfied in a properly governed Germany. The main obstacle to their satisfaction was *Jewish* (not German) capitalism and Jewish-inspired, internationalist socialism.[35]

The need for means of overcoming ideological divergences within the potential support bases of the DNVP and other conservative organizations also greatly affected their use of imperialist ideas. Quite apart from the strong convictions that many conservative leaders had that an active imperialist policy was essential for Germany, imperialism had become important to the consensus-building aspect of generalized conservative political action. But as the ideological heritage of German imperialism was split and as each of the major versions of imperialist ideology contained elements or connotations obnoxious to one group of potential conservative voters or another, some kind of reworking was necessary to create the semblance, at least, of an integrated conservative-imperialist ideology. The general line taken by practically all groups seeking conservative ideological integration was that pioneered by the Pan-Germans and by such writers as Bernhardi before the war, although substantial modifications in specifics occurred in the 1920s.

As in the past, the main framework for ideological integration was provided by the many-sided "threat" to Germany as a nation and to the Germans as a people, which all conservative political organizations decried. The fact that Germany was plainly surrounded by enemies who had taken from her in 1918 many of the things that her people needed for survival required not only that Germany adopt a form of government that could lead the country effectively and unify the actions of its population, but also that all potential sources of strength be marshalled. Thus, although industrialization and its consequences were obnoxious in a certain sense to all right-thinking Germans, the nation's ability to defend itself against its enemies depended on maintaining German industrial superiority. Not only that, but national security required that industry possess the raw materials necessary to keep it in operation and the markets needed to produce a profit. Hence a proper national policy would include provisions for maintaining and advancing the interests of the industrial sector— subject always to the requirement that pursuing such interests not be ultimately inimical to the other needs of the German people.[36] German culture in its broadest sense—the basic elements of the distinctive German personality and the qualities that defined the essence of the *Volk*— still needed to be protected against the disintegrating effects of modernity and industrialization. This could best be accomplished by the construction of a society and economy based on the peasant farmer, a construction to be accomplished primarily through inner colonization. Unless the essence of *Deutschtum* were thus protected, the attempt to regain German power and security through military and industrial strength would go for nought.

Both the aim of industrial advancement and the goal of protecting German culture were compatible if somehow national priorities were kept straight.[37]

The traditional structure of the *Lebensraum* argument, reinforced by the "scientific" notion of living space propagated by the geopoliticians of the 1920s, was generally an adequate means of presenting the long-term goal of cultural protection through settlement. Both overseas and continental European versions of *Lebensraum* were advanced, with different degrees of emphasis, in the programs of various groups. Practically all conservative organizations (indeed, practically all parties of whatever stripe, except those on the far left) formally demanded a return of Germany's lost colonies.[38] On the whole, conservative groups also favored a degree of overseas colonial expansion beyond Germany's limited pre-1914 holdings under the assumption that a great power, which Germany had to be, required a great overseas empire. Among the reasons prominently given for the reacquisition of an overseas empire was the standard *Lebensraum* one of finding settlement room for small farmers to relieve population pressure in Germany and to spare as many Germans as possible from the debilitating effects of living in an industrial setting.[39] Some groups, preeminently the Colonial Society, strongly emphasized the need for overseas colonization as opposed to policies directed toward the European continent. Most conservative organizations, however, ranging from the DNVP to the Nazis, tended to place their emphasis on *Lebensraum* transported to Europe—particularly to the areas removed from Germany by the Versailles treaty, to "underused" agricultural areas within Germany itself, and to areas to the east beyond Germany's 1914 borders.[40] In this respect, conservative ideology was following the directions that had been developing within *Lebensraum* since before the First World War.

The problem, of course, was to integrate an updated, Europe-oriented *Lebensraum* advertised as a primary goal of policy with a policy that recognized the "needs" of industry as well. It was something that the legitimacy of industrial production as a means to the end of securing German culture was acknowledged within the structure of conservative ideology, but how were expansionary aims in the service of industry to be reconciled with *Lebensraum?* (It must be remembered that there were *real* industrial interests involved. To be successful, conservative policy aims had to be compatible with the actual investment and marketing intentions of a large part of organized business.)[41] Rohrbach's approach before the war—giving settlement colonialism priority in certain colonies and framing policy in central Europe and in other colonies in terms of *Weltpolitik*—would not work in the context of a *Lebensraum* displaced to Europe. The answer that was found was the concept of economic autarky.

We have examined the emergence of the idea of autarky in the years just before and during the First World War.[42] An intrinsically appealing concept at a very superficial level during times of war and international tension, it had acquired its specific meaning in German political discourse as an extension of the *Lebensraum* version of central and eastern European economic union. The idea of autarky in this context had resulted from the lack of interest outside Germany in a form of international economic integration that simultaneously created protected industrial markets for Germany *and* protected German grain agriculture. Such a regime could only be established through a massive use of force by Germany. This could be done in wartime, but it required some sort of logical justification in the face of the *Weltpolitikers'* argument that the system thus established would be extremely inefficient (unlike their own proposals, which would sacrifice German grain agriculture in order to create the necessary exchanges within the system). Autarky—a condition of economic self-sufficiency constructed on a network of production and exchange entirely encompassed within an integrated geographic area under a single overall authority—was justified not by economic efficiency but by the supposed requirements of war. Military success could only be achieved if the economic foundations on which victory rested were secure from outside interference. Coincidentally, the political structure established to operate the autarkic economic system in the heartland of Europe would also protect the interests of the major economic groups in Germany.

The autarkic economic model remained a part of the *Lebensraum* ideological aggregation after 1918. Its appeal derived from several sources: its widespread acceptance on the political right during the war; the fact that autarky as an implicit aim of national policy had received official sanction during the war; the belief of many Germans that Germany's postwar condition constituted a demonstration of the need to secure sources of national economic strength; the belief of many politicians that the concept of autarky had great potential as a conservative integrating force. The problems of the DNVP and the other organizations seeking conservative consensus in the 1920s were in many ways the same as those facing their predecessors. *Lebensraum* connected to an autarkic economic scheme still incorporated a potentially useful package of appeals to industrialists, *Mittelstand,* and agrarians, given the assumption that a national emergency continued to exist.[43]

The key, of course, was the extent to which the package could attract the support of organized big business. Although the integrative effects of the idea always had a considerable amount of appeal, the practicality of autarky as a policy goal in Germany's weakened state between 1918 and the mid-1920s seemed to be highly questionable to the leadership of groups such as the RdI. Under the favorable economic circumstances of the period 1924 to 1929, the Stresemann approach to economic diplomacy appeared to be much more reasonable, even to many of the most conservative of business leaders.[44] The distinction between heavy industry (metals and coal) and the finished goods and chemical industries, which has been heavily used by historians of Weimar and the Nazi period in explaining the complexities of interest-group involvement in politics, has some bearing here. On the whole, the heavy-industrial organizations tended to accept the idea of autarky more readily than did the representatives of the other major industrial agglomerations, both because they had a long history of attempting to accommodate the agrarian right and because their export aims were still largely directed toward continental Europe and thus could be to some extent encompassed within an autarkic economic policy. On the other hand, banks, industries dependent on extra-European imports, and industries with diversified markets abroad found the prospect of an autarkic economic policy less attractive under normal circumstances.[45] Most industrial groups maintained their connections with all "respectable" political organizations of the right and center in Weimar politics and were careful not to disassociate themselves from any ideological tendency that might be useful to them, either for immediate purposes of pursuing particular economic interests or as a means of defending capitalism as an economic system. But in general, concepts of economic autarky—the establishment of a closed economic system controlled by Germany and containing essentially all of Germany's markets, investment areas, and sources of raw materials—were relatively ineffective in appealing to organized big business until the coming of the depression in 1929.

From the standpoint of practical politics, the depression provided the ideal occasion for a revival of the concept of autarky. The emergency created by the depression sufficiently resembled that of the war to give a strong suggestion of verisimilitude to ideological constructs that had originally built their legitimacy on the conditions of world war. Many business leaders (indeed, people in all walks of life) concluded that the depression was a fundamental crisis of capitalism as an economic system and that it might be attended by a working-class revolution. The times demanded a rallying of the center and right and brought to the forefront ideologies that could contribute to a full reconciliation of all potential elements of a conservative consensus.[46] *Lebensraum* attached to the notion of autarky was one of the most obvious of these. Furthermore, the idea of direct government intervention in the rest of Europe to secure markets completely free of competition became suddenly more appealing to industrialists as they observed aggregate demand rapidly dissolve throughout the industrial world and protectionist sentiment arise everywhere. Autarky might not be the ideal end of national policy, but responding favorably to political groups (the DNVP, the *Stahlhelm,* eventually even the Nazis) that strongly pushed autarkic policies after 1929 might well be a good way to encourage the formation of a political bloc that could protect capitalism in extremis and that could, if it attained power, meet many of the immediate needs of industry in its external marketing areas.[47]

The policy aims pursued under Stresemann did not die with the coming of the depression, but their ability to elicit consensus within the business community certainly diminished. The Brüning government had neither the intention of following an autarkic policy nor, given Germany's actual diplomatic and military position, the means of doing so. Although it greatly modified the direction of Germany's economic diplomacy in accordance with its reading of the post-1929 situation and its own ideological predilections, its policies with respect to the questions of importance to imperialist ideology cannot be regarded as a switch to an alternative ideological foundation, except perhaps in the matter of economic assistance to agriculture in the eastern districts.[48] Nevertheless, the economic policies of the Stresemann era clearly lost their *political* effectiveness in the wake of the depression and with the renewal of the appeal of the concept of autarky in connection with *Lebensraum*.

The attempt to integrate industrial concerns and some elements of economic imperialism into a framework of ideology founded on the *Lebensraum* tradition was not the only important development in *Lebensraum* imperialism in the Weimar era. There were changes in the colonial aspect of *Lebensraum*, changes also in the way that *Lebensraum* concepts were presented in the guise of legitimate science, and a substantial expansion of the impact of imperialist ideas (especially ones derived from *Lebensraum*) on the public consciousness. These changes will be considered in the later sections of the present chapter. A further change was the development of a relatively new, if fundamentally absurd, argument within the context of *Lebensraum* connecting the traditional *Lebensraum* conceptions with racist ideas.

Racism had never been completely absent from presentations of *Lebensraum* imperialism since the emergence of the latter as a radical conservative ideology in the 1890s. The racism connected with *Lebensraum* as an imperialist ideology, however, was not particularly distinctive; racism was inherent in practically every European imperialist ideology in the late nineteenth century. As an ideology operative in domestic German politics, *Lebensraum* picked up racist elements—particularly anti-Semitism and antipolonism—from its close association with the other ideological components of pre-1914 German radical conservatism. It would be difficult to argue, however, as we saw in the analysis of Bernhardi's writings in Chapter Seven, that these were successfully integrated into the structure of *Lebensraum*. The basic assumptions of *Lebensraum* ideology focused on culture and environment, not race. Both intellectually and in terms of constructing a politically effective argument, the functional link between *Lebensraum* and biological racism was made in the 1920s.

The linkage was manifested, among other places, in the Nazi concept of *Blut und Boden*, but it was made almost simultaneously under various names throughout the radical right in the 1920s.[49] The intellectual problem was to reconcile the arguments of *Lebensraum*, which held that ideal national personality characteristics and social and cultural forms were products of the interactions between peoples and their environments, with the "scientific" racism that had demonstrated its popularity since the late nineteenth century and was especially useful as an explanation of the right of a particular people to dominate others. The obviously materialistic origins of racist thinking were also difficult to reconcile with the traditions from which much of *Lebensraum* sprang. In the 1920s, it became customary to argue that *both* genetic *and* environmental factors played significant roles in the composition of a *Volk* and that the true German *Volk* could not survive and prosper without a national policy that took account of both. The physical and mental strength of the Germanic race lay in its unusual ability to realize its full potential through interaction with nature in a challenging rural environment. Other races, confronted with such an environment, were genetically incapable of making as much of it as the Germans were. Races such as the Slavs and the Jews, for example, were unsuited to efficient individual peasant farming and could not, even under the best of circumstances, play their proper, biologically determined roles in such a setting. On the other hand, a German people degenerated by racial intermixture or the physical effects of the modern urban environment could not do so either. Racial purity and the proper environment were inseparable requirements for German culture. Indeed, the rural small-farm environment was seen as a means of maintaining racial purity because it would limit opportunities for degenerative interracial breeding.[50]

This kind of argument became an important basis for Nazi policymaking during World War II and eventually the special preserve of the SS. It was immediately important to radical-conservative groups in the 1920s in two ways: it helped to smooth over a rough part of the general radical-conservative ideological set where a contradiction was particularly likely to be noticed by the public, and it created a means by which possible dissonance in the belief patterns of conservative politicians themselves could be overcome. It is possible that one of the reasons that *Blut-und-Boden* thinking played such an important role in the conscious political thought of radical-conservatives was that it provided a way around a problem that impeded their own ability to believe in their ideological pronouncements wholeheartedly.

Colonialism and the Colonial Movement

The history of the German colonial movement during the Weimar and Hitler periods has been rather thoroughly investigated, especially by Klaus Hilderbrand and Wolfe Schmokel, and need not be discussed in detail here.[51] What is necessary is that we attempt to fit the ideological positions taken by the colonial movement into the general framework of interpretation presented in the rest of this chapter.

Patterns of organizational and ideological continuity in imperialism were especially pronounced in the Weimar colonial movement, as were the tendencies toward imperialist ideological integration in response to the political circumstances of the era. The organizational center of German colonialism remained the German Colonial Society. Indeed, because the colonial administration and several of the old colonial-interest groups ceased to exist with the loss of the colonial empire, the Colonial Society was left in a more significant position with respect to German colonialism as a whole than it had previously occupied. Moreover, public support for the positions taken by the Colonial Society was probably much more extensive than it had ever been before. In part, this was a result of the provisions of the Versailles treaty, which stripped Germany of her colonies on the grounds that she had proven herself "unfit" to govern an overseas empire. This gave the demand for the return of the colonies, which was the Colonial Society's central program point, major symbolic importance as a rejection of the Versailles treaty and the logic that lay behind it. The Colonial Society argued with some justice that Germany's colonial rule had been no harsher or more inept than that of the victorious powers. It also argued, with very little justice, that Germany's former colonies were vital to her economic and political future. If both points were true, then under any reasonable interpretation of the "laws" of international politics, the Versailles treaty was unfair and Germany's colonies ought to be returned to her. More than that, most spokespersons of the colonial movement argued that, in fact, Germany had done an unusually good job of conducting native policy and therefore ought to assume an even greater share of the burden of "civilizing" the non-European world through colonialism. Also, since the German colonies, although vital to the German economy, were unable to provide all of the benefits that colonies were supposed to do because of their relatively small extent and population, the same logic that required the return of the overseas empire also required its expansion.[52]

The Colonial Society itself and the larger union of colonialist organizations which it sponsored and dominated generally advanced these aims as a call for a comprehensive agreement with the Versailles signatory powers that would recognize the justice of Germany's case; but they were willing to consider practically any policy approach that would yield the basic end of a reacquisition of Germany's overseas empire. Almost all organized political pressure groups (except those on the far left), all the major political parties from the SPD to the DNVP (including the Nazis but excluding the Communists), and practically all economic lobbying organizations rallied behind this general aim.[53] One of the things that kept the Colonial Society going in the absence of a colonial empire was the financial and political support it received almost across the board in German politics—a situation radically different from that in which the colonial movement had operated before the war.

As Hildebrand has pointed out, the leadership of the Colonial Society retained its prewar connections to the social and political elite into the 1920s. Its executive committee and the committees of its local branches were filled with industrialists, bankers, nobles, and politicians (usually, but not always, conservative ones.)[54] There was one major difference, however. The full-time leaders of the society, the people who occupied the chief positions in its hierarchy and who had the greatest influence on its political direction, were almost all retired colonial officials—mostly ex-colonial governors such as Theodor Seitz and Heinrich Schnee (both of whom also served as presidents of the society). Colonial officials had played a relatively small role in the domestic colonial movement before the war. During Weimar, with nothing much else to do and with a definite axe to grind (having had their careers cut short just as some of them might have attained really high bureaucratic rank), they literally took over the running of the Colonial Society and invested it with their own interests. It was thus not simply as an establishment organization that the Colonial Society functioned in Weimar politics, but also as the representative of a particular small interest group with little access to political power apart from whatever image the idea of overseas empire could conjure up in the minds of the public and whatever leverage the symbolic value of the lost empire gave them in the context of anti-Versailles politics.

These circumstances help to explain the position of the Colonial Society with respect to the ideological traditions of German colonialism and imperialism. It was presented fortuitously with an issue—the return of the empire—over which few political groups could afford to disagree with the society. The parties of the right had to adopt a colonialist line because any other would have been inconsistent with the attack on Versailles. Business interest groups such as the RdI had to do the same because otherwise they would have appeared as "antinational" before public opinion. (In addition, the directors of some businesses thought that a return of the colonies would produce favorable investment opportunities overseas.) The pro-Weimar parties—the DVP, the DDP, and the SPD—were under such constant attack from the right for their willingness to operate for the time being under the shadow of Versailles that they grasped eagerly at the opportunity to support the colonial movement, which gave them the appearance of defending a vital national interest and of opposing Versailles without risking very much.[55]

This does not mean that the expressions of colonialist sentiment by such groups were insincere. Stresemann himself had always been a conscientious imperialist, and there was nothing feigned in his assurances to the Colonial Society that he believed Germany should have a large colonial empire. In Stresemann's case, it was a question of priorities. It was more important for Germany in the immediate future to obtain the cooperation of the other Western European powers in diplomatic matters and then to build a system of European economic relations dominated by German industry than it was to obtain overseas colonies.[56] Once the primary objectives had been met, the reversion of the colonial empire (indeed, its expansion into *Mittelafrika,* which was still constantly discussed in colonialist circles) would be obtained without difficulty. For the time being, Stresemann found it expedient to placate the colonialists, insist publicly on Germany's "right" to colonies, but to do nothing unless an unusual opportunity arose. Similarly, the fact that, in part for political reasons, conservative politicians emphasized the return of the colonies and the eventual expansion of the colonial empire did not mean that they were necessarily hypocritical about colonies. It was again a matter of priorities. The tendency of conservative ideologists to emphasize *Lebensraum* and eastward expansion over colonial expansion during the 1920s did not imply a rejection of colonialism altogether. But European aims came first, and it appeared to increasing numbers of conservatives that colonies could never be expected to achieve all of the benefits for German society that the convinced colonialists claimed.[57]

The leaders of the Colonial Society thus had good reason to believe that the widespread support they obtained so easily from political and lobbying organizations lacked something in depth, no matter how sincere the personal assurances of people such as Stresemann might be. Throughout the 1920s, they could regularly rely on the participation of most political groups in the Colonial Society's activities and on statements of support from almost everybody who mattered to them, but they could neither persuade the German government to make return of the colonies a matter of major national priority nor convince any significant political bloc to put the kind of pressure on the government that was needed to change this situation. They could organize and finance a colonial propaganda campaign of unparalleled scope—a campaign that dwarfed prewar efforts—because of the generous support of big business, but they were aware that such support was granted more for the political statement that it made about the patriotism of the organizations that afforded it than for any depth of conviction about the importance of colonies among the nation's priorities. Hildebrand argues that this realization was one of the factors that led the society after 1928 to investigate the possibility of cooperation with the Nazis—a party that had shown little more than the obligatory interest in colonies up until that time.[58] If properly "educated" on colonial matters, Hitler might provide the popular backing that the colonial movement needed and a means of exerting effective pressure on policy.

The Colonial Society's stance on ideological matters reflected its leadership's conception of its political position. The society generally avoided political statements that would offend any of its actual or potential supporters or would divide its leaders (who belonged to several different conservative and moderate parties). With respect to the ideological dichotomy that was all too obvious in the German imperialist tradition, the Colonial Society did its best to avoid occasions for conflict. Most of the society's leaders (with the exception of former Colonial Secretary Lindequist and a few retired military officers active in the colonial veterans' association) were strongly identified with the colonial aspects of the *Weltpolitik* ideology. Schnee himself had been an object of some displeasure on the part of settlement colonialists during his term as governor of

East Africa immediately before the outbreak of the war, although he had shown considerable skill in compromising with them without surrendering policy direction entirely.[59] Under the circumstances obtaining in the postwar period, however, it was to the advantage of Schnee and the other leaders of the movement to seek to downplay all ideological differences within the ranks of colonialists.

The Colonial Society had always tried to accommodate both settlement enthusiasts and economic colonialists; now the society made a determined effort actually to integrate the two directions into a single ideological pattern. This was easier to do after 1918 when, in the absence of actual colonies, annoying issues arising from the formulation and implementation of real policies did not appear. The propaganda of the Colonial Society argued, for example, that the overseas colonies were absolutely vital to the continued growth and security of German industry because they would be markets and sources of industrial raw materials for the future. Colonialists still generally referred to the future because the past had not provided too convincing a proof of the colonialists' case. On the other hand, the society also liberally employed *Lebensraum* arguments about the need to find an outlet for Germany's "excess" population and to relieve the pressure on the country's overcrowded, morally depressing cities. It was argued, Rohrbach fashion, that different parts of the empire would accommodate different policies—especially if the African colonies were expanded into *Mittelafrika*.[60] Confronted with the threat that the inner colonization idea and the eastward direction of 1920s *Lebensraum* ideology might weaken the support base of the colonial movement, the Colonial Society countered with a vigorous affirmation of the social and cultural benefits of colonial settlement.[61] Rather than rejecting the dangerous *Lebensraum* view of eastward expansion, the Colonial Society played the same priorities game that everyone else did. Colonial settlement could be effectuated more readily in the immediate future; inner colonization and eastern settlement were possibilities for later. A serious problem appeared in the late 1920s when a radical-conservative, *Lebensraum*-oriented movement arose among the colonialists and attempted to get the Colonial Society to adopt a strongly settlement-oriented program that explicitly acknowledged the priority of a continental European settlement policy. The society's leaders, when they found that they could not put the *Lebensraum* colonialists off, firmly rejected their efforts.[62] For all of their pronouncements about settlement, the leaders of the Colonial Society remained primarily *Weltpolitiker* and economic colonialists at heart, and they would continue to be so into the Nazi era.

The colonial pronouncements of most of the conservative parties of the 1920s, including both the DNVP and the Nazis, similarly included elements derived both from *Lebensraum* and economic imperialism. Considerable play was given to the idea of *Mittelafrika*, which had been, even before the war, the kind of expansionary colonial aim that practically all segments of imperialist opinion could agree about.[63] Overseas colonialism attained an unprecedented breadth of superficial support among conservatives, while it moved even farther in reality from the center of their political concerns.

Geopolitics

Of the many intellectual movements at the boundary between academia and politics with which the Weimar era abounded, probably none was more important to the development of Nazi imperialist ideology than the group that sponsored the notion of geopolitics. The geopoliticians were significant for two reasons. In the first place, they developed the most superficially convincing and successful intellectual structure within which imperialist ideas could be legitimated as "science" and to some extent integrated into one program. Second, geopolitics may have exercised influence over the formulation of Adolf Hitler's imperialist conceptions. One root of the amazingly eclectric imperialist ideology enunciated after the early 1920s by the Nazis was the work of Karl Haushofer, the founder of the German school of geopolitics, and his followers.[64] Haushofer's ideas exerted influence through Rudolf Hess, who had been a student of Haushofer's at the University of Munich just after the war.

Haushofer (1869–1946) was a retired Bavarian general who held a university doctorate, had travelled widely before the First World War, and had become a professor at Munich at the war's conclusion.[65] Here he gathered around himself and his *Zeitschrift für Geopolitik* students and junior academics who were attracted by Haushofer's conservative ideas and his systematic conception of a link between geography and politics. The geopoliticians trained and influenced by Haushofer actually held a variety of political opinions within the broad scope of German conservatism, and their emphases within the conceptual inventory of geopolitics varied considerably, largely according to their specific political predilections. Although Haushofer himself favored such radical-conservative ideas as the creation of a political consensus around a "national" form of socialism, nevertheless, he operated most effectively among conservative elite groups and felt distinctly uncomfortable among such "unrefined" conservatives as the Nazis. He was, however, willing to accommodate himself to any political group that he thought could set Germany on the right political course and that would accept his own views as bases for foreign policy. Like many other leading German conservatives, he believed that once an integrated nationalist movement was established, with the assistance if necessary of radical conservatism as an ideology and a political force, it would be readily subject to control by the educated elite—especially if that elite had a clear idea of the foundations of proper German policy as provided by geopolitics. To Haushofer, the idea of geopolitics held one of the keys both to the creation of conservative consensus and to the making of correct national policy. Many of his disciples were much more wholehearted radical conservatives than he.[66] We shall concentrate here on Haushofer's version of geopolitics rather than the somewhat divergent views of his more radical followers because of Haushofer's more extensive reputation and his influence on the Nazis.

For all of its obvious political motivation and ideological content, Haushofer's geopolitics stood in a long line of genuine social scientific thinking about the physical environment and its relationship to society and politics. The line, it is true, was inextricably linked to politics throughout its length and suffered as theory from this linkage. But geopolitics could, nevertheless, appear to be, and to some extent was, a policy-oriented variant of the legitimate academic discipline of geography. Haushofer acknowledged Friedrich Ratzel as the main intellectual precursor of geopolitics and acknowledged also the influence of the Swedish political scientist Rudolf Kjellén, the inventor of the term *geopolitics*. Also important in Haushofer's thinking was the military tradition of strategic thought in a theoretical geographic context that dated back to General von Roon, Prussian war minister during the early Bismarck era.[67] From the standpoint of our subject, however, the influence of Ratzel and his theories is most significant. Haushofer accepted most of Ratzel's general analysis of the relationship between environment and society, with substantial modification in detail. Haushofer made extensive use of Ratzel's concept of *Lebensraum,* a term he helped to popularize in both its narrow Ratzelian meaning and in the broader sense in which the word is used in the present study. As we have already seen, Ratzel's ideas of *Lebensraum* implicitly contained many of the most important elements of the *Lebensraum* imperialist ideology; so it continued to do with Haushofer. Moreover, Haushofer also adopted Ratzel's previously described technique of linking different conceptions of imperialism through the use of a supposedly "scientific" hierarchy of relationships between man and his environment.[68] Using these and other approaches, Haushofer managed to construct an intellectual framework that could represent itself as a broad scientific theory and simultaneously incorporate together most of the *Lebensraum* ideology and key elements of the *Weltpolitik* imperialist tradition.

Following Ratzel, Haushofer implicitly defined the fundamental organizational unit of history—the *Volk,* represented socially as the nation and politically as the state—in cultural, economic, and geographic terms rather than racial ones. Although some of his disciples brought racial factors to the forefront in their approaches to geopolitics, Haushofer, while not openly rejecting racist thinking, perceived the incompatibilities between racialist social science and the kind of environmental view that he himself took. The *Volk* was a product of interactions between a group of people (however biologically constituted) and a highly complex, changing physical environment. The environment, in changing, altered the *Volk,* but the environment could also be significantly changed *by* the *Volk* through purposeful political and military action as well as the application of technology. The "science" of geopolitics focused on the identification of the environmental factors required for the maintenance, growth, and strength of a *Volk* and its associated nation and state. Once these factors and any deficiencies in their attainment by a particular state were identified, geopolitics supposedly provided the objective basis for making policy to correct the deficiencies. Geopolitics was "the science of the relationship between space and politics which particularly attempts to show how geographical knowledge can be transformed into intellectual equipment for political leaders."[69]

The most important of these factors was the possession of an adequate amount of *Lebensraum*. Haushofer employed an exceptionally broad conception of living space. He argued that each *Volk* needed a certain amount of geographic space in which to live and that a vigorous, growing people like the Germans needed an increasing amount of it. If the Germans were to stop growing in numbers or if their access to new living space were cut off, they would be doomed in their competition with other peoples.[70] Beneath this argument lay a complicated system of circular reasoning resting in the duality of "people" and "environment" within a logical structure in which the two items in the duality, when they were defined at all, were defined in terms of each other. To claim to reveal a *Volk*'s "objective" requirements for environmental change when a *Volk* was itself treated as a *product* of present and past environments opened the door to innumerable tautologies. One could claim that practically any territorial policy one wished to advocate was based on the needs of the *Volk* without much fear of effective contradiction within the scope of geopolitical thinking. This made ultimately for poor, untestable theory and therefore for poor policy recommendations, but it was extremely useful for legitimating imperialist policies and the ideologies that lay behind them in terms that were supposedly scientific. It was also useful for reconciling apparent contradictions between different expansionary policies derived from different ideological traditions.

Haushofer, like Ratzel before him, saw *Lebensraum* as a highly complex entity that consisted of several different forms of relationship between human society and the environment. He used, as Ratzel had, a hierarchical categorization of these forms to relate them to each other and develop implications for action. In keeping with the ideological tradition of *Lebensraum,* Haushofer claimed that the most fundamental form of living space was the land a people needed to support its agricultural population—in the case of the Germans, as individual peasant farmers. According to Haushofer, the peasant regime brought with it all of the advantages that the *Lebensraum* tradition assigned to it: it preserved the "true" character of the people; it secured the fundamental basis on which their entire economy rested; it was the ultimate recourse in case a real policy of economic autarky was forced on the nation; and so on. Peasant agricultural living space provided the "roots" of the German *Volk,* without which the effective maintenance of other forms of living space was impossible.

Although Haushofer gave a conventional priority to the traditional, narrow view of living space, with all of its implications for continually expanding borders and for limitations on the process of industrialization, it was precisely this part of his theories with which Haushofer appeared to be the least happy. In concrete terms, the resources that Germany would have to devote to securing the necessary space to put a settlement program into effect and to make it work would be immense and would undoubtedly divert attention from the other necessary parts of a proper program of geopolitics. Furthermore, under normal conditions, it was far from clear that a system of extensive peasant farms would be economically efficient as an agricultural complement to the industrial sector. Probably because of considerations of this sort, Haushofer tended to downplay the agricultural settlement aspect of geopolitics after stating it and giving it theoretical priority.[71] From a political standpoint, it was necessary that it be included in the total scheme if Haushofer wanted his ideas to serve as an effective integrating force on the German political right, but he was not inclined to push the idea too far in his recommendations for policy.

Haushofer was much more interested in the other forms of living space to which he nominally accorded a lower priority in his hierarchy of relationships. One aspect of *Lebensraum* encompassed the geographic surface area needed to conduct a successful military defense of the nation (and to conduct successful aggression as well). Here, Haushofer managed to incorporate into his "scientific" theory the very important integrating and legitimizing device of military security. Another form of living space was defined by the area covered by the system of economic exchanges on which a modern people with an industrial economy depended. A large industrial sector was necessary for national autonomy and survival. The maintenance of the industrial sector must not be permitted to restrict the area needed for the peasant "roots" of the people and must not be allowed to sap the people's vigor; apart from that, a correct national policy had to encompass the security and expansion of industry. A nation should possess some form of control over its markets and sources of raw materials; as the needs of the nation expanded with rising population, these controlled markets and sources of raw materials had to expand as well.[72]

Haushofer's model for the successful pursuit of policy according to these maxims was Japan, which he contrasted to the *Kaiserreich*—a failure in the search for economic *Lebensraum*.[73] The major differences were two. First, Japan's leaders understood the basic principles of geopolitics, which the old German political elite had not. The Japanese established a firm foundation for the domestic economy by developing industries and protecting their domestic markets. Only then did they pursue a course of overseas expansion; when they did, it was always with a clear conception in mind of how each new acquisition and each penetration into a new market could be related to the overall aim of an integrated economic system extending out from Japan. The German *Reich* before the war had not been able to get its priorities straight and had vacillated from one goal to another, seeking colonies at one time and continental economic domination at another. This failing was explicable through the second difference between Japan and Germany. The elite of Japan (according to Haushofer) was united in its outlook toward the rest of the world and capable of putting a coherent rational policy into effect. Moreover, the Japanese people were united in their support for the government and in their willingness to accept the discipline that a successful expansionary policy required. Not so the Germans. Germany therefore required unified leadership, discipline, and consensus.

These were not, however, qualities that arose entirely outside the context of imperialist policy. Haushofer obviously believed that his own clear exposition of the logic of national policy would be a major force for building internal unity. Moreover, he implied that emphasizing particular aspects of *Lebensraum* could elicit the required behavior patterns among the German population. He argued, for instance, that the Japanese government's version of migrationist colonialism (that overcrowded Japan needed settlement areas abroad to relieve population pressure) was not entirely an expression of the fundamental aims of policy. It was also a means by which the government built consensus among the Japanese population. Haushofer seems to imply that, although peasant-settlement considerations at the "root" of the concept of *Lebensraum* had a long-term (and fairly abstract) validity for Germany, their immediate utility lay in the effects that enunciating them could have in creating support for a "correct" national policy and for a government that might implement such a policy.[74] This is a point of considerable importance. Geopolitics, at least in Haushofer's rendition of it, was not simply an expression of *Lebensraum* imperialism in pseudoscientific terms with a number of elements of economic imperialism thrown in. From the standpoint of its potential function as a component of imperialist ideology, Haushofer's geopolitics provided a means by which a great many of the concerns of *Weltpolitik* itself could be integrated with *Lebensraum*. It was possible, if Haushofer's ideas were interpreted in a certain way, for one to pursue the basic *Weltpolitik* aims of economic network building and market and investment security as policy aims without rejecting the notion that agricultural living space was a long-run necessity—indeed, while playing the latter idea for all it was worth. Thus, leaders following Haushofer's prescriptions could legitimately emphasize agricultural *Lebensraum* in public pronouncements, yet consciously follow other aims, economic-imperialist aims, for the time being.

The extent to which Haushofer's geopolitics encompassed *Weltpolitik* can be seen in a number of ways. Haushofer's view of Germany's relationship with Britain, for example, came almost directly out of the *Weltpolitik* tradition. Britain and Germany were obvious partners in geopolitical expansion, not enemies. Each, together with other powers such as the United States and Japan, could be accommodated with a secure economic empire upon which their own prosperity and the prosperity of the world would depend. Conflict was, of course, required in creating and maintaining these empires. Britain would have to be forced to acknowledge the role of Germany in the world. But, for the foreseeable future, most necessary aggression could be directed toward smaller states.[75] Haushofer was far from sanguine about the actual possibility of avoiding war with Britain, but he thought that avoidance would be highly desireable.

Haushofer's conception of the system by which German industry should be secured is also very close to that of the traditional *Weltpolitiker*. Although it is true that Haushofer adjusted his economic conceptions to fit the increasing popularity of autarkic ideas in the 1930s, the geopoliticians in general had quite a complex view of economic integration.[76] The industrial base of a major power had to be within the political boundaries of the country, as did a significant proportion of its sources of raw materials and its markets. With respect to Germany in the 1920s, this meant the reacquisition of the areas lost in the war and the establishment of complete sovereignty over the Ruhr, the Rhineland, and the Saar as well as unification with Austria. Under wartime conditions, other neighboring areas might be added, but the main reasons for further outright annexation lay in the realms of strategy and settlement. A state did not need to administer directly its economic periphery in toto. What it had to control was the key transportation media and the geographic centers of exchange. Germany already effectively did this with respect to most of central and much of eastern Europe, and its dominance would become close to complete if unification with Austria and the return of the Polish corridor were effected. Under such circumstances, Germany, with its great economic strength and its central geographic situation, would be able (if it pursued a "sensible" policy) to create a European economic union connected to an overseas empire. The aim would not, in fact, be absolute economic autarky but rather a sufficient degree of centralized German control over the union and empire that economic interactions between Germany and the major industrial states would not threaten Germany's political independence and power. The system of external economic relations had to be so constructed, however, that temporary autarky in the event of a major war would be possible.

Haushofer's geopolitics was therefore both more than a particular development within German policy science and more than a scientific-sounding recapitulation of a number of elements of conservative ideology. It was those things, but it was also an important step toward the ideological amalgamation of *Lebensraum* and *Weltpolitik*. Geopolitics received considerable public attention, widely publicizing imperialist ideas and legitimating them as a "scientific" approach to policy formulation. Its influence on Hitler was probably significant, although Haushofer was by no means the only source of Nazi imperialist thinking. We shall examine the relationship between geopolitics and Naziism in Chapter Ten.

Hans Grimm and the Popularization of *Lebensraum*

One of the most popular German novels of the Weimar era was Hans Grimm's *Volk ohne Raum,* first published in 1926.[77] The reasons for its popularity may seem somewhat mysterious to a modern reader. The book is immensely long (between 1300 and 1500 pages in its various editions). By most current standards, it is not well written. Grimm's prose seems flat, his diction stylized and repetitive, and his descriptions of action—usually the saving grace of a lengthy popular novel—monumentally inept. Most of his characters are merely mouthpieces for political positions and devices for connecting the fragments of the book's episodic plot. Even the main character of this supposed *Bildungsroman,* the peripatetic cabinet-maker and colonial settler Cornelius Friebott, really "develops" only in his political opinions. *Volk ohne Raum,* nevertheless, sold 315,000 copies by 1935 and received considerable, although not universal, critical acclaim.[78] To some extent this may have resulted from comparisons between Grimm's novel and the average run of radical-conservative fiction, by which standard *Volk ohne Raum* may perhaps be said to approach excellence. But the main reason for its popularity was clearly its political message. *Volk ohne Raum* was one of the most comprehensive statements of the major elements of German radical conservatism ever made, which was the reason that Hitler and Goebbels pushed sales of the book and publicly identified their party with its contents, even though the Nazis' relations with its author were highly ambiguous. More important from our standpoint is the fact that Grimm framed his radical-conservative message within the structure of migrationist colonialism and *Lebensraum.*

It was probably not an accident that such a successful exposition of *Lebensraum* ideology and of radical conservatism in general should have taken a fictional form. In many ways, a novel is the ideal medium for the presentation of a composite ideology. The plot of *Volk ohne Raum,* which revolves around the experiences of its hero in "real" historical circumstances between the 1890s and the early 1920s, was consciously constructed to convey an ideological message. The hero, Friebott, develops a conception of Germany's destiny and the correct political direction for the nation as each alternative political view (especially, but not exclusively, Marxian socialism) is "proven" to be faulty through the experiences of Freibott and others. Grimm's attempt to give an air of factuality to his descriptions of places and historical events reinforces this appearance of reality. Inconsistencies in the ideological message are overcome simply by describing episodes in which things that seem irreconcilable are reconciled. Thus, for example, Friebott is unable to live happily in Germany because his "true" German personality, formed in a setting of rural agriculture, cannot be accommodated within an industrial economy. He can live successfully in German Southwest Africa, however, because the colonial setting, with its wide expanses of unoccupied space under German control, permits him to follow his occupations of skilled artisan and farmer without conflict with the processes of industrialization in Germany and within the colony itself. Why this is possible is not really explained; it is merely asserted, and its "proof" is given by fictional description.

With *Volk ohne Raum,* we come to a topic that has not been given a prominent place thus far in our study: the popularization of imperialist ideology. Before the 1920s, groups advocating imperialist policies usually relied on programmatic statements of their positions, conveyed in journalistic literature and official organizational pronouncements, to get their message across to the public. There were some exceptions, such as the ambitious and multisided publicity campaign organized by the Navy League before the war to assemble support for increased fleet building.[79] But, on the whole, the techniques of dissemination that were employed in conjunction with the new ideologies of political aggregation were woefully inadequate to their tasks before Weimar. The Weimar era saw substantial advances in the technical aspects of German popular politics, with the mass-propaganda campaigns of the various interest groups, the expansion of the Hugenberg publishing and propaganda empire on the political right, and eventually the highly effective approach to mass politics adopted by the Nazis.[80] The rapid growth of an imperialist fictional literature—especially a colonial literature—in the 1920s was a part of this process. Grimm was not the only German writer to explore colonial themes with an overtly political purpose in mind.[81] He was, however, the most popular and successful, and his success inspired a host of imitators.

Grimm (1875–1959), a journalist who had been in the export business in South Africa for many years before the First World War, was entirely open about what he was trying to do with *Volk ohne Raum.* He believed that a true *Dichter* (as opposed to a *Schriftsteller*) had a responsibility to display to the rest of his nation its own inner meaning, its destiny, and the political path that lay before it.[82] A writer should be "political" in this general sense, but not an advocate for any particular party. True to his beliefs, Grimm did not overtly act as a spokesperson for the DNVP, the *Stahlhelm,* or the Colonial Society, although he was closely associated with all of them and took part in many of their activities. Despite considerable pressure, he declined to join the National Socialist party (NSDAP) throughout the 1930s. Not only would membership compromise his literary position, but Grimm did not always approve of the Nazis. They were, in his opinion, about as close as an organization was likely to come to being an embodiment of the real political spirit of Germany, but Grimm regarded their program as too "socialist" and disliked the uncouth behavior of much of their following.[83] This did not, however, prevent his turning his major novel into a propaganda device that could be employed by the Nazis and by practically every other group in Germany that accepted the *Lebensraum* view of imperialism and its connection to the vast, ramshackle edifice of radical conservatism.

This is not the place to detail the entire plot of *Volk ohne Raum,* but it is necessary to summarize it because its structure is important to the exposition of Grimm's major themes. Briefly, the hero, Friebott, is the son of a family of small independent farmers descended from a decayed line of lower *Bildungsbürger*. He grows up to be an embodiment of the "true" German, with strong rural roots, a highly developed sensibility to nature, a virtuous character, and a deep appreciation of learning. His plans to become a teacher are crushed, however, when the loss of the family livestock cannot be rectified because of lack of capital. Friebott's father must go to work in a quarry, and Friebott must become an apprentice cabinetmaker. Grimm represents this and related developments as instances of the decay of traditional values and their supporting social structure in the environment of advancing capitalism. Friebott, after completing his apprencticeship, does his military service in the navy. While in the navy, he has his first contact with socialism in the person of Martin Wessell, a young man very much like Friebott who has, however, fallen prey to the allure of Marxism. In contrast, Friebott resists Marxism for the time being. He serves on a cruiser off the coast of Africa at the time of the Jameson raid. There he receives his first introduction to the international problems of the German people and to the hatred that the British have for the Germans.

Grimm's position on Britain is rather interesting. He evinces an intense, deep-seated dislike of the British, a dislike characteristic of the adherents of the *Lebensraum* tradition and one which Grimm apparently came by honestly enough in South Africa.[84] He seems to regard a life-and-death struggle with England as highly likely. On the other hand, at various points in the novel, he has Friebott put forward a viewpoint of Anglo-German relations that seems quite similar to, for example, that of Rohrbach. The British have partly avoided the cultural decay attendant on the materialism and industrialization of their society through the possession of an overseas empire, which has preserved opportunities for some of their people to realize their economic and social aspirations in the expansive environment of colonies. The British want to preserve their control of such opportunities throughout the world, especially in South Africa, and they do so in cooperation with their main allies: the Jews, the prime bearers of soulless, materialistic culture (represented by one of the characters in the novel, a German Jew who adapts himself easily to British cultural forms in South Africa). The main object of British fear is the German people, who are the only other people with the intelligence and the character to demand a share of the geographic space necessary for personal and national development. The Germans can, however, withstand the British if they respond to them firmly, and most important if they develop their own colonial empire. If the proper environment can be found in which to preserve the true characteristics of the German people, the British will be forced to admit the equality of the Germans. It is possible that this can be done peacefully and that the British and Germans can, in fact, become partners in dominating the world, at least temporarily. In the long run, of course, Grimm implies that if the Germans can resist tendencies toward social and cultural decay, they will replace the British as the world's paramount people. There is, in other words, an element of the *Weltpolitik* attitude toward Britain in Grimm's thought, but it is constrained within a general framework of attitudes that corresponds to the traditional outlook of the *Lebensraum* imperialists.

Friebott returns from military service with a heightened political consciousness, but this is of little help in obtaining employment as a skilled cabinetmaker in his home community. He works as a common laborer, but an unfair accusation that he is a "red" forces him to move to the industrial city of Bochum. Grimm frequently uses the theme of false accusation; it is his way of saying that not everyone who is (like Friebott) dissatisfied with the existing state of things in Germany is an unpatriotic socialist, despite what the capitalists may say. In Bochum, Friebott experiences all the moral and physical ills of the modern industrial city. On the other hand, he *does* find acceptable work, combining his skills as an artisan with industrial employment. (He becomes a model maker in a factory.) This introduces an important theme of Grimm's, one that he shared with radicals in the DNVP and throughout the German right: that the integration of traditional and modern economic forms is *not* impossible, any more than is the reconciliation of the best aspects of traditional German culture with modernity.[85] Good will and an environment conducive to integration are, however, necessary. These are lacking, as is demonstrated when Friebott is again fired on a false charge of being a socialist.

Friebott now really *does* become a Social Democrat, although he is neither a convinced nor a convincing one. Grimm portrays socialism as a false solution to Germany's problems. It is based on incorrect assumptions about human nature and society, it is international (and Jewish) in conception rather than national and German, and its emphasis on class conflict makes it inherently divisive of the proper unit of human organization: the *Volk*. On the other hand, Grimm professes great sympathy for the *motive* that leads people like Friebott to socialism: frustration at the restrictions on human development imposed by modern industrial society. This motivation must be harnessed by a political movement truer to the German character than socialism. Such a movement, Grimm implies, must be really radical, in the sense that it must not become coopted by the existing capitalist order but rather must arise from the "people." Most important, the movement must be built around the goal of colonial expansion overseas because only by means of such expansion can real personal and national development be accomplished.[86]

Friebott takes a job as a miner and is jailed for criticizing his employers after an accident. After his release, he decides that he cannot build a future in the socially and physically restricted space of Germany, and he emigrates to South Africa. Here he is entranced by the openness of the landscape and the opportunities available to a person of skill and intelligence. His aim is not to get rich, but to acquire enough capital to become an independent farmer. South Africa seems the ideal place to achieve his aim, but there is one catch: *Germans* may not take full advantage of South Africa's opportunities because of British discrimination and because of pressure on Germans to drop their native culture. Despite his difficulties, however, Friebott finds a place as a handyman on a farm and as the lover of the young German–Boer widow who owns it. This idyllic interlude is interrupted by the Boer War in 1899, in which Friebott serves on the Boer side and is quickly captured, spending the remainder of the war engaged in diligent self-education as a prisoner.

At war's end, Friebott learns that his lover has died in a concentration camp. He joins Martin Wessell—his socialist friend who has also immigrated to South Africa—as a skilled worker in the booming Johannesburg construction business. This rather complicated episode demonstrates the impossibility of adequate personal development for Germans in a British-controlled overseas world, and it provides Grimm the opportunity to turn Friebott away from socialism—in contrast to Wessell, who wrongheadedly retains his political opinions. In writing this section, Grimm was clearly attempting to appeal to socialist-oriented workers among his readers, showing them that their best interests would be served by adherence to a politically radical, but socially and economically conservative, nationalist movement.

In 1907, Friebott decides his future can only lie in a German colony. He therefore emigrates to German Southwest Africa. On the way, he meets Hans Grimm himself as he was in 1907—a Cape Colony merchant. The character Grimm summarizes, in private thought, the meaning of Friebott's previous adventures: Friebott is an example of the true German arising from the common people, to whom Germany must now turn for leadership because the old elites of birth and education (in which Grimm counts himself) have failed. The experience is, in its effects on character, essential for Germany's future.

Friebott arrives in Southwest Africa just at the end of the Nama rebellion. He participates in the suppression of the last part of the rebellion, gaining thereby a heightened sense of national purpose and of the role of colonial settlement in it. Because bureaucratic delays prevent his immediate occupation of his homestead, he goes to work successfully for a building contractor in the boom town of Lüderitz. Here Friebott again demonstrates that it is quite possible to mix economic modernization with the craftsmanship and small-unit agriculture that are the economic underpinnings of true German culture—given the conditions obtaining in a really *German* colony. Unfortunately, however, the discovery of diamonds in Southwest Africa in 1908 (a real event, it will be recalled) starts a diamond rush that threatens the ability of the colony to perform its major social and cultural functions. Unscrupulous foreign speculators flood the colony, and Colonial Secretary Dernburg promulgates regulations giving the diamond profits almost entirely to international big-business interests rather than diverting them to encourage settlement. Grimm comes down completely on the side of the anti-Dernburg, prosettler position in the diamond dispute, claiming that Dernburg threw away the best chance Germany ever had of creating a real settlement colony capable of solving the problems of social and cultural decay in Germany.

After various complications arising out of the diamond problem, Friebott eventually settles on his farm. Finding the leisure to read extensively, he finally puts his ideas and experiences together during a visit to Germany just before the outbreak of the First World War. He realizes that Germany's social order must be remade. In the geographic setting of large and expanding German colonies, the remaking can occur freely; the extensiveness of the geographic setting can bring out the full potential of the German character. The best of the old and the new can be reconciled, and the reconciliation can eventually affect Germany itself.[88]

War starts soon after Friebott's return to Southwest Africa. He is imprisoned during the South African occupation but eventually escapes, only to find that Germany has ignominiously surrendered. He returns to Germany to propagate his ideas about expansion and Germany's future and is killed by a Social Democrat who regards Friebott as a traitor to his former comrades.

As one can see from this summary of the plot of *Volk ohne Raum,* Grimm strongly emphasizes the basic assumptions of *Lebensraum* and builds a generalized radical conservative message into a *Lebensraum* format. In a very real sense, Grimm's approach makes radical conservatism an aspect of *Lebensraum* rather than the other way around. If the German people are to survive without losing the fundamental spiritual and material elements of their culture, if individual Germans are to fulfill themselves, and if Germany as a political entity is not to be destroyed by foreign enemies and internal division, Germans require large spaces for expansion—spaces that must be found overseas rather than in overcrowded Europe. Grimm was unusual among major radical conservative publicists in the 1920s and 1930s in his extremely strong emphasis on overseas colonial settlement and his opposition to the ideas of inner colonization and peasant settlement in Eastern Europe. Grimm's opposition to an eastward policy was, in fact, the main reason that his work was attacked by an important segment of Nazi opinion in the 1930s, led especially by Walther Darré. Darré was formerly an ardent settlement colonialist and a graduate of the Colonial School at Witzenhausen, but by 1930 he had become an equally ardent advocate of eastern settlement as the Nazis' "peasant expert."[89] There are practically no elements of economic imperialism in Grimm's colonial conception. The reason for a colonial empire lies purely and simply in its capacity for protecting German culture and the German character against the onslaught of modernization. Except in the position that Grimm takes on relations with England, there is little effort to integrate *Lebensraum* imperialism with *Weltpolitik* in *Volk ohne Raum.*

The political nature of Grimm's "radicalism" can be seen in various parts of the novel, especially in the places in which Grimm appears to be advocating colonialism as a means of building a sense of equality, almost a democratic spirit, among Germans in a frontier setting.[90] This "democratic" outlook results from a realization of the irrelevance of European class distinctions when Europeans are confronted with the vast spaces of the colonial world and from the experience of becoming members of a functioning master race with non-European subjects. Grimm's version of equality is therefore a highly specious one, similar to that employed by the Nazis. It is constructed on a foundation of racial inequality and it suggests no structural means by which equality can be permanently guaranteed or directed toward any tangible social result. Although Grimm, like Hitler, may have genuinely believed that the supposedly egalitarian element in his political conception differentiated his views from those of the old-line class-conscious conservatives of the DNVP, the fact remains that the very structure and assumptions that underlay this element made it functionally sterile, except as a means of soliciting support from groups with a grudge against the upper classes.

Grimm's novel is important in the history of German imperialist ideology in a number of ways. Because of its large readership, it probably brought the *Lebensraum* ideological set and its connection with the other elements of radical conservatism to a wider public than any other medium before the later years of the Nazi regime. It helped to create the widespread consensus that apparently existed in Germany in the late 1920s and early 1930s about Germany's vital need for living space. Grimm did not, in fact, use the term *Lebensraum* and, although his conception of the spatial dimension of social and cultural existence was quite similar to that of the geopoliticians, he did not derive his ideas directly from geopolitical literature. Haushofer helped to publicize Grimm's work among the conservative intelligentsia, but he never claimed that Grimm's notions were anything but a parallel development from the same general intellectual source from which geopolitics also arose.[91] But *Volk ohne Raum* did popularize much of the vocabulary that the geopoliticians used, and more important, it gave the notions that lay behind the vocabulary an aspect of believability that could not come from their identification as "science." The credibility of the *Lebensraum* ideas as represented by Grimm arose instead from his exploitation of the unique capabilities of fiction as a means of propagating ideology.

CHAPTER TEN

Nazi Imperialism

The culmination of the development of imperialism as a political ideology in Germany took place during the Nazi period. The Nazis managed to combine the major tendencies in German imperialism much more successfully than any previous political organization, mainly by fitting them into a larger ideological structure embodied in the party's program. They employed imperialist ideology probably to the limits of its effectiveness as a means of creating consensus, but this was not the most important result of the Nazis' connection with imperialism. Because much of the Nazi leadership firmly believed that the entire Nazi program (including its heterogeneous imperialist elements) constituted a correct guide for political action as well as a means of soliciting support, they attempted when in power to implement imperialist policies more broadly, completely, and systematically than any previous German government had done. In pursuing their expansionary course during the Second World War, the Nazis decisively demonstrated the fatal contradictions in their own program, the flaws embedded in the traditions of German imperialist ideology, and the terrible dangers lurking in the presence of imperialism in the domestic politics of a nation.

At the beginning of this book, it was indicated that the subject of the study was not Nazi imperialism itself but rather the process by which imperialism came to be a significant part of the Nazi program and a major influence on Nazi policy. Most of that process has already been described in the account given in the previous chapters of the evolution of the German imperialist ideologies as a function of domestic politics. As imperialists, the Nazis were the inheritors of a long and complex ideological tradition. They adopted much of the *Lebensraum* ideological aggregation in the 1920s, including the newly constructed bridges between *Lebensraum* and the industrial interest and the latest means of legitimating and popularizing imperialism. Hitler himself also managed (as we shall see) to incorporate into his general scheme for German expansion a substantial amount of the *Weltpolitik* approach as well. He reconciled these differing elements through an elaborate system of temporal priorities, possibly derived from such sources as Haushofer's geopolitics.[1]

It would certainly not go beyond the scope of a study such as this to include at the end a detailed analysis of the imperialist aspect of Naziism. Fortunately, it is unnecessary to do so. There exists an extensive literature on the subject, including Norman Rich's two-volume work on Hitler's war aims, studies of Nazi foreign policy by Gerhard Weinberg, Andreas Hillgruber, Klaus Hildebrand, and Hans-Adolf Jacobsen, and Hildebrand's lengthy examination of the relationship between the Nazis and the colonial movement.[2] The main deficiency in this literature has been the absence of a serious consideration of the historical development of the imperialist ideology adopted by the Nazis—a deficiency that the earlier chapters of the present study have attempted to correct. What remains now is to discuss in general terms, employing the work of those who have examined Nazi expansionism in detail, the ways in which imperialism was used by the Nazis and how it affected them.

Nazi Ideology

Recent studies have reinforced the already-common historical perception of the heterogeneous, changing ideological character of the Nazi program. Nazi ideology was a patchwork of political notions, many of them radically inconsistent with one another and few of them original. This was true even of the formal, programmatic statements of Naziism such as the "twenty-five points" of February 1920, Hitler's *Mein Kampf,* the comprehensive pronouncements on Nazi policy of 1930 and 1932, and the various statements that date from the years after 1933. Emphases within the program changed over time, depending on the political situation and the composition of the party's leadership. Especially before 1933, the Nazi ideological aggregation was like a magnet, attracting any form of ideological material that had an affinity to the radical-conservative sentiments of the party's leadership or that the Nazis thought might be useful in attracting support.[3]

Nazi ideology is, in fact, an extreme example of the type of aggregate political ideology described in Chapter One and employed as a model in the subsequent chapters. From the standpoint of the support aggregation function that such ideologies perform in modern political systems, the reason for the heterogeneous character of Nazi ideology was the desire of the NSDAP to appeal to an unusually wide array of social classes, opinion groups, and other political organizations. As we have seen, neither the aim of support aggregation nor the use of a composite ideology as one means of accomplishing it nor, indeed, the presence in the resulting political program of inconsistencies and contradictions was a unique characteristic of Naziism. What *was* unusual about Nazi ideology was the astounding breadth and variety of its conceptual content and the horrendous consequences of the attempt to carry out a substantial proportion of its policy implications. Several factors need to be considered in explaining why Naziism was so conceptually extensive and how so blatantly eclectic an ideology could generate widespread belief. We shall leave the question of the consequences until later.

In the first place, it is clear that the peculiar conditions of German politics in the interwar period help to account for the ability of the Nazis to employ successfully a program that, in most other modern industrial countries, would have seemed so heterogeneous and internally discordant as to be useless in building consensus. The circumstances noted in the previous chapter—the widespread attitude that both the loss of the war and the existence of the republic were temporary phenomena, the radical swings in the German economy in the 1920s, the continuation into the Weimar era of many of the institutional sources of indecisiveness in the political system—all contributed to insulating certain types of political ideology from the effects of a critical examination of their structures and assumptions. But this kind of explanation involves an obvious environmental fallacy.[4] *Any* political development of the interwar period could be similarly explained. What is required is a more specific set of reasons that the Nazi ideology *in particular* was so well suited to the political environment of the 1920s and 1930s.

One of the crucial factors has less to do with the content than with the means of propagating the ideology. The pioneers of modern mass political technique in post-1918 Germany mostly stood on the radical right.[5] The Nazis were not quite as original in their development of systems of slogans, their creation of a public image of a charismatic leader, and their use of new media such as film as they are sometimes regarded as having been, but they learned quickly from the other groups on the right who also took part in the process of modernizing German popular politics. Moreover, the Nazi propaganda organization was probably more efficient in the long run than any other in German politics. Its pronouncements could carry more conviction among the voting public than could those of, for example, the Hugenberg wing of the DNVP. Most national political groups advocating radical conservative policies in the 1920s were clearly led by members of the established elite classes; the Nazis clearly were not. Their supposed defense of the "little man" against the forces of change rang considerably truer than that of parties known to be associated with big business. In an environment in which modern mass propaganda and the techniques of image creation in place of formal ideological presentation were novelties, the first practitioners of such approaches had a decided advantage. Because the Nazis' program was presented through a different array of media from those of their competitors, it gave the appearance of really *being* something else, something not subject to the usual criteria by which political pronouncements were judged.[6]

But not just any ideological aggregation can be successfully put across to the public in a modern industrial society. The Nazis' ideological message may have been heterogeneous and highly self-contradictory in logic and in empirical referents, but the elements of which it was composed had almost all been thoroughly legitimated in the course of their political employment during the previous two or three generations. The process by which racism, anti-Semitism, and the peculiarly sterile form of conservative anti-industrialism adopted by the Nazis had come to be legitimated in pre-Hitler and pre-Weimar Germany is well known.[7] In earlier chapters, the parallel processes in the case of the imperialist elements of the Nazi program were examined. But the legitimacy and popularity of the *elements* of an aggregate ideology are not the only internal factors influencing the ideology's political success. The *structure* of the ideology, the ways in which the elements are put together for presentation, the means by which apparent or real contradictions between constituent elements are resolved, all of these have a bearing on its political effectiveness and on its ability to instill belief. One of the reasons that the Nazi ideology was so successful in eliciting support for the party and consensus behind its program was that its structure was built around central concepts that, in the political environment of interwar Germany, appeared to integrate the disparate individual elements of the party's program in a convincing fashion. Imperialism played an extremely important role in this regard.

The existence or supposition of a powerful exogenous threat to the national collectivity can be a significant means of resolving contradictions within an ideological program.[8] The utility of external threats in consensus politics is, of course, well known from centuries of experience in practically all polities. It is usually explained in rather general psychological terms: people of different social strata with differing interests will feel themselves to be part of the same social entity if they are collectively threatened. They will therefore be amenable to appeals to work together and, in the process, forego some of the aims of their particular social groups.[9] Within the structure of a composite ideology, however, the notion of an external threat, the avoidance of which takes precedence over all other considerations, can do more than simply elicit a unifying emotional response. It can reconcile ideological differences. In the earlier discussion of imperialist ideology in World War I, for example, we saw that agrarian and industrial interests were reconciled within a framework of modified *Lebensraum* through the idea of economic autarky necessitated by total war. In post-1918 Germany, the utility of the idea of an external threat as a device for resolving ideological differences in political programs was obvious, and such a threat was easy enough to claim. But it was the ideological traditions of German imperialism that largely defined the nature of the threat, predicted the likely forms of its future manifestation, and provided guidelines for action to repel it.

The *Weltpolitik* tradition indicated a threat to Germany's economic and social future if she could not regain her place in international politics and insist on her rightful role in the economic development of the world. The threat came from the interest groups in other industrial countries that sought to take advantage of Germany's weakened state by prohibiting her from economic expansion. The *Lebensraum* tradition identified a threat from the foreign powers that would hem the German people in territorially, preventing them from acquiring the space needed to protect their national culture and the source of their strength. In either case, the use of an external threat as an integrating and legitimating device within the structure of a composite ideology required not just the assertion that a threat existed, but also the adoption of the whole ideological entity that gave it meaning.[10] Imperialist ideological traditions were extremely well developed in Germany, and they became more convincing and more widely accepted than ever during the Weimar period. A political organization that could make maximum use of the external threat to Germany as defined by *both* of the imperialist ideologies as a justification for the inclusion in its program of discordant elements, each of which individually attracted support from certain groups, could potentially assemble considerable support. As we shall see, the Nazis attempted to use imperialism in precisely this way.

The displacement feature of imperialist ideologies—the fact that they characteristically displace the political actions that will achieve the multiple results that they call for to geographic locations not yet under the home country's control or not yet completely exploited under that control—also plays an important role in their apparent resolution of contradictions. We have seen this on numerous occasions in the preceding chapters. The Nazis, by strongly emphasizing the imperialist aspect of their program and by doing so more convincingly than any of their competitors, could harmonize a multitude of potential dissonances. Many of the apparently contradictory aims of National Socialism—the protection and extension of peasant agriculture while seeking full industrial and commercial employment, the protection of the German race from degeneration through the industrial environment while maintaining German industrial supremacy, the simultaneous promotion of an egalitarian folk consciousness, a "natural aristocracy," and a culturally distinct *Mittelstand*—could be achieved if Germany could be sufficiently expanded, if the German *Volk* possessed sufficient living space. Even that other major resolver of contradictions in radical conservative ideology—racism, especially in its anti-Semitic and anti-Slavic forms—became fully effective only when placed in a radical imperialist context. If the Jewish threat to *Deutschtum* was an international one, complete protection from it could only be afforded if Judaism were destroyed internationally—hence imperial expansion. The threat of communism (fundamentally a combined Jewish and Slavic threat) could only be dealt with ultimately by the destruction of the Communist homeland, Russia.[11] The occupation of Russia would also, of course, provide much of the living space needed for German peasant agriculture. From the standpoint of the process of ideological development discussed in this book, from the standpoint of the study of ideology as a major component of political structure, it could be argued that Naziism from the late 1920s onward was *primarily* an imperialist ideology, that imperialism provided much of the functional framework that held Nazi ideology together, and that this was one of the reasons for the National Socialists' political success. It was also, of course, one of the reasons for their ultimate failure in the Second World War.

To understand the function of imperialism within the larger framework of Nazi ideology, we must modify slightly one of the conventional explanations for the heterogeneity of the Nazi program: that Naziism was simply a combination of appeals to the interests of the different strata of German society that Hitler managed to play off against each other.[12] Within this pattern of explanation, the expansionary element takes on the character of a rather crude form of social imperialism—the advocacy of aggression as one of the ways in which the interests of the individual social groups could each be satisfied or appear to be satisfied. That the Nazis saw their ideology as a means of aggregating the support of a variety of social groups is undeniable, but the explanation leaves a number of unanswered questions. Why, for instance, could the members of each of the discrete social classes to which the Nazis appealed not see that Hitler, after promising them something, would promise to another conventionally antagonistic class something else not readily compatible with what had been promised to them? Because the conduct of a policy of social imperialism generally implies a clear idea on the part of the social imperialist of those interests that are to be taken seriously and those that are addressed merely to acquire the support of the group that possesses them, why is it that the evidence suggests that Hitler had no such conception of the absolute paramountcy of one part of his program over another? Hitler appears to have accepted it all as the basis for policy, differentiating between elements only on grounds of temporal priority in execution.[13]

What is missing from this view is a consideration of ideology as an element of the environment in which political actors operate. The Nazis, like all other political parties, were not, in fact, working with raw, unmediated data about social and economic relationships in the 1920s and 1930s but rather with a complex of ideas, attitudes, perceptions, resentments, and affectations that motivated people to political action. A large number of these factors were organized, as in any political situation, into composite ideologies; some of these ideologies were more characteristic of certain identifiable social groups than others but to some extent they also helped to define those groups in political terms. The *Mittelstand,* for example, was as much an artifact of the previous half-century's political and ideological development as it was a discrete, identifiable social category, yet it was capable of being manipulated and mobilized for political action nonetheless.[14] The ideologies that create consensus and the basis for joint action across a large part of a nation's social spectrum are those that have connections to the dominant ideological aggregations of the individual groups that make up the spectrum. The question is thus not whether the members of one group can see that other groups are being told different things by a political party, but rather whether the program of that party is constructed in such a way as to make the things that the party says appear to be compatible in terms of the internal logic of all groups' political outlooks. Under the circumstances of interwar German politics noted earlier, people who accepted the Nazis' arguments were not being entirely irrational in the sense of being stupid or being governed solely by unconsidered emotions and antipathies. The irrationality lay in the contradictory, tautological nature of the ideological systems that they used to construct their view of the political world. These systems were built into the political environment, protected from effective critical scrutiny by the same historical process that had produced the ideological systems in the first place. At the same time, it is clearly incorrect to explain people's acceptance of Naziism on the basis of perceptions of class position alone. If the Nazis' program had rested only on its appeal to a multitude of discrete, self-conceived class interests, it is unlikely that they would have been able to overcome the distrust within one class that deliberate appeals to the self-interest of other classes would have entailed.[15]

The problem posed by the apparent belief of many Nazi leaders themselves, especially Hitler, in the inherent truth of practically all parts of their program is a complex one that cannot be solved here. It can be suggested, however, that the use of a broad composite ideology to generate support and consensus in no way precludes implicit belief in the ideology on the part of the user. Although the elements and structure of such an ideology may be constructed over time by individuals seeking to achieve particular political ends and although at any time there might be a considerable amount of hypocrisy, or at least motivational duality, involved in the process, there is no reason that the logic of an ideological aggregation cannot be as convincing to a politician espousing it as it is to a member of the public accepting it. This is especially true when considerable time has elapsed between the period in which the central tenets of the ideology were put together and the time at which a new political organization such as the NSDAP comes to use it. It may also be that ideological conviction and political success are related to each other, that the most successful proponents of an ideological position are those who actually believe in it, no matter how absurd or dangerous it may appear to be on the basis of dispassionate, objective analysis.

Part of the reason for the Nazis' political success then probably lay in the nature of their ideology and the manner in which they presented it. One of the keys to the successful functioning of their ideology in the political environment of interwar Germany was, in turn, their use of the traditions of German imperialist ideology, both as sources of particular ideas that appealed to specific social and political groups and as agents for integration and legitimation within the overall structure of the Nazi program. There was, of course, one major problem: the duality of the imperialist ideological tradition in Germany. The Nazis had to confront the same problems that had faced earlier groups attempting to create an integrated imperialism around which to build a broadly based conservative, nationalist political movement. The use of one of the major tendencies in imperialist thinking ran the risk of automatically alienating the groups that adhered to the other tendency. We have already seen that during the First World War and the Weimar era, considerable strides had been taken on the radical right toward the addition of economic-imperialist elements to the structure of *Lebensraum*. The Nazis, especially Hitler himself, took advantage of many of these developments and carried them forward. The disparity between *Lebensraum* and *Weltpolitik* was not, however, eliminated even by Hitler. In fact, the two terms are often used, and rightly, to indicate two sides of a general tension that existed in the Nazi foreign policy process in the 1930s.[16] What the Nazis did was to incorporate them both into one grandiose structure of imperialist plans and expectations—grandiose because it had to be in order to accommodate *Lebensraum* and *Weltpolitik* simultaneously. What resulted was an ideological entity containing at least two fundamentally irreconcilable frameworks for national political action, treated as though they had, in fact, been reconciled. As several historians have pointed out, similar tensions and similar contradictions that were unresolvable when they were turned into policy were present in other areas of Nazi ideology as well.[17] Altogether, for all of its undoubted advantages in the process of consensus building and support aggregation, Nazi ideology added up to a formula for national disaster when it was taken seriously as a basis for policy.

The Imperialist Aspect of Nazi Ideology

Of all of the major spokespersons of Naziism, the one most responsible for the strongly imperialist direction of the Nazi program as it evolved in the 1920s and 1930s was Hitler himself. This should not be surprising, despite the questions that have been raised about the extent of Hitler's influence on the ideology of the party. Whatever his failings as a coherent political thinker, Hitler more than any other leading Nazi emphasized the need for a close connection between a composite *Weltanschauung* (by which he seems to have meant more or less what is understood here as ideology) and the function of support aggregation through propaganda that he saw as vital to the success of a political movement.[18] He clearly perceived the potential integrating role of imperialism within a radical-conservative composite ideology. The dominance of Hitler over the foreign policy aspects of the Nazi program and over the making of German foreign policy under the Nazi regime has been recognized by the majority of recent students of the subject. Consensus has emerged among them that Hitler's long-range view of foreign policy, full of delusions and contradictions though it was, constituted the basis on which the most crucial decisions on foreign relations were made in Germany from 1933 to 1945.

Hitler genuinely believed in the accuracy of his assessment of proper German foreign policy, holding to it even when its divergence from reality became abundantly clear to others in the early 1940s.[19] He developed his view of foreign policy, however, in the historical context of German imperialist ideology—not only through cogitating "objectively" about Germany's role in the world, but also through exploring the uses of imperialism in domestic politics.

Imperialism was formally a part of Nazi ideology at least from the latter's first programmatic statement in the "twenty-five points" of February 1920—a document the authorship of which has been disputed, but which does not seem to have involved a substantial input from Hitler.[20] The first of the points, although it was specifically directed against the removal of parts of German territory by the Versailles treaty, comes from the Pan-German imperialist tradition: "We demand the union of all Germans—on the basis of the right of self-determination of all peoples—in a Greater Germany." The third point is unquestionably imperialistic: "We demand land and soil (colonies) for the nourishment of our people and for the settlement of our excess population." When these items are taken together with others calling for the prevention of non-German immigration and the protection of peasant agriculture, it is clear that the imperialist element of early formal Naziism was derived directly from the *Lebensraum* ideology. No mention is made of the need for markets, raw materials, the protection of commerce, or the other trappings of *Weltpolitik;* no mention is made, in fact, even of economic autarky.

Although the imperialist sections of the 1920 program come early in the list of points, they are otherwise given little prominence as party goals. They are not explicated at any length, and no attempt is made to link them to the rest of the program, which concentrates on such domestic matters as the need for radical measures against aliens (especially Jews) within German society and the necessity of "breaking the bondage of interest." Most of the evidence about the early Nazi ideologues (Gottfried Feder, Alfred Rosenberg, etc.) indicates that, although they were not untouched by the currents of imperialist ideology, imperialism even of the *Lebensraum* variety played a comparatively small role in their thinking before the late 1920s. *Lebensraum* imperialism seems to have been adopted by the early NSDAP because it was a common part of conservative and radical-conservative political thought; to have left it out would have brought the party's nationalist credentials into question. But on the whole, the early National Socialists appear to have been a good deal less imperialistic and a good deal more radical in a domestic social-political sense than most of their rivals on the right. As Hildebrand has pointed out, the Nazis' relative lack of interest in the specifically colonial forms of imperialism persisted up to the late 1920s. The NSDAP had, moreover, in its left wing led by Gregor Strasser, a consciously anti-imperialist group up until 1932.[21]

During Hitler's early years in the party, he does not seem to have been particularly committed to imperialism either, except in a very broad and conventional sense. He shared the general view that Versailles needed to be overcome, most likely by force, and he appears in the early 1920s to have given considerable thought to the foreign policy failings of the *Kaiserreich*. Besides that, he seems to have accepted (without thinking especially hard about it) the standard *Lebensraum* view that an overcrowded Germany required more agricultural space to feed its people, to maintain its culture, and to accommodate population growth. Solving the problems defined by *Lebensraum* ideology was desirable, a proper goal of policy, but there is little evidence that Hitler gave it more than cursory attention before about 1924. This is of some importance, however. Like most conservatives, radical or otherwise, he had been politically socialized to accept the tenets of *Lebensraum* uncritically as part of a larger ideological set (radical conservatism). When he came to focus on imperialism later, it was not with any thought of fundamentally criticizing assumptions to which he had previously subscribed rather casually.[22]

In the aftermath of the Beer Hall *putsch* in 1923 and during the writing of *Mein Kampf* in 1924, Hitler's views on foreign policy became increasingly formalized and important in the overall structure of his world view. This development has been interpreted in various ways. Some have seen it as the result of Hitler's confrontation with the problems of foreign affairs while trying on the costume of "German statesman." Others have made particular reference to Hitler's enforced leisure in prison in 1924, where he wrote *Mein Kampf* and where he is supposed to have read a substantial amount of geopolitical literature.[23] The question of which books and articles Hitler read is still debated and probably unanswerable. As we have seen, however, if he seriously attempted to acquaint himself with the main currents of conservative political thought in the early and middle 1920s, he could hardly have avoided reading a lot of imperialist and geopolitical material. At some point, either then or shortly after, Hitler certainly became acquainted with the writings of Haushofer and his school.[24]

Account must, however, also be taken of the political context in which Hitler's growing emphasis on foreign policy took place, which helps to explain why imperialist ideologies increasingly informed his views. It was in the years 1924–25 that Hitler began the construction of his comprehensive scheme for taking power by "legal" means—an enterprise that encompassed considerably more than a determination to observe the formal legalities of political behavior.[25] The scheme was structured around the aim of building a broad political consensus behind the NSDAP that would bring the party to power through an electoral victory. It led to many developments in party organization and to the implementation of new propaganda techniques; from the standpoint of this study, however, the most important consequence was a strong effort to extend the Nazi ideology as a vehicle for support aggregation. Hitler and other Nazi ideologues who concurred with the new strategy engaged in an extended review of conventional political ideas that were or could be related to the general framework of radical conservatism already adopted by the NSDAP. With a few possible exceptions, this did not involve the wholesale, hypocritical adoption of previously uncongenial political ideas for the sake of their appeal to potential supporters but rather a tendency to emphasize certain acceptable ideas with consensus-building capacity to a greater extent than the Nazis had previously done. In some cases, for example, when Hitler adopted a more favorable attitude toward capitalism for the sake of attracting business support, it was necessary to work hard to find ways of reconciling the new emphases with other elements of Nazi ideology that seemed to contradict them.[26] Imperialism played an important role in this process.

In the first place, the various versions of imperialist ideology in Germany had, or were thought to have, considerable appeal to different segments of German society, appeal that often cut across class lines. Second, imperialism was particularly valuable as a framework within which divergent interests and ideological directions could apparently be reconciled. Third, and perhaps most crucially, the very same features of imperialist ideology that made it seem so useful to Hitler and his associates in their campaign for consensus probably also impressed on Hitler's mind the value of imperialism as a guide for policy—as a delineator of goals for national political action and as a means of achieving other goals. In a manner not uncommon among politicians who undertake their own political education in the very process of striving for power, Hitler had to deal in the middle and late 1920s with a wider variety of political opinions than those to which he had previously paid much attention. He required integrative ideological structures for his own use as well as for the assembly of political support, and he found one of them in imperialism. To Hitler, as to a great many other politicians, the problems of how to get power and what to do with it afterward were not separable. Forced as he was after 1924 to find ways to incorporate highly diverse policy goals into the Nazi program for political purposes, he needed also a means of incorporating them together into a single program to avoid excessive cognitive dissonance in his own mind.[27] He tended to use imperialism for both purposes, which helps to explain the continuous movement toward expansionism in the Nazis' public program from the late 1920s onward and Hitler's increasing emphasis in his own political outlook on a foreign policy defined largely in terms of imperialism. But for Hitler and the other Nazi ideologues to employ imperialist ideology in these ways, they had to solve the problem of the *Weltpolitik–Lebensraum* dichotomy in the German imperialist tradition. They proceeded to do precisely that, following for the most part directions already taken by other radical conservative imperialists and by the geopoliticians. They made particular use of the notion of a comprehensive imperialist policy to be implemented by stages as their most important integrative device and as their most significant "contribution" to German imperialist ideology.

Hitler's outlook on foreign policy and the framework of his scheme for German expansion appear to have taken their final form by 1930 and to have been modified only in detail thereafter—as befitted the system of ideas of a politician who prided himself on being able to take advantage of opportunities as they arose without losing sight of his ultimate goals.[28] Because Hitler's expansionary program has been discussed in great detail in other studies, we shall concentrate here on summarizing its major elements and the structure of their relationships to one another according to the categories of our earlier analysis of German imperialist ideology.

In many respects, the basic concepts of *Lebensraum* remained fundamental to Hitler's expansionary thought and to his conception of German foreign policy. In *Mein Kampf* and in his unpublished "second book" he used the term *Lebensraum* itself frequently as a description of one of the central criteria of national policy. He claimed, for example, that the unavoidable antagonism between Germany and France could only have meaning to the extent that it "builds the framework for the expansion of the *Lebensraum* of our *Volk* in Europe."[29] Although Hitler employed the term in a number of different contexts, it is clear that he understood by it what most others did: space required for the maintenance and propagation of an independent peasantry—the foundation of a true German culture. As he stated in one of his speeches:

> History has taught us that a nation can exist without cities, but history would have taught us one day, if the old system had continued, that a nation cannot exist without farmers. . . . Lasting successes a government can win only if the necessity is recognized for the securing of a people's *Lebensraum* and thus of its own agricultural class.[30]

In common with the majority of *Lebensraum*-oriented conservatives during the interwar years, Hitler believed that adequate living space could only be found in eastern Europe, particularly in Russia. Although he was not opposed to a German colonial empire, he initially regarded the demand for the immediate return and expansion of the German colonies simply as a part of the general attack on Versailles. Colonial expansion played a role in Hitler's imperialist thinking beyond the immediate circumstances of the 1920s and 1930s, but at no time did colonies take priority over the need for eastern expansion to acquire *Lebensraum*. "Obviously, such a land policy cannot find its fulfillment in Cameroon, but today exclusively only in Europe."[31] Hitler also ruled out inner colonization (strictly defined as the turning of land within the present *Reich* over to peasant farming) as inadequate to the needs of a rapidly growing German population. *Lebensraum* in the classical sense was to Hitler the sine qua non of German foreign policy; after the overturning of Versailles, it was Hitler's immediate external aim as potential German leader, and he did not deviate from his concentration on the *Lebensraum* problem after taking power in 1933.[32]

Hitler added very little directly to the conventional notion of living space. For example, although in *Mein Kampf* he indicated the existence of a relationship between land and race (specifically, between land farmed by German peasants and the characteristics of the Germanic race), his presentation of the idea was extremely superficial.[33] It was left to Walther Darré, the Nazi peasant leader in the 1930s and the main theoretician of eastward continental expansion and agricultural settlement, to adapt to Nazi purposes the *Blut-und-Boden* concept—the idea that a necessary affinity existed between the optimal exploitation of a certain type of natural environment and a certain pure racial type. As we saw in the previous chapter, *Blut und Boden* was an especially useful means of reconciling the basically cultural and environmental orientations of *Lebensraum* ideology with the "positivist" scientism of biological racism. In a broader sense, it was one of the elements of Nazi ideology that appeared to reconcile the antimodern, anti-industrial bias of much of German conservative thought with the obvious attractions of scientific modernity.[34]

But *Lebensraum,* even updated through *Blut und Boden* and similar constructs, was not the limit of Nazi imperialism. By the late 1920s, Hitler's imperialist ideology also incorporated a substantial number of economic-imperialist ideas, including many from the tradition of *Weltpolitik* that were, both in fact and by convention, incompatible with the *Lebensraum* to which he gave conceptual priority. The immediate reason for the addition of these ideas was of course Hitler's desire to attract support from business-interest groups to which they already appealed and to devise a comprehensive imperialist program that would create consensus among many different segments of the population simultaneously—generally by displacing the solution to each group's perceived problems to some place beyond Germany's current borders.[35] Hitler followed the directions toward imperialist ideological integration already laid out by the geopoliticians and the conservative theorists of economic autarky, but he and his associates took the process a great deal further.

The economics of autarky is a case in point. Notions of autarky current in German political and economic thought in the late 1920s and early 1930s varied considerably, from highly impractical schemes for the total separation of a German-controlled central European economic union from the rest of the industrial world to ideas of European economic integration that were largely extensions of the kind of thinking normally associated with *Weltpolitik*. The Nazis, in fact, simultaneously adopted practically all versions of integration that featured the assumption of unquestioned economic domination by Germany over her neighbors. They adopted also the unproven (and logically highly suspect) idea, commonly held throughout the political right, that a massive peasant-settlement program was compatible with—indeed, required as a prerequisite—the establishment of a German-dominated economic structure for east and central Europe.[36] This was, as we have seen, one of the prime ideological means by which conservative politicians attempted to reconcile industrial and

agrarian interests. Within this broad framework, it was possible for different interest groups and for people with quite different conceptions of
what autarky meant to identify policy goals with which they agreed and to
convince themselves that Hitler thought much the same way—which, to
some degree, he usually did.

The Nazi view of autarky, as presented in the late 1920s and throughout the 1930s, could be read in at least three ways. At its narrowest,
autarky could be defined as a strategic concept that stood beyond the
range of individual petty interests. National security and political independence required safe markets and sources of raw materials for the
economy. Germany must of necessity encompass large areas outside the
boundaries of the *Reich*. This concept could, if it were not too specifically
described, appeal to nationalists and conservatives of all stripes and could
provide a useful excuse for cooperation between the government and big
business in penetrating the economies of eastern Europe in the 1930s.[37]
To others—especially people such as Darré, Himmler, and Alfred Rosenberg—autarky implied not simply an unassailable economic basis for
future military action, but also a policy of deliberately seeking such extensive political domination over a large section of the European continent
that a peasant-settlement policy could be put into effect in the face of
contrary economic realities. Autarky, according to this second conception, was therefore a means to an end defined by *Lebensraum*.[38]

It was, however, also possible to interpret the Nazi version of autarky
as a sort of exaggerated *Mitteleuropa* in the *Weltpolitik* tradition, to which
Hitler had added meaningless references to living space and absolute
economic self-sufficiency mainly as political window dressing. There is
good evidence that a large part of the managerial and financial elite of
Germany in the early and mid-1930s treated the Nazi exposition of economic autarky in precisely this way—rather like the way many of them
regarded Hitler himself as a fundamentally "sound" conservative who
made radical anticapitalist statements to increase his public support and
placate the left wing of the party.[39] Hitler certainly encouraged this view;
many of his statements to business and bureaucratic groups led them to
believe that the aim of economic autarky was a flexible one that could
take a number of forms, including comprehensive economic agreements
with other states that would not require the open exercise of force for
their achievement. Hjalmar Schacht, an orthodox economist and former
Weltpolitiker who was Hitler's economics minister in the 1930s, believed
that Hitler agreed with the policy Schacht advocated of building up trade
agreements with central and eastern European states into a cooperative
system centering around industrial Germany.[40] This idea was clearly a
continuation of Weimar policies and an updated version of the *Weltpolitikers' Mitteleuropa*. To this continental economic system would be added
overseas colonies to supply additional raw materials and markets. Autarky would exist only in a relative sense, one compatible with external
trade and investment, with the rationalization of the capitalist economy

through trusts that many people like Schacht believed to be the "real" historical function of the Third Reich—a function not inconsistent with the traditions of *Weltpolitik*. The financial planners of the major investment institutions, especially the *Deutsche Bank,* accepted this version of autarky, as did many of the *Reich* government departments in the years after 1933.[41]

They were not entirely wrong. Hitler was not, in fact, simply leading them on. He clearly believed that *one* of the aspects of his overall policy included the establishment of a form of German economic hegemony over a vaguely defined (but large) segment of the European continent. This was, moreover, a relatively immediate aim of policy. What Schacht and a large part of the business community did not understand was that the obvious incompatibility of this notion of autarky with more radical forms of the idea (the hermetically sealed economy, totally safe from the effects of economic changes in the outside world) and with the idea of acquiring vast living space was not obvious to Hitler. The flexibility of many aspects of Nazi ideology permitted each group to read into the ideology what it wanted to, up to a point. In the matter of economic expansion beyond the *Reich*, that point was reached when, in World War II, Germany actually had the opportunity to impose policies on the whole continent. Under such circumstances, the Nazi government moved in a multitude of contradictory, ultimately disastrous directions. But up to the start of the war, much of the German policy toward central and eastern Europe—focusing on the establishment of privileged relations between Germany and countries such as Rumania—was entirely compatible with the neo-*Weltpolitik* interpretation of what was meant by autarky; indeed, it was carried out by people like Schacht who actually believed in it.[42]

Some of the most basic aims of Hitler's foreign policy came directly from *Lebensraum.* Germany needed living space for her people, which could only be found in the east, particularly in Russia. Therefore, although Germany might for short periods maintain cooperative relations with Russia, a fundamental anti-Russian bias must be a cornerstone of German policy. Furthermore, Russia as the center of Bolshevism had to be destroyed, and not in the distant future. Germany's need for hegemony on the European continent also made it certain that her relations with France would be essentially unfriendly in the long run. Much had to be recovered from France, and only force would accomplish the recovery.[43]

But the conclusions Hitler drew from these fixed circumstances, although not unique on the radical right, were sufficiently unusual to set him off from the majority of radical-conservative theorists of foreign policy. Because the future relations of Germany with the other major continental powers (except Italy) were set by the objective nature of Germany's place in the world and were fundamentally hostile, Germany had of necessity to seek the support and cooperation of Great Britain. It was here that *Weltpolitik* asserted itself. At various critical junctures right up to 1941, Hitler appeared far more willing to make substantial concessions to Britain in foreign affairs than had been customary on the radical right since the beginning of the century, even among conservatives who drew the same general conclusions about Germany's position vis-à-vis Russia and France that Hitler did.[44] It was as though Hitler, having determined a general course on the basis of an oversimplified view of international politics, turned to the most obvious framework of ideas that explained how the course could be carried through—which in the environment of German political thought meant *Weltpolitik*. It is also likely that Hitler understood that a substantial part of the German business and government establishment (those to whom *Weltpolitik* traditionally appealed) regarded a foreign policy couched in terms familiar from the *Weltpolitik* of old as more "responsible" than the anglophobic ravings of other radical conservatives. British public opinion probably did the same.[45]

To Hitler, as to the *Weltpolitiker*, Britain was Germany's "natural" ally.[46] At least in the immediate future, the world was big enough for both powers, and it was in the interests of both to understand this. Hitler rather unfairly chided the policymakers of the *Kaiserreich* for not having followed a consistent policy of alliance with Britain from a position of German strength. The inconsistency of Wilhelmian policy had been its major weakness, alternating between unbecoming courtship of Britain and dangerous threats to her overseas interests. Hitler argued that Germany was naturally a military, continental power. Her immediate objectives (living space, autarky, etc.) lay in Europe. Britain was a seapower, and her best interests lay in good relations with the hegemonial power in Europe that could most efficiently organize the continent—Germany. With British assistance or, at least, benevolent neutrality, Germany could assert herself over France, establish control over central and eastern Europe, and smash Soviet Russia. Germany had, of course, important overseas economic interests that had to be satisfied with a substantial colonial empire and a large share of world trade. These were, however, secondary to her continental interests and could, moreover, be satisfied without a substantial threat to Britain—for the time being. The problem was, as usual, getting the British to comprehend their own interests and cooperate with Germany. Hitler believed after coming to power that the best chance for cooperation lay in eventual British recognition that he, Hitler, was strong enough and determined enough to follow a consistent policy not immediately dangerous to Britain. Hence Hitler, like a number of Foreign Office officials, believed that, for example, the Anglo-German naval agreement of 1935 was a decisive step on the road to achieving a major aim of German policy that extended back to the early Wilhelmian period.[47]

Hitler was, of course, wrong about British motives and reactions to his own policies in much the same way that the *Weltpolitiker* had been wrong before 1914. To Hitler, the proper way to encourage Britain to take the correct attitude toward Germany was, besides following consistent lines on foreign policy, to make Germany strong. A militarily and economically powerful Germany would be safe from the malice of Jewish-inspired groups in Britain who argued against alliance with Germany and pushed for reducing Europe to the status of a colony. A strong Germany would be self-evidently worthy of alliance. Similarly, Germany's assertion of her colonial rights could be used to encourage the British government to accommodate itself to a hegemonial Germany in Europe. It was not simply that Germany's demand for the return of her colonies would give her a bargaining chip in negotiating for an expansion of her control in Europe—one that was not needed in 1937–38. The demand for colonies, the building up of a certain amount of naval power, and similar attributes of "world policy" would demonstrate to the British what might happen if accommodation with Germany were not forthcoming. In arguing in this fashion, Hitler was speaking the language of *Weltpolitik* and thus falling into an ideological appraoch to policy that was already legitimated by use, but he was also accepting without adequate criticism a set of assumptions about British reactions that had time and again been proven incorrect—and would, of course, be so proven once more.[48]

It should also be noted that Hitler's assessment of relations with Britain was based primarily on the same sort of consideration that had informed the *Weltpolitikers'* view: the necessities of power politics and the "obvious" advantages to a limited number of major powers of possessing international spheres of influence. It was not founded on the idea of "racial" similarities between the Germans and British, although Hitler believed that such similarities existed. Hitler took racist ideas as seriously as he did any other part of his *Weltanschauung*. But no more than in the case of his position on relations with Italy and Japan did he treat racial factors as the prime determinant of policy toward England—in the short run. Although he shared the conservative antimodernist distaste for the "materialism" of industrial Britain and for her supposedly "Jewish-dominated" economy, this did not stop him from believing that an understanding with Britain was a vital factor in Germany's successful pursuit of foreign policy.[49]

There are certain broader connections between Hitler's imperialist ideology and the intellectual ethos of *Weltpolitik*. Several students of Hitlerian Germany have noticed a tension between the obvious antimodernist, anti-industrial bias of much of Nazi radical conservatism and the appeal to technocratic rationality that was also a significant part of the Nazi ideological aggregation. The latter is, of course, best known from Albert Speer's description of the factors that attracted him to Hitler and the Nazis.[50] The tension, which had deep precedents in the development of radical conservatism in Germany, resulted in the case of the Nazis from a very deliberate integration of technocratic ideas with the rest of the Nazi ideological mixture. Hitler, Goebbels, and others spoke of the opportunities available under the Nazi regime for an aristocracy of talent, especially in fields of engineering and science, and they gave every sign that they meant it. In the area of imperialism, this technocratic tendency was reflected from 1933 in the proliferation of planning activities and programs devoted to preparing for Germany's reentry into the ranks of the great imperialist powers. Not only were offices set up to plan for the economic transformation of Europe, but even in the colonial sphere, to which Hitler gave a lower priority, planning for overseas expansion and the gathering of scientific information about colonies took place at an unprecedented level in various agencies of the government, party, and "coordinated" colonial movement.[51]

What was the significance of this technocratic aspect of Nazi imperialism and of all this planning? In part, one may presume, it represents an attempt to persuade a variety of interest and occupational groups that the new *Reich* intended to follow through on its commitments. If, for example, Hitler intended for the time being in the 1930s to do nothing substantial about acquiring an overseas empire (his public statements to the colonial movement notwithstanding), it was still useful to make the leading colonialists and important imperialists like Schacht *think* that he was serious about expansion by promoting a highly visible planning effort.[52] It was useful to keep the political support of technical occupational groups whose pet projects could not be funded for the moment by giving them at least the suggestion that the future would bring more progress. As we shall see shortly, this process of putting elements of the Nazi program into a time perspective was one of Hitler's most important ideological techniques.

There was, however, more to it than that. Encompassed within Hitler's "leader principle" was the notion that the manifold problems of social fragmentation, political indecisiveness, and the conflict of apparently irreconcilable interest groups could be solved by the application of reason and planning, if reason and planning were directed toward the proper political ends and if they were coordinated by an all-powerful central authority. Other Nazi ideologues had earlier made similar arguments about technocracy within the framework of a corporate state.[53] The propensity of the Nazis for planning and rationalization thus resulted in part from one of the inherent tendencies in Nazi ideology, however badly that tendency fitted with the rest of the Nazi ideological aggregation. The political effect of all this was to reconcile a substantial body of opinion oriented toward modernism and science with the Nazis and the Third Reich. Among the imperialist ideologies in Germany, *Weltpolitik* had always been closely related to modernism. The emphasis on "scientific" imperialism and colonialism in the 1930s and early 1940s that accompanied the various planning projects therefore represented an incorporation of *Weltpolitik* concepts into a composite scheme of imperialism, regardless of the fact that a considerable amount of the rest of that scheme was inconsistent with the thrust of scientific and technocratic modernism.

There still remain certain important problems in understanding the nature and workings of Nazi imperialism seen as an ideological entity. These can be illustrated by summarizing Hitler's relationship with German colonialism. Hitler was originally little interested in overseas colonialism, except in the context of the general attack on Versailles. That is, he believed that the main reason Germany should demand the return of her colonies was not because of their intrinsic economic or cultural importance, but simply because they had been unjustly taken from her under the provisions of Versailles. He originally thought of colonies in the conventional migrationists sense, and like most other Nazi leaders (including the former colonialist Darré) came to the conclusion that such colonies made much more sense in Russia than in Africa. This remained, incidentally, Hitler's view of settlement colonies right to the end, occasional bows to the migrationist in the colonial movement notwithstanding. At most, he was willing to concede that *if* overseas colonies were acquired, a German population would be one of the better ways of retaining them. Even in the context of the attack on Versailles, Hitler originally accorded the return of the colonies a relatively low priority, and he reiterated this priority in 1937–38 when he had the opportunity to regain the colonies by foregoing continental expansion.[54] Thus, although Hitler accepted the major premises of the tradition of migrationist colonialism as transmitted through *Lebensraum* ideology, he did not really think that *overseas* settlement colonies were all that important as a goal of policy.

Klaus Hildebrand describes the way in which the Nazis and the Colonial Society moved closer together between 1928 and 1933 as the result of a complex of motives on both sides (the elitist Colonial Society needing the popular base and possible access to power that the Nazis could supply, the Nazis finding the political support of the Society useful in making themselves more "respectable" and in acquiring credibility among imperialists of all social classes).[55] Even before that time, the NSDAP, with Hitler's blessing, had adopted a call for *Mittelafrika*—an expanded, integrated colonial empire in Africa beyond the boundaries of the old colonies—as part of their program. Although the concept of *Mittelafrika* among prewar and wartime German imperialists had transcended the boundaries between *Lebensraum* and *Weltpolitik* and although it was included in the programs of a number of different political organizations during Weimar, it made sense primarily in the context of *Weltpolitik* colonialism—which was mainly how the Nazis used it. In moving toward the colonialists, Hitler adopted the *Weltpolitik* version of colonialism. He and the party's propagandists argued that an extensive overseas empire was needed to secure German markets, sources of raw materials, and investment areas against the possibility of exclusion by competing powers. They also argued that an extensive overseas empire was the best guarantee of German access to noncolonial markets and that such an empire could be set up without major conflict with Great Britain. Occasional references were made to colonial settlement, but it was clear that settlement in the future was primarily to be undertaken in Europe.[56]

The problem that arises, as it does with a large part of the Nazi program, is how seriously we should take Hitler's colonialism. Among other things, in adopting his colonial program, Hitler was attempting to broaden his support base by incorporating the colonialists. His subsequent statements to the leaders of the Colonial Society and to colonialists such as Schacht that he thought colonies important for Germany in the long run, his willingness to permit extensive planning for a future colonial empire, and his emphasis on colonial affairs in the later 1930s could thus be interpreted as a complicated political ploy or as an opportunistic exploitation of domestic and international circumstances for short-term gains. Hildebrand and other recent students of Hitler's relationship to colonialism, however, show that this view is much too simple.[57] Hitler certainly took advantage of every oportunity colonialism presented to him, and he certainly led the colonial movement to believe that overseas colonial expansion had a higher priority on his list of national aims than, in fact, it turned out to do. On the other hand, there is good evidence that Hitler actually came to believe that an overseas colonialist and economic-imperialist policy would be desirable for Germany. Massive overseas settlement of the sort advocated by Hans Grimm made no great sense to Hitler, which was one of the reasons for the tension that existed between Grimm and the Nazis, but Hitler seems to have been convinced that in the long run a large overseas empire was a necessary concomitant to great power status. In the *very* long run, he seems also to have considered that Germany would have to acquire absolute world hegemony for economic reasons. Even in the later 1920s, Hitler had been willing to offend the generally anticolonialist Strasser wing of the NSDAP by openly advocating *Weltpolitik*-style imperialism. By the 1940s, the eventual acquisition of an empire that would span the continents was a widely accepted goal of Nazi policy.[58] How is this to be reconciled with the *Lebensraum* orientation of much of the rest of Hitler's expansionary policy and with the clear preference that Hitler gave in immediate decision making to continental economic autarky and the need to seize living space in Europe?

Here we come to one of the most important characteristics of Hitler's approach to ideology, particularly imperialist ideology: his technique of regarding incongruent ideological entities as separate program goals in a *time dimension*. As we have already seen, Hitler was by no means original in his exploration of what was called in Chapter One the "temporal displacement" attribute of ideology. To some degree practically everyone who employs ideologies as means of support aggregation or as guides to policy does something of the sort. But Hitler clearly went farther than anyone else discussed in this study in employing the concept of a schedule of imperialist expansion as a means of reconciling otherwise irreconcilable notions. Because this schedule is extremely well known from the extensive research that has been done on Nazi war aims, it is necessary only to outline it here in the context of ideological resolution. That the outlines of Hitler's expansionary program were clear in his own mind by the early 1930s is now generally accepted by most historians. The specifics of direction and timing, of course, depended on opportunities as they arose. The extent to which part or all of the program was revealed by Hitler at any one time depended on the context in which the revelation occurred: whether the program was being used in a (more-or-less) public political setting to attempt to create consensus by reconciling incompatible program goals or whether Hitler was using it to set policy by reconciling divergent elements in his own ideological framework. The crucial point is that as far as Hitler was concerned, the very same framework of ideas was applicable to both contexts. Only the immediate specifics and how much of the schedule was revealed varied with the circumstances.[59]

Up to 1936, of course, the immediate aim of Hitler's policy, the first stage in the Nazi imperialist program, was the achievement of Germany's independence and the reacquisition of power in world affairs. This was to be undertaken partly by the repudiation of reparations and international payments, withdrawal from the League of Nations, and the effective rejection of the Versailles treaty, but the primary agency of change was to be rearmament. Rearmament also played a vital role in the Nazis' plans for economic recovery from the depression. Practically the entire political center and right and most of the interest groups with which the Nazis were concerned could concur in the need to achieve these aims. The next stage, entered after 1936, was the establishment of the political dominance over central and eastern Europe, which was needed to acquire living space and to create a regime of economic autarky. The annexation of Austria and the occupation of Czechoslovakia were the actual initial steps in this second stage. In terms of consensus politics, the second stage represented the fulfillment of the aims of the groups that subscribed to the extended *Lebensraum* ideological set. Those oriented toward *Weltpolitik* and toward overseas economic imperialism were to be appeased with the promise, manifested in extensive planning efforts, of a third stage of expansion once the second was realized.[60]

Ultimately, the achievement of *Lebensraum* in the second stage meant destroying the Soviet Union and totally defeating France—hopefully without interference from Britain. In 1939, Hitler was perfectly willing to countenance an understanding with the Soviet Union so as to undertake the next immediate steps toward *Lebensraum:* the capture of Poland and the defeat of France. As we have already seen, however, in Hitler's view (like that of the majority of the adherents of *Lebensraum* and of the *Lebensraum*-derived idea of autarky), neither economic autarky nor an adequate amount of living space—even for short-term purposes—could be attained without seizing a substantial amount of Russia. Once the process of creating a German-dominated Europe had commenced, its completion implied an attack on the Soviet Union just as soon as the benevolent neutrality of the Russians was no longer necessary.

The most crucial of Hitler's foreign policy decisions then, the one which by practically any criterion external to the structure of *Lebensraum* imperialism stands out as his most outrageous mistake—the 1941 invasion of Russia—followed directly from his conception of the second or *Lebens-*

raum stage of his imperialist program. It was the "logical" consequence of the successful pursuit of German aims up to 1941. The immediate circumstances were opportune. Stalin apparently suspected nothing and most observers in 1941 believed the Soviet Army incapable of effective resistance. Moreover, the failure of Britain to play her ordained role in the second stage—to signify acceptance of Germany's domination of the continent through an alliance, imperial partnership, or friendly neutrality—also seemed to dictate action against Russia. If the fall of France and the blitz had not convinced the British that their best interests lay in accommodation, the fall of Russia certainly would.[61]

In the structure of the first two segments of Hitler's imperialist schedule can also be seen at least some of the reasons for a number of other important decisions that Hitler and the German government made in the late 1930s and early 1940s. The 1937–38 decision to occupy Austria and Czechoslovakia rather than pressing for the return of the former German colonies was not based on a rejection by Hitler of the desirability of colonies but on the more immediate priority that he gave to setting the stage for the expansion of living space and the establishment of economic autarky.[62] The decision to attack Poland in 1939 followed from the same priorities, as did the knocking out of France in 1940. Although many of these actions, like the invasion of Russia, may appear to have been irrational from the standpoint of German strength and economic needs, they seemed perfectly reasonable in the context of the *Lebensraum* segment of Hitler's imperialist thinking. Most Nazis and a great many other Germans thought about policy in this context, which perhaps explains why such decisions were not effectively opposed within the government and military. The position of Britain in Hitler's thinking was misconceived in large part because the view of Britain that had entered Nazi imperialism from *Weltpolitik* was misconceived as well. In some cases, ideologically derived expectations about British reactions to German moves were more "real" in the processes of Nazi decision making than was the evidence, available from half a century of experience, that these expectations were false.

The third stage of Hitler's policy framework might well be called the *Weltpolitik* stage because it was during the period after the basis for *Lebensraum* and autarky had been achieved and in which full-scale programs based on those ideas were being effectuated that Germany was to move toward a full exercise of her power in the greater world. At the height of Nazi success in 1940–41, the third stage was apparently expected to full up at least the first half of the decade. At other times it was less well defined, possibly extending for some generations to come.[63] Germany was to acquire strategically and economically advantageous colonies—including *Mittelafrika*—and economic hegemony over a substantial number of noncolonial areas (including a large portion of South America). The ideas that lay behind this policy stage came almost entirely from *Weltpolitik*. Little importance was ascribed to overseas settlement.

The aims of Nazi world policy were essentially economic, defined by the perceived needs of German industry. Many former *Weltpolitiker* in government and business took an active part in planning in the late 1930s and early 1940s for Germany's reemergence as a colonial and world-political power.[64]

It is essential to emphasize once again the three stages in the evolution of German policy discussed thus far were *ideological* entities, created not only because it is often convenient to organize projected political action into discrete steps, but more important, because the idea of stages provided a powerful means of reconciling divergent prescriptions for policy incorporated within the Nazis' composite ideology itself. Although the formulation of policy around these stages profoundly affected social reality external to the world of German political ideology, the stage approach to imperialism neither reflected external realities very accurately nor avoided actual logical inconsistencies, however much it may have disguised the latter. It was an excellent tool for reconciling divergent views of politics and imperialism, but it was a poor basis for policy. The first stage, the achievement of power and political independece, was something all imperialists could accept. The second or *Lebensraum* stage represented the need to achieve the aims prescribed by the *Lebensraum* ideological tradition (and to construct the means of achieving other radical goals of the Nazis, such as the eradication of European Jewry). The third stage—put temporally after the *Lebensraum* stage, in part to acknowledge the theoretical primacy of the ideas that made up *Lebensraum*—represented the supposedly valid elements of the *Weltpolitik* tradition that, in turn, represented the claims of modernity and industrialism on Nazi policymakers. According to Hitler's view, effective *Weltpolitik* could not be conducted without achieving at least the foundation for *Lebensraum* in Europe. At a minimum, it was the latter that he desired to secure before his own death.[65] The basis for the continued strength of German culture and the German *Volk* having been achieved, his successors could execute the world-political aspects of Nazi policy if he himself were not able to get around to them.

In actuality, of course, this clear differentiation of policy imperatives into discrete temporal and geographic spheres was an illusion. It was an illusion to think that locating *Lebensraum* at a certain stage and within a particular area (central and eastern Europe) could reconcile its logic with empirical economic reality. The resettlement progams in eastern Europe, which Himmler, Rosenberg, Darré, and the various organizations under them attempted to put into effect during World War II, ran into immediate difficulties because they were, at best, meaningless in terms of the German and European economics and, at worst, hindrances to the kinds of regional economic specialization and exchange that were the most coherent parts of the idea of autarky. Programs for occupying settlement land in the Ukraine and other parts of the Soviet Union made it difficult for the Germans to acquire the willing support of non-Russians in the captured territories, on which many of their plans for military success against the Soviets depended. The concept of economic autarky as a whole, although given a certain amount of meaning by wartime conditions, proved to be too vaguely defined and too full of ignored contradictions to serve as a basis for consistent policymaking. And so forth. The deficiencies of Nazi economic policy in Europe during the war are well known.[66]

It was moreover an illusion to think that *Weltpolitik* and *Lebensraum,* as frameworks for conducting national policy, could be reconciled with each other through temporal and geographic separation. Quite apart from the long-term difficulties that would obviously have been created by the need to coordinate continental economic policy with overseas policy, even the initial implementation of Nazi policies created insuperable problems. The fact that Germany did not, in 1940 and 1941, achieve all of Hitler's aims for those years (the acquisition of adequate living space and the forcing of Britain into accommodation) meant that the distinctions between imperialist stages became in reality hopelessly blurred. Hitler found himself after 1941 simultaneously attempting to complete the work of the *Lebensraum* stage by defeating Russia and Britain, to build the foundations of his New Order in Europe (based essentially on doctrines of *Lebensraum,* autarky, and racial purity), and to conduct a war that theoretically belonged to the third or *Weltpolitik* stage: the war against the United States.

During the third stage of expansion, Germany was supposed to create for herself an integrated overseas empire more-or-less equivalent to those of Britain and the United States and based largely on *Weltpolitik* conceptions of economic imperialism. Hitler's previous orientation toward Japan in international relations had partly been based on the recognition that Japan was also seeking to establish such an empire for herself, in an area of the world in which immediate conflicts of interest with Germany were relatively few. If Germany could create her own empire with the concurrence of either Japan or Britain (preferably both), only the United States would stand in the way of, for example, German imperialism in South America. In reality, of course, Britain remained hostile after the fall of France, supported by the United States. That left Japan as the key to the third stage. When the Japanese decided to attack the United States at the end of 1941, Hitler was, in his own framework of thought, forced to declare war on the United States in support of Japan so as not to jeopardize Japan's cooperation in Germany's future third-stage expansion and to take maximum advantage of Japan's new imperial bid.[67] In other words, Germany's seemingly unnecessary declaration of war on the United States, which drained further German resources from the achievement of the *Lebensraum* aims of policy, stemmed partly from Hitler's inability to maintain the temporal distinction between the *Lebensraum* and *Weltpolitik* elements of his imperialism and his unwillingness to forego either element in the long run. His supposed opportunism in supporting Japan was thus an opportunism in pursuit of an ideological aim that was, in the circumstances, self-defeating and hopelessly inconsistent with other aims.

There is considerable evidence of a fourth stage in the imperialist outlook of Hitler and several other Nazis, a stage that was to be reached after the secure acquisition of an overseas empire connected to a German-dominated European heartland. Unlike the *Weltpolitiker*, most of whom had refused to carry the logic of *Weltpolitik* out to its almost inevitable conclusion in German world domination, Hitler did not hesitate to foresee a world in which there would be not three or four great powers with attendant empires, but one: Germany. For the most part, the reasoning behind this view did not derive from *Lebensraum*. Germany's continental empire, if properly secured and exploited, ought to be able to provide sufficient living space for the nation's expanding population for centuries to come. But the resources of the overseas world in raw materials, markets, and investment areas were sure to become sources of conflict among the powers eventually, even if the number of such powers were reduced as Hitler intended. Even if Britain did accept accommodation with Germany as a result of persuasion (up to 1940) or force, the accommodation could not be a permanent one. Accommodation was to be based on guarantees of German military superiority, which would mean that when Germany eventually needed to secure a larger share of the world's economic resources, she could do so at the expense of Britain. Similarly, Germany needed to aim—during the third stage in which she acquired her worldwide economic empire—at securing strategic advantages that would allow her to win in the eventual showdown with the United States. This was the initial goal of war with the United States in 1941 rather than the complete defeat of the Americans. Even Japan would have to be contended with in the long run, but geography might put that event off for a while. Although Hitler's extension of *Weltpolitik* into world domination was not very clearly conceived, it followed directly from the structure and assumptions of the Nazis' composite imperialist ideology.[68]

Conclusion

Obviously, one cannot argue that all of the disastrous decisions made by the Nazi regime and everything that went wrong for Germany in the 1940s were directly due to deficiencies in the imperialist ideology that the Nazis had concocted and adopted. Even within the realm of ideologically determined policy, many of the most horrendous of Nazi actions (especially the massacre of the Jews) and many of the self-defeating economic initiatives of the German government before and during the World War had comparatively little to do with the specifically imperialist parts of the Nazi program. Nevertheless, opportunistic as Hitler was in terms of short-term political and diplomatic moves, it remains the case that most of the

German actions leading to the Second World War were based on policy goals derived from Nazi ideology. I have attempted to show the extent to which those segments of the Nazi program that most influenced the various decisions to go to war and that shaped many of the crucial German decisions during the war were connected to the ideological traditions of German imperialism.

If there was continuity in German imperialism between Bismarck's time and Hitler's time, it consisted mainly of a line of ideological development commencing before the middle of the nineteenth century and extending down to the collapse of 1945. Bismarck, Bülow, Stresemann, and Hitler are connected along this line because the political environment in which each worked included the then-current imperialist ideologies. These ideologies were not just intellectual constructs, abstracted from the political and economic events going on around them, nor were they simply disguises for specific interests. Rather, they were collections of ideas and attitudes from many different sources, organized primarily for purposes of interest aggregation and political mobilization under the circumstances then prevailing. Each era did not, however, construct its own imperialism from new materials. Each was presented with ideological aggregations from the previous period, aggregations that already possessed meaning in terms of possibilities for national policy and in terms of the perceived concerns of different interest groups. Politicians, including successive German chancellors, could choose to employ imperialism in their conduct of politics or they could choose not to do so, but they could not ignore its presence. And as time went on, as the imperialist ideologies were adapted to changing political needs, as they absorbed the particular outlooks of additional social groups and political organizations, and as they demonstrated capacity for creating partial political consensus, they gradually joined the array of concepts imparted to new generations of Germans through the processes of political socialization. By this and other means, the ideologies themselves—not just some of their elements—became frameworks for the conscious construction of national policy options. Within the various sectors of the political elite by the time of the First World War and among large segments of the public at large, people actually believed in the accuracy of political analyses based on the imperialist ideologies and in the efficacy of actions that followed from them. And here, of course, was one of the roots of the tragedy of German imperialism, because the imperialist ideologies contained a host of fallacies, contradictions, and self-defeating proposals for action—the legacy of their origins in the politics of consensus building.

One of the most distinctive features of imperialist ideology in pre-Hitler Germany was its dualistic nature. Despite overlap in content and frequent attempts at integration, *Weltpolitik* and *Lebensraum* remained fundamentally different—and usually antagonistic—ideologies from the early 1890s down to the Hitler era. Ideological differences can be found in the imperial histories of other countries, sometimes along lines akin to the *Welt-*

politik–Lebensraum split. The debate in British official circles just after the turn of the century about whether or not to turn Kenya into a white settlement colony comes immediately to mind. But in Britain and France, such differences appear to have been shorter lived and more specific, and they were generally overshadowed by the question of whether imperialism was in any case a good idea.

Why was this ideological dualism so pronounced and continuous in Germany? Probably for a great many reasons, but the most apparent is that the level of political and social fragmentation there in the late nineteenth century—the period in which the dualism became fixed—was extremely high. This, in turn, as we saw in Chapter Three, was due to many factors, including rapid industrialization, "unbalanced" social and political modernization, and the preexisting structures of German ideology. As the two imperialist ideologies diverged in the course of their employment by different, often competing, groups seeking to aggregate political support, the differences between *Lebensraum* and *Weltpolitik* became an enduring feature of German politics, even as the socioeconomic fragmentation that gave rise to the differences diminished. Attempts to overcome the differences and to produce a single, composite imperialist ideology as a means of creating national consensus failed until the rise of the Nazis. Even the Nazis' version succeeded only because of their full exploitation of new means of opinion manipulation and the changes in public attitudes caused by the First World War. Ideological integration did not eliminate the logical and empirical weaknesses in *Lebensraum* and *Weltpolitik,* but rather enhanced their seriousness.

By 1942, Germany found herself in possession of one of the most impressive territorial empires in modern history. She was also, however, at war with major powers on all sides. She need not have been at war with at least two of them—the Soviet Union and the United States—and would perhaps have had the strength to defeat the third, Great Britain, if she had not been. As it was, Germany was engaged in an impossible war in the east that had been deliberately started to achieve an end, *Lebensraum,* that made practically no sense except within the framework of one version of German imperialist ideology. Instead of knocking Britain out of the war, Germany had augmented Britain's strength by going to war with the United States in pursuit of world-political aims that were at best vaguely defined and at worst thoroughly contradictory to other aspects of German policy. Within Europe, policies derived from *Lebensraum* imperialism conflicted with others connected with economic imperialism and *Weltpolitik.* Neither imperialist ideological tradition by itself was an adequate basis for effective policy; both together created unresolvable conflicts among the goals of policy and among the institutions pursuing them. Settlement policies in Russia interfered with the attempt to rally anticommunist elements against the Soviet government. Successful continental autarky depended on maximizing the agricultural production of non-German areas of eastern and central Europe; agrarianism and settlement imperialism required the protection (indeed, the multiplication) of inefficient small German producers and the maintenance of artificially high food prices. The war itself increasingly came to provide the main criterion of policy in the absence of effective direction from the Nazi ideological program. The war, in other words, which had been started to a large extent in pursuit of the goals laid out by Nazi imperialism, had become the major goal in itself, the overriding social activity that appeared to dissolve the contradictions found in Nazi imperialism and everywhere else in the Nazi ideology. The traditions of German imperialist ideology had finally and decisively demonstrated their bankruptcy as foundations for national political action.

Notes

ABBREVIATIONS USED IN NOTES:

AV	*Alldeutscher Verband* (Pan-German League)
BA	*Bundesarchiv* Koblenz
CDI	*Centralverband deutscher Industrieller*
DKB	*Deutsches Kolonialblatt*
DKG	*Deutsche Kolonialgesellschaft* (German Colonial Society)
DKZ	*Deutsche Kolonialzeitung*
GP	Johannes Lepsius et al., eds., *Die Grosse Politik der Europäischen Kabinette, 1871–1914.* 40 vols. Berlin, 1922–27.
LC	Library of Congress, Washington, DC
NA	National Archives, Washington, DC
SPD	German Social Democratic Party
Sten. Ber.	*Stenographische Berichte über die Verhandlungen des Reichstages*
VDES	*Verein deutscher Eisen- und Stahlindustrieller* (metals lobby)
ZStA (Hoover microfilm)	*Zentrales Staatsarchiv* Potsdam (microfilms of German Colonial Office and Colonial Society files from Potsdam maintained at the Hoover Institution, Stanford, CA)

CHAPTER ONE

1. The classic interpretation of Hitler as opportunist is A. J. P. Taylor, *The Origins of the Second World War* (London, 1961), which is discussed from various perspectives in Wm. Roger Louis, ed., *The Origins of the Second World War: A. J. P. Taylor and His Critics* (New York, 1972).
2. Hans-Adolf Jacobsen, *Nationalsozialistische Aussenpolitik 1933–1938* (Frankfurt am Main and Berlin, 1968), pp. 446–63.
3. See, for example, the studies collected in Helmuth Stoecker, ed., *Drang nach Afrika* (Berlin, 1977); also A. S. Jerussalimski, *Die Aussenpolitik und die Diplomatie des deutschen Imperialismus Ende des 19. Jahrhunderts* (Berlin, 1954).

4. The most notable and important of these studies in recent years has been Geoff Eley, *Reshaping the German Right: Radical Nationalism and Political Change after Bismarck* (New Haven and London, 1980).

5. Fritz Fischer, *Germany's Aims in the First World War* (New York, 1967; orig. German ed., 1961); Fritz Fischer, *War of Illusions: German Policies from 1911 to 1914* (New York, 1975; orig. German ed., 1969). Fischer was not, of course, the first to focus on the political and social effects of modernization as the motivating forces behind German imperialism, only the first to push such an analysis to the forefront of German historical consciousness. Fischer's predecessors in this respect (both of them, in fact, more comprehensive in the scope of their approach) were Eckart Kehr and George W. F. Hallgarten. See Eckart Kehr, *Battleship Building and Party Politics in Germany 1894–1901*, tr. P. R. and E. N. Anderson (Chicago and London, 1973); Eckart Kehr, *Der Primat der Innenpolitik. Gesammelte Aufsätze zur preussisch-deutschen Sozialgeschichte im 19. und 20. Jahrhundert*, ed. H. -U. Wehler (Berlin, 1965); also George W. F. Hallgarten, *Imperialismus vor 1914* (2 vols.; Munich, 1951).

6. See, for example, Imanuel Geiss, *German Foreign Policy, 1871–1914* (London and Boston, 1976). Fischer himself considerably broadened his political analysis in *War of Illusions*.

7. Many of the positions taken on Fischer's work are summarized in J. A. Moses, *The Politics of Illusion: The Fischer Controversy in German Historiography* (London, 1975).

8. Hans-Ulrich Wehler, *Bismarck und der Imperialismus* (Cologne, 1969); Hans-Ulrich Wehler, *Krisenherde des Kaiserreichs 1871–1918. Studien zur deutschen Sozial- und Verfassungsgeschichte* (Göttingen, 1970).

9. See H. Pogge von Strandmann and Imanuel Geiss, *Die Erforderlichkeit des Unmöglichen* (Frankfurt am Main, 1965).

10. For evaluations of social imperialism, see Paul M. Kennedy, "German Colonial Expansion: Has the Manipulated Social Imperialism Been Antedated?" *Past and Present* 54 (1972), pp. 134–41; Geoff Eley, "Defining Social Imperialism: Use and Abuse of an Idea," *Social History* 3 (1976), pp. 265–90; and Wolfgang J. Mommsen, ed., *Der moderne Imperialismus* (Stuttgart, 1971).

11. Eley, *Reshaping the German Right*, pp. 1–16, 101–235, 349–61.

12. Wehler himself makes little of it: Wehler, *Bismarck und der Imperialismus*, pp. 155–57. The most thorough study to date of any aspect of German colonial politics—Klaus J. Bade, *Friedrich Fabri und der Imperialismus in der Bismarckzeit: Revolution-Depression-Expansion* (Freiburg, 1975), pp. 354–68—similarly cannot adequately accommodate the *Auswanderung* idea within a Wehlerian framework.

13. The classic presentation of the Nazis as the front men for capitalism is Franz Neumann, *Behemoth: The Structure and Practice of National Socialism 1933–1944* (rev. ed.; New York, 1944). Contrary views are summarized in Pierre Ayçoberry, *The Nazi Question. An Essay on the Interpretation of National Socialism (1922–1975)* (New York, 1981), pp. 149–215.

14. Klaus Hildebrand, *Deutsche Aussenpolitik 1933–1945. Kalkül oder Dogma?* (Stuttgart, 1971); Gerhard L. Weinberg, *The Foreign Policy of Hitler's Germany: Diplomatic Revolution in Europe, 1933–1936* (Chicago, 1970); Norman Rich, *Hitler's War Aims: Ideology, the Nazi State, and the Course of Expansion* (2 vols.; New York, 1973, 1974). See also Andreas Hillgruber, *Germany*

and the Two World Wars (Cambridge, MA, and London, 1981), pp. 49–98; Jacobsen, *Nationalsozialistische Aussenpolitik.*

15. Heinz Gollwitzer, *Geschichte des weltpolitischen Denkens* (2 vols.; Göttingen, 1972, 1982); Heinz Gollwitzer, *Die gelbe Gefahr. Geschichte eines Schlagwortes* (Göttingen, 1962); Wolfgang J. Mommsen, *Das Zeitalter des Imperialismus* (Frankfurt am Main, 1969).

16. Paul M. Kennedy, *The Rise of the Anglo-German Antagonism 1860–1914* (London, 1980).

17. This is essentially the way ideology is treated in Daniel Bell, *The End of Ideology: On the Exhaustion of Political Ideas in the Fifties* (2nd rev. ed.; New York, 1962).

18. Karl Mannheim, *Ideology and Utopia* (New York, 1954).

19. Clifford Geertz, *The Interpretation of Cultures. Selected Essays* (New York, 1973).

20. See Joyce Appleby's rather similar use of the concept of ideology in her article "Ideology and Theory: The Tension between Political and Economic Liberalism in Seventeenth-Century England," *American Historical Review* 81 (1976), pp. 499–515.

21. The literature on ideology is immense. For a sampling, see David E. Apter, ed., *Ideology and Discontent* (New York, 1964); Edward Shils, "The Concept and Function of Ideology," in *International Encyclopedia of the Social Sciences* (New York, 1968), 7: pp. 66–76; Harry M. Johnson, "Ideology and the Social System," in *International Encyclopedia of the Social Sciences* (New York, 1968), 7: pp. 76–85; and Talcott Parsons, *Essays in Sociological Theory* (2nd ed.; London, 1954), pp. 19–33. A theoretical treatment of ideology that comes close (in a vastly more sophisticated way) to the approach taken in the present study is Peter L. Berger and Thomas Luckmann, *The Social Construction of Reality. A Treatise in the Sociology of Knowledge* (Garden City, NY, 1966). See, for example, Berger and Luckmann's treatment (pp. 71–72) of the specific point discussed in our text. Berger and Luckmann do not, however, employ the structural-functionalist framework used in the present study.

22. Parsons, *Essays,* pp. 19–33.

23. Mannheim, *Ideology and Utopia,* pp. 192–211.

24. See Eric Stokes, *The English Utilitarians and India* (London, 1959).

25. This point is discussed in Chapter Five. See also Berger and Luckmann, *Social Construction of Reality,* pp. 80–128.

26. The problem of *belief* is one of the most difficult aspects of any analysis of ideology. In the present study, the issue arises primarily in the context of explaining how politicians can simultaneously treat an aggregate ideology as an instrument of domestic politics and as a genuine guide to national policy. Barring conscious hypocrisy (which, of course, often enters into politics), there are two approaches applied here—neither of which is pursued at length. It is argued that a politically successful ideology (i.e., successful at attracting support in competition with other ideologies) will be absorbed into processes of socialization and thus come to be implicitly believed over time—a progression from partial to total belief over the space of two or more generations. In addition, it is argued (especially in the case of Hitler discussed in Chapter Ten) that the qualities of a successful ideology that allow it to appear to reconcile contradictions among the outlooks of different groups or organizations *also* often enable the ideology to reconcile contradictions among the

ideas present in an individual policymaker's mind. The prevalence of ideologies in politics may ultimately be due to their ability to reduce dissonances among inconsistent notions and images in the cognitive frameworks of individuals. Cognitive dissonance theories in psychology may provide the outline of an explanation for this phenomenon, although to present such an explanation would exceed the practical limits of our study. On dissonance theory, see Leon Festinger, *A Theory of Cognitive Dissonance* (New York, 1957).

CHAPTER TWO

1. The most complete discussion of the *Auswanderung* and its connection to nineteenth-century German politics is Mack Walker, *Germany and the Emigration, 1816–1885* (Cambridge, MA, 1964).
2. See, for example, Robert Mohl, "Ueber Auswanderung," *Zeitschrift für die gesammte Staatswissenschaft* 4 (1847), pp. 320–49. See also Heinrich Sieveking, *Karl Sieveking 1787–1847* (Hamburg, 1929), pp. 518–25.
3. Leonard Krieger, *The German Idea of Freedom: History of a Political Tradition* (Boston, 1957), pp. 280–96; James J. Sheehan, *German Liberalism in the Nineteenth Century* (Chicago and London, 1978), pp. 5–48.
4. See Friedrich Hundeshagen, *Deutsche Auswanderung als Nationalsache* (Frankfurt am Main, 1849).
5. Mohl, "Auswanderung," pp. 320–49.
6. See, for example, the attitude of the prominent liberal leader Heinrich von Gagern in *Deutscher Liberalismus im Vormärz: Heinrich von Gagern, Briefe und Reden 1815–1848* (2 vols.; Göttingen, 1959), 2: pp. 243–45, 277–80.
7. Hundeshagen, *Deutsche Auswanderung*, pp. 38–42.
8. E. Bekerath et al., eds., *Friedrich List: Schriften, Reden, Briefe* (10 vols.; Berlin, 1952), 5: pp. 418–547.
9. See Emil Lehmann, *Die deutsche Auswanderung* (Berlin, 1861); and Wilhelm Roscher, *Kolonien, Kolonialpolitik und Auswanderung* (2nd ed.; Leipzig and Heidelberg, 1856).
10. Donald G. Rohr, *The Origins of Social Liberalism in Germany* (Chicago, 1963), pp. 121–30.
11. See Walker, *Germany and the Emigration*. An example of a proposal for a voluntary migration society is C. von Werner, *Antrag des Abgeordneten von Werner, die Bildung eines Emigrations- und Colonisations-Verein betreffend* (n.p., n.d., c.1842), pp. 1–12 (in LC collection of photostats of Prussian Foreign Ministry records relating to emigration.)
12. Mohl, "Auswanderung."
13. Ibid.; Hundeshagen, *Deutsche Auswanderung*.
14. See Lehmann, *Deutsche Auswanderung;* Roscher, *Kolonien;* Mohl, "Auswanderung;" and Hundeshagen, *Deutsche Auswanderung*. See especially Julius Fröbel, *Die deutsche Auswanderung und ihre kulturhistorische Bedeutung* (Leipzig, 1858).
15. Frederick List, *National System of Political Economy,* tr. G. A. Matile (Philadelphia, 1856), pp. 77–78, 490–97.
16. Franz Wigard, ed., *Stenographischer Bericht über der deutschen constituierenden Nationalversammlung zu Frankfurt am Main* (9 vols.; Leipzig, 1848), 2: pp. 1055–62; Günther Wollstein, *Das "Grossdeutschland" der Paulskirche: Nationale Ziele in der bürgerlichen Revolution, 1848/49* (Düsseldorf, 1977).

17. See, for example, Friedrich Kapp, *Über Auswanderung* (Berlin, 1871).
18. Marcus L. Hansen, *German Schemes of Colonization before 1860* (North-hampton, MA, 1923–24). Although emigration in the period 1831–40 had totalled 167,700 and in the decade 1841–50 had come to 469,300, it shot up to 1,075,000 in the 1850s. Gustav Stolper et al., *Deutsche Wirtschaft seit 1870* (Tübingen, 1964), p. 27.
19. The connection between rural economic change and the growth of interest in emigration, both as a social phenomenon and as an ideological entity, is discussed in Walker, *Germany and the Emigration,* pp. 153–74.
20. On post-1848 reappraisals of the political importance of the rural lower classes, see Theodore S. Hamerow, *Restoration Revolution Reaction: Economics and Politics in Germany 1815–1871* (Princeton, 1958), pp. 219–37, and Klaus Bergmann, *Agrarromantik und Grossstadtfeindschaft* (Meisenheim am Glan, 1970), pp. 33–39. Eley, *Reshaping the German Right,* pp. 19–24, discusses the relationship of liberalism to its rural constituency.
21. See, for example, Friedrich Ratzel's article in DKZ, 15 January 1885, pp. 38–44; Friedrich Ratzel, *Wider die Reichsnörgler. Ein Wort zur Kolonialfrage aus Wählerkreisen* (Munich, 1884); Rudolf Virchow, *Sozialismus und Reaktion* (Berlin, 1878).
22. Roscher, *Kolonien;* Fröbel, *Deutsche Auswanderung.*
23. Fröbel, ibid., pp. 86–92.
24. Heinrich von Treitschke, *Politics,* tr. B. Dugdale and T. de Bille (2 vols; London, 1916), 1: pp. 403–4; Bergmann, *Agrarromantik,* pp. 33–69.
25. Lehmann, *Deutsche Auswanderung,* pp. 86–87; Ratzel, *Wider die Reichs-nörgler.*
26. Hans Rosenberg, *Grosse Depression und Bismarckzeit: Wirtschaftsablauf, Gesellschaft und Politik in Mitteleuropa* (Berlin, 1967), pp. 38–40; Bergmann, *Agrarromantik,* pp. 33–62; John G. Gagliardo, *From Pariah to Patriot: The Changing Image of the German Peasant 1770–1840* (Lexington, KY, 1969), pp. 211–306.
27. See, for example, Friedrich Kapp's anticolonialist opinions in Friedrich Kapp, *Vom radikalen Frühsozialisten des Vormärz zum liberalen Parteipolitiker des Bismarckreichs: Briefe, 1843–1884,* ed. H.-U. Wehler (Frankfurt am Main, 1969), pp. 32–34.
28. See Bernard Semmel, *The Rise of Free-Trade Imperialism: Classical Political Economy, the Empire of Free Trade and Imperialism 1750–1850* (Cambridge, 1970), pp. 82–91, 100–29.
29. This is the kind of thinking to which Hans-Ulrich Wehler gives special weight in his classic *Bismarck und der Imperialismus,* pp. 112–26.
30. List, *National System,* pp. 70–82, 458–97; Bekerath et al., eds., *Friedrich List,* 5: pp. 195–96.
31. For Bucher's ideas in the 1860s, see Lothar Bucher, *Kleine Schriften politischen Inhalts* (Stuttgart, 1893), pp. 180–219. See also *Norddeutsche Allgemeine Zeitung,* 16, 17, 19, 21, 22 February 1867; and Bade, *Fabri,* pp. 58–59.
32. General summaries of Germany's initial colonial expansion can be found in: Wehler, *Bismarck und der Imperialismus;* Woodruff D. Smith, *The German Colonial Empire* (Chapel Hill, 1978), pp. 20–39; Bade, *Fabri,* pp. 80–314.
33. Bade, *Fabri,* pp. 85–97. This point was made by Ratzel in *Wider die Reichsnörgler.*
34. On the 1879 tariff and its general background, see Helmut Böhme, *Deutsch-*

lands Weg zur Grossmacht: Studien zum Verhältnis von Wirtschaft und Staat während der Reichsgründungszeit 1848–1881 (Cologne, 1966), pp. 211–416. On the position of light and export-import industry, see BA R13I/12 (draft history of the VDES by C. Klein), pp. 115–22.

35. On Woermann, see DKZ, 27 May 1911, pp. 354–55.
36. Wehler, *Bismarck und der Imperialismus*, pp. 215–23; R. P. Gilson, *Samoa 1830–1900: The Politics of a Multi-Cultural Community* (Melbourne, 1970), pp. 276–395.
37. The most important of these organizations were the *Verein für Handelsgeographie und Förderung deutscher Interessen im Ausland* of Leipzig and, later, the *Westdeutscher Verein für Colonisation und Export*. These are best treated in Bade, *Fabri,* pp. 102–5, 136–69.
38. Ibid.
39. Wehler, *Bismarck und der Imperialismus,* pp. 112–26, 142–55; Bade, *Fabri,* pp. 67–85. Friedrich Fabri (1824–1891) was a theologian, Protestant minister, and, from 1857, inspector (chief administrator) of the Rhine Mission of Barmen, Germany's largest missionary organization. His appointment led him into the politics of industrialization in Barmen and involved him in questions of overseas expansion. By the 1870s, he had developed important national political connections and a procapitalist, conservative social ideology. His 1879 pamphlet *Bedarf Deutschland der Colonien?* propelled him into the intellectual leadership of the German colonial movement. He was instrumental in creating several of the early imperialist organizations of the 1870s and 1880s, including the *Kolonialverein*. Fabri also led the colonialist opposition to Bismarck after 1887 when it became clear that the chancellor was not interested in further colonial expansion. Fabri's activities as a publicist, which expanded in the 1880s, cost him his job in 1884. He was still a major figure in the colonial movement at his death in 1891.

    Wilhelm Hübbe-Schleiden (1846–1917), a law graduate, served briefly in the consular service and spent the 1870s as a traveler, a merchant in West Africa, a Hamburg lawyer, and a journalist. Physically weak and severely neurotic, Hübbe-Schleiden was incapable of holding a permanent job. His brief period of notoriety came with his procolonial journalistic activities in the early 1880s. His impact on the colonial movement was smaller than Fabri's because of his instability and lack of organizing skill, but he can be regarded as one of the most important early radical conservative ideologists. Most of his later life was spent in straitened economic circumstances and in pursuit of a growing interest in the occult.

40. The main examples of this kind of argument are Friedrich Fabri, *Bedarf Deutschland der Colonien?* (Gotha, 1879); Wilhelm Hübbe-Schleiden, *Deutsche Colonisation* (Hamburg, 1881); and Ernst von Weber, *Die Erweiterung des deutschen Wirtschaftsgebiets und die Grundlegung zu überseeischen deutschen Staaten* (Leipzig, 1879).
41. Bade, *Fabri,* pp. 140, 172, 175. The opportunistic, mainly passive role of the big industrial organizations is documented in CDI and VDES files: BA R13I/162, pp. 11–17, 30–44, 65–74 (VDES meetings, 1882, 1884, 1886).
42. BA R13I/162, pp. 65–74 (VDES meeting, 1886).
43. BA R13I/161, pp. 128–31 (VDES report, November 1879); 169–75 (VDES report, December 1881).

44. BA R13I/173, pp. 240–47, contains an example of colonialist propaganda aimed at heavy industry.
45. Wehler, *Bismarck und der Imperialismus,* pp. 215–23.
46. Bade, *Fabri,* pp. 181–85; Fabri, *Bedarf Deutschland,* pp. 27–50.
47. Fabri, *Bedarf Deutschland,* pp. 30–32; Wilhelm Hübbe-Schleiden, *Überseeische Politik, eine culturwissenschaftliche Studie* (Hamburg, 1881).
48. See Richard Victor Pierard, *The German Colonial Society, 1882–1914* (Ph.D. diss., State University of Iowa, 1964), pp. 118–62.
49. See, for example, Wehler, *Bismarck und der Imperialismus,* pp. 155–57; and Bade, *Fabri,* pp. 354–68.
50. Pierard, *German Colonial Society,* pp. 118–62. Woermann did little to promote settlement once he got what he wanted in West Africa. On Peters, the propaganda campaigns of the early 1880s, and Peters's own views, see Carl Peters, *Gesammelte Schriften,* ed. Walter Frank (3 vols.; Munich, 1943), 1: 54–64, 332–41; Carl Peters, *Zum Weltpolitik* (Berlin, 1912); BA Frank papers, no. 8 (copy of letter: Peters to J. Scharlach, 3 December 1898).
51. See the furious argument at the *Verein*'s organizational meeting between Fabri and H. H. Meier of North German Lloyd over whether Germany should aim at trading or settlement colonies: DKG, *Die Deutsche Kolonialgesellschaft* (Berlin, 1908), p. 20. See also Ernst Hasse, "Was können und sollen wir jetzt für die deutsche Auswanderung thun?", DKZ, 15 December 1884.
52. Carl Peters (1856–1918), a university graduate without other career plans, returned to Germany from a stay in England in 1883 intending to become the leader of a movement to seize for Germany a huge colonial empire. He formed the GfdK in 1884 as a rival to the *Kolonialverein* and used it to back his treaty-signing trip to East Africa in that year. Although Bismarck accepted Peters's treaties, he moved effectively to keep German East Africa out of Peters's hands and to circumscribe Peters's activities. Peters was active in imperialist politics until 1896, leading the German Emin Pasha expedition to Uganda, helping to found the Pan-German movement, politicking to become head of the Colonial Department, and serving briefly as imperial commissioner in the Kilimanjaro region in East Africa. In 1896, a scandal arising from Peters's misbehavior in the last-named office led to criticism by the Social Democratic party (SPD) and gave the colonial director, Paul Kayser, the opportunity to dismiss him. Thereafter, Peters lived in England and South Africa and engaged in dubious colonial development schemes. He remained active in imperialist journalism while in exile and received official rehabilitation in 1907 through the help of the leadership of the Free Conservative party. He returned to Germany in 1914. Vain, psychologically unstable, violent, and unreliable, Peters was, nonetheless, one of the most effective journalistic proponents of German imperialism.
53. Smith, *German Colonial Empire,* pp. 40–45; Friedrich Fabri, *Fünf Jahre deutscher Kolonialpolitik* (Gotha, 1889). For a later example, see *Verhandlungen des Deutschen Kolonialkongresses 1902* (Berlin, 1903), pp. 597–610.
54. For a summary of the positions on the issue of Bismarck's colonialism, see Smith, *German Colonial Empire,* pp. 238–40. Major interpretations include the following works: Wehler, *Bismarck und der Imperialismus:* Henry Ashby Turner, Jr., "Bismarck's Imperialist Venture: Anti-British in Origin?" in Prosser Gifford and Wm. Roger Louis, eds., *Britain and Germany in Africa:*

Imperial Rivalry and Colonial Rule (New Haven, 1967), pp. 49–82; Hartmut Pogge von Strandmann, "Domestic Origins of Germany's Colonial Expansion under Bismarck," *Past and Present* 42 (1969), pp. 140–59; A. J. P. Taylor, *Germany's First Bid for Colonies, 1884–1885* (London, 1938); William O. Aydelotte, *Bismarck and British Colonial Policy; the Problem of South West Africa, 1883–1885* (Philadelphia, 1937); Stoecker, ed., *Drang nach Afrika*, pp. 15–27; and Kennedy, *Anglo-German Antagonism*, pp. 167–83.

55. These arguments are made by Aydelotte, *Bismarck and British Colonial Policy*, and by Wehler, *Bismarck und der Imperialismus*, pp. 180–93, 412–503, respectively.

56. For a cogent discussion of the background to Bismarck's later colonial policy, see Pogge von Strandmann, "Domestic Origins," pp. 156–59. On the left liberals, see Sheehan, *German Liberalism*, pp. 204–18.

57. Fabri, *Fünf Jahre.*

CHAPTER THREE

1. For general discussions of Wilhelmian society and politics, see Michael Stürmer, ed., *Das kaiserliche Deutschland. Politik und Gesellschaft 1870–1918* (Düsseldorf, 1970); James J. Sheehan, ed., *Imperial Germany* (New York and London, 1976); and Kennedy, *Anglo-German Antagonism*.

2. On the shopkeepers, see Robert Gellately, *The Politics of Economic Despair: Shopkeepers and German Politics, 1890–1914* (Beverley Hills, 1974). For master artisans, see Shulamit Volkov, *The Rise of Popular Antimodernism in Germany: The Urban Master Artisans, 1873–1896* (Princeton, 1978), pp. 123–325.

3. See, for example, Volkov, *Rise of Pupular Antimodernism*, pp. 32–60, 172–91, 215–36.

4. See the discussion of the responses of British and German parties to the changed conditions of the latter part of the nineteenth century in Kennedy, *Anglo-German Rivalry*, pp. 59–86, 146–53.

5. See, for example, Ernst Hasse, *Deutsche Politik*. Vol. 1: *Das Deutsche Reich als Nationalstaat* (Munich, 1905), nos. 1, 2, and 3.

6. See Wehler's treatment of ideology in *Bismarck und der Imperialismus*, pp. 112–26, 412–23, 454–502.

7. Paul Rohrbach, *Der deutsche Gedanke in der Welt* (Düsseldorf and Leipzig, 1912), pp. 5–63; Friedrich Naumann, *Demokratie und Kaisertum: Ein Handbuch für innere Politik* (Berlin, 1900); Hans-Jürgen Puhle, "Parlament, Parteien und Interessenverbände 1890–1914," in Stürmer, ed., *Das kaiserliche Deutschland*, pp. 340–77.

8. Gabriel A. Almond and C. Bingham Powell, Jr., *Comparative Politics: System, Process, and Policy* (2nd ed.; Boston, 1978), pp. 198–231.

9. This argument is made in a broader context in Woodruff D. Smith, *European Imperialism in the Nineteenth and Twentieth Centuries* (Chicago, 1982), pp. 81–85.

10. For examples of this approach, see the articles in Stürmer, ed., *Das kaiserliche Deutschland*, and Sheehan, ed., *Imperial Germany*.

11. On the Junkers, see Hans-Jürgen Puhle, *Agrarische Interessenpolitik und preussischer Konservatismus in Wilhelmischen Reich, 1893–1914* (Hanover, 1966), pp. 14–28.

12. Volkov, *Rise of Popular Antimodernism*.

13. See, for example, Rohrbach, *Deutsche Gedanke;* Naumann, *Demokratie und Kaisertum;* Friedrich Naumann, *Mitteleuropa* (Berlin, 1915), pp. 58–101; Hasse, *Deutsche Politik,* 1, 1: pp. 13–29.
14. On the continuance of traditional class structures and their adaptability to new conditions, see Arno J. Mayer, *The Persistence of the Old Regime: Europe to the Great War* (New York, 1981), pp. 79–187.
15. Rosenberg, *Grosse Depression,* pp. 49–77.
16. Ibid., pp. 78–82, 88–117; Kenneth D. Barkin, *The Controversy over German Industrialization 1890–1902* (Chicago and London, 1970), pp. 60–67, 131–85.
17. Puhle, *Agrarische Interessenpolitik,* pp. 14–22.
18. Volkov, *Rise of Popular Antimodernism,* pp. 3–60.
19. Rosenberg, *Grosse Depression,* pp. 62–78.
20. See, for example, Rohrbach, *Deutsche Gedanke,* pp. 36–61, 126; Eley, *Reshaping the German Right,* pp. 41–100; Abraham J. Peck, *Radicals and Reactionaries: The Crisis of Conservatism in Wilhelmine Germany* (Washington, 1978), pp. 17–48.
21. Richard S. Levy, *The Downfall of the Anti-Semitic Political Parties in Imperial Germany* (New Haven, 1975); Puhle, *Agrarische Interessenpolitik,* pp. 133–41.
22. This can be seen clearly in much of the discussion that took place during the founding of the Pan-German movement, which was supposed to be a consensus-building nationalist movement using imperialism as its central ideological focus. BA Frank papers, no. 9 (transcripts of Carl Peters's Pan-German correspondence) and no. 7 (letters: Peters to Otto Arendt, 15 July 1891; 28 July 1891; 8 October 1891; 28 November 1891).
23. On the question of modernization in German politics, see Dirk Stegmann, *Die Erben Bismarcks. Parteien und Verbände in der Spätphase des Wilhelmischen Deutschlands* (Cologne, 1970); and Dankwart Guratzsch, *Macht durch Organisation. Die Grundlegung des Hugenbergschen Presseimperiums* (Düsseldorf, 1974), pp. 26–62.
24. On Tirpitz, the Navy League, and public relations, see Eley, *Reshaping the German Right,* pp. 68–84, 101–59, 207–11; and Jonathan Steinberg, *Yesterday's Deterrent: Tirpitz and the Birth of the German Battle Fleet* (New York, 1965), pp. 125–63. Eley, although acknowledging the navy's leading role in government public relations, claims that nationalist organizations such as the Navy League were more innovative.
25. Peter Molt, *Der Reichstag vor der improvisierten Revolution* (Cologne and Opladen, 1963), comes to this conclusion.
26. Woodruff Smith and Sharon A. Turner in "Legislative Behavior in the German Reichstag, 1898–1906," *Central European History* 14 (1981), pp. 3–29, provide the evidence for this assertion. Although confirming previous assessments of social heterogeneity and nonrepresentativeness, the research reported in this article reveals several ways in which the Reichstag apparently was tending to perform some of the functional roles of a parliament. Indices of party cohesiveness on roll call votes were relatively high, indicating the existence of a degree of party discipline comparable to that found in most modern European parliaments. Other analyses showed that party affiliation was vastly more important in influencing members' votes than any other sociopolitical characteristic in their backgrounds. Factor analysis of samples of roll calls indicated substantial consistency in the voting patterns of sets of

parties and individual members on clusters of issues over time. All of this appears to show the appearance of a "normal" pattern of parliamentary behavior in the Reichstag and an important integrative role for many of its parties. See also Manfred Rauh, *Die Parlamentarisierung des Deutschen Reiches* (Düsseldorf, 1977).

CHAPTER FOUR

1. For a discussion of the term *Weltpolitik* in its broadest sense and its uses in Germany, see Gollwitzer, *Geschichte des weltpolitischen Denkens,* 2: pp. 23–82, 217–52; see also Fischer, *Germany's Aims,* pp. 20–38.

2. Bernhard Fürst von Bülow, *Denkwürdigkeiten* (4 vols.; Berlin, 1930), 1: pp. 415–16.

3. For *Weltpolitik* in the Foreign and Colonial offices and the *Deutsche Bank,* see Fischer, *War of Illusions,* pp. 310–18. For the importance of *Weltpolitik* in the relations between government departments and business organizations, see Lamar Cecil, *Albert Ballin: Business and Politics in Imperial Germany, 1818–1918* (Princeton, 1967), pp. 175–213.

4. An example of this argument is contained in a report dated 24 November 1913 from the German representative in Portugal, Friedrich Rosen, to Bethmann Hollweg. In it, Rosen details the means by which the Warburg Bank wants to safeguard its role in German policymaking in central and southern Africa in return for its investment in areas of Angola that the government wants to annex. NA, T–149, roll 136. This kind of belief underlay many of the arrangements made for the Baghdad Railway. See John G. Williamson, *Karl Helfferich, 1872–1924: Economist, Financier, Politician* (Princeton, 1971), pp. 80–96.

5. On antimodernism, see George L. Mosse, *The Crisis of German Ideology: Intellectual Origins of the Third Reich* (New York, 1964); Fritz Stern, *The Politics of Cultural Despair: A Study in the Rise of the Germanic Ideology* (Berkeley, 1961); and Volkov, *Rise of Popular Antimodernism.* For the less studied modernist attitude, see Barkin, *German Industrialization,* pp. 186–207. The connection between the modernist impulse and *Weltpolitik* is illustrated in the passage from Bülow quoted above. See also, among countless other examples that could be cited, Robert Wuttke, "Der Kampf um der Weltmarkt," *Die Grenzboten* 62 (1903), no. 27, pp. 1–10; no. 28, pp. 71–81; and Alexander Tille, "Die wirtschaftliche Grundlage und die Entwickelung der deutschen Auswanderung seit 1871," *Verhandlungen des Deutschen Kolonialkongresses 1902,* pp. 597–609, which is attacked (pp. 609–10) as being too modernist and materialistic in approach by an advocate of *Lebensraum.*

6. The Colonial Department of the Foreign Office became the Colonial Office, a *Reich* ministry in its own right, in 1907. On the Foreign Office, see Lamar Cecil, *The German Diplomatic Service, 1871–1914* (Princeton, 1976). On the fall of Bismarck and the groups responsible for it, see John C. G. Röhl, *Germany without Bismarck: The Crisis of Government in the Second Reich, 1890–1900* (Berkeley and Los Angeles, 1967), pp. 27–84.

7. In the Foreign Office after the 1890s there was little overt opposition to *Weltpolitik* assumptions, although the core *Weltpolitiker,* even by 1914, were still only a segment within the ministry. See Fischer, *War of Illusions,* p. 310. In the Colonial Office, where *Weltpolitik* clearly dominated, there were some

officials who tended more toward *Lebensraum* imperialism. The most impor-
tant of these was Friedrich Lindequist, whose career is discussed in Chapter
Six. In the Prussian Interior Ministry, which strongly influenced eastern European policy during the First World War, there was a fairly clearly defined
Lebensraum group associated, through official and business ties, with Alfred
Hugenberg. The most important of this group was probably Friedrich von
Schwerin. On Schwerin, see Fischer, *Germany's Aims,* pp. 115–16, 162–63,
273–74; Guratzsch, *Macht durch Organisation,* pp. 39–47; BA Sering papers,
no. 17, pp. 1–14 (wartime report by Schwerin and Lindequist on eastern
settlement.) Even during World War I, many senior Foreign Office personnel, including Foreign Secretary Gottlieb von Jagow, were basically traditional Bismarckian diplomats who gave the considerations that were central
to *Weltpolitik* a peripheral status in their thinking without necessarily disparaging them.

8. The initial group of *Weltpolitiker* in the Foreign Office is fairly clearly indicated by the correspondence of its leading figures. They were not so much an
organized party as they were a group of individuals sharing, among other
things, similar views about the relationship of foreign policy to business. They
also shared similar individual relationships to the axis around which the German foreign policy mechanism rotated in the early 1890s: the link between
Holstein and the emperor's confidant, Philipp Eulenburg. This was true not
only of Kayser and Kiderlen, but also of Marschall, Holstein's putative superior, who constantly needed Holstein's expertise and Eulenburg's support.
For examples of these connections in operation, see John C. G. Röhl, ed.,
Philipp Eulenburgs politische Korrespondenz (2 vols.; Boppard am Rhein,
1976), 2: pp. 529–30 (letter: Holstein to Eulenburg, 11 April 1890); 586–88
(letter: Holstein to Eulenburg, 31 October 1890). On the workings of the
Foreign Office Political Department during the Holstein era, see Cecil, *German Diplomatic Service,* pp. 257–81, esp. 266–67. For Cecil's analysis of the
eventual falling-out between Holstein and Kayser in 1896, see p. 252. A
graphic picture of the situation of one of the first *Weltpolitiker* is provided by
the letters of Paul Kayser to his uncle, the legal scholar Julius Baron of Bonn
University, included in BA Frank papers, no. 14. The letter of 20 September
1895, for example, describes the relationships among Kayser, Kiderlen, and
the Holstein/Eulenburg connection—in this case, considering the possibility
of a separate colonial ministry under Kayser. The Frank papers are an important source on Kayser, but they must be used with caution. They consist of
lengthy transcripts of official files made by the pro-Nazi historian Walter
Frank in the early 1940s for a projected biography of Carl Peters. Kayser, an
enemy of Peters and a person of Jewish descent, was intended to be one of
the major villains. There is, however, no indication that Frank falsified his
notes and transcripts. BA Frank papers, no. 14, also contains drafts of some
of Kayser's key comprehensive statements of *Weltpolitik* ideology, especially
his memorandum of summer 1890 to Caprivi on the projected consequences
of the Zanzibar-Heligoland treaty. Other material on Kayser can be found in
BA *Kleine Erwerbungen,* no. 10 (letters to Kayser, 1879–1897).

9. On the relationship between imperialism and other factors in the international outlooks of Bülow and Holstein, see Kennedy, *Anglo-German Antagonism,* pp. 223–88; Peter Winzen, *Bülows Weltmachtkonzept. Untersuchungen
zur Frühphase seiner Aussenpolitik 1897–1901* (Boppard am Rhein, 1977),

pp. 129–351; Norman Rich, *Friedrich von Holstein: Politics and Diplomacy in the Era of Bismarck and Wilhelm II* (2 vols.; Cambridge, 1965), 1: pp. 325–74; 2: pp. 555–601.

10. Some indication of the role of *Weltpolitik* in the Wilhelmian Foreign and Colonial offices and of the existence of perceived differences among groups of officials with respect to the degree of their acceptance of *Weltpolitik* can be found in the correspondence of Wilhelm Solf. The existence of a group of *Weltpolitiker* surrounding Kiderlen before 1912 is discussed in a letter of 31 January 1913 from Solf to Glasenapp, the vice president of the Reichsbank, in BA Solf papers, no. 33, p. 222. Differences of opinion between groups in the Foreign Office about the importance of an imperial understanding with Britain are referred to in BA Solf papers, no. 116, pp. 19–20 (letter: Kühlmann to Solf, 12 June 1912); in pp. 54–58, a 1915 exchange of letters between Kühlmann and Solf, both men refer to the continuous existence of a body of opinion connected with particular personnel (apparently including both Jagow and Arthur Zimmermann) that had emphasized the overwhelming need for an understanding with Russia to balance power in Europe—a different set of policy priorities from that of the self-professed *Weltpolitik* group to which Kühlmann and Solf belonged. Solf is the subject of an excellent biography: Eberhard von Vietsch, *Wilhelm Solf, Botschafter zwischen den Zeiten* (Tübingen, 1961).

11. Tirpitz's use of *Weltpolitik* will be discussed later in the present chapter. In general, this view corresponds to the one most frequently found among students of Tirpitz's role—that his main interest was in building the strongest navy in the world and that he used several different ideological approaches (all of them more or less congruent with his personal outlook) to achieve the desired end, one that he could not express in public.

12. William II's imperialist views are discussed in Röhl, *Germany without Bismarck*, pp. 156–99.

13. Cecil, *German Diplomatic Service*, pp. 260–61.

Paul Kayser (1845–1898) graduated in law and occupied various legal posts in the Prussian Interior Ministry. Because of his expertise on social and insurance questions, he was transferred to the Chancery and the Reich Insurance Office in 1884. Apparently because of his ambition for higher things, he got himself translated into the Foreign Office in 1885 and bounced between that ministry and others for the next five years. In 1890, attaching himself to Holstein and William II, Kayser played a part in the removal of Bismarck and was rewarded with the leadership of the Colonial Department of the Foreign Office. Kayser's activities in office are described in Chapter Six. After breaking with Holstein, he was forced to leave the Foreign Office in 1896 and was given a seat on the Imperial Supreme Court. Information on Kayser can be found in BA Frank papers, no. 14, in BA *Kleine Erwerbungen,* no. 10, and in Heinrich Schnee, ed., *Deutsches Kolonial-Lexikon* (3 vols.; Leipzig, 1920), 2: p. 257.

Alfred von Kiderlen-Wächter (1852–1912) came from a mercantile family in Württemberg, although his father had been ennobled and had court connections. After legal studies, Kiderlen entered first the consular and then the diplomatic service. After service in various capitals, he was appointed *Referent* specializing in oriental affairs in the Political Department in 1888. Kiderlen became close to William II and joined Bismarck's opponents at the chancellor's fall in 1890. Kiderlen was a central figure at the Foreign Office until 1894 when a duel made it necessary to post him out of Berlin. As was the case with many senior officials, he continued to spend much of his time in Berlin anyway. Kiderlen's rather coarse humor lost him the emperor's favor in 1899 and led to his "banishment" as minister to Rumania—which, because of growing German investment in Turkey and the Balkans, turned out to be an important post after all. With Marschall (then ambassador in Constantinople), Kiderlen was one of the major forces behind the *Weltpolitik* approach to foreign policy after 1900, continuously pushing for an understanding with Britain and a comprehensive policy of economic expansion. He served as temporary foreign secretary in 1908–9 and held the job permanently from 1910 to his death in December 1912. Sources for Kiderlen are Ernst Jäckh, ed., *Kiderlen-Wächter, der Staatsmann und Mensch. Briefwechsel und Nachlass* (2 vols.; Stuttgart, 1924) and *Neue Deutsche Biographie* (Berlin, 1953 ff.).

Baron Adolf von Marschall von Bieberstein (1842–1912) was the son of a Baden diplomat. After legal studies at Heidelberg and Berlin, he entered the Baden civil service. In 1883, he became Baden's representative on the *Bundesrat* and in 1884 the *Bundesrat*'s representative in the Reich insurance office. His appointment by the emperor in 1890 as foreign secretary—a position for which he had few conventional qualifications—was a surprise, and he depended heavily on Holstein while in office. He was forced out under agrarian attack in 1897 and was appointed ambassador to Turkey, where he came into his own as one of the most influential and effective of the *Weltpolitiker*. He had just been transferred to the crucial London embassy when he died in September 1912. See David Burnett King, *Marschall von Bieberstein and the New Course* (Ph.D. diss., Cornell University, 1962); and Erich Lindow, *Marschall von Bieberstein als Botschafter in Konstantinopel 1897–1912* (Danzig, 1934).

14. Albrecht Freiherr von Rechenberg (1859–1935), son of a diplomat, was born in Madrid. He entered the Foreign Office in 1889 and was assigned to the colonial administration in East Africa in 1893. From 1896 he held a succession of consular posts, notably in Moscow and Warsaw, where he acquired a reputation as an expert in eastern European affairs. In 1906, Rechenberg was named governor of German East Africa, where the massive Maji Maji rebellion was underway. During the next six years, Rechenberg undertook a program of colonial development according to the *Weltpolitik* model, which became a major symbol of the ideology in action. He temporarily retired in 1912, was elected to the Reichstag as a Center party deputy, and reentered active service at the Foreign Office prior to the outbreak of hostilities in 1914. During the war, Rechenberg served as one of the government's leading experts on eastern European affairs and central European economic integration. See Schnee, *Kolonial-Lexikon*, 3: p. 133.

15. Richard von Kühlmann (1873–1948) was something of a born *Weltpolitiker*. He was born in Constantinople, the son of a director of the Anatolian railway who was also a senior figure in the *Deutsche Bank*'s network of industrial investments. After graduating in law at Heidelberg, Kühlmann entered the diplomatic service in 1899. He served in various foreign posts for short periods and on special assignments to international conferences until he became councilor in the London embassy in 1908. In that post, Kühlmann was one of the central figures in attempts to reconcile Britain and Germany. He was also

one of the acknowledged leaders of the *Weltpolitik* school of thought in the Foreign Office. In 1915, Kühlmann was made minister in The Hague and in 1916, ambassador to Turkey. In August 1917, at the emperor's wish and against the desires of the army command and the political right, he was appointed foreign secretary. He took part in the negotiations at Brest-Litovsk. Kühlmann was forced to resign in July 1918, in part because of pressure from the radical right. Thereafter, he was senior director of the industries of his wife's family, the Stumms. Richard Kühlmann, *Erinnerungen* (Heidelberg, 1948).

16. On the relationship between the Political Department and the other branches of the Foreign Office, see Cecil, *German Diplomatic Service,* pp. 6—14. On ideological currents in the Colonial Department and later in the Colonial Office, see Smith, *German Colonial Empire,* pp. 130–40.

17. See the discussion of Kayser and his ideas in Röhl, ed., *Eulenburgs politische Korrespondenz,* 1:pp. 443 (letter: Eulenburg to William II, 7 February 1890); 529–30 (letter: Holstein to Eulenburg, 11 April 1890); 586–88 (letter: Holstein to Eulenburg, 31 October 1890). Kayser's Jewish origins and the problems they caused him in his career are discussed in a letter from Count Wilhelm ("Bill") von Bismarck to Kayser, 14 October 1886 in BA *Kleine Erwerbungen,* no. 10, pp. 21–23.

18. The connection between imperialism, industrialization, and social progress is explicated in a great many sources, both from within government circles and from public debate. It was also a defining characteristic of one common approach to *Sozialpolitik* in the *Verein für Sozialpolitik* as well as the *Weltpolitik* version of social imperialism. See Röhl, *Eulenburgs politische Korrespondenz,* 1: pp. 440–42 (letter: Kayser to Eulenburg, 6 February 1890, later forwarded to William II); BA Frank papers, no. 14 (draft of journal article on colonial policy by Kayser, 1890/91); Dieter Lindenlaub, *Richtungskämpfe im Verein für Sozialpolitik, Beihefte* 52 and 53 of *Vierteljahrshefte für Sozial- und Wirtschaftsgeschichte* (Wiesbaden, 1967), 52: 44–83; Wolfgang J. Mommsen, *Max Weber und die deutsche Politik* (2nd rev. ed.; Tübingen, 1974), pp. 73–96. Classic statements of this view are Moritz J. Bonn, *Die Neugesteltung unserer kolonialen Aufgaben* (Tübingen, 1911), pp. 4–7, 30–40; and Bernhard Dernburg, *Koloniale Lehrjahre* (Stuttgart, 1907), pp. 6–8, 12–13. Another comprehensive statement by Bonn is contained in BA Bonn papers, no. 1 (draft of study of *Kolonialpolitik.*)

19. One exception was the industrialist Walther Rathenau, a late convert to *Weltpolitik* in the decade before the First World War, who possessed a science degree. Ernst Schulin, *Walther Rathenau. Repräsentant, Kritiker und Opfer seiner Zeit* (Göttingen, 1979), pp. 18–23.

20. Even Ballin and Rathenau, although clearly members of the stratosphere of business management, were technically salaried employees of their firms and did not possess the status of the Krupps or Stumms.

Albert Ballin (1857–1918), son of a Jewish businessman, started in his father's business and in the 1880s built up Hamburg's most aggressive shipping line. After a period of vicious competition with the Hamburg-America line (HAPAG), Ballin agreed in 1886 to sell out to HAPAG and became a director of the firm. From 1899 to 1918, he was general director. In that capacity, he became one of the prime leaders of German business, influential with the emperor, the Foreign Office, the navy, and several of the Reichstag parties. Originally a supporter of fleet-building schemes, he eventually turned against Tirpitz as a threat to *Weltpolitik*-style policy. See Lamar Cecil, *Albert Ballin: Business and Politics in Imperial Germany 1888–1918* (Princeton, 1967).

Walther Rathenau (1867–1922) was the son of the electrical pioneer Emil Rathenau. After university studies and an attempt at an army commission (which his Jewish origins prevented), Rathenau became a manager in a succession of enterprises connected to AEG, the giant electrical conglomerate of which his father was president. In the 1890s, driven by contradictory ambitions, Rathenau commenced a supplementary literary career with the help of Maximillian Harden. In 1899, he became a director of AEG, from whose board he had to resign temporarily in 1902 because his schemes for "rationalizing" management were rejected. Thereafter, Rathenau pursued an erratic course as a minor litterateur, AEG manager, and would-be politician who used personal contacts with William II, Bülow, Dernburg, and others to attempt to create a political career. In the period 1907–14, he became an identifiable *Weltpolitiker,* accompanying Dernburg on his well-publicized inspection tours in Africa in 1907–8. He took part, with Ballin and others, in the attempt after 1912 to prevent a coalition of heavy-industrial and radical conservative groups from seizing the political initiative in Germany. During World War I, while achieving the presidency of AEG against considerable opposition, Rathenau became the main coordinator of war-materials planning for the Reich. His career as foreign minister during the early years of Weiman, which led to his assassination, is well known. See Schulin, *Rathenau.*

Karl Helfferich (1872–1924) also became one of the leading figures of the early Weimar Republic, although on the opposite side from Rathenau. The son of a minor Bavarian industrialist, Helfferich was a university-trained economist specializing in money and banking. He first attracted notice for his defense of the gold standard and industry during the economic controversies of the 1890s. During that time, he became closely connected to important government and business leaders and earned the enmity of agrarians and of bimetalists such as the Free Conservative politician, Otto Arendt, a founder of the Pan-German League. In 1901, he was hired by the Colonial Department as a special assistant and thereafter made a career of alternating between bureaucratic positions in government and business. He became a major spokesman of the economic elements of *Weltpolitik* in his successive jobs with the Colonial Department (whose directorship he rejected in 1906) and the *Deutsche Bank* (1906–14). In the latter capacity, he was in charge of the bank's Baghdad Railway project, working closely with Arthur Gwinner of the *Deutsche Bank* and Marschall and Kiderlen in the Foreign Office. Helfferich was also active in organizing *Weltpolitik*-oriented interests against the political right and left in 1912–14. In January 1915, Helfferich was appointed Reich treasury secretary and in May 1916 he became deputy chancellor and interior minister. He was Bethmann Hollweg's most important advisor and supporter during the war. Helfferich survived Bethmann-Hollweg's fall but was forced to resign because of Reichstag pressure in November 1917. After the war, Helfferich became a major leader of the conservative German National People's party. See Williamson, *Helfferich.*

Arthur Gwinner (1856–1931) was born in Frankfurt to a family of civil servants and bankers. After an early career in international banking, Gwinner entered the *Vorstand* of the *Deutsche Bank* in 1894. In 1900, he took over from Georg von Siemens control of the bank's foreign investments, which included the Baghdad Railway, the development of the Rumanian oil fields, and interests in central Africa. See *Neue Deutsche Biographie.*

21. Werner Schieffel, *Bernhard Dernburg, 1865–1937: Kolonialpolitiker und Bankier in Wilhelmischen Deutschland* (Zurich and Freiburg, 1974).

22. BA Dernburg papers, no. 11 (uncompleted draft of Dernburg's autobiography), pp. 64–65.

23. Ibid., p. 72.

24. On the politics of the Caprivi period, see Röhl, *Germany without Bismarck,* pp. 56–117; Kennedy, *Anglo-German Antagonism,* pp. 205–22; Barkin, *German Industrialization,* pp. 44–102.

25. For a general study of the involvement of entrepeneurs in politics, see Hans Jaeger, *Unternehmer in der deutsche Politik, 1890–1918* (Berlin, 1967). An appreciation of the use of imperialism as an ideological force that business and government could use against left and right is indicated in BA Dernburg papers, no. 47 (letter: Gustav Stresemann, writing as a syndic of the League of Saxon Industries, to Dernburg, 20 March 1907).

26. See Baldur Kaulisch, "Centralverband Deutscher Industrieller und Sozialdemokratie um die Jahrhundertwende," in Fritz Klein, ed., *Studien zum deutschen Imperialismus vor 1914* (Berlin, 1976), pp. 115–41; Lindenlaub, *Richtungskämpfe,* 52: pp. 44–83; Hans-Peter Ullmann, *Der Bund der Industriellen. Organisation, Einfluss und Politik klein- und mittelbetrieblicher Industrieller im Deutschen Kaiserreich 1895–1914* (Göttingen, 1976), pp. 108–9, 165–75, 186–221; Guratzsch, *Macht durch Organisation,* pp. 66–70.

27. On Rohrbach's entry into a journalistic career, see Paul Rohrbach, *Um des Teufels Handschrift. Zwei Menschenalter erlebter Weltgeschichte* (Hamburg, 1953), pp. 13–54; and Walter Mogk, *Rohrbach und das "Grössere Deutschland": Ethischer Imperialismus im Wilhelmischen Zeitalter* (Munich, 1972), pp. 22–34.

28. On the professional politician, see Molt, *Reichstag,* pp. 274–76; Smith and Turner, "Legislative Behavior;" and James J. Sheehan, "Political Leadership in the German Reichstag, 1871–1918," *American Historical Review* 74 (1968), pp. 511–28.

29. Donald Warren, Jr., *The Red Kingdom of Saxony: Lobbying Grounds for Gustav Stresemann 1901–1909* (The Hague, 1964), pp. 25–47.

30. On the disputes over the Caprivi government's policies, see Barkin, *German Industrialization.* The development and spread of *Weltpolitik* opinion can be traced in BA Frank papers, no. 14, especially Kayser's memorandum to Caprivi on the 1890 treaty with Britain—an early comprehensive statement of *Weltpolitik* ideology. Also relevant in the same file are the previously cited (Chapter 4, Note 18) draft of Kayser's article on colonial policy and his letters to Professor Baron of 6 July 1890, 16 July 1890, 12 November 1890, 16 January 1892, 4 February 1892, and 24 April 1892.

31. Fischer, *Germany's Aims,* p. 13.

32. On the reserve market idea and related economic matters, see Wehler, *Bismarck und der Imperialismus,* pp. 95–111; and Kennedy, *Anglo-German Antagonism,* pp. 4–58, 291–320.

33. The reserve market idea was much discussed in the VDES in the 1890s: BA R13I/12, pp. 229–304; R13I/53, pp. 169–75; R13I/162, pp. 11–17.

34. See Paul Dehn, *Von deutscher Kolonial- und Weltpolitik* (Berlin, 1907), pp. 1–26; Bonn, *Neugestaltung,* pp. 34–38; Rohrbach, *Deutsche Gedanke,* pp. 76–79. Also, BA R13I/162, pp. 85–97 (VDES, *Vorstand* meeting 1887).

35. For Karl Helfferich's views on these points, see Williamson, *Helfferich,* pp. 49–55; see also Rohrbach, *Deutsche Gedanke,* pp. 72–77.

36. Julius Scharlach, *Koloniale und politische Aufsätze und Reden* (Berlin, n.d.), pp. 1–11; Dernburg, *Zielpunkte des deutschen Kolonialwessens* (Berlin, 1907), pp. 10–12, 19–20, 25–26, 34–35, 49–51; Bonn, *Neugestaltung,* pp. 25, 30, 32–40; F. Wohltmann, "Die wirtschaftliche Entwickelung unserer Kolonien," *Verhandlungen des Deutschen Kolonialkongresses 1902,* pp. 494–507.

37. Fischer, *Germany's Aims,* pp. 41–49. If one compares measures of capital availability for Britain and Germany, for example, one finds a startling expansion of German capital during the Wilhelmian era. For instance: totals of deposits in savings and commercial banks, in millions of £ (1 £ = 20M):

	Germany	Britain
1890	331.2	780.6
1900	628.3	1037.0
1910	1340.4	1089.3

(Calculated from tables in B. R. Mitchell, *European Historical Statistics* [2nd rev. ed.; London, 1975], pp. 716–32. See also Williamson, *Helfferich,* pp. 111–14.)

38. This attitude was noted by Bernhard Dernburg, who had to confront it throughout his business career: BA Dernburg papers, no. 11, pp. 58–72, 122–45.

39. See the able summary of the problems of financing the railway in Williamson, *Helfferich,* pp. 80–96.

40. Geo A. Schmidt, *Das Kolonial-Wirtschaftliche Komitee* (Berlin, 1934), pp. 5–18; BA Dernburg papers, no. 49 (letter: 13 June 1907, Karl Supf, President of KWK, to Dernburg).

41. Woodruff D. Smith, "Julius Graf Zech auf Neuhofen (1868–1914)," in L. H. Gann and Peter Duignan, eds., *African Proconsuls. European Governors in Africa* (New York, 1978), pp. 473–91.

42. For useful summaries, see Bonn, *Neugestaltung,* and J. K. von Vietor, "Der Handel der deutschen Kolonien," *Verhandlungen des Deutschen Kolonial-kongresses 1905* (Berlin, 1906), pp. 629–37.

43. John E. Schrecker, *Imperialism and Chinese Nationalism: Germany in Shantung* (Cambridge, MA, 1971), pp. 23–30, 140–209.

44. For an overview of *Mittelafrika,* see Helmuth Stoecker, "Die Expansionsbestrebungen in Mittelafrika 1898–1914," in Stoecker, ed., *Drang nach Afrika,* pp. 207–15.

45. For economic policy in the German colonies, see Smith, *German Colonial Empire,* pp. 66–107, 162–68; and Rainer Tetzlaff, *Koloniale Entwicklung und Ausbeutung. Wirtschafts- und Sozialgeschichte Deutsch-Ostafrikas, 1885–1914* (Berlin, 1970).

46. See, for example, Rohrbach, *Deutsche Gedanke,* pp. 133–60.

47. Evidence of the thinking that went into plans for *Mittelafrika* is contained in BA Solf papers, no. 4, pp. 64–67 (memorandum: Solf to Foreign Secretary, 20 April 1914), and no. 33, pp. 274–77 (Solf memorandum, 7 January 1912).

48. For the notion of parallel imperial economic systems as the future of the

world economy (usually represented as British, Russian, German, and American), see Rohrbach, *Deutsche Gedanke,* pp. 161–216; and Naumann, *Mitteleuropa,* pp. 164–98. Similar ideas can be found in BA Solf papers, no. 42, pp. 212–14 (clipping of American journal article quoting Solf, 14 July 1914).

49. Smith, *German Colonial Empire,* pp. 51–115; Tetzlaff, *Koloniale Entwicklung;* Smith, "Zech," pp. 473–91.

50. For classic statements of the major contrasting positions on native and development policy, both clearly within the framework of *Weltpolitik,* see J. K. von Vietor, *Wirtschaftliche und kulturelle Entwicklung unserer Schutzgebieten* (Berlin, 1913) for the peasant-development argument and Scharlach, *Aufsätze und Reden* for the contrary view. See also *Verhandlungen des Deutschen Kolonialkongresses 1902,* pp. 507–35, where the question is debated by, among others, Vietor, Scharlach, and Gustav Schmoller.

51. See Rohrbach, *Deutsche Gedanke,* pp. 5–63; Naumann, *Mitteleuropa,* pp. 177–78, 199–228; Bülow, *Denkwürdigkeiten,* 1: pp. 415–16; Bonn, *Neugestaltung,* pp. 34–40.

52. Rohrbach, *Deutsche Gedanke,* pp. 5–63; BA Solf papers, no. 33, pp. 77–79 (letter: Solf to Bethmann Hollweg, 15 August 1913, on the stance to be taken toward Britain over the economic development of central Africa.)

53. Smith, *German Colonial Empire,* pp. 159–62; Paul Rohrbach, *Die Bagdadbahn* (2nd ed.; Berlin, 1911), pp. 21–27; Williamson, *Helfferich,* pp. 80–110; BA Dernburg papers, no. 11 (draft autobiography), pp. 108–14, 137–43; ZStA (Hoover microfilm) *Kolonialrat,* vol. 2, no. 4287 (Kayser's speech to *Kolonialrat,* 1 June 1891), reported in DKZ, 27 June 1891, pp. 85–87; Kurt Riezler, *Tagebücher, Aufsätze, Dokumente,* ed. K. D. Erdmann (Göttingen, 1972), pp. 41–44.

54. The literature on Tirpitz and the politics of his building program is enormous. See Volker R. Berghahn, *Der Tirpitz-Plan. Genesis und Verfall einer innerpolitischen Krisenstrategie unter Wilhelm II* (Düsseldorf, 1971); Kehr, *Battleship Building;* Steinberg, *Yesterday's Deterrent;* Eley, *Reshaping the German Right,* pp. 68–73.

55. Kennedy, *Anglo-German Antagonism,* pp. 184–222. Classic statements of this view are contained in BA Frank papers, no. 14 (Kayser's 1890 memorandum to Caprivi on the Heligoland-Zanzibar treaty) and BA Solf papers, no. 99, pp. 85–92 (letter: Solf to Hans Delbrück, 1 August 1927, in which Solf ruefully discusses the prewar attitudes toward Britain of himself and his associates).

56. Kennedy, *Anglo-German Antagonism,* pp. 184–250.

57. For evidence of the difficulty *Weltpolitiker* had in comprehending British responses to German initiatives, see Walther Rathenau, *Tagebuch 1907–1922,* ed. H. Pogge von Strandmann (Düsseldorf, 1967), p. 8; and Theodor Schiemann, *Wie England eine Verständigung mit Deutschland verhinderte* (Berlin, 1915).

58. Hübbe-Schleiden, *Überseeische Politik,* pp. 12–19, 33–35; Friedrich von Bernhardi, *Deutschland und der nächste Krieg* (Stuttgart and Berlin, 1912), pp. 83, 174–88.

59. Kennedy, *Anglo-German Antagonism,* pp. 103–23; Rohrbach, *Deutsche Gedanke,* pp. 76–77, 126, 207–8; BA Solf papers, no. 99, pp. 85–92 (letter: Solf to H. Delbrück, 1 August 1927); and no. 36 (Solf's diary), passim, especially pp. 40–43. Kurt Riezler (Bethmann Hollweg's wartime secretary), cited En-

glish free-trade and colonial policies as examples for Germany, not just in terms of specifics but also of general political attitudes: "Not from pride, but from enlightened self-interest, England lets . . . the other peoples participate in the economic affairs of the lands which she rules. It is . . . the most grandiose example of far-sighted moderation that the history of great world-empires has to show" (Riezler, *Tagebücher*, p. 44).

60. Lindenlaub, *Richtungskämpfe*, 53: pp. 393–409; Mommsen, *Weber*, pp. 97–146; Naumann, *Mitteleuropa*, pp. 229–62.

61. Rohrbach, *Deutsche Gedanke*, pp. 120–21. By the 1920s, however, Rohrbach had changed his views on liberal democracy, precisely because he had come to believe that it promoted integration: Paul Rohrbach, *Briefe über Demokratie und Pazifismus* (Dresden, 1925), pp. 5, 37–38.

62. G. R. Searle, *The Quest for National Efficiency: A Study in British Politics and Political Thought, 1899–1914* (Oxford, 1971), pp. 54–57.

63. BA 13I/12 (Klein's history of VDES), p. 62.

64. Fischer, *Germany's Aims*, pp. 11–20; Dehn, *Kolonial- und Weltpolitik*, pp. 65–70.

65. Kennedy, *Anglo-German Antagonism*, pp. 290–305; BA Dernburg papers, no. 36 (letter: Max Warburg to Dernburg, 4 September 1909).

66. Schmidt, *Kolonial-Wirtschaftliche Komittee;* Ullmann, *Bund der Industriellen*, pp. 108–9, 165–75.

67. Extensive statements of this view are collected in BA Dernburg papers, no. 35 (materials on Dernburg's 1909 visit to England).

68. Ibid., no. 49 (letter: Karl Supf to Dernburg, 13 June 1907); see also Dehn, *Kolonial- und Weltpolitik*, pp. 71–102.

69. Schmidt, *Kolonial-Wirtschaftliche Komitee*, pp. 27–30.

70. Smith, *German Colonial Empire*, pp. 66–73; and Smith, "Zech."

71. The KWK was discussed, for example, in glowing terms by the *Vorstand* of the metals lobby: BA R13I/177 (VDES circular, 19 January 1912).

72. This belief is expressed in Dernburg's 1907 pamphlet on colonial policy: Dernburg, *Koloniale Lehrjahre*, pp. 12–13. See also BA Dernburg papers, no. 49 (letter: Supf to Dernburg, 13 June 1907).

73. BA Dernburg papers, no. 35 (1909 visit to England).

74. The standard work on the *Mitteleuropa* concept is Henry Cord Meyer, *Mitteleuropa in German Thought and Action, 1815–1945* (The Hague, 1955). For a view of the idea from the turn of the century, see Friedrich Ratzel, "Die mitteleuropäische Wirtschaftsverein," *Die Grenzboten* 63 (1904), no. 5, pp. 253–59. See also Lindenlaub, *Richtungskämpfe*, 52: pp. 178–80.

75. The classic statement of these ideas is of course Naumann, *Mitteleuropa*, especially pp. 102–33, 164–228. See also Bonn, *Neugestaltung*, p. 40.

76. Barkin, *German Industrialization*, pp. 44–49; Cecil, *German Diplomatic Service*, p. 261.

77. BA R13I/162, pp. 111–20, 123–34, 138–48, 151–63, 169–79 (VDES annual reports, 1888–92).

78. See report of Caprivi's 1891 speech on colonial estimates in the Reichstag in DKZ, 12 December 1891, pp. 178–79. See also the assessment of the Caprivi tariff policy and its relationship to economic imperialism contained in Ratzel, "Mitteleuropäische Wirtschaftsverein," and the responses of the Colonial Society and of one of the early Pan-German formulators of *Lebensraum* (H. Denicke) to the tariff policy in DKZ, 9 January 1892, pp. 3–4. Also relevant

to the discussion of attitudes are Kayser's letters to Professor Baron of 16 January, 4 February, and 24 April 1892 in BA Frank papers, no. 14.

79. The question of changing geographic orientations in German imperialism has been the subject of much discussion. Geiss, *German Foreign Policy*, pp. 60–71, sees a general tendency away from Bismarck's continental orientation and toward overseas imperialism during the early Caprivi era (despite Caprivi's own concentration on Europe.) Others, especially H. Pogge von Strandmann, tend to assign the decisive break to about 1897, more or less as a result of Tirpitz's fleet-building campaign. Either way, the current orthodoxy is that a continental orientation reappeared in the years just before the First World War, partly because of certain developments in internal German politics. See H. Pogge von Strandmann, "Nationale Verbände zwischen Weltpolitik und Kontinentalpolitik," in Herbert Schottelius and Wilhelm Deist, eds., *Marine und Marinepolitik im kaiserlichen Deutschland 1871–1914* (Düsseldorf, 1972), pp. 296–317. These views all have a substantial basis in reality, but they also miss some crucial points because they do not adequately distinguish between the varieties of imperialist ideology. In Chapter Five, the question of a continental versus an overseas imperialist policy is discussed in the context of *Lebensraum* ideology and its relationship to Wilhelmian political trends. Among *Weltpolitiker*, one can detect changes in emphasis among individuals and groups that more or less correspond to the pattern noted above. Walther Rathenau, for instance, moved from an overseas to a continental orientation around 1909 (Schulin, *Rathenau*, pp. 31–37.) Against this case (and many others), one could cite that of Richard von Kühlmann, who strongly advocated an overseas direction for German policy and a dampening of dangerous continental initiatives in the period 1912–14. (Fischer, *War of Illusions*, pp. 310–15.) The important point is that few, if any, *Weltpolitiker* advocated a complete concentration in one direction as opposed to the other. The framework of *Weltpolitik* encompassed, and *had* to encompass, both European and extra-European elements. Kühlmann did not, in 1912–14, suggest a permanent abandonment of the attempt to integrate the economy of eastern and central Europe around Germany. What he recommended was a concentration of attention on overseas (especially African) aims for the time being because of the greater probability of their fulfillment and the greater danger of war inherent in the alternative. It is true, as Chapter Five will argue, that the notion of settlement colonization in Europe came to be more important in *Lebensraum* imperialism by 1914 than overseas settlement, but even this was not a universal phenomenon. Certainly, the varying geographic emphases within *Weltpolitik* were conceived of as being matters of temporal priority rather than complete redirections of policy.

80. Barkin, *German Industrialization*, pp. 40–89.

81. Ibid.; Puhle, *Agrarische Interessenpolitik*, pp. 28–36.

82. Besides Wehler, *Bismarck und der Imperialismus*, see Bernard Semmel, *Imperialism and Social Reform. English Social-Imperialist Thought 1895–1914* (Cambridge, MA, 1960), and Smith, *European Imperialism*, pp. 75–85.

83. The best case for social imperialist motivation in a particular instance of German imperialism is made by Bade, *Fabri*, pp. 80–135. Against this are the presentations of *Weltpolitik* ideology by Bonn, Kayser, Dehn, and even Rohrbach and Naumann, in which the social imperialist aspect plays the secondary and indirect role described in this chapter and in which the primary overt

domestic focus is on overcoming social and political fragmentation rather than on deliberately diverting the antagonism of the working classes.

84. Reference to the utility of imperialism in appealing directly to workers is contained in BA Dernburg papers, no. 47 (letter: Stresemann to Dernburg, 20 March 1907), which notes the appeal of colonialism to voters in "red-leaning Saxony." Most of the *Weltpolitik* works previously cited, however, are clearly directed toward an educated middle-class audience. They treat the imperialist appeal to the working class as a potential advantage of imperialism, not as the focus of their arguments per se. See, for example, Rohrbach, *Deutsche Gedanke*, pp. 86–132.

85. Sheehan, *German Liberalism*. For uses of the concept of liberal imperialism, see Mommsen, *Weber*, pp. 73–96, and Reinhard Opitz, *Der deutsche Sozialliberalismus 1917–1933* (Cologne, 1973), pp. 44–50.

86. Williamson, *Helfferich*, pp. 55–59. This point is made by Geoff Eley, who argues that the effect of agrarian antimodernism among nationalists opposed to liberalism has been exaggerated by historians: Eley, *Reshaping the German Right*, pp. 8–16, 101–235.

CHAPTER FIVE

1. Woodruff D. Smith, "Friedrich Ratzel and the Origins of Lebensraum," *German Studies Review* 3 (1980), pp. 51–68.

2. Bergmann, *Agrarromantik*, pp. 33–164; Puhle, *Agrarische Interessenpolitik*, pp. 72–110.

3. The most important analysis of *völkisch* ideology is Mosse, *Crisis of German Ideology*. Mosse does not claim, however, that all forms of new conservatism were *völkisch*. Eley, *Reshaping the German Right*, pp. 108–11, points out that many radical nationalists were by no means antimodern *völkisch* conservatives.

4. On illiberalism, see Fritz Stern, *The Failure of Illiberalism* (New York, 1972).

5. Eley, *Reshaping the German Right*, pp. 160–205, attempts to define the radical element in turn-of-the-century German nationalism and, in the process, perhaps excessively downplays its conservative aspects.

6. Puhle, *Agrarische Interessenpolitik*, pp. 72–110; Bergmann, *Agrarromantik*, pp. 38–85.

7. On Wagner and Sering, see Barkin, *German Industrialization*, pp. 138–85. See also the anonymous article "Zum Schutz der deutschen Landschaft," *Die Grenzboten* 51 (1892), no. 40, pp. 31–33.

8. See Puhle, *Agrarische Interessenpolitik*, pp. 23–37, 72–83; and Eley, *Reshaping the German Right*, pp. 8–12. Puhle tends to emphasize the manipulation of agrarianism by elite interest groups; Eley stresses the role of agrarian ideas as genuine expressions of peasant discontent.

9. See the discussion of the *Ostmarkverein* in Eley, *Reshaping the German Right*, pp. 58–68.

10. See Eduard Hahn, *Die Entstehung der wirtschaftlichen Arbeit* (Heidelberg, 1908), pp. 1–4, 102–4; and (in a colonial context) Paul Samassa, *Die Besiedlung Deutsch-Ostafrikas* (Berlin, 1909), pp. 2–3, 105–27.

11. Friedrich Ratzel, *Jugenderinnerungen* (Munich, 1966), pp. 107–47; Friedrich Ratzel, *Völkerkunde* (2 vols.; 2nd rev. ed.; Leipzig and Vienna, 1894), 2: pp. 370–83.

12. In this category, for example, could be included arguments for a hereditary,

privileged aristocracy based on its supposed utility to society as a whole as a source of leadership.

13. Puhle, *Agrarische Interessenpolitik,* pp. 274–90.
14. See the Pan-Germans' use of this notion of AV, *Zwanzig Jahre alldeutscher Arbeit und Kämpfe* (Leipzig, 1910), pp. 62–67 (1899 speech by E. Hasse).
15. Woodruff D. Smith, "The Emergence of German Urban Sociology, 1900–1910," *Journal of the History of Sociology* 1 (1979), pp. 1–16.
16. On *völkisch* agrarianism, see Puhle, *Agrarische Interessenpolitik,* pp. 85–98, and Mosse, *Crisis of German Ideology,* pp. 13–30.
17. For a classic statement of the idea that a peasantry is necessary for military security, see Dietrich Schäfer, "Die politische und militärische Bedeutung der Grossstädte," in Karl Bücher et al., *Die Grossstadt* (Dresden, 1903), p. 279.
18. This was true of Friedrich Ratzel and Ernst Hasse. Eley, *Reshaping the German Right,* pp. 58–68, shows the liberal connections of some of the leaders of the *Ostmarkverein.* His article, "Some Thoughts on the Nationalist Pressure Groups in Imperial Germany," in Paul M. Kennedy and Anthony Nicholls, eds., *Nationalist and Racialist Movements in Britain and Germany Before 1914* (London, 1981), pp. 40–67, especially p. 66, fn. 26, makes this point more broadly.
19. Eley, *Reshaping the German Right,* pp. 19–36. *Populism* is, of course, a difficult term to define and to employ accurately in political history, especially because it seldom appears as the single, distinctive ideology of a political organization. For present purposes, it is sufficient to use the term quite broadly to refer to a tendency in nineteenth- and twentieth-century Western political thought that called stridently for wide participation in politics, that regarded elites (whether traditional or modern) with distrust as exploiters of the "little man," and that tended to see more dangers than advantages in modernization and large-scale capitalism. Populism could be attached, in Germany as elsewhere, to any of a number of political ideologies and movements. Except perhaps in the United States, organized national populist movements capable of strongly influencing national politics did not appear before 1914, but populism constituted an important element of the approaches of many parties and pressure groups in very different parts of the political spectrum.
20. This point was clearly recognized by Max Weber after studying the sociopolitical situation in eastern Prussia in the early 1890s. Mommsen, *Weber,* pp. 58–59.
21. Lindenlaub, *Richtungskämpfe,* 53: pp. 393–409.
22. Ibid., 52: pp. 53–83.
23. See the discussion of tariff revision and agrarianism in the lead editorial of the *Die Grenzboten* 62 (1903), no. 1, pp. 8–17; and in Robert Wuttke, "Der Arbeiter und der Getreidezoll," ibid., 62, no. 24, pp. 621–28.
24. See, for example, the remarkable argument by the Conservative spokesman von Böllendorff-Kölpin in a 1914 Reichstag debate on colonial policy: *Sten. Ber.,* 9 March 1914, pp. 7940–43.
25. Such contradictions manifested themselves, for instance, in the difficulties that Friedrich Ratzel experienced in reconciling his fundamentally cultural emphasis in human geography with biological racism: Friedrich Ratzel, "Mythen und Einfälle über den Ursprung der Völker," *Globus* 78, no. 2 (1900), pp. 21–25. See also Alfred Kelly, *The Descent of Darwin. The Popu-*

larization of Darwinism in Germany, 1860–1914 (Chapel Hill, 1981), pp. 57–74.

26. For the League's pre-Class position on the Jewish segment of the German population, see Hasse, *Deutsche Politik*, 1, 1: pp. 139–45. See also Eley, *Reshaping the German Right*, p. 245.

27. Mosse, *Crisis of German Ideology*, pp. 126–45.

28. See Hasse, *Deutsche Politik*, 1, 1: pp. 30–48; and Samassa, *Besiedlung Deutsch-Ostafrikas*, pp. 1–6.

29. Samassa, ibid., pp. 105–27; Volkov, *Rise of Popular Antimodernism*, pp. 123–46, 192–214.

30. Samassa, *Besiedlung Deutsch-Ostafrikas*, pp. 105–27; Dehn, *Kolonial- und Weltpolitik*, pp. 31–33.

31. Compare the *Lebensraum* approach with the radical antimodern utopias described in Mosse, *Crisis of German Ideology*, pp. 108–25.

32. None of the pressure organizations that actively advanced *Lebensraum* ideology before the First World War (including the Colonial Society and the Pan-German League) drew a substantial part of their membership or leaders from the so-called "declining" agrarian elite. Although all groups considered that a large part of their audience consisted of peasants and the segments of the lower *Mittelstand* threatened by economic change, none of them drew many members from those groups. Only the Navy League, which employed all sorts of imperialist arguments in its propaganda, came close to being a "mass" organization. See Eley, *Reshaping the German Right*, pp. 118–40, 196–203.

33. Bonn, *Neugestaltung*, pp. 3–5; Reichstag speech of SPD delegate Dittmann, *Sten. Ber.*, 7 March 1914, pp. 7898–99.

34. Mildred S. Wertheimer, *The Pan-German League, 1890–1914* (New York, 1924), pp. 179–201.

35. Friedrich Lindequist, the later colonial secretary, noted the split among the National Liberals in 1898. As one of the few officials who took a *Lebensraum*-oriented view of colonial policy, he identified mainly with the *Lebensraum* group led by Ernst Hasse and Ernst Lehr of the Pan-German League, who had just been elected National Liberal Reichstag deputies. BA *Kleine Erwerbungen*, no. 275 (Lindequist's draft autobiography), p. 73.

36. On the Colonial Society, see Pierard, *German Colonial Society*, and Smith, *German Colonial Empire*, pp. 40–42.

37. On the early history of the Pan-German League, see Wertheimer, *Pan-German League*, pp. 22–48; Guratzsch, *Macht durch Organisation*, pp. 22–26; and the foreword to AV, *Zwanzig Jahre*. The last is a collection of material on the history of the league put together in celebration of the twentieth anniversary of the Pan-German movement.

38. See the discussion of the "style" of the radical right in Geoffrey Searle, "The 'Revolt from the Right' in Edwardian Britain," in Kennedy and Nicholls, eds., *Nationalist and Racialist Movements*, pp. 21–39. See also Kennedy's introduction to the same volume.

39. Eley, *Reshaping the German Right*, pp. 41–58; lengthy telegram from Alfred Hugenberg to Carl Peters, c. July–August 1890, in BA Frank papers, no. 9; Guratzsch, *Macht durch Organisation*, pp. 22–26.

40. On Weber's membership in the Pan-German movement, see Mommsen, *Weber*, pp. 58–59.

41. Eley, *Reshaping the German Right,* pp. 49–50; BA Frank papers, no. 8 (letter: W. Schroeder-Poggelow to Heinrich Peters [Carl's brother] 1892 n.d.)
42. Ernst Hasse, "Was können und sollen wir," DKZ, 15 December 1884, pp. 485–92; Friedrich Ratzel, "In welcher Richtung beeinflussen die afrikanischen Ereignisse die Thätigkeit des Kolonialvereins?", DKZ, 15 January 1885, pp. 38–44; Guratzsch, *Macht durch Organisation,* pp. 22–26, 39–47. Of interest are Bernhard Dernburg's comments on Siemens and Gwinner in BA Dernburg papers, no. 11, pp. 63–72, 108–43, passim.
43. BA Frank papers, no. 9 (draft circulars of 1891 program).
44. This point is contained in a minute of a September 1890 conversation between Carl Peters and other prospective founders of a Pan-German movement contained in BA Frank papers, no. 9.
45. On the change in direction and leadership in the movement, see Guratzsch, *Macht durch Organization,* pp. 24–25; Eley, *Reshaping the German Right,* p. 50; Wertheimer, *Pan-German League,* pp. 40–42. For a treatment of the radicalism of the Pan-German League and its relationship to German culture, see Roger Chickering, *We Men Who Feel Most German: A Cultural Study of the Pan-German League 1886–1914* (London, 1984), which unfortunately appeared too late for its findings to be incorporated in this study.
46. On Hasse and other leading Pan-Germans, see Eley, *Reshaping the German Right,* pp. 50–53, 284–85, and Wertheimer, *Pan-German League,* pp. 43–48. Hasse differed from his successor, Class, in that he insisted on a high level of local autonomy for local chapters and an openness to differences of opinion at national meetings. As a result, a great deal of variation existed on practically all questions among the Pan-Germans. This variation must be borne in mind whenever we refer to any particular position as being that of the league as a whole.
47. The 1894 program is contained in AV, *Zwanzig Jahre,* pp. 11–13. It may be compared with later versions of the program in the same source.
48. Ibid., pp. 251–53 (1904 speech by Heinrich Class on possibilities of settlement in Morocco); Samassa, *Besiedlung Deutsch-Ostafrikas,* pp. 1–6.
49. Comprehensive statements of the Pan-German position on colonial settlement may be found in AV, *Zwanzig Jahre,* pp. 137–42 (report by Hasse at 1902 *Verbandstag*) and 157–89 (speech by Class at 1903 *Verbandstag.*)
50. See Hasse's speech to the 1899 *Verbandstag,* ibid., pp. 68–71.
51. *Alldeutsche Blätter,* 30 April 1899, pp. 145–47; Mommsen, *Weber,* p. 59.
52. *Verhandlungen des Deutschen Kolonialkongresses 1902,* pp. 609–10, 627–36 (speeches by Alexander Tille and Dr. Hindorf); *Verhandlungen des Deutschen Kolonialkongresses 1905,* pp. 807–22, 972–86 (speeches by Dr. Arning and Paul Rohrbach); Bernhardi, *Deutschland und der nächste Krieg,* pp. 86–88.
53. It should be noted that the Pan-German League in addition maintained a strong interest in German settlement in non-German lands in Europe and America, an interest also pursued by the Colonial Society. Among other things, the Pan-Germans argued that *Ausland* Germans should be afforded continued connection to the Reich through the retention of citizenship and cultural contacts so that Germany would continue to benefit from the experiences of her settlers abroad. See AV, *Zwanzig Jahre,* pp. 27–31, 133.
54. Wertheimer, *Pan-German League,* pp. 111–31, 160–78; Eley, *Reshaping the German Right,* pp. 206–35.

55. Eley, *Reshaping the German Right*, pp. 57–58.
56. Mommsen, *Weber*, pp. 62–63; R. W. Tims, *Germanizing Prussian Poland. The H-K-T Society and the Struggle for the Eastern Marches in the German Empire 1894–1919* (New York, 1941).
57. H. H. Gerth and C. Wright Mills, eds., *From Max Weber: Essays in Sociology* (New York, 1958), pp. 34, 363–85.
58. *Alldeutsche Blätter*, 30 April 1899, pp. 145–47; AV, *Zwanzig Jahre*, pp. 71–75 (Theodor Reismann-Grone's speech at 1899 *Verbandstag.*)
59. AV, *Zwanzig Jahre*, pp. 11–12, 13–22, 42–43, 45–47, 53–54, 59–62; Mommsen, *Weber*, pp. 58–59.
60. AV, *Zwanzig Jahre*, pp. 5–11 (1894 article on "Der preussische Staat als Polonisator").
61. Eley, *Reshaping the German Right*, pp. 41–98; Peck, *Radicals and Reactionaries*, pp. 17–48.
62. AV, *Zwanzig Jahre*, pp. 2–3, 23–24, 50–51, and especially 137–42.
63. Ibid., p. 150 (article from *Alldeutsche Blätter*, 1902); also pp. 62–67, 88–92.
64. See, for example, Hasse's 1902 statement on colonial policy, ibid., pp. 137–42.
65. For one Pan-German's attempt to reconcile *Lebensraum* and *Weltpolitik*, see Dehn, *Kolonial- und Weltpolitik*. Dehn was a leading Pan-German ideologue who was personally much more attracted by *Weltpolitik* than by *Lebensraum*. In this book, Dehn attempts not only to reconcile *Lebensraum* and economic imperialism, but also tries to paper over the split that was appearing within the league over whether Germany should aim at overseas expansion or continental security. On this point, see Pogge von Strandmann, "Nationale Verbände."
66. Richard Blanke, "Bismarck and the Prussian Polish Policies of 1886," *Journal of Modern History* 45 (1973), pp. 211–39.
67. On the *Ostmarkverein* (H-K-T Society), see Tims, *Germanizing Prussian Poland*. The left wing inner colonization movement was led by the journalist Hans Ostwald, whose correspondence with Max Sering is included in BA Sering papers, no. 28.
68. On Sering, see Barkin, *German Industrialization*, pp. 147–50. Sering's major work on inner colonization was his *Die innere Kolonisation in östlichen Deutschland* (Leipzig, 1893).
69. Mommsen, *Weber*, pp. 58–62; *Alldeutsche Blätter*, 30 April 1899, pp. 145–47.
70. Puhle, *Agrarische Interessenpolitik*, pp. 23–37.
71. Barkin, *German Industrialization*, pp. 178–80. An anonymous Pan-German memorandum dated 12 January 1902, advocating the imposition of internal colonization on Junker estates, is printed in AV, *Zwanzig Jahre*, pp. 114–26. The editor indicates that the memorandum was not published until 1910—an indirect criticism of Hasse and Lehr. By 1910, eastern colonization had become so closely linked to territorial expansion in Pan-German thinking that such proposals could be reported—almost as historical items—without much political risk.
72. Wollstein, *Das "Grossdeutschland" der Paulskirche*.
73. Eastern annexationism began appearing in pamphlet literature associated with the Pan-Germans in the 1890s: "Alldeutsch," *Grossdeutschland und Mitteleuropa um das Jahr 1950* (2nd ed.; Berlin, 1895). Pan-German leaders, including Hasse, began moving in the same direction after 1900. The process

is traced in Martin Hobohm and Paul Rohrbach, *Die Alldeutschen* (Berlin, 1919), pp. 180–314. See also Klaus Wernecke, *Der Wille zur Weltgeltung. Aussenpolitik und Öffentlichkeit im Kaiserreich am Vorabend des ersten Weltkrieg* (Düsseldorf, 1970), pp. 98–99, 300–3; and Pogge von Strandmann, "Nationale Verbände." Pogge argues that the league advocated overseas expansion primarily when naval armament was a hot issue but turned to continental expansion in the years just before 1914 to benefit from growing interest in army expansion and reform.

74. Bernhardi, *Deutschland und der nächste Krieg*, pp. 85–86, 113; AV, *Zwanzig Jahre*, pp. 267–71 (1905 speech by Reismann-Grone.)

75. Bernhardi, *Deutschland und der nächste Krieg*, pp. 189–208. Examples of how readily inner colonization ideas could be transformed into annexationist programs can be found in G. A. Fabarius, *Neue Wege der deutschen Kolonialpolitik nach dem Kriege* (Berlin, 1916), pp. 7–20; and BA Sering papers, no. 17 (report by Lindequist and Schwerin on settlement in Baltic lands, August 1917). For a prewar example, see Samassa, *Besiedlung Deutsch-Ostafrikas*, pp. 105–27.

76. Lindenlaub, *Richtungskämpfe*, 52: pp. 178–80; AV, *Zwanzig Jahre*, pp. 224–26 (1904 article by P. Samassa); Hobohm and Rohrbach, *Die Alldeutschen*, p. 199; Wernecke, *Wille zur Weltgeltung*, pp. 288–310.

77. Ratzel, "Mitteleuropäische Wirtschaftsverein"; Fritz Klein, "Innere Widersprüche im Bündnis zwischen Deutschland und Österreich-Ungarn zu Beginn der imperialistischen Epoche (1897 bis 1902)," in Klein, ed., *Studien zum deutschen Imperialismus*, pp. 225–62.

78. On the effort to create a national opposition before the First World War, see Eley, *Reshaping the German Right*, pp. 316–34; Peck, *Radicals and Reactionaries*, pp. 82–134; Ullmann, *Bund der Industriellen*, pp. 222–33; and Guratzsch, *Macht durch Organisation*, pp. 85–117.

79. On *Kontinentalpolitik*, see Pogge von Strandmann, "Nationale Verbände"; on radical reactions to the takeover of nationalist organizations by the establishment, see Eley, *Reshaping the German Right*, pp. 267–79.

80. AV, *Zwanzig Jahre*, pp. 267–72.

81. Wernecke, *Wille zur Weltgeltung*, pp. 300–303.

82. See DKZ, 5 March 1892, pp. 31–33; AV, *Zwanzig Jahre*, pp. 12–13, 27–31, 113–14.

CHAPTER SIX

1. Smith, *German Colonial Empire*, pp. 121–22.

2. For examples of the political use of the Reichstag budget hearings, see *Sten. Ber.*, 7–9 March 1914, pp. 7897–7949; DKZ, 8 February 1900, pp. 51–52; and 15 February 1900, pp. 65–66.

3. Röhl, *Germany without Bismarck*, pp. 30, 36, 48, 60.

4. BA Frank papers, no. 14 (letters: Kayser to Professor Baron, 16 January, 4 February, and 22 November, 1892).

5. Ibid., no. 14 (letter: Kayser to Professor Baron, 20 June 1889); Röhl, ed., *Eulenburgs Korrespondenz*, 1: pp. 440–42 (letter: Kayser to Eulenburg, 9 February 1890); 1: pp. 586–88 (letter: Holstein to Eulenburg, 31 October 1890).

6. Smith, *German Colonial Empire,* pp. 159–62; ZStA (Hoover microfilm), *Kolonialrat* 2: no. 4287; DKZ, 27 June 1891, pp. 85–87.

7. Kolonialabteilung, *Denkschrift über die im südwestafrikanischen Schutzgebiete tätigen Land- und Minengesellschaften. Beilage* 6 to DKB, 1905 (Berlin, 1905); E. Th. Foerster, *Das Konzessionsunwesen in den Deutschen Schutzgebieten* (Berlin, 1903), pp. 5–6.

8. Wehler, *Bismarck und der Imperialismus,* pp. 412–502.

9. ZStA (Hoover microfilm), *Kolonialrat* 2: no. 4287 (Kayser's speech opening *Kolonialrat*); and BA Frank papers, no. 14 (letter: Kayser to Professor Baron, 22 November 1892).

10. Smith, *German Colonial Empire,* p. 47; DKZ, 27 June 1891, pp. 75–76; ZStA (Hoover microfilm), *Kolonialrat,* 4: nos. 8748, 9217 (materials relating to formation of *Kolonialrat.*) For a detailed treatment of the *Kolonialrat* and, more important, the issues discussed there in the broader context of imperialism, see Harmut Pogge von Strandmann, *The Kolonialrat, Its Significance and Influence on German Politics from 1890 to 1906* (D.Phil. thesis, Oxford University, 1970).

11. BA Frank papers, no. 14 (draft article by Kayser, c. 1890–91); Scharlach, *Aufsätze und Reden.*

12. Kolonialabteilung, *Denkschrift;* Foerster, *Konzessionsunwesen,* pp. 3–7, 14–16; Karin Hausen, *Deutsche Kolonialherrschaft in Afrika: Wirtschaftsinteressen und Kolonialverwaltung in Kamerun vor 1914* (Zurich, 1970), pp. 224–29.

13. Jesko von Puttkamer, *Gouverneursjahre in Kamerun* (Berlin, 1912), pp. 324–31; DKZ, 26 April 1900, pp. 181–84.

14. Puttkamer, *Gouverneursjahre,* pp. 104–5, 136–37; Hausen, *Deutsche Kolonialherrschaft,* pp. 229–48.

15. ZStA (Hoover microfilm), *Kolonialrat* 22: 2/6975/3 (minutes of 1900 *Kolonialrat* session).

16. DKZ, 14 November 1891, pp. 169–70; 9 January 1892, pp. 3–4; 30 April 1892, p. 63.

17. BA Frank papers, no. 8 (letter: Schroeder-Poggelow to Carl Peters, 13 January 1899.

18. For a treatment of events in Southwest Africa, see Helmut Bley, *South-West Africa under German Rule, 1894–1914,* tr. Hugh Ridley (Evanston, IL, 1971; orig. German ed., 1968).

19. See the position, for example, of Theodor Leutwein, governor of the colony, ZStA (Hoover microfilm), *Kolonialrat* 22: no. 6975; 24: no. 6976.

20. See AV, *Zwanzig Jahre,* pp. 84–86; DKZ, 19 April 1900, pp. 161–62; 3 May 1900, pp. 186–87.

21. DKZ, 7 February 1891, pp. 17–20.

22. See Detlef Bald, *Deutsch-Ostafrika 1900–1914* (Munich, 1970), pp. 35–71, 127–40; Hans Oelhafen von Schöllenbach, *Die Besiedlung Deutsch-Südwestafrikas bis zum Weltkriege* (Berlin, 1926), pp. 19–33.

23. Eley, *Reshaping the German Right,* pp. 83–84.

24. ZStA (Hoover microfilm), DKG *Vorstand,* meetings of 1 December 1900 and 9 October 1902; AV, *Zwanzig Jahre,* pp. 84–86; DKZ, 19 April 1900, pp. 161–62; 26 April 1900, *Beilage,* pp. 181–84; 3 May 1900, pp. 186–87.

25. *Verhandlungen des Deutschen Kolonialkongresses 1905,* pp. 807–22, 872–81, 972–86.

26. AV, *Zwanzig Jahre,* pp. 82–88, 137–42.

27. BA *Kleine Erwerbungen,* no. 275 (Lindequist autobiography), pp. 71–74; BA Frank papers, no. 7 (letter: O. Arendt to Carl Peters, 14 October 1898); no. 8 (letter: Schroeder-Poggelow to Carl Peters, 13 January 1899).

28. Barkin, *German Industrialization,* pp. 56–58; Puhle, *Agrarische Interessenpolitik,* pp. 199–201; Williamson, *Helfferich,* pp. 33–35.

29. See Smith, *German Colonial Empire,* pp. 159–62.

30. See Rohrbach, *Deutsche Gedanke,* pp. 146–47. For evidence of the nature of the new colonial service consensus on development policy, see Franz Stuhlmann, *Beiträge zur Kulturgeschichte von Ostafrika* (Berlin, 1909), pp. 4–9, 811–80; BA Solf papers, no. 26, pp. 19–33 (memorandum by Solf, 4 August 1905); no. 27, pp. 18–31 (memorandum by Solf, 7 May 1906); no. 131, pp. 78–84 (letter: Solf to Heinrich Schnee, 3 July 1902).

31. Hans Spellmeyer, *Deutsche Kolonialpolitik im Reichstag* (Stuttgart, 1931), pp. 87–90; AV, *Zwanzig Jahre,* pp. 84–85, 153–54; DKZ, 11 January 1900, p. 13; 8 February 1900, p. 51.

32. Spellmeyer, *Deutsche Kolonialpolitik,* pp. 87–90.

33. DKZ, 1 January 1903, p. 1; 15 January 1903, pp. 21–22; 19 February 1903, pp. 73–74; 26 February 1903, pp. 81–82; 5 March 1903, pp. 95–97; 26 March 1903, pp. 121–22; 7 May 1903, p. 183; 14 May 1903, pp. 190–91. BA Richthofen papers, no. 14 (letter: Duke of Mecklenburg to Oswald Freiherr von Richthofen, 19 April 1902).

34. Most studies, both at the time and since, have strongly indicated that the *Nordbahn* was a waste of money and that the *Zentralbahn,* although overly ambitious, was economically the more reasonable proposition. See John Iliffe, *Tanganyika under German Rule, 1905–1912* (Cambridge, 1969), pp. 118–32; Tetzlaff, *Koloniale Entwicklung und Ausbeutung,* pp. 281–85; and DKZ, 26 March 1903, pp. 121–22.

35. Smith, *German Colonial Empire,* pp. 185–91; Schieffel, *Dernburg,* pp. 30–45; BA Dernburg papers, no. 11 (Dernburg's draft autobiography), addendum, pp. 2–8; BA Richthofen papers, no. 14 (letters: Helfferich to Richthofen, 22 February 1905, 14 August 1905, 29 November 1905; letter: Richthofen to Bülow, 19 July 1905).

36. Dernburg, *Koloniale Lehrjahre;* and BA Dernburg papers, no. 11, addendum, pp. 3–11.

37. Dernburg, *Koloniale Lehrjahre,* pp. 14–16.

38. The dissolution of December 1906 and the ensuing election are discussed in George Dunlop Crothers, *The German Elections of 1907* (New York, 1941); Schieffel, *Dernburg,* pp. 48–62; BA Dernburg papers, no. 11, addendum, pp. 10–13.

39. DKZ, 2 February 1907, pp. 46–47; Eley, *Reshaping the German Right,* pp. 254–6.

40. Schieffel, *Dernburg,* pp. 62–142.

41. Ibid.; BA Dernburg papers, no. 49 (letter: Supf to Dernburg, 13 June 1907, with enclosures; draft telegram: Dernburg to Bülow, with reply, 10 October 1907); DKB, 15 December 1907, pp. 1195–1207.

42. On the Southwest African diamond issue, see Bley, *South-West Africa,* pp. 185–208; Paul Rohrbach, *Dernburg und die Südwestafrikaner* (Berlin, 1911), pp. 1–44; and Schieffel, *Dernburg,* pp. 73–80.

43. Rohrbach, *Dernburg,* pp. 45–90.

44. Probably the best summaries of the Colonial Office consensus are contained

in the policy statements of Wilhelm Solf (colonial secretary, 1911–18). See his *Kolonialpolitik: Mein politisches Vermächtnis* (Berlin, 1919) and his earlier, more private and comprehensive statements in position papers written while he was governor of Samoa: BA Solf papers, no. 26, pp. 19–33 (memorandum: Solf to Colonial Department, 4 August 1905); no. 27, pp. 64–113 (draft memorandum: November 1906).

45. For examples, see Samassa, *Besiedlung Deutsch-Ostafrikas;* and AV, *Zwanzig Jahre,* pp. 413–14.

46. The major source for Lindequist is his draft autobiography in BA *Kleine Erwerbungen,* no. 275.

47. On the humanitarian movement, see Smith, *German Colonial Empire,* pp. 215–19, and *Sten. Ber.,* 7 March 1914, pp. 7897–7935; 9 March 1914, pp. 7940–52.

48. Among many works on the Moroccan crises, the reader might consult Pierre Guillen, *L'allemagne et le Maroc de 1870 à 1905* (Paris, 1967); Fischer, *War of Illusions,* pp. 71–83; and Wernecke, *Wille zur Weltgeltung,* pp. 26–143.

49. Stoecker, ed., *Drang nach Afrika,* pp. 189–205; Claus H. Mannesmann, *Die Unternehmung der Brüder Mannesmann in Marokko* (Leipzig, 1931).

50. See Stoecker, ed., *Drang nach Afrika,* pp. 189–99; and Eugene N. Anderson, *The First Moroccan Crisis 1904–1906* (Chicago, 1930).

51. Joachim Graf von Pfeil, "Marokko," *Verhandlungen des Deutschen Kolonialkongresses 1905,* pp. 910–18; AV, *Zwanzig Jahre,* pp. 251–53.

52. NA, T–138, roll 51 (evaluations of Morocco by Freiherr Hans von Wangenheim, Foreign Office, 5 January 1908; and Hellmuth von Moltke, chief of general staff, 23 May 1908); Hartmut Pogge von Strandmann, "Rathenau, die Gebrüder Mannesmann und die Vorgeschichte der zweiten Marokkokrise," in Imanuel Geiss and Bernd Jürgen Wendt, eds., *Deutschland in der Weltpolitik des 19. und 20. Jahrhunderts* (Düsseldorf, 1973), pp. 251–70.

53. The question of the relative importance of business interests in Morocco as opposed to ideas about a future *Mittelafrika* or possible diplomatic advantages to be gained in informing German policy is a matter of some dispute, but current research tends to fall on the side of *Mittelafrika.* See Fischer, *War of Illusions,* pp. 71–83; Pogge von Strandmann, "Rathenau," pp. 251–70; Stoecker, ed., *Drang nach Afrika,* pp. 199–205. See also Kiderlen's argument of 20 July 1911 for seeking compensation in the Congo region in GP, 29: p. 295, fn. 1.

54. Rich, *Holstein,* 2: pp. 567–601. For extragovernment attitudes, see AV, *Zwanzig Jahre,* pp. 2–3, 50–51; also BA Frank papers, no. 7 (letter: Carl Peters to Arendt, 27 March 1889). On intragovernment attitudes, see BA Frank papers, no. 14 (Kayser's 1890 memorandum on Anglo-German treaty, with marginal comments by Caprivi); no. 18 (promemoria by Bismarck on German expansion in Africa, 14 September 1888).

55. On the 1890 negotiations and treaty, see Kennedy, *Anglo-German Antagonism,* pp. 205–12; BA Frank papers, no. 14 (Kayser's memorandum); and GP, 8:2, pp. 1–40. On the 1898 treaty, see Fritz Schwarze, *Das deutschenglische Abkommen über die portugiesischen Kolonien vom 30. August 1898* (Göttingen, 1931); Kennedy, *Anglo-German Antagonism,* pp. 251–88; BA Solf papers, pp. 84–91 (1914 Colonial Office summary of previous negotiations with Britain); Gerhard Ebel, ed., *Botschafter Paul Graf von Hatzfeldt nachgelassene Papiere 1838–1901* (2 vols.; Boppard am Rhein, 1976), 2: pp. 1169–73 (letter: Hatzfeldt to Holstein, 27 June 1898); GP 14:1.

56. See Pogge von Strandmann, "Rathenau," pp. 251–70.
57. A sequence of documents that illustrates the character of business-government discussions of central African policy (in this case, with particular reference to the Portuguese colonies) can be found in NA, T-149, roll 136. Particularly instructive is the interaction between the Warburg Bank and the Foreign Office, in which the initiating role is taken by the latter. See also BA Solf papers, no. 33, p. 270 (letter: Helfferich to Solf, 12 March 1912).
58. Schieffel, *Dernburg*, pp. 120–27; NA, T–149, rolls 135, 136 (Foreign Office material relating to Portuguese possessions in Africa, 1910–13); BA Dernburg papers, no. 36 (letter: M. Warburg to Dernburg, 4 September 1909, on prospectus for *Hansa-Bund*); BA Solf papers no. 33, pp. 77–79 (letter: Solf to Bethmann Hollweg, 15 August 1913, on negotiations with Britain), 87–89 (letter: Solf to Bethmann Hollweg, 28 November 1913, same subject).
59. Although various conceptions were discussed, both within the government and (after 1911) publicly, no single plan was agreed on by all departments. The closest to a general statement of aims is a secret internal Colonial Office memorandum dated 7 January 1912 (BA Solf papers, no. 33, pp. 274–77). The need for diplomatic flexibility was clearly paramount, which is made clear in correspondence on the subject contained in BA Solf papers, no. 4, pp. 64–67 (memorandum: Solf to foreign secretary, 20 April 1914) and no. 33, pp. 87–89 (letter: Solf to Bethmann Hollweg, 28 November 1913). In the former, the general economic aims of *Mittelafrika* are laid out together with various political possibilities.
60. An example of this sort of thinking can be seen in the formal discussions within the Colonial Office of war-aims policy in 1916: BA Solf papers, no. 48, pp. 145–69 (protocol of sittings of Second Commission of Colonial Office).
61. Bernhardi, *Deutschland und der nächste Krieg*, p. 115; Wernecke, *Wille zur Weltgeltung*, pp. 98–99.
62. This was a key point in the correspondence between Solf, in the Colonial Office, and Kühlmann, in the London embassy, between 1912 and 1914. BA Solf papers, no. 116, especially pp. 40–43 (letter: Solf to Kühlmann, 2 July 1913).
63. Schieffel, *Dernburg*, pp. 120–27.
64. For an appreciation of Kiderlen from a leading *Weltpolitiker* journalist, see Jäckh, ed., *Kiderlen-Wächter*.
65. Fischer, *War of Illusions*, pp. 64–111.
66. Cecil, *German Diplomatic Service*, pp. 309–14.
67. BA Solf papers, no. 44, pp. 84–91 (1914 summary of Anglo-German negotiations).
68. Fischer, *War of Illusions*, pp. 71–83; Jäckh, ed., *Kiderlen-Wächter*, 2: p. 228.
69. NA, T–138, roll 51 (1908 evaluations of Morocco by Moltke, Wangenheim).
70. BA Solf papers, no. 33, pp. 274–77 (Colonial Office memorandum, 7 January 1912).
71. AV, *Zwanzig Jahre*, pp. 259–61.
72. Fischer, *War of Illusions*, p. 72.
73. DKZ, 27 May 1911, p. 354; 8 July 1911, pp. 455–56; 22 July 1911, pp. 488–89; 29 July 1911, pp. 503–4.
74. Wernecke, *Wille zur Weltgeltung*, pp. 102–38; DKZ, 6 September 1911, pp. 619–21. Most segments of imperialist opinion expressed disappointment at the small extent of Germany's gains, but only the *Lebensraum* advocates could not be brought into line by the government.

75. Wernecke, *Wille zur Weltgeltung,* pp. 142–43; DKZ, 11 November 1911, pp. 747–48; *Koloniale Rundschau,* December 1911, pp. 721–23.

76. Wernecke, *Wille zur Weltgeltung,* pp. 139–43; DKZ, 28 October 1911, pp. 715–17; 11 November 1911, p. 747; ZStA (Hoover microfilm), DKG *Vorstand* meeting 21 November 1911; BA Solf papers, no. 33, pp. 309–15 (Solf's comments on treaty). For the public campaign in favor of *Mittelafrika,* see DKZ, 24 January 1914, pp. 51–52, 55–56; and Emil Zimmermann, *Neu-Kamerun. Reiseerlebnisse und wirtschaftspolitische Untersuchungen* (Berlin, 1913).

77. The classic statement of Pan-German expansionary aims (which encompassed central African expansion) is the "secret" 1914 memorandum by Class, to be found in Solf papers, no. 44, pp. 136–209. There is also a similar memorandum by G. Fabarius in BA Solf papers, no. 48, pp. 58–104.

78. BA Solf papers, no. 116, p. 48 (letter: Solf to Kühlmann, 28 July 1913).

79. These negotiations and their relationship to *Weltpolitik* and *Mittelafrika* can be followed in BA Solf papers, no. 116, pp. 1–52 (Solf's correspondence with Kühlmann, 1912–14.)

80. This is the view of most students of German colonial economic history. See Smith, *German Colonial Empire,* p. 220, and W. O. Henderson, *Studies in German Colonial History* (Chicago, 1962). For an attempt to demonstrate the economic potential of *Mittelafrika,* if not the reality of economic success in Cameroon, see Stoecker, ed., *Drang nach Afrika,* pp. 207–15.

81. BA Solf papers, no. 116, pp. 5–9 (letter: Kühlmann to Solf, 6 May 1912); pp. 40–43 (letter: Solf to Kühlmann, 2 July 1913).

82. The extent of their self-deception was eventually recognized by many *Weltpolitiker:* BA Solf papers, no. 99, pp. 85–92 (letter: Solf to Delbrück, 1 August 1927).

83. Cecil, *Ballin,* pp. 159–62, 169–213; BA Solf papers, no. 116, pp. 1–52. The *Weltpolitik* circle in the Foreign Office remained strong after Kiderlen's death, despite the loss of Kiderlen himself and of Marschall, who died in the same year. Kühlmann emerged as the most active spokesperson of the group, but the new undersecretary, Zimmermann, often sided with the *Weltpolitiker.* The position of the foreign secretary, Jagow, was not clearly defined, but he was not a strong figure. Bethmann returned to the pre-Kiderlen system of taking foreign policy decisions himself, and Bethmann was strongly influenced by the *Weltpolitiker.*

84. Cecil, *Ballin,* pp. 180–204. On Tirpitz's relationship with the radical right before 1914, see Eley, *Reshaping the German Right,* pp. 316–34.

85. Anonymous, *Deutsche Weltpolitik und kein Krieg!* (Berlin, 1913); Wernecke, *Wille zur Weltgeltung,* pp. 296–99. The actual author was Hans Plehn, a German journalist stationed in London and closely associated with Kühlmann.

86. Kühlmann's views can be traced in BA Solf papers, no. 116, p. 52 (letter: Kühlmann to Solf, 23 April 1914); pp. 54–55 (letter: Kühlmann to Solf, 28 July 1915); and 62–63 (letter: Kühlmann to Solf, 1 November 1915). On Rathenau's thinking, see Schulin, *Rathenau,* p. 51.

CHAPTER SEVEN

1. Social Darwinism is particularly emphasized as a source of imperialism by Wolfgang J. Mommsen, *Das Zeitalter des Imperialismus* (Frankfurt am Main,

1969); and W. H. Koch, *Der Sozialdarwinismus: Seine Genese und sein Einfluss auf das imperialistischen Denken* (Munich, 1973). See also Heinz Gollwitzer, *Europe in the Age of Imperialism 1880–1914* (London, 1969), pp. 60, 157–58, 179. Hans-Ulrich Wehler, while ascribing considerable importance to social Darwinist ideas in the composition of imperialist ideology, argues against treating social Darwinism as a *cause* of imperialism. Hans-Ulrich Wehler, "Sozialdarwinismus im expandierenden Industriestaat," in Geiss and Wendt, eds., *Deutschland in der Weltpolitik*, pp. 133–42.

2. For examples of this kind of argument, see AV, *Zwanzig Jahre*, pp. 50–51; and *Verhandlungen des Deutschen Kolonialkongresses 1905*, pp. 928–34 (speech by General Liebert). For a Socialist critique, see SPD, *Die deutsche Kolonialpolitik* (Berlin, n.d. [probably 1907], pp. 15–16.

3. This is one of the arguments used by Paul Rohrbach in his *Deutsche Gedanke*, pp. 5–10.

4. Smith, *German Colonial Empire*, pp. 141–43.

5. On Naumann, see Theodor Heuss, *Friedrich Naumann. Der Mann, das Werk, die Zeit* (Stuttgart, 1937).

6. On Fabri, see Bade, *Fabri*, pp. 30–79, 185–89.

7. Hausen, *Deutsche Kolonialherrschaft*, pp. 274–90. On German missionary activity in general, see Klaus J. Bade, ed., *Imperialismus und Kolonialmission. Kaiserliches Deutschland und koloniales Imperium* (Wiesbaden, 1982).

8. For expositions of this approach, see Vietor, *Wirtschaftliche und kulturelle Entwicklung;* Vietor's papers "Die Arbeiterfrage in den deutschen Kolonien," *Verhandlungen des Deutschen Kolonialkongresses 1902*, pp. 518–24; and "Der Handel der deutschen Kolonien," *Verhandlungen des Deutschen Kolonialkongresses 1905*, pp. 629–37.

9. See Smith, "Zech," pp. 473–91; and Tetzlaff, *Koloniale Entwicklung und Ausbeutung*, pp. 252–62.

10. As we have seen, Vietor, *Wirtschaftliche und kulturelle Entwicklung*, is largely an attack from a *Weltpolitik* standpoint on the views of Julius Scharlach, also a *Weltpolitiker*.

11. *Koloniale Rundschau*, January 1911, pp. 1–4; December 1911, pp. 721–23; BA Dernburg papers, no. 32 (letter: Vohsen to Dernburg, 20 January 1909). For the aims of this movement, see Vietor, *Wirtschaftliche und kulturelle Entwicklung;* Bonn, *Neugestaltung;* Vietor's article in DKZ, 11 April 1914, pp. 246–47.

12. Tetzlaff, *Koloniale Entwicklung und Ausbeutung*, pp. 259–60; DKZ, 28 March 1914, pp. 215–16; 4 April 1914, pp. 230–31; 11 April 1914, pp. 246–47; *Sten, Ber.,* 7 March 1914, pp. 7897–7930; 9 March 1914, pp. 7940–53.

13. Kelly, *Descent of Darwin*, pp. 57–74.

14. For particular case studies related to this subject, see Woodruff D. Smith, "The Social and Political Origins of German Diffusionist Ethnology," *Journal of the History of the Behavioral Sciences* 14 (1978), pp. 103–12, and Woodruff D. Smith, "The Emergence of German Urban Sociology, 1900–1910," *Journal of the History of Sociology* 1 (1979), pp. 1–16. See also Mommsen, *Weber*, pp. 36–72, 97–146; Lindenlaub, *Richtungskämpfe*, 52: pp. 14–43; and, for an encyclopedic treatment of the role of intellectuals in imperialist propaganda, see Rüdiger vom Bruch, *Weltpolitik als Kulturmission: Auswärtige Kulturpolitik und Bildungsbürgertum in Deutschland am Vorabend des Ersten Weltkrieges* (Paderborn, 1982).

15. See Fritz K. Ringer, *The Decline of the German Mandarins: The German Academic Community, 1890–1933* (Cambridge, MA, 1969), pp. 51–61; Mommsen, *Weber,* pp. 1–36; Smith, "Ratzel," pp. 51–68.

16. Kelley, *Descent of Darwin,* pp. 100–22; Daniel Gasman, *The Scientific Origins of National Socialism: Social Darwinism in Ernst Haeckel and the German Monist League* (London and New York, 1971), pp. 126–46.

17. See Hübbe-Schleiden, *Überseeische Politik* and *Deutsche Colonisation,* and Wehler, "Sozialdarwinismus."

18. See Smith, "Ratzel." For sympathetic presentations of Ratzel's life and thought, see Harriet Wanklyn (Mrs. J. A. Steers), *Friedrich Ratzel. A Biographical Memoir and Bibliography* (Cambridge, 1961); and Günther Buttmann, *Friedrich Ratzel. Leben und Werk eines deutschen Geographen* (Stuttgart, 1977). The biographical information cited in this section comes primarily from these three sources.

19. Friedrich Ratzel, *Die Erde und das Leben. Eine vergleichende Erdkunde* (2 vols.; Leipzig and Vienna, 1901), 2: pp. 3–17, 578–82, 652–77; Friedrich Ratzel, *Politische Geographie* (3rd ed.; Munich and Berlin, 1923), pp. 1–32.

20. Ratzel, *Völkerkunde,* 1: pp. 121–32; 2: pp. 372–73.

21. Wanklyn, *Ratzel,* pp. 11, 24–26; Buttmann, *Ratzel,* pp. 37–42, 61–72; Ratzel, *Die Erde und das Leben,* 2: p. 584; Moritz Wagner, *Die Darwinische Theorie und das Migrationsgesetz der Organismen* (Munich, 1868); Moritz Wagner and Carl Scherzer, *Die Republik Costa Rica in Central Amerika* (Leipzig, 1856); H. Ganslmayr, "Moritz Wagner und seine Bedeutung für die Ethnologie" in *Verhandlungen des XXXVIII. Internationalen Amerikanisten Kongresses . . . 1968* (Munich, 1969), 4: pp. 459–71.

22. Ratzel, "In welcher Richtung," DKZ, 15 January 1885, pp. 38–44.

23. Rudolf Virchow, "Acclimatisation," in *Verhandlungen der Berliner Gesellschaft für Anthropologie, Ethnologie und Urgeschichte* (Berlin, 1885), pp. 202–14.

24. Ratzel, *Jugenderinnerungen,* pp. 107–47.

25. Ratzel, *Politische Geographie,* p. 7; also see pp. 33–59, 90–121.

26. For Ratzel's views on these subjects and his relationship with the National Liberals, see his pamphlet *Wider die Reichsnörgler* and his article "Mitteleuropäische Wirtschaftsverein."

27. Friedrich Ratzel, "Der Lebensraum. Eine biogeographische Studie," in K. Bücher et al., *Festgaben für Albert Schäffle . . .* (Tübingen, 1901), pp. 101–89.

28. The *Volk,* a concept well known from politics, was a highly elastic one. Ratzel's *Lebensraum* theory (and social Darwinism in general) could be made to appear consistent by varying the implied definition of *Volk* from place to place in an argument. On *völkisch* thought, see Mosse, *Crisis of German Ideology.*

29. See Ratzel, "Lebensraum," pp. 111–12, 139–40.

30. Ratzel, *Die Erde und das Leben,* 2: pp. 659–63.

31. Ratzel, "Mitteleuropäische Wirtschaftsverein"; F. Ratzel (published anonymously), "Ein Beitrag zu den Anfängen der deutschen Kolonialpolitik," *Die Grenzboten* 62 (1903), no. 2, pp. 115–16.

32. Dernburg, *Koloniale Lehrjahre.* Dernburg's interest in applying science and technology to colonial development is attested by the materials on inventions (especially aircraft) he collected while in office, which are to be found in BA Dernburg papers, no. 46.

33. On racism and imperialism, see V. G. Kiernan, *The Lords of Human Kind. Black Man, Yellow Man, and White Man in an Age of Empire* (Boston, 1969).
34. BA Solf papers, no. 26, pp. 19–33 (Solf memorandum on Samoan policy, 9 August 1905).
35. Samassa, *Besiedlung Deutsch-Ostafrikas*, pp. 128–62.
36. Kelly, *Descent of Darwin*, pp. 57–74.
37. Hübbe-Schleiden, *Überseeische Politik*, pp. 66–67, 120–42.
38. On diffusionism and its relationship to politics and imperialism see Smith, "Social and Political Origins of Diffusionist Ethnology."
39. See Diedrich Westermann, *Afrika als europäische Aufgabe* (Berlin, 1941), pp. 112–18, 124–34, 208–17.
40. See Ratzel, "Lebensraum," pp. 111–12; Ratzel, *Die Erde und das Leben*, 2: pp. 652–67; Ratzel, "Geschichte, Völkerkunde und historische Perspektive," *Historische Zeitschrift* 93 (1904), pp. 1–46, especially pp. 10–12.
41. See, for example, the "scientific" speeches presented in *Verhandlungen des Deutschen Kolonialkongresses 1902*, pp. 148–74.
42. For a discussion of some of the immediate prewar expansionary literature, see Wernecke, *Wille zur Weltgeltung*, pp. 288–310.
43. On Bernhardi, see Fischer, *War of Illusions*, pp. 242–44.
44. Bernhardi, *Deutschland und der nächste Krieg*, pp. 9–55.
45. Ibid., p. 79.
46. Ibid., p. 113.
47. Ibid., pp. 74–88. It should be noted that many other imperialists tried to link race and culture. See, for example, Hübbe-Schleiden, *Überseeische Politik*, pp. 33–35, 120–42.
48. Bernhardi, *Deutschland und der nächste Krieg*, pp. 85–86, 298–325.
49. Ibid., p. 85.
50. Ibid., pp. 80–89.
51. For discussions of the growth of right-radicalism in connection with imperialism just before World War I, see Eley, *Reshaping the German Right*, pp. 316–34; and Wernecke, *Wille zur Weltgeltung*, pp. 180–310.
52. Kühlmann and Solf, for example, agreed that the Pan-Germans were a danger to peace and to the successful pursuit of *Weltpolitik* but that the radical right's effect on public opinion was so great that it had to be humored by playing on its recent adoption of *Weltpolitik* ideas. BA Solf papers, no. 116, pp. 40–43 (letter: Solf to Kühlmann, 2 July 1913).
53. *Sten. Ber.*, 7 March 1914, pp. 7916–21.
54. For an easily accessible treatment of imperialism by Weber late in his career, a treatment that takes the *Weltpolitik* system as its object from the position of an external observer and devotes precisely one sentence to *Lebensraum*, see Gerth and Mills, eds., *From Max Weber*, pp. 162–71 (an excerpt from Weber's *Wirtschaft und Gesellschaft*.)
55. On the VSP, see Lindenlaub, *Richtungskämpfe*, 52: pp. 1–43; Mommsen, *Weber*, pp. 22–36, 73–96.
56. Lindenlaub, *Richtungskämpfe*, 53: pp. 272–432.
57. Mommsen, *Weber*, pp. 58–59.
58. Lindenlaub, *Richtungskämpfe*, 53: pp. 238–71, 292–303.
59. Weber's Freiburg address is analyzed in Mommsen, *Weber*, pp. 73–96. The text of the address can be found in Max Weber, *Gesammelte politische Schriften*, ed. Johannes Winckelmann (3rd. ed.; Tübingen, 1971), pp. 1–25.

60. See Gerth and Mills, eds., *From Max Weber,* pp. 159–79.
61. Mommsen, *Weber,* pp. 94–96.
62. Ibid., pp. 22–36, 62–64, 77–78.
63. Ibid., pp. 73–76.
64. See Heuss, *Naumann;* and Naumann, *Demokratie und Kaisertum.*
65. See, for instance, Naumann's lead article in *Die Hilfe,* 14 July 1895, and his introduction to Paul Rohrbach, *Deutsch Südwestafrika, ein Ansiedlungsgebiet* (Berlin, n.d.), pp. 3–6 (published by *Die Hilfe*).
66. Mommsen, *Weber,* p. 96. See also Hannah Vogt's introduction to Friedrich Naumann, *Ausgewählte Schriften* (Frankfurt am Main, 1949), especially pp. 9–37.
67. On Rohrbach, see Mogk, *Rohrbach;* and Rohrbach, *Um des Teufels Handschrift.*
68. See, for example, Fischer, *Germany's Aims,* pp. 9–10.
69. Mogk, *Rohrbach,* pp. 97–140; Rohrbach, *Um des Teufels Handschrift,* pp. 61–181.
70. Rohrbach, *Deutsche Gedanke,* pp. 5–10.
71. Ibid., pp. 9–10. The organized attempt of German intellectuals before the First World War to export Germany's culture has recently been examined in Bruch, *Weltpolitik als Kulturmission.*
72. Rohrbach, *Deutsche Gedanke,* pp. 91, 107.
73. Ibid., p. 10.
74. Ibid., pp. 161–96. Cf. p. 10. The tragic consequences of this kind of contradiction were not apparent to Rohrbach even after 1918. See Rohrbach, *Um des Teufels Handschrift,* pp. 182–92.
75. Rohrbach, *Deutsche Gedanke,* p. 10.
76. Ibid., p. 17.
77. Ibid., pp. 21, 36–61.
78. Ibid., pp. 76–77, 137–39, 207–8; Rohrbach, *Um des Teufels Handschrift,* pp. 61–66, 76–77, 93–94, 141; Paul Rohrbach, *Die Kolonie* (Frankfurt am Main, 1907), pp. 14–48.
79. Rohrbach, *Deutsche Gedanke,* pp. 133–60.
80. Ibid., pp. 148–49.
81. Ibid., pp. 137–39.
82. BA Solf papers, no. 126 (Solf's correspondence with Rohrbach, 1913–18); BA *Kleine Erwerbungen,* no. 353/1, pp. 86–90 (letter: Rohrbach to Prince Rupprecht of Bavaria, 11 September 1918).
83. Rohrbach, *Um des Teufels Handschrift,* pp. 182–231; BA *Kleine Erwerbungen,* no. 353/2 (Rohrbach's wartime papers); Peter Borowsky, *Deutsche Ukrainepolitik 1918* (Lübeck and Hamburg, 1970), pp. 13–14.
84. Eley, *Reshaping the German Right,* pp. 101–59, argues that much of radical conservatism before 1914 consisted of attempts to introduce such innovations. See also Guratzsch, *Macht durch Organisation.*

CHAPTER EIGHT

1. Fischer, *Germany's Aims* and *War of Illusions.* See also Konrad H. Jarausch, "The Illusion of Limited War: Bethman Hollweg's Calculated Risk," *Central European History* 2 (1969), pp. 48–76.
2. Moses, *Politics of Illusion.*

3. The annexationist–antiannexationist dichotomy is employed by Hans W. Gatzke, *Germany's Drive to the West: A Study of Germany's Western War Aims During the First World War* (Baltimore, 1950), pp. 8–77, 132–38.

4. Ibid., pp. 38–54; Albrecht Mendelssohn-Bartholdy, *The War and German Society: The Testament of a Liberal* (New York, 1971), pp. 19–30, 44–52, 280–96.

5. See Rohrbach's account of his involvement with government propaganda in Rohrbach, *Um des Teufels Handschrift,* pp. 195–200, 206–10. The most notable case of extragovernment organization to influence public opinion was Hugenberg's propaganda network. See Guratzsch, *Macht durch Organisation,* pp. 127–343.

6. Fischer, *Germany's Aims,* p. 106. The September Program is quoted in detail on pp. 104–5.

7. Naumann, *Mitteleuropa.* See also Meyer, *Mitteleuropa,* pp. 236–39.

8. For example: BA Solf papers, no. 48, pp. 145–92 (Colonial Office planning committee reports, 1916); no. 44, p. 42 (note: Solf to Helfferich, 26 September 1914); no. 54, pp. 134–50 (memorandum: Feldmann to Solf, 15 July 1917). See also Fischer, *Germany's Aims,* pp. 201–8, 247–79.

9. Schulin, *Rathenau,* p. 54; Fischer, *Germany's Aims,* pp. 101–2.

10. Fischer, *Germany's Aims,* p. 104.

11. Naumann, *Mitteleuropa,* pp. 1–32, 177–78, 229–62. In a letter to Georg Gothein dated 30 September 1914, Naumann insisted that he was not advocating the forcible establishment of the union; the prospective members would join voluntarily. Gothein, who also favored economic union but did not trust the willingness of big business to forego the use of political control for selfish ends and an alliance with the Junkers, was not sure that *Mitteleuropa* would live up to Naumann's expectations. BA Gothein papers, no. 27, pp. 33–36.

12. Fischer, *Germany's Aims,* pp. 113–17.

13. Freiherr Albrecht von Rechenberg, "Kriegs- und Friedensziele," *Nord und Süd* 41 (1917), pp. 131–43.

14. Naumann, *Mitteleuropa,* pp. 14–15.

15. Ibid., pp. 134–63.

16. Fischer, *Germany's Aims,* p. 182; BA Solf papers, no. 44, pp. 54–57 (H. Class's memorandum on war aims, December 1914).

17. The official Colonial Office view of *Mittelafrika* is detailed in the 1916 reports of the departmental committee on war aims: BA Solf papers, no. 48, pp. 145–69. Also BA Solf papers, no. 116, pp. 54–55 (letter: Kühlmann to Solf, 28 July 1915) and pp. 56–58 (reply: 9 August 1915).

18. This is made clear in Solf's summary of the Colonial Office's war-aims position of 24 October 1917, BA Solf papers, no. 48, p. 277.

19. Fischer, *Germany's Aims,* pp. 184–246.

20. BA Solf papers, no. 51 (war-aims disputes between the Colonial Office and the navy, 1915–16). Admiral Henning von Holtzendorff's memorandum of 26 November 1916 (pp. 28–35) makes clear the extent of underlying similarities between the views of the two departments, despite differences over specifics.

21. This feature of government war-aims thinking is discussed extensively in Fischer, *Germany's Aims,* passim. See Albert Ballin's attitudes toward peace with Britain in Cecil, *Ballin,* pp. 261–84; and Rohrbach's conception of parallel postwar empires in his articles "England und Russland, unsere Gegner,"

Deutsche Politik, 1 January 1916, pp. 2–11; and "Das Kriegsziel im Schützgraben," *Deutsche Politik,* 4 February 1916, pp. 241–47.

22. Rohrbach, "England und Russland," pp. 2–11. BA Solf papers, no. 99, pp. 1–2 (letter: Solf to Hans Delbrück 6 October 1914) and no. 116, pp. 54–58 (exchange of letters, Solf and Kühlmann, July–August 1915) show these assumptions at work in discussions of war-aims politics.

23. Solf made this point in a conversation with Ludendorff as late as 22 July 1918: BA Solf papers, no. 54, pp. 334–38. He also made it in explaining the position of the government group to which he belonged—on the U-boat question in a private letter of 10 January 1917 (BA Solf papers, no. 54, p. 27): "The Chancellor cannot hold out the olive branch with one hand while blasting away with the U-boat pistol in the other." Paul Rohrbach made the same argument constantly in 1915–16, most vigorously in a secret collection of press reports circulated through the government on 26 July 1916 (BA Solf papers, no. 126, pp. 6–26). Rohrbach's view was based on his analysis of the close relationship between the conservative, anti-German segment of the British elite and the mass-circulation press: "Excessive war aims against Britain would play into the hands of this block."

24. Konrad H. Jarausch, *The Enigmatic Chancellor: Bethmann Hollweg and the Hubris of Imperial Germany* (New Haven and London, 1973), pp. 112–16, 270–85; Theobald von Bethmann Hollweg, *Betrachtungen zum Weltkriege* (2 vols.; Berlin, 1919), 1: pp. 43–70; 2: pp. 1–84.

25. See, besides Fischer's *Germany's Aims,* both Gatzke, *Germany's Drive,* and Ernst W. Graf von Lynar, ed., *Deutsche Kriegsziele 1914–1918* (Darmstadt, 1964).

26. See, for example, the lead article in *Die Post* (a newspaper controlled by heavy-industrial interests), 1 October 1913, attacking the *Hansa-Bund* and representing the CDI as the ally of the *Mittelstand.* The *Mittelstand* strategy, of which this article was a manifestation, was discussed by the directors of the CDI at their meeting of 6 September 1911: BA R13I/52, pp. 21–30. See also Guratzsch, *Macht durch Organisation,* pp. 106–7.

27. Eley, *Reshaping the German Right,* pp. 316–34.

28. Ibid., pp. 239–53; Peck, *Radicals and Reactionaries,* pp. 82–134. See also the leading article in *Die Post,* 1 October 1913 (Note 26 above).

29. See James J. Sheehan, "Conflict and Consensus among German Elites in the Nineteenth Century," in Sheehan, ed., *Imperial Germany,* especially pp. 77–84.

30. This was one of the major problems of political organizations that developed highly reactionary ideological lines before World War I (e.g., the advocates of a revived feudalism or a return to the social and cultural forms of the age of Arminius). They could acquire fervent supporters, but they could not generalize this support because even the conservative public could detect the impossibility of their schemes. The trick was to make it appear that reactionary ideas were not incompatible with an effective modern social order—a trick that the postwar radical conservatives learned. See Mosse, *Crisis of German Ideology,* pp. 52–87.

31. Peck, *Radicals and Reactionaries,* pp. 135–202, strongly emphasizes the political, ideological, and social differences impeding integration on the right. See also Guratzsch, *Macht durch Organisation,* pp. 88–89, 100–117.

32. Peck, *Radicals and Reactionaries,* pp. 119–81, 135–63.

33. The version of the Class memorandum used here is found, with covering material, in BA Solf papers, no. 44, pp. 136–209. The actual printed memorandum is Heinrich Class, *Denkschrift betreffend die national-, wirtschafts-, und sozialpolitischen Ziele des deutschen Volkes im gegenwärtigen Kriege* (privately printed, 22 December 1914). Page numbers cited in the following notes refer to pages in the printed text itself.
34. Fischer, *Germany's Aims,* pp. 106–8; Fischer, *War of Illusions,* pp. 517–18.
35. Class, *Denkschrift,* p. 9.
36. Ibid., pp. 8, 11, 13–19.
37. Ibid., p. 11.
38. Ibid., pp. 37–54.
39. Ibid., pp. 49–50, 51–53.
40. Compare Class's position, for example, with those summarized in Imanuel Geiss, *Der polnische Grenzstreifen 1914–1918* (Lübeck, 1960), pp. 48–55.
41. Class, *Denkschrift,* pp. 33–35.
42. Ibid., pp. 57–59. See also Fischer, *Germany's Aims,* pp. 106, 164. According to Fischer, *Mitteleuropa* was not originally among the aims decided on by the Pan-German executive committee in August 1914. It was added by Class to his memorandum, apparently with the approval of several important business leaders.
43. For example: BA R13I/52, pp. 276–81 (minutes of VDES *Vorstand* meeting, 23 October 1912).
44. Williamson, *Helfferich,* pp. 258–60.
45. Peck, *Radicals and Reactionaries,* pp. 164–85; Ullmann, *Bund der Industriellen,* pp. 222–33.
46. Fischer, *Germany's Aims,* pp. 370–75, 430–31, 575–76. Similar motives were present among the leaders of the Center party as well. Matthias Erzberger, partly because of his private connections with heavy industry and partly because of his aim of making the Center the core of a bourgeois consensus, also temporarily subscribed to a war-aims position very much like Class's. By 1917, however, convinced that the *Lebensraum* position reduced the likelihood of an early peace and that the *Lebensraum* advocates were using their external program to prevent political reform, Erzberger had switched camps to the *Weltpolitik*-oriented antiannexationist position.
47. Ibid., pp. 165–66.
48. Class, *Denkschrift,* pp. 22–35.
49. Fischer, *Germany's Aims,* pp. 108–10.
50. Class, *Denkschrift,* pp. 54–57.
51. The proposals of the Colonial Office in 1916 were more modest, although they subsequently expanded: BA Solf papers, no. 48, pp. 145–69 (1916 planning committee); no. 48, p. 277 (Solf's 1917 war-aims memorandum).
52. Class, *Denkschrift,* pp. 20–21.
53. Ibid., pp. 35–36.
54. This is not to say that Fischer is wrong in indicating that the actual *consequences* of the *Lebensraum* approach to war aims would have been little different from those of the *Weltpolitiker.* Both approaches, in the improbable event of their being effectuated, would necessarily have issued in German world hegemony or else have collapsed. The difference was the Class had no illusions about the necessity of hegemony in realizing his war aims, while the *Weltpolitiker,* true to the assumptions built into their ideology, did.

55. There was one major point on which Class and the most doctrinaire of the official *Weltpolitiker* agreed in 1915: that Bethmann Hollweg's idea of seeking a separate peace with Russia was silly. The idea was bruited about mainly by orthodox Prussian conservatives who saw imperial Russia as a prop for the old order. Class viewed Russia as a source of annexations; the *Weltpolitiker* such as Solf, Kühlmann, and Rathenau believed that Russia's ability to interfere with *Mitteleuropa* had to be eliminated and were, in any case, not interested in propping up a tottering autocracy. Kühlmann scornfully reminded Solf on 28 July 1915 that the idea of a special arrangement with Russia had a long history among conservatives on the Wilhelmstrasse (presumably including Foreign Secretary Jagow): "There must be basilisks in the walls and especially the furniture of the offices which infuse themselves into the successive occupants of these particular working places, giving their written and oral expressions a certain frightening family resemblance" BA Solf papers, no. 116, pp. 54–55.
56. Peck, *Radicals and Reactionaries,* pp. 135–63; Gatzke, *Germany's Drive,* pp. 170–76.
57. Jarausch, *Enigmatic Chancellor,* pp. 185–229, 355.
58. Guratzsch, *Macht durch Organisation,* pp. 39–47, 100–117, 150–63.
59. On planning for the border strip, see Geiss, *Grenzstreifen;* and Fischer, *Germany's Aims,* pp. 115–17.
60. Fischer, *Germany's Aims,* p. 159, describes this group as "Government-Liberal." He considers their program in some detail, arguing that it differed little from that of the Pan-Germans, although citing evidence that it did differ precisely along the lines discussed above in the comparison between Class's program and that of the Bethmann government. Both sides certainly *thought* there was a difference, despite points of overlap. One of the main reasons that they emphasized the differences was of course the political agendas that lay behind the war-aims positions. For an exposition of the reformist–*Weltpolitiker* position and its differences from that of the Pan-Germans, see Bernhard Dernburg, *"Unser Friede"* (Frankfurt am Main, 1918), pp. 1–5. Dernburg explicitly connects economic imperialism, a negotiated peace, and the vital aim of "democratizing and politicizing Germany" on the first page. For the 1917 Peace Resolution, see Fischer, *Germany's Aims,* pp. 401–4; and Dernburg, *"Unser Friede,"* pp. 4–5.
61. Dernburg, *"Unser Friede,"* p. 18. Much the same aims were expounded in private by the economist Lujo von Brentano: BA Brentano papers, no. 14, pp. 20–22 (letter: Brentano to Hans Delbrück, 7 July 1915). See also BA Sering papers, no. 17 (letter: Schulze-Gävernitz to Sering, 19 December 1917).
62. Dernburg, *"Unser Friede,"* p. 2; BA Solf papers, no. 124, pp. 6–8 (letter: Rathenau to Solf, 17 May 1918; reply: 8 June 1918).
63. Schulin, *Rathenau,* p. 63; Schieffel, *Dernburg,* pp. 155–61. Solf wrote a letter to the Emperor on 9 June 1917 arguing in favor of internal political reform on these grounds: BA Solf papers, no. 54, pp. 95–98.
64. Gatzke, *Germany's Drive,* pp. 117–26, 132–38; Williamson, *Helfferich,* pp. 199–211.
65. Gatzke, *Germany's Drive,* pp. 132–38. For an example of the vigor of the *Weltpolitikers'* attack on the Pan-Germans and the *Vaterlandspartei,* see Paul Rohrbach, ed., *Die alldeutsche Gefahr* (Berlin, 1918), pp. 5–15.

66. This was done most notably by Gerald D. Feldman, *Army Industry and Labor in Germany 1914–1918* (Princeton, 1966).

67. See Hoffmann's reports of disputes with Ludendorff over Brest-Litovsk in *Ursachen und Folgen. Vom deutschen Zusammenbruch 1918 und 1945 bis zur staatlichen Neuordnung in der Gegenwart,* ed. H. Michaelis (8 vols.; Berlin, 1959), 2: pp. 126–30, and Ludendorff's conception of war aims, 2: pp. 130–31. General Hans von Beseler, the military governor of occupied Poland, also expressed essentially a *Weltpolitik* view of Poland's future as a politically independent but economically subordinate nation, which was in opposition to extreme annexationist views: NA, T–120, roll 3241, fr. E550707 ff. (position paper by Beseler, 6 March 1918). Evidence of Ludendorff's apparent willingness to accommodate himself to *Weltpolitik* ideas of imperialism is found in Solf's report of a discussion with Ludendorff on 22 July 1918: BA Solf papers, no. 54, pp. 334–38.

68. Gatzke, *Germany's Drive,* pp. 139–94.

69. See ibid.; Williamson, *Helfferich,* pp. 151–238; and Gordon A. Craig, *The Politics of the Prussian Army 1640–1945* (New York, 1964), pp. 313–26.

70. So it was painted by Solf in a letter to a cousin on 10 January 1917: BA Solf papers, no. 54, p. 27. On the formation of the conservative connection, see Guratzsch, *Macht durch Organisation,* pp. 127–82, 363–79.

71. Jarausch, *Enigmatic Chancellor,* pp. 308–80.

72. On the Peace Resolution, see Williamson, *Helfferich,* pp. 219, 224, 229–33.

73. This point was made strongly in a letter from Solf to Chancellor Hertling on 18 January 1918: BA Solf papers, no. 54, pp. 267–71.

74. Jarausch, *Enigmatic Chancellor,* pp. 308–80.

75. Feldman, *Army Industry and Labor,* pp. 407–58.

76. See Peck, *Radicals and Reactionaries,* pp. 203–35; Feldman, *Army Industry and Labor,* pp. 430–31; *Ursachen und Folgen* 2: pp. 48–51.

77. BA Solf papers, no. 48, p. 277 (Solf war-aims memorandum, 24 October 1917).

78. Borowsky, *Deutsche Ukrainepolitik,* pp. 41–63; Fischer, *Germany's Aims,* pp. 444–72.

79. Rohrbach, "England und Russland;" Paul Rohrbach, "Klarheit im Osten," *Deutsche Politik,* 14 April 1916, pp. 705–11; Hans von Delbrück, editorial in *Preussische Jahrbücher* 161, 3 (1915), pp. 556–61.

80. Heinrich Class, *Zum deutschen Kriegsziel* (Munich, 1917).

81. BA Solf papers, no. 124, pp. 6–7 (letter: Rathenau to Solf, 17 May 1918); NA, T–137, fr. 1–156 (files of Foreign Office representative at GHQ on war-aims matters, 1917–18; especially protocol of meeting of emperor, Hertling, Kühlmann, and Ludendorff, 18 December 1917).

82. Rohrbach, *Um des Teufels Handschrift,* pp. 217–18; Paul Leutwein, *Mitteleuropa-Mittelafrika* (Dresden, 1917).

83. Friedrich von Schwerin, *Kriegersansiedlung vergangenen Zeiten* (Leipzig, 1917); H. L. Dannenberg, *Sieg ohne Landgewinn?* (Dresden, 1918); Hans Siegfried Weber, *Ansiedlung von Kriegsinvaliden* (Berlin, 1916); BA Sering papers, no. 17 August 1917 (report on Baltic settlement by Schwerin and Lindequist); *Ursachen und Folgen,* 2: pp. 128–30.

84. See, for example, the *Ostmarverein*'s interpretation of the economic functions of the "independent" Kingdom of Poland in *Ursachen und Folgen,* 1: p. 41. See also Class, *Zum deutschen Kriegsziel.*

85. See Naumann, *Mitteleuropa,* pp. 199–228.
86. On Brest-Litovsk, see J. W. Wheeler-Bennett, *Brest-Litovsk: The Forgotten Peace* (London, 1938); Fischer, *Germany's Aims,* pp. 475–509; Borowsky, *Deutsche Ukrainepolitik,* pp. 49–63.
87. Borowsky, *Deutsche Ukrainepolitik,* pp. 63–65; BA Solf Papers, no. 54, pp. 334–38 (report of conference, Solf and Ludendorff, 22 July 1918.)
88. Borowsky, *Deutsche Ukrainepolitik,* pp. 63–166.
89. Ibid., pp. 166–263, especially pp. 141–46; Fischer, *Germany's Aims,* p. 548; NA, T–134, roll 134 (protocol of meeting between the emperor and civilian and military chiefs at GHQ, 2 July 1918, at which Ludendorff explained his colonial schemes.)

CHAPTER NINE

1. On the role of liberal *Weltpolitiker* in the formation of the DDP and the early Weimar Republic, see Werner Stephan, *Aufstieg und Verfall des Linksliberalismus, 1918–1933: Geschichte der Deutschen Demokratischen Partei* (Göttingen, 1973); and Opitz, *Deutsche Sozialliberalismus,* pp. 18–21, 44–50.
2. Rohrbach, *Briefe über Demokratie und Pazifismus.* On Rohrbach during the Weimar era, see also Opitz, *Deutsche Sozialliberalismus,* pp. 21–44.
3. In Rohrbach, *Briefe,* p. 5, the connection between establishing a functioning democracy and attaining imperialist goals is made explicit when Rohrbach argues that democracy is a necessary means of reestablishing Germany's "right to existence and living-space."
4. Hans Delbrück made the same general argument in an article in the *Frankfurter Zeitung,* 13 November 1924. Wilhelm Solf wrote to Delbrück from Japan on 23 March 1925 in response to the article, agreeing with it partly on the grounds of the capacity of representative democracy for eliciting cooperation among disparate political organizations: BA Solf papers, no. 99, pp. 18–22.
5. Williamson, *Helfferich,* pp. 330–64.
6. Ibid., pp. 256–58, 369–70.
7. See Annelise Thimme, "Gustav Stresemann: Legende und Wirklichkeit," *Historische Zeitschrift* 181 (1956), pp. 287–338, and a contrary view by Robert Grathwol, "Gustav Stresemann: Reflections on His Foreign Policy," *Journal of Modern History* 45 (1973), pp. 52–70. The limits even of Stresemann's most secret designs on Poland are indicated in a memorandum ordering the funding of organizations to "strengthen *Deutschtum*" in Polish-occupied areas: NA, T–120, roll 1579, fr. D704698 ff.
8. From the draft of a position paper on foreign policy drawn up by Stresemann late in 1923 for cabinet presentation: NA, T–120, roll 1579, fr. D704485 ff. This draft gives an extremely comprehensive view of Stresemann's attitudes toward foreign policy and its relationship to economic matters. For a summary and analysis of Stresemann's aims, see John Jacobson, *Locarno Diplomacy. Germany and the West 1925–1929* (Princeton, 1972), especially pp. 40–43.
9. Wilhelm Solf noted the *Weltpolitik* predilections of Foreign Ministry personnal in his previously cited letter to Delbruck of 1 August 1927, BA Solf papers, no. 99, pp. 85–92. The persistence of *Weltpolitik* attitudes toward the relationship between foreign and economic policy in bureaucratic circles is

excellently illustrated by a memorandum of 17 December 1923, written by a Dr. Wohlmannsteter of the Ministry of Economics, advocating an "active" policy of trade expansion: NA, T–120, roll 1579, fr. D704820 ff.

10. On the relations between Weimar governments and the military over foreign affairs, see Gaines Post, Jr., *The Civil-Military Fabric of Weimar Foreign Policy* (Princeton, 1973).

11. Dieter Lohn, *Politik und Interesse: Die Interessenstruktur der Deutschen Volks- partei* (Meisenheim am Glan, 1970); Henry Ashby Turner, Jr., *Stresemann and the Politics of the Weimar Republic* (Princeton, 1963), pp. 27–34; DVP circular on party position, c. 1923, in NA, T–253, roll 52 (Karl Haushofer papers), fr. 1508116 ff.

12. See Dirk Stegmann, "Deutsche Zoll- und Handelspolitik 1924/25–1929 unter besonderer Berücksichtigung agrarischer und industrieller Interessen," in Hans Mommsen, Dietmar Petzina, and Bernd Weisbrod, eds., *Industrielles System und politische Entwicklung in der Weimarer Republik* (Düsseldorf, 1974), pp. 499–513.

13. Ibid., p. 502 n.

14. Ibid., pp. 499–513; NA, T–120, roll 1579, fr. 704485ff. (1923 Stresemann memorandum); fr. D704820 (Wohlmannsteter memorandum).

15. See William A. Hoisington, "The Struggle for Economic Influence in South- eastern Europe: The French Failure in Rumania, 1940," *Journal of Modern History* 43 (1971), pp. 468–82; and Bernd Jürgen Wendt, "England und der deutsche 'Drang nach Südosten': Kapitalbeziehungen und Warenverkehr in Südeuropa zwischen den Weltkriegen," in Geiss and Wendt, eds., *Deutsch- land in der Weltpolitik*, pp. 483–512.

16. Stegmann, "Deutsche Zoll- und Handelspolitik," pp. 499–513.

17. For Franco-German relations in general, see Michael-Olaf Maxelon, *Strese- mann und Frankreich 1914–1928. Deutsche Politik der Ost-West Balance* (Düsseldorf, 1972). An analysis of French public opinion by the German embassy in Paris dated 31 May 1924 describes German policy and French reaction to it in terms of long-run German-oriented continental economic integration: NA, T–120, roll 1580, fr. D705145 ff.

18. See Stresemann's message to the *Tagung der deutschen Auslandshandels-kam- mern*, c. October 1924, in NA, T–120, roll 1580, fr. D705751 ff.

19. NA, T–120, roll 1579, fr. D704485 ff.

20. BA Solf papers, no. 99, pp. 85–92 (letter: Solf to Delbrück, 1 August 1927).

21. On Stresemann's view of Britain, see Werner Weidenfeld, *Die Englandpolitik Gustav Stresemanns* (Mainz, 1972), pp. 89–140. The official attitude discussed here can be seen in a secret internal Foreign Ministry memorandum on possi- ble future developments in Anglo-German relations dated 13 October 1923: NA, T–120, roll 1579, fr. D704616 ff. For the recrudescence of a Tirpitz-like argument in favor of naval building, see speech by Defense Minister Wilhelm Groener to the Reichstag in *Sten. Ber.*, vol. 395, pp. 13, 377–84.

22. Stegmann, "Deutsche Zoll- und Handelspolitik," pp. 511–13; Kurt Goss- weiler, *Grossbanken Industriemonopole Staat. Ökonomie und Politik des staatsmonopolistischen Kapitalismus in Deutschland 1914–1932* (Berlin, 1971), pp. 355–94; David Abraham, *The Collapse of the Weimar Republic: Political Economy and Crisis* (Princeton, 1981), pp. 221–28.

23. See, for example, Ernst Tiessen, "Der Friedensvertrag von Versailles und die politische Geographie," *Zeitschrift für Geopolitik* 1 (1924), pp. 203–19; Karl

Haushofer, "Vergleich des Lebensraumes Deutschlands mit dem seiner Nach-barn . . . ," in Hans-Adolf Jacobsen, *Karl Haushofer—Leben und Werk* (2 vols.; Boppard am Rhein, 1979), 1: pp. 524–36.

24. Friedrich Ratzel, *Deutschland. Einführung in die Heimatkunde* (7th ed.; Berlin, 1943).

25. Tiessen, "Friedensvertrag," pp. 203–19; *Die bürgerlichen Parteien Deutschlands* (2 vols.; Leipzig, 1968), 1: p. 725.

26. On the later Pan-Germans, see *Die bürgerlichen Parteien,* 1: pp. 18–23; Robert P. Grathwol, *Stresemann and the DNVP: Reconciliation or Revenge in German Foreign Policy 1924–1928* (Lawrence, KS, 1980), pp. 11, 22, 74, 102–3, 142, 191, 200; Klaus Hildebrand, *Vom Reich zum Weltreich. NSDAP und koloniale Frage 1919–1945* (Munich, 1969), pp. 233–36.

27. The continued strength of *Lebensraum* concepts in politics and academic life can be seen in the various articles, clippings, and drafts on questions of inner colonization to be found in BA Sering papers, no. 22. See the cogent discussion of the political employment of *Lebensraum* by political organizations in Hildebrand, *Vom Reich zum Weltreich,* pp. 143–45, 156–73.

28. *Die bürgerlichen Parteien,* 1: p. 725.

29. This becomes clear when one compares Max Sering's argument for inner colonization after 1918 with the arguments he had made for external settlement colonization during the war. Cf. draft article on "Die Ziele des ländlichen Siedlungswerkes," 21 January 1919, BA Sering papers, no. 22, and draft of the article by Sering for *Der Panther,* 5 October 1916, BA Sering papers, no. 28.

30. For evidence of the diffusion of *Lebensraum* political aims throughout the right, see *Die bürgerlichen Parteien,* 1: pp. 19, 107, 390–407, 725. As we shall see in Chapter 10, the Nazis were calling for *Lebensraum*-style expansion as early as their first comprehensive program statement in 1920.

31. An excellent discussion of the political problems and approach of the DNVP before the ascendancy of Hugenberg is contained in Grathwol, *Stresemann and the DNVP,* especially pp. 8–16, 21–41. See also Lewis Hertzman, *DNVP: Right-Wing Opposition in the Weimar Republic, 1918–1924* (Lincoln, NE, 1963).

32. Grathwol, *Stresemann,* pp. 195–96; Williamson, *Helfferich,* pp. 332–35, 341, 368–71.

33. John A. Leopold, *Alfred Hugenberg: The Radical Nationalist Campaign against the Weimar Republic* (New Haven, 1977), pp. 55–106. However, it should be noted that, although the DNVP right wing was thoroughly anti-Semitic, Hugenberg himself was not.

34. On anti-Semitism in the DNVP and its role in the party's politics, see Mosse, *Crisis of German Ideology,* pp. 237–53; and Hertzman, *DNVP,* pp. 124–64.

35. Mosse, *Crisis of German Ideology,* pp. 253–65.

36. See Lebovics, *Social Conservatism and the Middle Classes in Germany 1914–1933,* (Princeton, 1969), pp. 79–108, for treatments of autarky and cultural protection by conservative intellectuals.

37. Ibid., pp. 109–38; Bergmann, *Agrarromantik; Die bürgerlichen Parteien,* 1: p. 725.

38. Hildebrand, *Vom Reich zum Weltreich,* p. 51.

39. Adolf Rüger, "Der Kolonialrevisionismus der Weimarer Republik," in Stoecker, ed., *Drang nach Afrika,* pp. 250–51, 267–68.

40. Hildebrand, *Vom Reich zum Weltreich,* pp. 143–45.
41. See ibid.; Gossweiler, *Grossbanken;* Rüger, "Kolonialrevisionismus," pp. 243–79.
42. See Class, *Zum deutschen Kriegsziel.*
43. Lebovics, *Social Conservatism,* pp. 79–138.
44. Grathwol, *Stresemann,* pp. 180–203; Gossweiler, *Grossbanken,* pp. 308–10.
45. Stegmann, "Deutsche Zoll- und Handelspolitik," pp. 511–13; Abraham, *Collapse of the Weimar Republic,* pp. 116–79; Roswitha Berndt, "Wirtschaftliche Mitteleuropapläne des deutschen Imperialismus (1926–31)," in Gilbert Ziebura, ed., *Grundfragen der deutschen Aussenpolitik seit 1871* (Darmstadt, 1975), pp. 305–34.
46. Abraham, *Collapse of the Weimar Republic,* pp. 180–228.
47. For a comprehensive statement of the conservative theory of autarky connected to other radical conservative notions (including anti-Semitism), see Paul Bang, *Deutsche Wirtschaftsziele* (Langensalza, 1926). Bang was an economic spokesperson of the DNVP and a prominent Pan-German. See also Günther Schmölders and Walther Vogel, *Wirtschaft und Raum* (Hamburg, 1937), pp. 109–10.
48. Dietmar Petzina, *Die deutsche Wirtschaft in der Zwischenkriegszeit* (Wiesbaden, 1977), pp. 96–107; Abraham, *Collapse of the Weimar Republic,* pp. 281–327.
49. See Mosse, *Crisis of German Ideology,* pp. 239, 246–48; Bang, *Wirtschaftsziele;* Ernst Nolte, *Three Faces of Fascism* (New York, 1966), pp. 332–33.
50. For a comprehensive statement of the *Blut-und-Boden* concept, see R. W. Darré, *Das Bauerntum als Lebensquell der nordischen Rasse* (Munich, 1929), which was probably written before Darré officially joined the Nazis.
51. Hildebrand, *Vom Reich zum Weltreich;* Wolfe W. Schmokel, *Dream of Empire: German Colonialism, 1919–1945* (New Haven, 1964); Rüger, "Kolonialrevisionismus"; Jolanda Ballhaus, "Kolonialziele und -vorbereitungen des faschistischen Regimes 1933–1939," in Stoecker, ed., *Drang nach Afrika,* pp. 281–314.
52. For a concise statement of this argument, constantly repeated by the Colonial Society, see Wilhelm Solf, *Germany's Right to Recover Her Colonies* (Berlin, 1919). See also DKZ, 14 August 1920, p. 74; Hildebrand, *Vom Reich zum Weltreich,* pp. 123–229.
53. Hildebrand, *Vom Reich zum Weltreich,* p. 51; Rüger, "Kolonialrevisionismus," pp. 248–57.
54. Hildebrand, *Vom Reich zum Weltreich,* pp. 100–12.
55. Ibid., pp. 135–57.
56. NA, T–120, roll 1579, fr. D704485 ff. (Stresemann's 1923 foreign policy review).
57. Hildebrand, *Vom Reich zum Weltreich,* pp. 51–62, 100–12, 123–27; Rüger, "Kolonialrevisionismus," pp. 258–71.
58. Hildebrand, *Vom Reich zum Weltreich,* pp. 173–87.
59. Smith, *German Colonial Empire,* pp. 216–17; Tetzlaff, *Koloniale Entwicklung und Ausbeutung,* pp. 229–32.
60. See the discussion of the colonial movement's program in Rüger, "Kolonialrevisionismus," pp. 273–75.
61. Hildebrand, *Vom Reich zum Weltreich,* pp. 100–12, 143–45.
62. Ibid., pp. 156–73.
63. Rüger, "Kolonialrevisionismus," pp. 272–78.

64. Karl Lange, "Der Terminus 'Lebensraum' in Hitlers 'Mein Kampf'," *Vierteljahrshefte für Zeitgeschichte* 13 (1965), pp. 426–37.
65. The standard study of Haushofer is Jacobsen, *Karl Haushofer.* See also Andreas Dorpalen, *The World of General Haushofer: Geopolitics in Action* (New York, 1942).
66. For Haushofer's ideas of national consensus and "national socialism" see Karl Haushofer, "Geopolitische Einflüsse bei den Verkörperungsversuchungen von nationalen Sozialismus und sozialer Aristokratie," *Zeitschrift für Geopolitik* 1 (1924), pp. 127–34. See also Jacobsen, *Karl Haushofer,* 1: pp. 178–278.
67. Smith, "Friedrich Ratzel;" BA Haushofer papers, no. HC 829 (draft of paper on "Geopolitische Grundlagen des heutigen Wehrwesens"); NA, T–253 (Haushofer files), roll 52, fr. 1507195 ff.
68. Karl Haushofer, *Weltpolitik von heute* (Berlin, 1936), pp. 22–50; BA Haushofer papers, no. HC 834 (draft essay "Was ist Geopolitik?", 28 May 1929); Lange, "Lebensraum," pp. 429–30.
69. Quoted in Dorpalen, *Haushofer,* p. 24.
70. Karl Haushofer, "Geographische Grundzüge auswärtiger Politik," *Süddeutsche Monatshefte* 24 (1926–27), pp. 258 ff. See also Fritz Hesse, "Das Gesetz der wachsende Räume," *Zeitschrift für Geopolitik* 1 (1924), pp. 1–4.
71. Haushofer, *Weltpolitik von heute;* Hesse, "Gesetz," pp. 1–4. Kurt Vowinckel, a close associate of Hauhofer's, gave a three-level definition of *Lebensraum:* "German Lebensraum is, first, wherever the German peasant has settled as a part of the German national body; second, wherever the economic structures of other states supplement and align themselves with that of the German heartland in common activity; and third, where German culture adds to or fertilizes alien cultures." Kurt Vowinckel, "Zum Begriff Lebensraum," *Zeitschrift für Geopolitik* 16 (1939), pp. 638–39.
72. Haushofer, "Geographische Grundzüge," pp. 258–61.
73. Karl Haushofer, *Das japanische Reich in seiner geographischen Entwicklung* (Vienna, 1921). See also the collection of material on this work contained in BA Haushofer papers, no. HC 917a.
74. BA Haushofer papers, no. HC 917a, pp. 190–243.
75. Haushofer, *Weltpolitik von heute,* pp. 48–50, 116–18; BA Haushofer papers, no. HC 829 ("Geopolitische Grundlagen").
76. Dorpalen, *Haushofer,* pp. 221–70; Schmölders and Vogel, *Wirtschaft und Raum.*
77. The edition cited here is the 1932 unabridged one-volume *Volksaufgabe.* The original edition was Hans Grimm, *Volk ohne Raum* (2 vols.; Munich, 1926). The present discussion is in some respects a summary of Woodruff Smith, "The Colonial Novel as Political Propaganda: Hans Grimm's *Volk ohne Raum,*" *German Studies Review* 6 (1983), pp. 215–35, which contains specific page references for the plot exposition.
78. Donald Ray Richards, *The German Bestseller in the 20th Century. A Complete Bibliography and Analysis 1915–1940* (Berne, 1968), pp. 55, 141; *Der Türmer* 19 (1926–27), p. 247; *Süddeutsche Monatshefte* 25 (1927–28), p. 290.
79. Eley, *Reshaping the German Right,* pp. 68–85.
80. On aspects of this process, see Leopold, *Hugenberg,* pp. 11–54; and Gary D. Stark, *Entrepreneurs of Ideology: Neoconservative Publishers in Germany, 1890–1933* (Chapel Hill, 1981).
81. Hildebrand, *Vom Reich zum Weltreich,* pp. 390–440.

82. For Grimm's background, see his autobiographical fragment *Suchen und Hoffen. Aus meinem Leben 1928 bis 1934* (Lippoldsberg, 1960); and *Neue Deutsche Biographie* (Berlin, 1966), 7: pp. 83–85. For his theory of literature, see Grimm, *Suchen und Hoffen*, pp. 27–28, and Hans Grimm, *Der Schriftsteller und die Zeit* (Munich, 1931).

83. For Grimm's relationship with the Nazis: Grimm, *Suchen und Hoffen*, pp. 10–12, 33, 80, 92; Hildebrand, *Vom Reich zum Weltreich*, pp. 164, 401, 412; Rolf Geissler, *Dekadenz und Heroismus. Zeitroman und völkisch-national sozialistische Literaturkritik* (Stuttgart, 1964), pp. 142–50.

84. Grimm, *Suchen und Hoffen*, p. 7; Grimm, *Volk ohne Raum*, pp. 588–94.

85. Grimm, *Volk ohne Raum*, pp. 255–96.

86. Ibid., pp. 725–30; Grimm, *Suchen und Hoffen*, pp. 48–55; Hans Grimm, *Von der bürgerlichen Ehre und bürgerlichen Notwendigkeit* (Munich, 1932).

87. Grimm, *Volk ohne Raum*, p. 662.

88. Ibid., pp. 958–63, 989–1007.

89. Hildebrand, *Vom Reich zum Weltreich*, pp. 220, 443; Barbara Miller Lane and Leila J. Rupp, *Nazi Ideology before 1933: A Documentation* (Austin, Texas, and London, 1978), p. 47; Schmokel, *Dream of Empire*, p. 51n; Lange, "Lebensraum," p. 435.

90. Grimm, *Volk ohne Raum*, pp. 713–16. This point is analyzed in Hugh Ridley, "Colonial Society and European Totalitarianism," *Journal of European Studies* 3 (1973), pp. 147–59, esp. pp. 154–56.

91. Jacobsen, *Karl Haushofer*, 1: p. 538; 2: pp. 77, 142–43.

CHAPTER TEN

1. For the possible influence of Haushofer on Hitler, see Lange, "Lebensraum."

2. Rich, *Hitler's War Aims;* Andreas Hillgruber, *Hitlers Strategie. Politik und Kriegführung 1940–1941* (Frankfurt am Main, 1965); Jacobsen, *Nationalsozialistische Aussenpolitik;* Hildebrand, *Deutsche Aussenpolitik;* Hildebrand, *Vom Reich zum Weltreich;* Weinberg, *Foreign Policy, 1933–1936;* Gerhard L. Weinberg, *The Foreign Policy of Hitler's Germany: Starting World War II, 1937–1939* (Chicago, 1980).

3. On Nazi ideology, see Lane and Rupp, *Nazi Ideology*, and Eberhard Jäckel, *Hitler's Weltanschauung: A Blueprint for Power*, tr. Herbert Arnold (Middletown, CT, 1972; orig. German ed., 1969).

4. That is, the fact that the Nazis were successful was presumably due to some combination of circumstances inhering in the political environment. But to characterize that environment in a particular way is not to demonstrate that the characteristics one cites were the ones that led to Nazi success.

5. On radical-conservative propaganda, see Guratzsch, *Macht durch Organisation*, pp. 183–343; Leopold, *Hugenberg*, pp. 84–97; Stark, *Entrepreneurs of Ideology;* Ernest K. Bramsted, *Goebbels and National Socialist Propaganda, 1925–1945* (East Lansing, 1965).

6. For a contemporary leftist commentary on Nazi use of new political techniques, see Serge Chakotin, *The Rape of the Masses: The Psychology of Totalitarian Political Propaganda* (London, 1940), esp. p. 191, where Chakotin compares Nazi techniques with those of the SPD. Hitler's own early views on propaganda can, of course, be found in *Mein Kampf*, especially vol. 1, ch. 6, and vol. 2, ch. 11. The edition of *Mein Kampf* used here is the 1939

English translation: Adolf Hitler, *Mein Kampf* (New York, 1939). Citations, however, will be given here by chapter to permit reference to the various editions of the book.

7. See, for example, Stern, *Politics of Cultural Despair;* Mosse, *Crisis of German Ideology.*

8. It must be remembered that when the text refers to the resolution of a contradiction within a set of ideological statements, this means only that a superficially plausible resolution within the intellectual framework of one or both parts of the contradiction has been presented. It does not mean that the resolution can meet an objective logical or empirical test successfully.

9. Hans J. Morgenthau, *Politics Among Nations: The Struggle for Power and Peace* (3rd. ed.; New York, 1965), pp. 106–9.

10. This can be seen, for example, in a comparison of the threat to Germany presented in NA, T–120, roll 1579, fr. D704820 ff. (Wohlmannsteter's 1923 review of Germany's economic relations, a document oriented toward *Weltpolitik* thinking) with that described in Grimm, *Volk ohne Raum,* pp. 588–94.

11. Jacobsen, *Nationalsozialistische Aussenpolitik,* pp. 446–63.

12. See, for example, Franz Neumann, *Behemoth,* pp. 37–39, 130–218.

13. Jäckel, *Hitler's Weltanschauung,* pp. 13–26.

14. Herman Lebovics, *Social Conservatism,* pp. 3–48, 205–20.

15. The broad social appeal of Naziism, beyond the limits of the lower middle class that was once thought to be the main support of the party, is demonstrated in Richard F. Hamilton, *Who Voted for Hitler?* (Princeton, 1982).

16. See, for example, Hildebrand, *Vom Reich zum Weltreich,* pp. 317–25.

17. See, for example, Neumann, *Behemoth,* pp. 459–76, on economic policy and political theory.

18. Jäckel, *Hitler's Weltanschauung,* pp. 13–26. See also Hitler's own discussion of *Weltanschauung* in *Mein Kampf* 2: chs. 1, 5.

19. On Hitler's role in foreign policy and the extent of his responsibility for establishing that policy's expansionary direction, see Rich, *Hitler's War Aims,* 1: pp. 3–80; and Hillgruber, *Germany and the Two World Wars,* pp. 49–55. See also Jacobsen, *Nationalsozialistische Aussenpolitik,* pp. 16–318, for an analysis of the structure of Nazi foreign policy determination, which involved an interplay of government and extragovernment interests in influencing Hitler's actions.

20. Lane and Rupp, *Nazi Ideology,* pp. 40–43; includes a translation of the text of the document.

21. Hildebrand, *Vom Reich zum Weltreich,* pp. 43, 56–62, 237–47.

22. Ibid., pp. 70–75; Jäckel, *Hitler's Weltanschauung,* pp. 28–31.

23. Jäckel, *Hitler's Weltanschauung,* pp. 32–34; Hildebrand, *Vom Reich zum Weltreich,* pp. 70–81; Hillgruber, *Germany and the Two World Wars,* pp. 49–55.

24. Lange, "Lebensraum," pp. 426–37. By Haushofer's own (admittedly suspect) account in a well-known letter of 24 December 1938 to his dean at the University of Munich, he had "stood close" to the NSDAP since 1919 but had not joined the party on "grounds of secrecy"—presumably so that he could achieve general political ends desired by the Nazis among groups suspicious of them. Haushofer claims to have been a substantial influence on the Nazis through his connection with his former student Rudolf Hess: NA, T–253, roll 54, fr. 1510339.

25. Karl Dietrich Bracher, *The German Dictatorship: The Origins, Structure, and Effects of National Socialism* (New York, 1970), pp. 122–68. Hildebrand, *Vom Reich zum Weltreich,* pp. 113–22, 173–87, notes the link between Hitler's movement toward "legal" politics and his growing interest in imperialism.

26. See the analysis of this process from the standpoint of anti-Semitism in Mosse, *Crisis of German Ideology,* pp. 299–301.

27. The effects of Hitler's personal need for ideological synthesis are described in Jäckel, *Hitler's Weltanschauung,* pp. 87–107, although not in connection with the political problem of support aggregation.

28. Hillgruber, *Germany and the Two World Wars,* pp. 49–55; Hildebrand, *Deutsche Aussenpolitik,* pp. 19–29; Rich, *Hitler's War Aims,* 1: pp. 3–16.

29. Quoted in Lange, "Lebensraum," p. 427.

30. Norman H. Baynes, ed., *The Speeches of Adolf Hitler April 1922–August 1939* (2 vols.; London, 1942; repr. New York, 1969), 1: p. 385.

31. Quoted in Hildebrand, *Vom Reich zum Weltreich,* p. 77; and Jäckel, *Hitler's Weltanschauung,* p. 34.

32. This point is strongly made by Rich, *Hitler's War Aims,* 1: pp. 7–10, 65, 82–83, 97.

33. See, for example, *Mein Kampf,* 2: chs. 2, 14.

34. On Darré and his views, see Darré, *Bauerntum;* Lane and Rupp, *Nazi Ideology,* pp. 103–6, 130–35, 147; and Rich, *Hitler's War Aims,* 1: p. 63.

35. Ballhaus, "Kolonialziele," pp. 281–303; Hildebrand, *Vom Reich zum Weltreich,* pp. 173–87.

36. See the still-useful discussion in Neumann, *Behemoth,* pp. 130–54, 327–37.

37. Ibid., pp. 327–37; Dorpalen, *Haushofer,* pp. 221–40; Berndt, "Mitteleuropapläne," pp. 305–34.

38. Hildebrand, *Vom Reich zum Weltreich,* pp. 317–29. As Rosenberg wrote in an official letter in 1943 during a discussion of policy priorities in the face of limited resources: "I remain convinced still that the ideological-political education of the country people [to be accomplished by, among other things, eastern settlement] is a matter for the whole party not of *secondary,* but of *primary* importance." NA, T–454, roll 89, fr. 22 ff.

39. For contrasting views of the Nazi's links to business, see Arthur Schweitzer, *Big Business and the Third Reich* (Bloomington, IN, 1964); and Henry Ashby Turner, Jr., *German Big Business and the Rise of Hitler* (New York, 1985).

40. Hildebrand, *Vom Reich zum Weltreich,* pp. 252–64; Weinberg, *Foreign Policy, 1933–1936,* pp. 220–22, 279–81, 350–55.

41. Ballhaus, "Kolonialziele," pp. 290–303; Richard Lakowski, "Der zweite Weltkrieg," in Stoecker, ed., *Drang nach Afrika,* pp. 315–19; Weinberg, *Foreign Policy, 1933–36,* pp. 279–81, 354–55.

42. Hoisington, "Struggle for Economic Influence," pp. 468–82; Wendt, "England und der deutsche 'Drang nach Südosten'," pp. 483–512. See also the interesting discussion of Germany's institutionalized relationship with the Balkans in Hans Krämer, "Zwischenstaatliche Wirtschaftslenkung nach strukturellen Massstäben," *Zeitschrift für Geopolitik* 16 (1939), pp. 377–82.

43. Hitler, *Mein Kampf,* 2: chs. 13, 14; Jacobsen, *Nationalsozialistische Aussenpolitik,* pp. 446–63; Jäckel, *Hitler's Weltanschauung,* pp. 27–38.

44. Hitler's attitude toward Great Britain is discussed in Rich, *Hitler's War Aims,* 1: pp. 157–64; Hildebrand, *Deutsche Aussenpolitik,* pp. 43–54; Hillgruber, *Hitlers Strategie,* pp. 144–91; Hildebrand, *Vom Reich zum Weltreich,* pp. 79,

441–42, 467, 652–73; Jäckel, *Hitler's Weltanschauung,* pp. 30–46. Even if one allows for the possible exaggeration of the enthusiasm Hitler shows for cooperation with Britain in *Mein Kampf,* 1: ch. 4; 2: chs. 13, 14, it remains the case that Hitler regarded Britain as a natural potential ally, along the lines laid down by the *Weltpolitik* tradition, from the mid-1920s down to 1941. Compare Hitler's view with, for example, that of Class discussed in Chapter Eight. In the 1920s, Class was still a figure of some importance.

45. See Franklin Reid Gannon, *The British Press and Germany 1936–1939* (Oxford, 1971), pp. 1–31.

46. Hitler, *Mein Kampf,* 2: chs. 13, 14. The overseas implications of Hitler's imperialism, not yet developed in *Mein Kampf* but fully present by the 1930s, are discussed in Hillgruber, *Germany and the Two World Wars,* pp. 49–55; and Hildebrand, *Vom Reich zum Weltreich,* pp. 441–67.

47. Jäckel, *Hitler's Weltanschauung,* p. 44.

48. Hildebrand, *Vom Reich zum Weltreich,* pp. 440–744 passim., presents a comprehensive analysis of the role of the colonial issue in the intricacies of Nazi policy toward Britain. In 1938, Ribbentrop summarized the ultimate aim of German policy with respect to Britain: a German alliance with Japan and other powers, like the other thrusts of German diplomacy, should threaten the British and ultimately force "England to reach an agreement with us after all," *Akten zur deutschen auswärtigen Politik 1918–1945,* Series D, 1 (1950): p. 135.

49. The negative side of Hitler's view of Britain is not apparent in *Mein Kampf,* but there is ample evidence of its existence. See Weinberg, *Foreign Policy, 1933–1936,* pp. 14–16. It became intense, however, only after the collapse of his delusions about British cooperation in 1941.

50. Albert Speer, *Inside the Third Reich,* tr. Richard and Clara Winston (New York, 1970), pp. 64–111; see also Neumann, *Behemoth,* pp. 470–76. Hitler's own early attempt to integrate a glorification of science with his other beliefs can be found in *Mein Kampf,* 2: ch. 2.

51. Lakowski, "Der zweite Weltkrieg," pp. 326–36.

52. Hildebrand, *Vom Reich zum Weltreich,* pp. 248–440.

53. Bracher, *German Dictatorship,* pp. 330–50; Hitler, *Mein Kampf,* 2: chs. 2, 4; Lane and Rupp, *Nazi Ideology,* pp. 32–40; Neumann, *Behemoth,* pp. 293–361.

54. Hildebrand, *Vom Reich zum Weltreich,* pp. 564–80; Schmokel, *Dream of Empire,* pp. 103–24; Ballhaus, "Kolonialziele," pp. 304–14.

55. Hildebrand, *Vom Reich zum Weltreich,* pp. 100–187.

56. Ibid., pp. 252, 263, 317–25, 390–440; Hillgruber, *Hitlers Strategie,* pp. 242–54; Ballhaus, "Kolonialziele," pp. 281–314.

57. Hildebrand, *Vom Reich zum Weltreich,* pp. 263, 441–42; Rich, *Hitler's War Aims,* 2: pp. 394–419.

58. Hildebrand, *Vom Reich zum Weltreich,* pp. 237–47, 652–711; Rich, *Hitler's Aims,* 2: pp. 394–419; Hildebrand, *Deutsche Aussenpolitik,* pp. 94–106.

59. Sources for the progressive, programmatic character of Hitler's war aims include Hildebrand, *Deutsche Aussenpolitik;* Hillgruber, *Germany and the Two World Wars;* Jacobsen, *Nationalsozialistische Aussenpolitik;* and Rich, *Hitler's War Aims.*

60. Once the war began, the navy became the main advocate of extra-European expansion within the government, although it had backing from other govern-

ment departments and financial concerns. Hildebrand, *Deutsche Aussenpolitik,* pp. 94–121; Lakowski, "Der zweite Weltkrieg," pp. 313–36.

61. Hillgruber, *Hitlers Strategie,* pp. 144–91, 207–41; Jäckel, *Hitler's Weltanschauung,* pp. 45–46.

62. Hildebrand, *Deutsche Aussenpolitik,* pp. 43–93.

63. Ibid., pp. 94–106. Hitler's most comprehensive statement of his expansionary intentions was, of course, the one noted in the famous Hossbach memorandum, a report of a meeting of Hitler, Foreign Minister Neurath, and the military service chiefs in November 1937. (*Akten zur deutsche auswärtigen Politik,* D, 1: no. 19.) This document deals primarily with the necessity of preparing the ground for the *Lebensraum* stage. The outlines of the *Weltpolitik* stage were delineated later.

64. Lakowski, "Der zweite Weltkrieg," pp. 314–51. On the whole, the senior colonial and foreign service officials who had been active in the colonial movement were bypassed in later Nazi colonial planning, as were suspect publicists such as Paul Rohrbach, despite the latter's attempt to make his peace with the regime. It was rather men who had held middle-level appointments at the end of the old Reich and who had been thoroughly socialized into the *Weltpolitik* ideology—people such as the former colonial officials Rudolf Asmis and Theodor Gunzert—who did the work of overseas colonial planning under Hitler. Asmis had started his career as the right-hand man of Governor Julius Graf Zech in Togo; Gunzert had been a highly reputed district officer in East Africa under Rechenberg and Schnee: impeccable credentials for *Weltpolitik* colonialists.

65. This set of priorities is made clear in the Hossbach memorandum and elsewhere. See Rich, *Hitler's War Aims,* 1: pp. 63–65, 82–83, 97.

66. On the German economy in wartime, see Alan S. Milward, *The German Economy at War* (London, 1965). On the contradictions in German Eastern policy, see Gerald Reitlinger, *The House Built on Sand: The Conflicts of German Policy in Russia, 1939–1945* (New York, 1960); and Robert L. Koehl, *RKFDV: German Resettlement and Population Policy, 1939–1945* (Cambridge, MA, 1957). Reflections of contradictions in eastern policy during the war can be found in practically any collection of records of agencies charged with implementing such policies. For example, a dispute arose late in 1939 about compensating German owners of large estates in Poland and the Baltic states whose property had been expropriated after World War I by giving them similar estates in newly occupied land. Large estates would make more sense in terms of augmenting the autarkic economy of Germany but would go against the *Lebensraum* notion of small pioneer farmsteads. Himmler decided on the latter, despite their probable immediate economic inefficiency. NA, T–454, roll 89, fr. 58 ff. (letter: Himmler to Rosenberg, 29 December 1939).

67. On the background to Hitler's declaration of war on the United States, see Hillgruber, *Hitlers Strategie,* pp. 192–206; and Rich, *Hitler's War Aims,* 1: pp. 224–46. Even before 1941, however, the ambiguities of Germany's interests in China had suggested serious problems for future German–Japanese relations.

68. Rich, *Hitler's War Aims,* 2: pp. 394–419.

Bibliography

Archival sources

Bundesarchiv Koblenz
> Bestand R13I (records of *Wirtschaftsgruppe Eisenschaffende Industrie,* incorporating records of VDES)
> Moritz Bonn papers
> Lujo von Brentano papers
> Leo von Caprivi papers
> Bernhard Dernburg papers
> Walter Frank papers
> Georg Gothein papers
> Karl Haushofer papers
> *Kleine Erwerbungen,* nos. 10, 12, 141, 275, 353
> Oswald Freiherr von Richthofen papers
> Max Sering papers
> Wilhelm Solf papers

Hoover Institution, Stanford, California
> Microfilms of records from the files of the German Colonial Office relating to meetings of the *Vorstand* of the German Colonial Society and to meetings of the *Kolonialrat;* originals in the *Zentrales Staatsarchiv,* Potsdam.

Library of Congress, Washington, DC
> Microfilms of German Foreign Office records relating to Franco–German relations
> Photostats of German Foreign Ministry records relating to emigration to the United States

National Archives, Washington, DC
> Microfilms of German Foreign Office records (T–120, 137–139, 149, 291)
> Microfilms of German Navy records (T–1022)
> Microfilms of Karl Haushofer papers (T–253)
> Microfilms of records of Reich Ministry for the Occupied Eastern Territories 1941–1945 (T–454)

Government Publications

Akten zur deutschen auswärtigen Politik 1918–1945, Series D, 1 (1950).
Kolonialabteilung. *Denkschrift über die im südwestafrikanischen Schutzgebiete tätigen Land- und Minengesellschaften.* Berlin, 1905.
————. *Die Entwicklung unserer Kolonien.* Berlin, 1892.
Stenographische Berichte über die Verhandlungen des Reichstages

Newspapers and periodicals

Alldeutsche Blätter
Deutsche Kolonialzeitung
Deutsche Politik
Deutsches Kolonialblatt
Frankfurter Zeitung
Globus
Die Grenzboten
Die Hilfe
Historische Zeitschrift
Koloniale Rundschau
Norddeutsche Allgemeine Zeitung
Nord und Süd
Preussische Jahrlbücher
Süddeutsche Monatshefte
Der Türmer
Zeitschrift für die gesammte Staatswissenschaft
Zeitschrift für Geopolitik

Primary sources

"Alldeutsch." *Grossdeutschland und Mitteleuropa um das Jahr 1950.* 2nd ed. Berlin, 1895.
Alldeutscher Verband. *Zwanzig Jahre alldeutscher Arbeit und Kämpfe.* Berlin, 1910.
Anonymous. *Deutsche Weltpolitik und kein Krieg!* Berlin, 1913.
————. "Zum Schutz der deutschen Landschaft." *Die Grenzboten* 51 (1892), no. 40, pp. 31–33.
Bang, Paul. *Deutsche Wirtschaftsziele.* Langensalza, 1926.
Baynes, Norman H. Ed. *The Speeches of Adolf Hitler April 1922–August 1939.* 2 vols. London, 1942. Repr. New York, 1969.
Bekerath, E., et al. Eds. *Friedrich List: Schriften, Reden, Briefe.* 10 vols. Berlin, 1952.
Bericht über die Verhandlungen des 19. Kongresses deutscher Volkswirte in Berlin. Berlin, 1880.
Bernhard, Georg. *Land oder Geld?* Berlin, 1916.
Bernhardi, Friedrich von. *Deutschland und der nächste Krieg.* Stuttgart and Berlin, 1912.
Bethmann Hollweg, Theobald von. *Bertrachtungen zum Weltkriege.* 2 vols. Berlin, 1919.
Bodner, M.J. *Ein neuer Staatenbund und das Ostjuden Problem.* Berlin, 1916.

Bongard, Oskar. *Staatsekretär Dernburg in Britisch- und Deutsch-Südafrika.* Berlin, n.d.

Bonn, Moritz J. *Die Neugestaltung unserer kolonialen Aufgaben.* Tübingen, 1911.

Brauns, Ernst. *Ideen über die Auswanderung nach Amerika.* Göttingen, 1827.

Brentano, Lujo. *Mein Leben im Kampf um die soziale Entwicklung Deutschlands.* Jena, 1931.

Bucher, Lothar. *Kleine Schriften politischen Inhalts.* Stuttgart, 1893.

Bücher, Karl, et al. *Die Grossstadt.* Dresden, 1903.

Bülow, Bernhard Fürst von. *Denkwürdigkeiten.* 4 vols. Berlin, 1930.

Chakotin, Serge. *The Rape of the Masses: The Psychology of Totalitarian Political Propaganda.* London, 1940.

Class, Heinrich. *Denkschrift betreffend die national-, wirtschafts-, und sozialpolitischen Ziele des deutschen Volkes im gegenwärtigen Kriege.* N.p., 1914.

―――. *Wider den Strom. Vom Werden und Wachsen der nationalen Opposition im alten Reich.* Leipzig, 1932.

―――. *Zum deutschen Kriegsziel.* Munich, 1917.

Dannenberg, H. L. *Sieg ohne Landgewinn?* Dresden, 1918.

Darré, R. W. *Das Bauerntum als Lebensquell der nordischen Rasse.* Munich, 1929.

Dehn, Paul. *Von deutscher Kolonial- und Weltpolitik.* Berlin, 1907.

Dernburg, Bernhard. *Koloniale Lehrjahre.* Stuttgart, 1907.

―――. *"Unser Friede."* Frankfurt am Main, 1918.

―――. *Zielpunkte des deutschen Kolonialwesens.* Berlin, 1907.

Deutsche Kolonialgesellschaft. *Die Deutsche Kolonialgesellschaft.* Berlin, 1908.

Deutsches Kolonial-Handbuch. 1913 edition. Berlin, 1913.

Ebel, Gerhard. Ed. *Botschafter Paul Graf von Hatzfeldt nachgelassene Papiere 1838–1901.* 2 vols. Boppard am Rhein, 1976.

Erzberger, Matthias. *Die Kolonial-Bilanz.* Berlin, 1906.

Fabarius, G. A. *Neue Wege der deutschen Kolonialpolitik nach dem Kriege.* Berlin, 1916.

Fabri, Friedrich. *Bedarf Deutschland der Colonien?* Gotha, 1879.

―――. *Fünf Jahre deutscher Kolonialpolitik.* Gotha, 1889.

Foerster, E. Th. *Das Konzessionsunwessen in den Deutschen Schutzgebieten.* Berlin, 1903.

Fonck, Hh. *Farbige Hilfsvölker. Die militarische Bedeutung von Kolonien für unsere nationale Zukunft.* Berlin, 1917.

Friedrich, J. K. Julius. *Kolonialpolitik als Wissenschaft. Ein neues Forschungsgebiet der Rechtphilosophie.* Berlin and Leipzig, 1909.

Frobenius, Leo. *Die Möglichkeit einer deutsch-innerafrikanischen Luftflottenstation.* Berlin, 1913.

Fröbel, Julius. *Die deutsche Auswanderung und ihre kulturhistorische Bedeutung.* Leipzig, 1858.

"Frymann, Daniel." (Heinrich Class). *Wenn ich der Kaiser wär. Politische Wahrheiten und Notwendigkeiten.* Leipzig, 1912.

Gagern, Heinrich von. *Deutscher Liberalismus im Vormärz: Heinrich von Gagern, Briefe und Reden 1815–1848.* 2 vols. Göttingen, 1959.

Gerth, H. H., and Mills, C. Wright. Eds. *From Max Weber: Essays in Sociology.* New York, 1958.

Götzen, Gustav Adolf, Graf von. *Deutsch-Ostafrika im Aufstand 1905/6.* Berlin, 1909.

Grimm, Hans. *Der Schriftsteller und die Zeit.* Munich, 1931.
———. *Suchen und Hoffen. Aus meinem Leben 1928 bis 1934.* Lippoldsberg, 1960.
———. *Volk ohne Raum.* Munich, 1932.
———. *Von der bürgerlichen Ehre und bürgerlichen Notwendigkeit.* Munich, 1932.
Hahn, Eduard. *Die Entstehung der wirtschaftlichen Arbeit.* Heidelberg, 1908.
Hasse, Ernst. *Deutsche Politik,* 3 vols. in 19 parts. Munich, 1905.
———. "Was können und sollen wir jetzt für die deutsche Auswanderung thun?" *Deutsche Kolonialzeitung,* 15 December 1884.
Haushofer, Karl. "Geographische Grundzüge auswärtiger Politik." *Süddeutsche Monatshefte* 24 (1926–27). Pp. 258 ff.
———. "Geopolitische Einflüsse bei den Verkörperungsversuchungen von nationalen Sozialismus und sozialer Aristokratie." *Zeitschrift für Geopolitik* 1 (1924). Pp. 127–34.
———. *Das japanische Reich in seiner geographischen Entwicklung.* Vienna, 1921.
———. *Weltpolitik von heute.* Berlin, 1936.
Helfferich, Karl. *Zur Reform der kolonialen Verwaltungs-Organisation.* Berlin, 1905
Hesse, Fritz. "Das Gesetz der wachsende Räume." *Zeitschrift für Geopolitik* 1 (1924). Pp. 1–4.
Hitler, Adolf. *Mein Kampf.* New York, 1939.
Hobohm, Martin, and Rohrbach, Paul. *Die Alldeutschen.* Berlin, 1919.
Hoffmann, Karl. *Das Ende des kolonialpolitischen Zeitalters.* Leipzig, 1917.
Hübbe-Schleiden, Wilhelm. *Deutsche Colonisation.* Hamburg, 1881.
———. *Überseeische Politik, eine culturwissenschaftliche Studie.* Hamburg, 1881.
Hundeshagen, Friedrich. *Deutsche Auswanderung als Nationalsache.* Frankfurt am Main, 1849.
Jäckh, Ernst. *Der goldene Pflug. Lebensernte eines Weltbürgers.* Stuttgart, 1954.
———. Ed. *Kiderlen-Wächter, der Staatsmann und Mensch. Briefwechsel und Nachlass.* 2 vols. Stuttgart, 1924.
Kapp, Friedrich. *Über Auswanderung.* Berlin, 1871.
———. *Vom radikalen Frühsozialisten der Vormärz zum liberalen Parteipolitiker des Bismarckreichs: Briefe, 1843–1884.* Ed. Hans-Ulrich Wehler. Frankfurt am Main, 1969.
Kardorff, Wilhelm von. *Bebel oder Peters?* Berlin, 1907.
Karstedt, Oskar. *Deutschlands koloniale Not.* Berlin, 1917.
Krämer, Hans. "Zwischenstaatliche Wirtschaftlenkung nach strukturellen Masstäben." *Zeitschrift für Geopolitik* 16 (1939). Pp. 377–82.
Kühlmann, Richard. *Erinnerungen.* Heidelberg, 1948.
Lehmann, Emil. *Die deutsche Auswanderung.* Berlin, 1861.
Lepsius, Johannes, et al., Eds. *Die Grosse Politik der europäischen Kabinette, 1871–1914.* 40 vols. Berlin, 1922–27.
Leutwein, Paul. *Mitteleuropa–Mittelafrika.* Dresden, 1917.
Leutwein, Theodor. *Elf Jahre Gouverneur in Deutsch Südwestafrika.* Berlin, 1908.
Liebert, Eduard von. *Aus einem bewegten Leben. Erinnerungen.* Munich, 1925.
List, Frederick. *National System of Political Economy.* Tr. G. A. Matile. Philadelphia, 1856.

Lynar, Ernst W. Graf von Lynar. Ed. *Deutsche Kriegsziele 1914–1918.* Darmstadt, 1964.

Memoirs of Prince Chlodwig of Hohenlohe-Schillingsfuerst. Tr. and Ed. G. W. Chrystal. 2 vols. New York, 1966.

Mendelssohn-Bartholdy, Albrecht. *The War and German Society: The Testament of a Liberal.* New York, 1971.

Michaelis, H. Ed. *Ursachen und Folgen. Vom deutschen Zusammenbruch 1918 und 1945 bis staatlichen Neuordnung Deutschlands in der Gegenwart.* 8 vols. Berlin, 1959.

Mohl, Robert. "Ueber Auswanderung." *Zeitschrift für die gesammte Staatswissenschaft* 4 (1847). Pp. 320–49.

Mosse, George W. *The Crisis of German Ideology: Intellectual Origins of the Third Reich.* New York, 1964.

Naumann, Friedrich. *Ausgewählte Schriften.* Frankfurt am Main, 1949.

———. *Demokratie und Kaisertum: Ein Handbuch für innere Politik.* Berlin, 1900.

———. *Mitteleuropa.* Berlin, 1915.

Noske, Gustav. *Kolonialpolitik und Sozialdemokratie.* Stuttgart, 1914.

Obst, Erich. *Die Vernichtung des deutschen Kolonialreichs in Afrika.* Berlin, 1921.

Peters, Carl. *Gesammelte Schriften.* Ed. Walter Frank. 3 vols. Munich, 1943.

———. *Zum Weltpolitik.* Berlin, 1912.

Pfeil, Joachim Graf von. "Marokko." *Verhandlungen des Deutschen Kolonialkongresses 1905.* Pp. 910–18.

Puttkamer, Jesko von. *Gouverneursjahre in Kamerun.* Berlin, 1912.

Radlauer, Ernst Ludwig. *Die lokale Selbstverwaltung der kolonialen Finanzen.* Breslau, 1909.

Rathenau, Walther. *Tagebuch 1907–1922.* Ed. H. Pogge von Strandmann. Düsseldorf, 1967.

———. *Von kommenden Dingen.* Berlin, 1917.

Ratzel, Friedrich (published anonymously). "Ein Beitrag zu den Anfängen der deutschen Kolonialpolitik." *Die Grenzboten* 62 (1903), no. 2, pp. 115–16.

———. *Deutschland. Einführung in die Heimatkunde.* 7th ed. Berlin, 1943.

———. *Die Erde und das Leben. Eine vergleichende Erdkunde.* 2 vols. Leipzig and Vienna, 1901.

———. "Geschichte, Völkerkunde und historische Perspektive." *Historische Zeitschrift* 93 (1904). Pp. 1–46.

———. *Jugenderinnerungen.* Munich, 1966.

———. "Der Lebensraum. Eine biogeographische Studie," in K. Bücher et al., *Festgaben für Albert Schäffle* . . . Tübingen, 1901. Pp. 101–89.

———. "Die mitteleuropäische Wirtschaftsverein." *Die Grenzboten* 63 (1904), no. 5, pp. 253–59.

———. "Mythen und Einfälle über die Ursprung der Völker." *Globus* 78 (1900), no. 2, pp. 21–25.

———. *Politische Geographie.* 3rd ed. Munich and Berlin, 1923.

———. *Völkerkunde.* 2 vols. 2nd rev. ed. Leipzig and Vienna, 1894.

———. "In welcher Richtung beeinflussen die afrikanischen Ereignisse die Thätigkeit des Kolonialvereins?" *DKZ*, 15 January 1885. Pp. 38–44.

———. *Wider die Reichsnörgler. Ein Wort zur Kolonialfrage aus Wählerkreisen.* Munich, 1884.

Rechenberg, Albrecht Freiherr von. "Kriegs- und Friedensziele." *Nord und Süd* 41 (1917). Pp. 131–43.

Rich, Norman, and Fisher, M. H. Eds. *The Holstein Papers.* Cambridge, 1955.

Riezler, Kurt. *Tagebücher, Aufsätze, Dokumente.* Ed. K. D. Erdmann. Göttingen, 1972.

Rodbertus-Jagetzow, Carl. *Zur Beleuchtung der socialen Frage.* Eds. A. Wagner and T. Kozak. Berlin, 1875.

Röhl, John C. G. Ed. *Philipp Eulenburgs politische Korrespondenz.* 2 vols. Boppard am Rhein, 1976.

Rohrbach, Paul. Ed. *Die alldeutsche Gefahr.* Berlin, 1918.

———. *Die Bagdadbahn.* 2nd ed. Berlin, 1911.

———. *Briefe über Demokratie und Pazifismus.* Dresden, 1925.

———. *Dernburg und die Südwestafrikaner. Diamantenfrage, Selbstverwaltung, Landeshilfe.* Berlin, 1911.

———. *Der deutsche Gedanke in der Welt.* Düsseldorf and Leipzig, 1912.

———. *Deutsch Südwestafrika, ein Ansiedlungsgebiet.* Berlin, n.d.

———. "England und Russland, unsere Gegner." *Deutsche Politik,* 1 January 1916. Pp. 2–11.

———. "Klarheit im Osten." *Deutsche Politik,* 14 April 1916. Pp. 705–11.

———. *Die Kolonie.* Frankfurt am Main, 1907.

———. "Das Kriegsziel im Schützgraben." *Deutsche Politik,* 4 February 1916. Pp. 241–47.

———. *Um des Teufels Handschrift. Zwei Menschenalter erlebter Weltgeschichte.* Hamburg, 1953.

———. "Weltvolk—Seevolk." *Deutsche Politik,* 8 February 1916. Pp. 337–42.

Rohrbach, Paul, and Rohrbach, Justus. *Afrika heute und morgen.* Berlin, 1939.

Roscher, Wilhelm. *Kolonien, Kolonialpolitik, und Auswanderung.* 2nd ed. Leipzig and Heidelberg, 1856.

SPD. *Die deutsche Kolonialpolitik.* Berlin, 1907.

Samassa, Paul. *Die Besiedlung Deutsch-Ostafrikas.* Berlin, 1909.

Schäfer, Dietrich. *Kolonialgeschichte.* 2 vols. Berlin, 1922.

———. *Mein Leben.* Berlin, 1926.

———. "Die politische und militärische Bedeutung der Grossstädte," in K. Bücher et al., *Die Grossstadt.* Dresden, 1903. Pp. 231–82.

Scharlach, Julius. *Koloniale und politische Aufsätze und Reden.* Berlin, n.d.

Schiemann, Theodor. *Wie England eine Verständigung mit Deutschland verhinderte.* Berlin, 1915.

Schmidt, Geo A. *Das Kolonial-Wirtschaftliche Komitee.* Berlin, 1934.

Schmölders, Günther, and Vogel, Walther. *Wirtschaft und Raum.* Hamburg, 1937.

Schnee, Heinrich. Ed. *Deutsches Kolonial-Lexikon.* 3 vols. Leipzig, 1920.

Schöllenbach, Hans Oelhafen von. *Die Besiedlung Deutsch-Südwestafrikas bis zum Weltkriege.* Berlin, 1926.

Schütze, Woldemar. *Schwarz gegen Weiss. Die Eingeborenenfrage als Kernpunkt unserer Kolonialpolitik in Afrika.* Berlin, 1908.

Schwerin, Friedrich von. *Kriegersansiedlung vergangenen Zeiten.* Leipzig, 1917.

Sering, Max. *Die innere Kolonisation in östlichen Deutschland.* Leipzig, 1893.

Solf, Wilhelm. *Germany's Right to Recover her Colonies.* Berlin, 1919.

———. *Kolonialpolitik. Mein politisches Vermächtnis.* Berlin, 1919.

———. *Die Lehren des Weltkriegs für unsere Kolonialpolitik.* Berlin, 1916.

————. *Die Missionen in den deutschen Schutzgebieten*. Berlin, 1918.

————. *Die Zukunft Afrikas*. Berlin, 1918.

Speer, Albert. *Inside the Third Reich*. Tr. Richard and Clara Winston. New York, 1970.

Stern, Jacques. *"Mitteleuropa." Von Leibniz bis Naumann über List und Frantz, Planck und Lagarde*. Stuttgart and Berlin, 1916.

Stuhlmann, Franz. *Beiträge zur Kulturgeschichte von Ostafrika*. Berlin, 1909.

Tiessen, Ernst. "Der Friedensvertrag von Versailles und die politische Geographie." *Zeitschrift für Geopolitik* 1 (1924). Pp. 203–19.

Tille, Alexander. "Die wirtschaftliche Grundlage und die Entwickelung der deutschen Auswanderung seit 1871." *Verhandlungen des Deutschen Kolonialkongresses 1902*. Pp. 597–609.

Treitschke, Heinrich von. *Politics*. Tr. B. Dugdale and T. de Bille. 2 vols. London, 1916.

Verhandlungen des Deutschen Kolonialkongresses 1902. Berlin, 1903.

Verhandlungen des Deutschen Kolonialkongresses 1905. Berlin, 1906.

Verhandlungen des Deutschen Kolonialkongresses 1910. Berlin, 1910.

Vietor, J. K. von. "Die Arbeiterfrage in den deutschen Kolonien." *Verhandlungen des Deutschen Kolonialkongresses 1902*. Berlin, 1903. Pp. 518–24.

————. "Der Handel der deutschen Kolonien." *Verhandlungen des Deutschen Kolonialkongresses 1905*. Berlin, 1906. Pp. 629–37.

————. *Wirtschaftliche und kulturelle Entwicklung unserer Schutzgebieten*. Berlin, 1913.

Virchow, Rudolf. "Acclimatisation," in *Verhandlungen der Berliner Gesellschaft für Anthropologie, Ethnologie und Urgeschichte*. Berlin, 1885. Pp. 202–14.

————. *Sozialismus und Reaktion*. Berlin, 1878.

Vowinckel, Kurt. "Zum Begriff Lebensraum." *Zeitschrift für Geopolitik* 16 (1939). Pp. 638–39.

Wagner, Moritz. *Die Darwinische Theorie und das Migrationsgesetz der Organismen*. Munich, 1868.

Wagner, Moritz, and Scherzer, Carl. *Die Republik Costa Rica in Central Amerika*. Leipzig, 1856.

Weber, Ernst von. *Die Erweiterung des deutschen Wirtschaftsgebiets und die Grundlegung zu überseeischen deutschen Staaten*. Leipzig, 1879.

Weber, Hans Siegfried. *Ansiedlung von Kriegsinvaliden*. Berlin, 1916.

————. *Rucksiedlung Auslanddeutscher nach dem Deutschen Reiche*. Jena, 1915.

Weber, Max. *Gesammelte politische Schriften*. Ed. Johannes Winckelmann. 3rd ed. Tübingen, 1971.

Werner, C. von. *Antrag des Abgeordeneten von Werner, die Bildung eines Emigrations- und Colonisations-Verein betreffend*. N.p., n.d., c. 1842.

Westermann, Diedrich. *Afrika als europäische Aufgabe*. Berlin, 1941.

Wigard, Franz. Ed. *Stenographischer Bericht über der deutschen constituierenden Nationalversammlung zu Frankfurt am Main*. 9 vols. Leipzig, 1848.

Wirth, Albrecht. *Deutschland und der Orient*. Frankfurt am Main, n.d.

Wohltmann, F. *Der Landwirt und die deutschen Kolonien*. Flysheet, KWK. N.p., n.d.

————. *Die nationale und ethische Bedeutung unserer Kolonien*. Berlin, 1908.

————. "Die wirtschaftliche Entwickelung unserer Kolonien." *Verhandlunen des Deutschen Kolonialkongresses 1902*. Berlin, 1903. Pp. 494–507.

Wuttke, Robert. "Der Arbeiter und der Getreidezoll." *Die Grenzboten* 62 (1903), no. 24, pp. 621–28.

————. "Der Kampf um der Weltmarkt." *Die Grenzboten* 62 (1903), no. 27, pp. 1–10; no. 28, pp. 71–81.

Zimmermann, Alfred. *Geschichte der Deutschen Kolonialpolitik.* Berlin, 1914.

Zimmermann, Emil. *Das deutsche Kaiserreich Mittelafrika als Grundlage einer neuen deutschen Weltpolitik.* Berlin, 1917.

————. *Kann uns Mesopotamien eigene Kolonien ersetzen?* Berlin, 1917.

————. *Mittelafrika als deutsche Kolonie.* Berlin, n.d., c. 1914–18.

————. *Neu-Kamerun. Reiseerlebnisse und wirtschaftspolitische Untersuchungen.* Berlin, 1913.

Secondary sources

Abraham, David. *The Collapse of the Weimar Republic: Political Economy and Crisis.* Princeton, 1981.

Albertini, Rudolf von. *Europäische Kolonialherrschaft 1880–1940.* Zurich, 1976.

Almond, Gabriel, and Powell, C. Bingham, Jr. *Comparative Politics: System, Process, and Policy.* 2nd ed. Boston, 1978.

Anderson, Eugene N. *The First Moroccan Crisis 1904–1906.* Chicago, 1930.

Anderson, Pauline. *The Background of Anti-English Feeling in Germany, 1890–1902.* New York, 1969 (repr.).

Appleby, Joyce. "Ideology and Theory: The Tension between Political and Economic Liberalism in Seventeenth-Century England." *American Historical Review* 81 (1976). Pp. 499–515.

Apter, David E. Ed. *Ideology and Discontent.* New York, 1964.

Ayçoberry, Pierre. *The Nazi Question. An Essay on the Interpretation of National Socialism (1922–1975).* New York, 1981.

Aydelotte, William O. *Bismarck and British Colonial Policy; The Problem of South-West Africa, 1883–1885.* Philadelphia, 1937.

Bade, Klaus J. *Friedrich Fabri und der Imperialismus in der Bismarckzeit: Revolution-Depression-Expansion.* Freiburg, 1975.

————. Ed. *Imperialismus und Kolonialmission. Kaiserliches Deutschland und koloniales Imperium.* Wiesbaden, 1982.

Bald, Detlef. *Deutsch-Ostafrika 1900–1914.* Munich, 1970.

Ballhaus, Jolanda. "Kolonialziele und -vorbereitungen des faschistischen Regimes 1933–1939," in H. Stoecker, ed., *Drang nach Afrika.* Berlin, 1970. Pp. 281–314.

Barkin, Kenneth D. *The Controversy over German Industrialization 1890–1902.* Chicago and London, 1970.

Bell, Daniel, *The End of Ideology: On the Exhaustion of Political Ideas in the Fifties.* 2nd rev. ed. New York, 1962.

Berger, Peter L., and Luckmann, Thomas. *The Social Construction of Reality. A Treatise in the Sociology of Knowledge.* Garden City, NY, 1966.

Berghahn, Volker R. *Germany and the Approach of War in 1914.* London, 1973.

————. *Der Tirpitz-Plan. Genesis und Verfall einer innerpolitischen Krisenstrategie unter Wilhelm II.* Düsseldorf, 1971.

Bergmann, Klaus. *Agrarromantik und Grossstadtfeindschaft.* Meisenheim am Glan, 1970.

Berndt, Roswitha. "Wirtschaftliche Mitteleuropapläne des deutschen Imperialismus (1926–31)," in Gilbert Ziebura, ed., *Grundfragen der deutschen Aussenpolitik seit 1871.* Darmstadt, 1975. Pp. 305–34.

Betts, Raymond F. *The False Dawn: European Imperialism in the Nineteenth Century.* Minneapolis, 1975.

Blanke, Richard. "Bismarck and the Prussian Polish Policies of 1886." *Journal of Modern History* 45 (1973). Pp. 211–39.

Bley, Helmut. *South-West Africa under German Rule 1894–1914.* Tr. Hugh Ridley. Evanston, IL, 1971.

Böhme, Helmut. "Big Business, Pressure Groups, and Bismarck's Turn to Protectionism, 1873–1879." *Historical Journal* 10 (1967). Pp. 224–35.

———. *Deutschlands Weg zur Grossmacht: Studien zum Verhältnis von Wirtschaft und Staat während der Reichsgründungszeit 1848–1881.* Cologne, 1966.

Borowsky, Peter. *Deutsche Ukrainepolitik 1918.* Lübeck and Hamburg, 1970.

Bracher, Karl Dietrich. *The German Dictatorship: The Origins, Structure, and Effects of National Socialism.* New York, 1970.

Bramsted, Ernest K. *Goebbels and National Socialist Propaganda, 1925–1945.* East Lansing, 1965.

Bruch, Rüdiger vom. *Weltpolitik als Kulturmission: Auswärtige Kulturpolitik und Bildungsbürgertum in Deutschland am Vorabend des Ersten Weltkrieges.* Paderborn, 1982.

Brunschwig, Henri. *L'expansion allemande outre-mer du xve siècle à nos jours.* Paris, 1957.

Die bürgerlichen Parteien Deutschlands. 2 vols. Leipzig, 1968.

Buttmann, Günther. *Friedrich Ratzel. Leben und Werk eines deutschen Geographen.* Stuttgart, 1977.

Cecil, Lamar. *Albert Ballin: Business and Politics in Imperial Germany, 1888–1918.* Princeton, 1967.

———. *The German Diplomatic Service, 1871–1914.* Princeton, 1976.

Chickering, Roger. *We Men Who Feel Most German: A Cultural Study of the Pan-German League 1886–1914.* London, 1984.

Craig, Gordon A. *The Politics of the Prussian Army 1640–1945.* New York, 1964.

Crothers, George Dunlop. *The German Elections of 1907.* New York, 1941.

Dorpalen, Andreas. *The World of General Haushofer: Geopolitics in Action.* New York, 1942.

Drechsler, Horst. *Südwestafrika unter deutscher Kolonialherrschaft.* Berlin, 1966.

Earle, Edward Meade. *Turkey, the Great Powers, and the Baghdad Railway: A Study in Imperialism.* New York, 1923.

Eley, Geoff. "Defining Social Imperialism: Use and Abuse of an Idea." *Social History* 3 (1976). Pp. 265–90.

———. *Reshaping the German Right: Radical Nationalism and Political Change after Bismarck.* New Haven and London, 1980.

———. "Some Thoughts on the Nationalist Pressure Groups in Imperial Germany," in P. M. Kennedy and A. Nicholls, eds., *Nationalist and Racialist Movements in Britain and Germany Before 1914.* London, 1981. Pp. 40–67.

Epstein, Klaus W. *Matthias Erzberger and the Dilemma of German Democracy.* Princeton, 1959.

Feldman, Gerald D. *Army Industry and Labor in Germany 1914–1918.* Princeton, 1966.

———. *German Imperialism, 1914–18: The Development of a Historical Debate.* New York, 1972.

Festinger, Leon. *A Theory of Cognitive Dissonance.* New York, 1957.

Fischer, Fritz. *Germany's Aims in the First World War.* New York, 1967.

————. *War of Illusions: German Policies from 1911 to 1914.* New York, 1975.

Gagliardo, John G. *From Pariah to Patriot: The Changing Image of the German Peasant 1770–1840.* Lexington, KY, 1969.

Gann, L. H., and Duignan, Peter. Eds. *African Proconsuls. European Governors in Africa.* New York, 1978.

————. *The Rulers of German Africa 1884–1914.* Stanford, CA, 1977.

Gannon, Franklin Reid. *The British Press and Germany 1936–1939.* Oxford, 1971.

Ganslmayr, H. "Moritz Wagner und seine Bedeutung für die Ethnologie," in *Verhandlungen des XXXVIII. Internationalen Amerikanisten Kongresses . . . 1968.* Munich, 1969. Vol. 4. Pp. 459–70.

Gasman, Daniel. *The Scientific Origins of National Socialism: Social Darwinism in Ernst Haeckel and the German Monist League.* London and New York, 1971.

Gatzke, Hans W. *Germany's Drive to the West: A Study of Germany's Western War Aims During the First World War.* Baltimore, 1950.

Geertz, Clifford. *The Interpretation of Cultures. Selected Essays.* New York, 1973.

Geiss, Imanuel. *German Foreign Policy, 1871–1914.* London and Boston, 1976.

————. *Der polnische Grenzstreifen 1914–1918.* Lübeck, 1960.

Geiss, Immanuel, and Wendt, Bernd Jürgen. Eds. *Deutschland in der Weltpolitik des 19. und 20. Jahrhunderts.* Düsseldorf, 1973.

Geissler, Rolf. *Dekadenz und Heroismus. Zeitroman und völkisch-nationalsozialistische Literaturkritik.* Stuttgart, 1964.

Gellately, Robert. *The Politics of Economic Despair: Shopkeepers and German Politics, 1890–1914.* Beverly Hills, 1974.

Gifford, Prosser, and Louis, Wm. Roger. Eds. *Britain and Germany in Africa: Imperial Rivalry and Colonial Rule.* New Haven, 1967.

Gilson, R. P. *Samoa 1830–1900: The Politics of a Multi-Cultural Community.* Melbourne, 1970.

Gollwitzer, Heinz. *Europe in the Age of Imperialism 1880–1914.* London, 1969.

————. *Die gelbe Gefahr. Geschichte eines Schlagwortes.* Göttingen, 1962.

————. *Geschichte des weltpolitischen Denkens.* 2 vols. Göttingen, 1972, 1982.

Gordon, Michael R. "Domestic Conflict and the Origins of the First World War." *Journal of Modern History* 46 (1974). Pp. 191–226.

Gossweiler, Kurt. *Grossbanken Industriemonopole Staat. Ökonomie und Politik des staatsmonopolistischen Kapitalismus in Deutschland 1914–1932.* Berlin, 1971.

Grathwol, Robert. "Gustav Stresemann: Reflections on His Foreign Policy." *Journal of Modern History* 45 (1973). Pp. 52–70.

————. *Stresemann and the DNVP: Reconciliation or Revenge in German Foreign Policy.* Lawrence, KS, 1980.

Guillen, Pierre. *L'allemagne et le Maroc de 1870 à 1905.* Paris, 1967.

Guratzsch, Dankwart. *Macht durch Organisation. Die Grundlegung des Hugenbergschen Presseimperiums.* Düsseldorf, 1974.

Hallgarten, George W. F. *Imperialismus vor 1914.* 2 vols. Munich, 1951.

Hamerow, Theodore S. *Restoration Revolution Reaction: Economics and Politics in Germany 1815–1871.* Princeton, 1958.

————. *The Social Foundations of German Unification, 1858–71.* 2 vols. Princeton, 1969, 1972.

Hamilton, Richard F. *Who Voted for Hitler?* Princeton, 1982.

Hansen, Marcus L. *German Schemes of Colonization before 1860.* Northampton, MA, 1923–24.

Hausen, Karin. *Deutsche Kolonialherrschaft in Afrika: Wirtschaftsinteresse und Kolonialverwaltung in Kamerun vor 1914.* Zurich, 1970.

Heckart, Beverly. *From Bassermann to Bebel: The Grand Bloc's Quest for Reform in the Kaiserreich, 1900–1914.* New Haven, 1974.

Henderson, W. O. *Studies in German Colonial History.* Chicago, 1962.

Hertzman, Lewis. *DNVP: Right-Wing Opposition in the Weimar Republic, 1918–1924.* Lincoln, NE, 1963.

Herwig, Holger. *The German Naval Officer Corps: A Social and Political History, 1890–1918.* New York, 1973.

Heuss, Theodor. *Friedrich Naumann. Der Mann, das Werk, die Zeit.* Stuttgart, 1937.

Hildebrand, Klaus. *Deutsche Aussenpolitik 1933–1945. Kalkül oder Dogma?* Stuttgart, 1971.

———. *Vom Reich zum Weltreich. NSDAP und koloniale Frage 1919–1945.* Munich, 1969.

Hillgruber, Andreas. *Germany and the Two World Wars.* Cambridge, MA, 1981.

———. *Hitlers Strategie. Politik und Kriegführung 1940–1941.* Frankfurt am Main, 1965.

Hoisington, William A. "The Struggle for Economic Influence in Southeastern Europe: The French Failure in Rumania, 1940." *Journal of Modern History* 43 (1971). Pp. 468–82.

Hubatsch, Walther. *Die Ära Tirpitz. Studien zur deutschen Marinepolitik 1890–1918.* Göttingen, 1955.

Iliffe, John. *Tanganyika under German Rule, 1905–1912.* Cambridge, 1969.

International Encyclopedia of the Social Sciences. 18 vols. in 9 books. New York, 1968.

Jacobsen, Hans-Adolf. *Karl Haushofer—Leben und Werk.* 2 vols. Boppard am Rhein, 1979.

———. *Nationalsozialistische Aussenpolitik 1933–1938.* Frankfurt am Main and Berlin, 1968.

Jacobson, John. *Locarno Diplomacy. Germany and the West 1925–1929.* Princeton, 1972.

Jäckel, Eberhard. *Hitler's Weltanschauung: A Blueprint for Power.* Tr. Herbert Arnold. Middletown, CT, 1972.

Jaeger, Hans. *Unternehmer in der deutsche Politik, 1890–1918.* Berlin, 1967.

Jarausch, Konrad H. *The Enigmatic Chancellor: Bethmann Hollweg and the Hubris of Imperial Germany.* New Haven and London, 1973.

———. "The Illusion of Limited War: Bethmann Hollweg's Calculated Risk," *Central European History* 2 (1969). Pp. 48–76.

Jerussalimski, A. S. *Die Aussenpolitik und die Diplomatie des deutschen Imperialismus Ende des 19. Jahrhunderts.* Berlin, 1954.

Kaelble, Hartmut. *Industrielle Interessenpolitik in der Wilhelmischen Gesellschaft. Centralverband deutscher Industrieller, 1885–1914.* Berlin, 1967.

———. "Social Mobility in Germany, 1900–1960." *Journal of Modern History* 50 (1978). Pp. 439–61.

Kehr, Eckart. *Battleship Building and Party Politics in Germany 1894–1901.* Tr. P. R. and E. N. Anderson. Chicago and London, 1973.

———. *Der Primat der Innenpolitik. Gesammelte Aufsätze zur preussisch-*

deutschen Sozialgeschichte im 19. und 20. Jahrhundert. Ed. H.-U. Wehler. Berlin, 1965.

Kelly, Alfred. *The Descent of Darwin. The Popularization of Darwinism in Germany, 1860–1914*. Chapel Hill, 1981.

Kennedy, Paul M. "German Colonial Expansion: Has the Manipulated Social Imperialism Been Antedated?" *Past and Present* 54 (1972). Pp. 134–41.

———. *The Rise of the Anglo-German Antagonism 1860–1914*. London, 1980.

———. *The Samoan Tangle: A Study in Anglo–German–American Relations, 1878–1900*. New York, 1977.

Kennedy, Paul M., and Moses, John A. Eds. *Germany in the Pacific and Far East, 1870–1914*. St. Lucia, 1977.

Kennedy, Paul M., and Nicholls, Anthony. Eds. *Nationalist and Racialist Movements in Britain and Germany Before 1914*. London, 1981.

Kiernan, V. G. *The Lords of Human Kind. Black Man, Yellow Man, and White Man in an Age of Empire*. Boston, 1969.

King, David Burnett. *Marschall von Bieberstein and the New Course*. Ph.D. diss., Cornell University. 1962.

Klein, Fritz. Ed. *Studien zum deutschen Imperialismus vor 1914*. Berlin, 1976.

Koch, W. H. *Der Sozialdarwinismus: Seine Genese und sein Einfluss auf das imperialistischen Denken*. Munich, 1973.

Koehl, Robert L. *RKFDV: German Resettlement and Population Policy, 1939–1945*. Cambridge, MA, 1957.

Krieger, Leonard. *The German Idea of Freedom: History of a Political Tradition*. Boston, 1957.

Kruck, Alfred. *Geschichte des Alldeutschen Verbandes*. Wiesbaden, 1954.

Kuczynski, R. R. *"Living Space" and Population Problems*. Oxford, 1939.

Lafeber, Walter. *The New Empire. An Interpretation of American Expansion 1860–1898*. Ithaca, NY, 1963.

Lakowski, Richard. "Der zweite Weltkrieg," in H. Stoecker, ed., *Drang nach Afrika*. Berlin, 1977. Pp. 315–51.

Lane, Barbara Miller, and Rupp, Leila J. Eds. *Nazi Ideology before 1933: A Documentation*. Austin, TX, and London, 1978.

Lange, Karl. "Der Terminus 'Lebensraum' in Hitlers 'Mein Kampf'." *Vierteljahrshefte für Zeitgeschichte* 13 (1965). Pp. 426–37.

Langer, William L. *The Diplomacy of Imperialism 1890–1902*. 2nd ed. New York, 1951.

Lebovics, Herman. *Social Conservatism and the Middle Classes in Germany 1914–1933*. Princeton, 1969.

Leopold, John A. *Alfred Hugenberg: The Radical Nationalist Campaign against the Weimar Republic*. New Haven, 1977.

Levy, Richard S. *The Downfall of the Anti-Semitic Political Parties in Imperial Germany*. New Haven, 1975.

Lindenlaub, Dieter. *Richtungskämpfe im Verein für Sozialpolitik. Beihefte* 52 and 53 of *Vierteljahrshefte für Sozial- und Wirtschaftsgeschichte*. Wiesbaden, 1967.

Lindow, Erich. *Marschall von Bieberstein als Botschafter in Konstantinopel 1897–1917*. Danzig, 1934.

Lohn, Dieter. *Politik und Interesse: Die Interessenstruktur der Deutschen Volkspartei*. Meisenheim am Glan, 1970.

Louis, Wm. Roger. Ed. *The Origins of the Second World War: A. J. P. Taylor and His Critics*. New York, 1972.

Lütge, Friedrich. *Deutsche Sozial- und Wirtschaftsgeschichte*. Berlin, 1952.

Mannesmann, Claus H. *Die Unternehmung der Brüder Mannesmann in Marokko*. Leipzig, 1931.

Mannheim, Karl. *Ideology and Utopia*. New York, 1954.

Markov, Walter. Ed. *Études africaines*. Leipzig, 1967.

Maxelon, Michael-Olaf. *Stresemann und Frankreich 1914–1928. Deutsche Politik der Ost-West Balance*. Düsseldorf, 1972.

Mayer, Arno J. *Dynamics of Counterrevolution in Europe, 1870–1956: An Analytic Framework*. New York, 1971.

———. "The Lower Middle Class as an Historical Problem." *Journal of Modern History* 47 (1975). Pp. 409–36.

———. *The Persistence of the Old Regime: Europe to the Great War*. New York, 1981.

Meyer, Henry Cord. *Mitteleuropa in German Thought and Action, 1815–1945*. The Hague, 1955.

Mielke, Siegfried. *Der Hansa-Bund für Gewerbe, Handel und Industrie 1909–1914. Der gescheiterte Versuch einer antifeudalen Sammlungspolitik*. Göttingen, 1976.

Milward, Alan S. *The German Economy at War*. London, 1965.

Mitchell, B. R. *European Historical Statistics*. 2nd rev. ed. London, 1975.

Mitzman, Arthur. *The Iron Cage: An Historical Interpretation of Max Weber*. New York, 1969.

———. *Sociology and Estrangement. Three Sociologists of Imperial Germany*. New York, 1973.

Mogk, Walter. *Rohrbach und das "Grössere Deutschland": Ethischer Imperialismus im Wilhelmischen Zeitalter*. Munich, 1972.

Molt, Peter. *Der Reichstag vor der improvisierten Revolution*. Cologne and Opladen, 1963.

Mommsen, Wolfgang J. *Max Weber und die deutsche Politik*. 2nd rev. ed. Tübingen, 1974.

———. Ed. *Der moderne Imperialismus*. Stuttgart, 1971.

———. *Das Zeitalter des Imperialismus*. Frankfurt am Main, 1969.

Morgenthau, Hans J. *Politics Among Nations: The Struggle for Power and Peace*. 3rd ed. New York, 1965.

Moses, J. A. *The Politics of Illusion: The Fischer Controversy in German Historiography*. London, 1975.

Mosse, George L. *The Crisis of German Ideology: Intellectual Origins of the Third Reich*. New York, 1964.

Neue Deutsche Biographie. Berlin, 1953 ff.

Neumann, Franz. *Behemoth: The Structure and Practice of National Socialism 1933–1944*. Rev. ed. New York, 1944.

Nolte, Ernst. *Three Faces of Fascism*. New York, 1966.

Opitz, Reinhard. *Der deutsche Sozialliberalismus 1917–1933*. Cologne, 1973.

Owen, Roger, and Sutcliffe, Bob. Eds. *Studies in the Theory of Imperialism*. London, 1972.

Parsons, Talcott. *Essays in Sociological Theory*. 2nd ed. London, 1954.

Peck, Abraham J. *Radicals and Reactionaries: The Crisis of Conservatism in Wilhelmine Germany*. Washington, 1978.

Pehl, Hans. *Die deutsche Kolonialpolitik und das Zentrum, 1884–1914*. Lemburg, 1934.

Petzina, Dietmar. *Die deutsche Wirtschaft in der Zwischenkriegszeit.* Wiesbaden, 1977.

Pierard, Richard Victor. *The German Colonial Society, 1882–1914.* Ph.D. diss., State University of Iowa, 1964.

Pogge von Strandmann, Hartmut. "Domestic Origins of Germany's Colonial Expansion under Bismarck." *Past and Present* 42 (1969). Pp. 140–59.

———. *The Kolonialrat, Its Significance and Influence on German Politics from 1890 to 1906.* D. Phil. thesis, Oxford University. 1970.

———. "Nationale Verbände zwischen Weltpolitik und Kontinentalpolitik." In Herbert Schottelius and Wilhelm Deist, eds., *Marine und Marinepolitik im kaiserlichen Deutschland 1871–1914.* Düsseldorf, 1972. Pp. 296–317.

———. "Rathenau, die Gebrüder Mannesmann und die Vorgeschichte der zweiten Marokkokrise," in I. Geiss and B. J. Wendt, eds., *Deutschland in der Weltpolitik des 19. und 20. Jahrhunderts.* Düsseldorf, 1973. Pp. 251–70.

Pogge von Strandmann, Hartmut, and Geiss, Imanuel. Eds. *Die Erforderlichkeit des Unmöglichen.* Frankfurt am Main, 1965.

Post, Gaines, Jr. *The Civil-Military Fabric of German Foreign Policy.* Princeton, 1973.

Puhle, Hans-Jürgen. *Agrarische Interessenpolitik und preussischer Konservatismus im Wilhelmischen Reich, 1893–1914.* Hannover, 1966.

———. "Parlament, Parteien und Interessenverbände 1890–1914," in M. Stürmer, ed., *Das kaiserliche Deutschland.* Düsseldorf, 1977. Pp. 340–77.

Rauh, Manfred. *Die Parlamentarisierung des Deutschen Reiches.* Düsseldorf, 1977.

Reitlinger, Gerald. *The House Built on Sand: The Conflicts of German Policy in Russia, 1939–1945.* New York, 1960.

Reshetar, John S. *The Ukrainian Revolution, 1917–1920: A Study in Nationalism.* Princeton, 1952.

Rich, Norman. *Friedrich von Holstein: Politics and Diplomacy in the Era of Bismarck and William II.* 2 vols. Cambridge, 1965.

———. *Hitler's War Aims: Ideology, the Nazi State, and the Course of Expansion.* 2 vols. New York, 1973, 1974.

Richards, Donald Ray. *The German Bestseller in the 20th Century. A Complete Bibliography and Analysis 1915–1940.* Berne, 1968.

Ridley, Hugh. "Colonial Society and European Totalitarianism." *Journal of European Studies* 3 (1973). Pp. 147–59.

Ringer, Fritz K. *The Decline of the German Mandarins: The German Academic Community, 1890–1933.* Cambridge, MA, 1969.

Röhl, John C. G. *Germany without Bismarck: The Crisis of Government in the Second Reich, 1890–1900.* Berkeley and Los Angeles, 1967.

Rohr, Donald G. *The Origins of Social Liberalism in Germany.* Chicago, 1963.

Rosenberg, Hans. *Grosse Depression und Bismarckzeit: Wirtschaftsablauf, Gesellschaft und Politik in Mitteleuropa.* Berlin, 1967.

Ross, Ronald J. *Beleaguered Tower: The Dilemma of Political Catholicism in Wilhelmine Germany.* Notre Dame and London, 1976.

Roth, Guenther. *The Social Democrats in Imperial Germany: A Study of Working-Class Isolation and National Integration.* Totowa, NJ, 1963.

Rüger, Adolf. "Der Kolonialrevisionismus der Weimarer Republik," in H. Stoecker, ed., *Drang nach Afrika.* Berlin, 1977. Pp. 243–79.

Saul, Klaus. *Staat, Industrie, Arbeiterbewegung im Kaiserreich.* Düsseldorf, 1974.

Schieffel, Werner. *Bernhard Dernburg, 1865–1937: Kolonialpolitiker und Bankier in Wilhelmischen Deutschland.* Zurich and Freiburg, 1974.

Schmokel, Wolfe W. *Dream of Empire: German Colonialism, 1919–1945.* New Haven, 1964.

Schrecker, John E. *Imperialism and Chinese Nationalism: Germany in Shantung.* Cambridge, MA, 1971.

Schröder, Hans-Christoph. *Sozialismus und Imperialismus: Die Auseinandersetzung der deutschen Sozialdemokratie mit dem Imperialismus und "der Weltpolitik" vor 1914.* Hannover, 1968.

Schulin, Ernst. *Walther Rathenau. Repräsentant, Kritiker und Opfer seiner Zeit.* Göttingen, 1979.

Schwarze, Fritz. *Das deutsch-englische Abkommen über die portugiesischen Kolonien vom 30. August 1898.* Göttingen, 1931.

Schweitzer, Arthur. *Big Business and the Third Reich.* Bloomington, IN, 1964.

Searle, G. R. *The Quest for National Efficiency: A Study in British Politics and Political Thought, 1899—1914.* Oxford, 1971.

——. "The 'Revolt from the Right' in Edwardian Britain," in P. M. Kennedy and A. Nicholls, eds., *Nationalist and Racialist Movements.* London, 1981. Pp. 21–39.

Semmel, Bernard. *Imperialism and Social Reform. English Social-Imperial Thought 1895–1914.* Cambridge, MA, 1960.

——. *The Rise of Free-Trade Imperialism: Classical Political Economy, the Empire of Free Trade and Imperialism 1750–1850.* Cambridge, 1970.

Sheehan, James J. *German Liberalism in the Nineteenth Century.* Chicago and London, 1978.

——. Ed. *Imperial Germany.* New York and London, 1976.

——. "Political Leadership in the German Reichstag, 1871–1918." *American Historical Review* 74 (1968). Pp. 511–28.

Sieveking, Heinrich. *Karl Sieveking 1787–1847.* Hamburg, 1929.

Smith, Woodruff D. "The Colonial Novel as Political Propaganda: Hans Grimm's *Volk ohne Raum." German Studies Review* 6 (1983). Pp. 215–35.

——. "The Emergence of German Urban Sociology, 1900–1910." *Journal of the History of Sociology* 1 (1979). Pp. 1–16.

——. *European Imperialism in the Nineteenth and Twentieth Centuries.* Chicago, 1982.

——. "Friedrich Ratzel and the Origins of Lebensraum." *German Studies Review* 3 (1980). Pp. 51–68.

——. *The German Colonial Empire.* Chapel Hill, 1978.

——. "Julius Graf Zech auf Neuhofen (1868–1914)," in L. H. Gann and P. Duignan, eds., *African Proconsuls. European Governors in Africa.* New York, 1978. Pp. 473–91.

——. "The Social and Political Origins of German Diffusionist Ethnology." *Journal of the History of the Behavioral Sciences* 14 (1978). Pp. 103–12.

Smith, Woodruff, and Turner, Sharon A. "Legislative Behavior in the German Reichstag, 1898–1906." *Central European History* 14 (1981). Pp. 3–29.

Spellmeyer, Hans. *Deutsche Kolonialpolitik im Reichstag.* Stuttgart, 1931.

Spidle, Jake Wilton, Jr. "Colonial Studies in Imperial Germany." *History of Education Quarterly* 13 (1973). Pp. 231–47.

Stark, Gary D. *Entrepreneurs of Ideology: Neoconservative Publishers in Germany, 1890–1933.* Chapel Hill, 1981.

Stegmann, Dirk. "Deutsche Zoll- und Handelspolitik 1924/25–1929 unter besonderer Berücksichtigung agrarischer und industrieller Interessen," in Hans Mommsen, Dietmar Petzina, and Bernd Weisbrod, eds., *Industrielles System und politische Entwicklung in der Weimarer Republik*. Düsseldorf, 1974. Pp. 499–513.

———. *Die Erben Bismarcks. Parteien und Verbände in der Spätphase des Wilhelmischen Deutschlands*. Cologne, 1970.

Steinberg, Jonathan. *Yesterday's Deterrent: Tirpitz and the Birth of the German Battle Fleet*. New York, 1965.

Steiner, Zara S. *The Foreign Office and Foreign Policy 1898—1914*. Cambridge, 1969.

Stephan, Werner. *Aufstieg und Verfall des Linksliberalismus, 1918–1933: Geschichte der Deutschen Demokratischen Partei*. Göttingen, 1973.

Stern, Fritz. *The Failure of Illiberalism*. New York, 1972.

———. *Gold and Iron. Bismarck, Bleichröder and the Building of the German Empire*. New York, 1977.

———. *The Politics of Cultural Despair. A Study in the Rise of the Germanic Ideology*. Berkeley, 1961.

Stoecker, Helmuth. *Deutschland und China im 19. Jahrhundert. Das Eindringen des deutschen Kapitalismus*. Berlin, 1958.

———. Ed. *Drang nach Afrika*. Berlin, 1977.

———. Ed. *Kamerun unter deutscher Kolonialherrschaft*. 2 vols. Berlin, 1960, 1968.

Stokes, Eric. *The English Utilitarians and India*. London, 1959.

Stolper, Gustav, et al. *Deutsche Wirtschaft seit 1870*. Tübingen, 1964.

Stürmer, Michael. Ed. *Das kaiserliche Deutschland. Politik und Gesellschaft 1870–1918*. Düsseldorf, 1970.

Taylor, A. J. P. *Germany's First Bid for Colonies, 1884–1885*. London, 1938.

———. *The Origins of the Second World War*. London, 1961.

Tetzlaff, Rainer. *Koloniale Entwicklung und Ausbeutung. Wirtschafts- und Sozialgeschichte Deutsch-Ostafrikas, 1885–1914*. Berlin, 1970.

Thimme, Annelise. "Gustav Stresemann: Legende und Wirklichkeit." *Historische Zeitschrift* 181 (1956). Pp. 287–338.

Tims, R. W. *Germanizing Prussian Poland. The H-K-T Society and the Struggle for the Eastern Marches in the German Empire 1894–1919*. New York, 1941.

Townsend, Mary E. *The Rise and Fall of Germany's Colonial Empire 1884–1918*. New York, 1930.

Turner, Henry Ashby, Jr. "Bismarck's Imperialist Venture: Anti-British in Origin?" in Gifford and Louis, eds., *Britain and Germany in Africa: Imperial Rivalry and Colonial Rule*. Pp. 49–82.

———. *German Big Business and the Rise of Hitler*. New York, 1985.

———. *Stresemann and the Politics of the Weimar Republic*. Princeton, 1963.

Ullmann, Hans-Peter. *Der Bund der Industriellen. Organisation, Einfluss und Politik klein- un mittelbetrieblicher Industrieller im Deutschen Kaiserreich 1895–1914*. Göttingen, 1976.

Vietsch, Eberhard von. *Wilhelm Solf, Botschafter zwischen den Zeiten*. Tübingen, 1961.

Volkov, Shulamit. *The Rise of Popular Antimodernism in Germany: The Urban Master Artisans, 1873–1896*. Princeton, 1978.

Walker, Mack. *Germany and the Emigration, 1816–1885*. Cambridge, MA, 1964.

Wanklyn, Harriet. *Friedrich Ratzel. A Biographical Memoir and Bibliography.* Cambridge, 1961.

Warren, Donald, Jr. *The Red Kingdom of Saxony: Lobbying Grounds for Gustav Stresemann. 1901–1909.* The Hague, 1964.

Washausen, Helmut. *Hamburg und die Kolonialpolitik des Deutschen Reiches, 1880 bis 1890.* Hamburg, 1968.

Wehler, Hans-Ulrich. *Bismarck und der Imperialismus.* Cologne, 1969.

———. *Krisenherde des Kaiserreichs 1871–1918. Studien zum deutschen Sozial- und Verfassungsgeschichte.* Göttingen, 1970.

———. "Sozialdarwinismus im expandierenden Industriestaat," in I. Geiss and B. J. Wendt, eds., *Deutschland in der Weltpolitik.* Düsseldorf, 1977. Pp. 133–42.

Weidenfeld, Werner. *Die Englandpolitik Gustav Stresemanns.* Mainz, 1972.

Weinberg, Gerhard L. *The Foreign Policy of Hitler's Germany: Diplomatic Revolution in Europe, 1933–1936.* Chicago, 1970.

———. *The Foreign Policy of Hitler's Germany: Starting World War II, 1937–1939.* Chicago, 1980.

Wendt, Bernd Jürgen. "England und der deutsche 'Drang nach Südosten': Kapitalbeziehungen und Warenverkehr in Südeuropa zwischen den Weltkriegen," in I. Geiss and B. J. Wendt, eds., *Deutschland in der Weltpolitik.* Düsseldorf, 1977. Pp. 483–512.

Wernecke, Klaus. *Der Wille zur Weltgeltung. Aussenpolitik und Öffentlichkeit am Vorabend des ersten Weltkriegs.* Düsseldorf, 1970.

Wertheimer, Mildred S. *The Pan-German League, 1890–1914.* New York, 1924.

Wheeler-Bennett, J. W. *Brest-Litovsk: The Forgotten Peace.* London, 1938.

White, Dan S. *The Splintered Party. National Liberalism in Hessen and the Reich 1867–1918.* Cambridge, MA, 1976.

Willequet, Jacques. *Le Congo belge et la Weltpolitik (1894–1914).* Brussels, 1962.

Williamson, John G. *Karl Helfferich 1872–1924: Economist, Financier, Politician.* Princeton, 1971.

Winkler, H. A. Ed. *Organisierter Kapitalismus, Voraussetzungen und Anfänge.* Göttingen, 1974.

Winzen, Peter. *Bülows Weltmachtkonzept. Untersuchungen zur Frühphase seiner Aussenpolitik 1897–1901.* Boppard am Rhein, 1977.

Witt, Peter Christian. *Die Finanzpolitik des Deutschen Reiches von 1903 bis 1913.* Lübeck, 1970.

Wolf, John B. *The Diplomatic Background of the Baghdad Railroad.* Columbia, MO, 1936.

Wollstein, Günther. *Das "Grossdeutschland" der Paulskirche: Nationale Ziele in der bürgerlichen Revolution, 1848/49.* Düsseldorf, 1977.

Zeender, John K. *The German Center Party 1890–1906.* Philadelphia, 1976.

Index

DATE DUE		
DEC 1 0 2009		
JUN 1 1 2010		